RANCHO CUCAMONGA
PUBLIC LIBRARY
W9-BAH-974

Mayflower

THE VOYAGE THAT CHANGED THE WORLD

CHRISTOPHER HILTON

SUTTON PUBLISHING

First published in the United Kingdom in 2005 by
Sutton Publishing Limited · Phoenix Mill
Thrupp · Stroud · Gloucestershire · GL5 2BU

British Library Cataloguing in Publication Data
A catalogue record for this book is available from the British Library.

ISBN 0-7509-3654-1

Typeset in 11/14.5pt Sabon.
Typesetting and origination by
Sutton Publishing Limited.
Printed and bound in England by
J.H. Haynes & Co. Ltd, Sparkford.

Contents

Acknowledgements

An American producer was making a documentary for the Discovery channel on the Berlin Wall the other month, and came over to interview me. That done, we fell to chatting and I told him I was working on the story of the *Mayflower*. 'Interesting,' he said, 'because I don't really know much about it.' I suppose most people are the same. They know, perhaps vaguely, the basic outline but little or nothing beyond that: not the sequence of improbable and astonishing events, the religious fervour which tore the fabric of old England, the little group – now called the Pilgrim Fathers – from an obscure village who were swept up in that fervour, their harrowing flight to Holland to avoid persecution, their dangerous journey across the Atlantic in winter to found their own new world, their clinging on to survive . . .

This book is that story.

There are very few primary sources, and all who approach the story have to use them. The most important is *Of Plymouth Plantation* by William Bradford, who was a witness throughout and Governor of the Plantation. His prose is evocative and sometimes genuinely dramatic but at crucial moments maddeningly imprecise. This has fed a subsequent industry of assumption and speculation.

Mourt's Relation (London, 1622) by Edward Winslow and other, anonymous, writers are eyewitness accounts of the very beginnings of the Plantation. *Good News from New England* (London, 1624), also by Winslow, continues the story.

Caleb Johnson (and his wife Anna) have produced a memorial volume – *The Complete Works of the Mayflower Pilgrims* – which contains all the above, and just about everything else the Pilgrims wrote, in its 1,173 pages. It has been a bedrock for me and has the feel of a labour of love about it. (He says it took 'thousands of hours of transcribing, typing, and editing'.) I used it constantly for reference and have quoted Bradford and Winslow throughout (but with a caveat: see the section immediately below). Mr Johnson graciously said he had no problem with this. 'The very purpose of *Complete Works* was to make these sources readily available to authors, reasearchers and historians.' He printed 100 copies and I got the last of them! He is, however, considering republishing either the whole or some of its constituent parts, and he has a comprehensive website www.mayflowerhistory.com. The *Complete Works* and other material are on his Mayflower History Reference Collection CD-ROM available on the website. At present he is working on a new book *The Mayflower and Her Passengers*. I offer him my sincere thanks – and gratitude for the job he has done.

The historian is immediately confronted with what is *not* known. Many good men and true have toiled among parchments and records, teasing out fragments of information. A couple of outstanding practitioners of this are Jeremy D. Bangs, director of the Leiden American Pilgrim Museum, Holland, and the late Harold Kirk-Smith, whose book *William Brewster, 'The Father of New England'* contains invaluable original research. I am deeply grateful to Mr Kay for permission to quote from it. I have done so extensively.

The rendering of old English into modern is a problem which must be faced. Bradford's and Winslow's works are very heavy going (not to mention archaic words, long out of use) and Caleb Johnson has taken the sensible precaution of rendering them into more modern English. As he says, he 'transcribed from originals or public domain editions, modernising the spelling but only very lightly touching up punctuation'. I have accentuated this, notably in smoothing and sometimes stripping out punctuation as well as clumsy and/or ambiguous phrases.

In the time covered by the book, people spelt their names freely – which is a polite way of saying several different ways. For example, John Smyth appears as Smith in various sources but I have standardised it to Smyth to avoid confusion.

The nomenclature needs resolving, too, because popularly the voyage from Plymouth, England, to Plymouth, Massachusetts, was undertaken by the Pilgrim Fathers. This term was first used much later and in any case is not all-embracing, because many who made the voyage were nothing to do with the original religious group but adventurers out to make whatever they could. However, once their destinies had intertwined, as inevitably they did, they all became part of a greater group. I have called them just settlers.

Time is tricky, too. Up to 1572, the Julian Calendar (known as Old Style) was used in England. This was inaccurate and by 1582 required adjustment: it was done by advancing ten days in October. This was called the Gregorian Calendar (known as New Style), after the Pope of that name – and the English wouldn't use it. This explains why the same event can be ten days apart, depending on which Calendar was being used by whom. For uniformity, because the Pilgrims used the Old Style I have stayed with that.

I need to thank many people for their help. Malcolm J. Dolby, a resident of Scrooby and formerly of the Bassetlaw Museum in Retford, took pains to give me invaluable background; Dr Andy Russel, Archaeology Unit Manager at Southampton City Council, gave his time to fleshing out many details; John Cammack gave me insights into what happened at Boston (and a funny footnote or two); Maurice Barrick explored the mystery of where exactly the Pilgrims did try to sail from when they first decided to leave England for Holland; Nigel Overton, Maritime Heritage Officer at Plymouth City Museum and Art Gallery, sent a superb five-page response to my many specific queries – and thanks to Tammy Baines of the Chief Executive's Department for steering me in the right direction. The respective staffs of the Greenwich Naval and Lambeth House libraries took me by the hand and led me to their treasures.

I am particularly indebted to Professor Robert Bliss, Dean, Pierre Lacede Honors College, University of Missouri–St Louis, for the breadth of his insights and explanations in Chapter 12, and grateful to Kenneth Bowling, Adjunct Associate Professor of History, the George Washington University, Washington DC for acting as a conduit to Professor Bliss, and Helen Veit, Bowling's assistant, for making sure it all happened.

There is a bibliography at the end of the book, but I want to set down here my gratitude to the following for permission to quote from their work: Dr David Beale, Professor of Church History at Bob Jones University and Seminary, Greenville, South Carolina for extracts from his *The Mayflower Pilgrims*; Crispin Gill for his book *Mayflower Remembered*; Joanne Smith, Senior Archivist at Southampton City Council for the Mayflower pamphlet; Pearsons for *The Stuart Age* by Barry Coward and *The Age of Plunder* by W.G. Hoskins; Kevin Knight for the *Catholic Encyclopedia* website; Miss K.L. Merritt for a piece she wrote on Immingham; Blackwell Publishing for *Reformation Thought* by Alister E. McGrath; Jordan S. Dill for extracts from the *Tolatsga* website; Henry B. Hoff, Editor, for words from an article by Anthony R. Wagner, 'The Origin of the Mayflower Children: Jasper, Richard and Ellen Moore', in *The New England Historical and Genealogical Register* 114 (1960): 163–8; Penguin for *The History of the Church, Volume 3: The Reformation* by Owen Chadwick; Joke Kardux and Eduard van de Bilt for their *Newcomers in an Old City*; Random House for *Puritanism and Revolution* by Christopher Hill and *A Place for Habitation* by Francis Dillon.

Laurel Guadazno, visitor services manager of the Pilgrim Monument and Provincetown Museum, Massachusetts, extended a memorably warm welcome and was kind enough to take me around all the places I needed to see in the Provincetown area. She also allowed me to quote from her published material. Of course the name Plymouth, Massachusetts is now firmly embedded in world history, and rightly so, but the great adventure opened right around Cape Cod Bay, at Provincetown. Here is where they waded ashore for the first time and put their (soaking) boots on *terra firma*.

There might be confusion over the nomenclature: Plymouth, Plimoth Plantation and Plymouth Colony.

Plymouth is the generic term for the place in general.

Bradford's book is called *Of Plimoth Plantation*. I am indebted to Caleb Johnson for this definition: 'I do not believe that "Plimoth Plantation" has any formal definition, it is a more colloquial "common name," which to my hearing has an agrarian sense to it. I personally would only use "Plimoth Plantation" to describe the town in its earliest years (before the founding of Duxbury), and I would probably not use it in any legal or political sense. If I were writing about raising corn, or an Indian visit in the early years, or something along those lines, I would be more inclined to use Plantation than Colony.'

I have been guided by this and used Plantation to mean the town which the settlers built and the land immediately around it.

Plymouth Colony, Johnson says, 'was a political/governmental/legal entity. It originally consisted of just Plymouth itself, plus the Colony's various land and trading rights that were established under English authority. The colony later grew over time to include other townships including Duxbury, Marshfield, Scituate, Barnstable, Sandwich, Yarmouth, Taunton, and others, all of which were under the jurisdiction of the Plymouth Colony Court.'

I have been guided by this, too, and have used Colony to mean the enterprise as a whole.

In days of olde, spelling conventions were much looser than now and I'm indebted to Nigel Overton for tracing the various versions of England's Plymouth.

He says: 'In terms of names and spellings I do not think there was one hard and fast rule. In most cases it would be the record keeper's or cartographer's spelling of the word. There was not always consistency; sometimes names would be spelt phonetically based on how they were heard, so accents could play a role too!' So here goes: 1308, Bordeaux Custom's Records, Plomuth; unknown source, Plymme; chart from about 1539, Plymmouth; 1590/91 map, Plommowth; 1592 map, Plymouth; 1592 map, Plimmouthe; 1593 map, Plimouthe; 1601/02 Italian maps, Pleymouth and Plimouth; 1643 siege map, Plymouth; 1646 map, Plimouth; 1665 plan, Pleymouth; eighteenth-century French map, Plimouth. From the sixteenth century, however, Plymouth was the more general usage and Mr Overton stresses that.

In other words, Plimoth Plantation is quite entitled to retain that spelling, and the towns in Massachusetts and Devon are quite entitled to call themselves Plymouth. Looking at Overton's list, it is a mercy that we only have two versions to deal with. Incidentally, I have used a capital P for the Plantation throughout because, all else aside, it deserves one.

The People

Allerton, Isaac (1583/6–1658/9) One of the Leiden congregation who sailed on the *Mayflower*. A tailor, he became an assistant governor of Plymouth.

Allerton, John (before 1591–1620/1) Presumed to be a relative of Isaac Allerton (perhaps brother), he came from the Leiden congregation and sailed on the *Mayflower*. He was to return to Leiden to bring over more of the congregation later.

Arminius, Jacobus (1560–1609) A resident of Leiden, he was a controversial theologian at the University. His followers' theory of salvation rejected predestination. He was – briefly – a contemporary of the English congregation in the town.

Boleyn, Anne (*c.* 1507–36) Henry VIII's second wife, who bore him a daughter, Elizabeth, but no male heir. Anne was executed on dubious charges so Henry could marry Jane Seymour.

Bradford, William (1590–1657) The central pillar of the Plymouth Colony, its governor and guide. His sense of vision, justice and firmness may have been the key to its survival.

Brewster, William (1566/7–1644) The elder of the Scrooby church and postmaster. Served with diplomat Sir William Davison in Holland. Printed controversial material in Leiden and sailed on the *Mayflower*. He was the oldest passenger at the first Thanksgiving.

Browne, Robert (1550?–1633) A Cambridge University man, he was a leading independent (his followers were known as 'Brownists'): he demanded freedom of conscience in religion, invoking separatism from the Church.

Catherine of Aragon (1485–1536) Henry VIII's first wife, the widow of his brother Arthur, Prince of Wales. Henry and Catherine had a daughter, Mary. When he wanted an annulment the Pope refused, which led to the break between the Church of England and Rome.

Charles I, King of England (1600–49) He dissolved Parliament and ruled personally for eleven years before having to accept restrictions on his power. He was beheaded.
Clyfton, Richard (?–1616) The Separatist pastor at Babworth, near Scrooby who eventually moved to Holland.
Corbitant (?–?) He was the chief of the Nemasket tribe and opposed to any dealings with the English settlers, against whom he conspired with other tribes. Eventually he befriended the settlers.
Cranmer, Thomas (1489–1556) As Archbishop of Canterbury, he was a pivotal figure in shaping the Church of England. Under the Catholic Queen Mary, he was burnt at the stake for heresy.
Elizabeth I, Queen of England (1533–1603) The daughter of Henry VIII and Anne Boleyn, she reversed the moves to Catholicism instituted by Mary. An enigmatic and accomplished woman, she never married.
Henry VIII, King of England (1491–1547) A giant figure, he became king on the death of his father, Henry VII, in 1509. He created the schism with Rome over his marriage to Catherine of Aragon, and married a further five times. He bent the Church of England to his will and plundered the monasteries. He can be seen as the bridge between the Middle Ages and modernity.
Hobomok (?–before 1643) An Indian of the Wampanoag, he spoke a little English and settled with his family near Plymouth, acting as interpreter. There are suggestions that he leant towards Christianity.
James IV of Scotland and James I of England (1566–1625) The son of Mary Queen of Scots, he was, however, a staunch Protestant; he tried to accommodate the Puritans at the Hampton Court Conference, and hoped to become a European peacemaker, but failed.
Mary, Queen of England (1516–58) She ascended the throne in 1553, was without any preparation for government and restored the papal position in England and punished leading Protestants, sometimes with violence.
Massasoit (*c.* 1590–1661) A chief of the Wampanoag tribe, it seems that he saw the future because he concluded a peace treaty with the settlers which was never broken.

Robinson, John (1575–1625) The pastor of the Pilgrims' church at Leiden, he remained in Holland when the *Mayflower* sailed, intending to follow when the colony was established. He died in Holland soon after.

Samoset (?–?) He belonged to a tribe – of the Algonquins – then in Maine and spoke broken English which he had picked up from the fishermen on the coast. Of all the Indians, he was the first the settlers met: he suddenly came 'boldly among them'.

Smyth, John (1570–1612) An ordained Anglican priest, he fell into dispute with the Church of England and moved to Holland, where he founded the first General Baptist Church.

Squanto (*c.* 1590–1622) A member of the Patuxtet tribe, he was taken to England by an expedition under Captain Weymouth, returned and befriended the settlers at Plymouth teaching them how to sow Indian corn. He played politics, too.

Standish, Myles (*c.* 1584–1656) A military man with a temper, he served as a soldier in Holland, travelled on the *Mayflower* and took responsibility for defence.

Weston, Thomas (1584–1647) A London ironmonger, he also sold cloth in Holland and heard that the Leiden congregation wanted to emigrate. He more than anyone put the whole project together, although he was of dubious integrity.

Winslow, Edward (1595–1655) He sailed on the *Mayflower*, was thrice governor of Plymouth and brought the first European livestock across the Atlantic in 1624.

Wyclif, John (*c.* 1329–84) A religious reformer who campaigned against wealth among the clergy and was a vociferous critic of the basis of Catholicism.

Maps

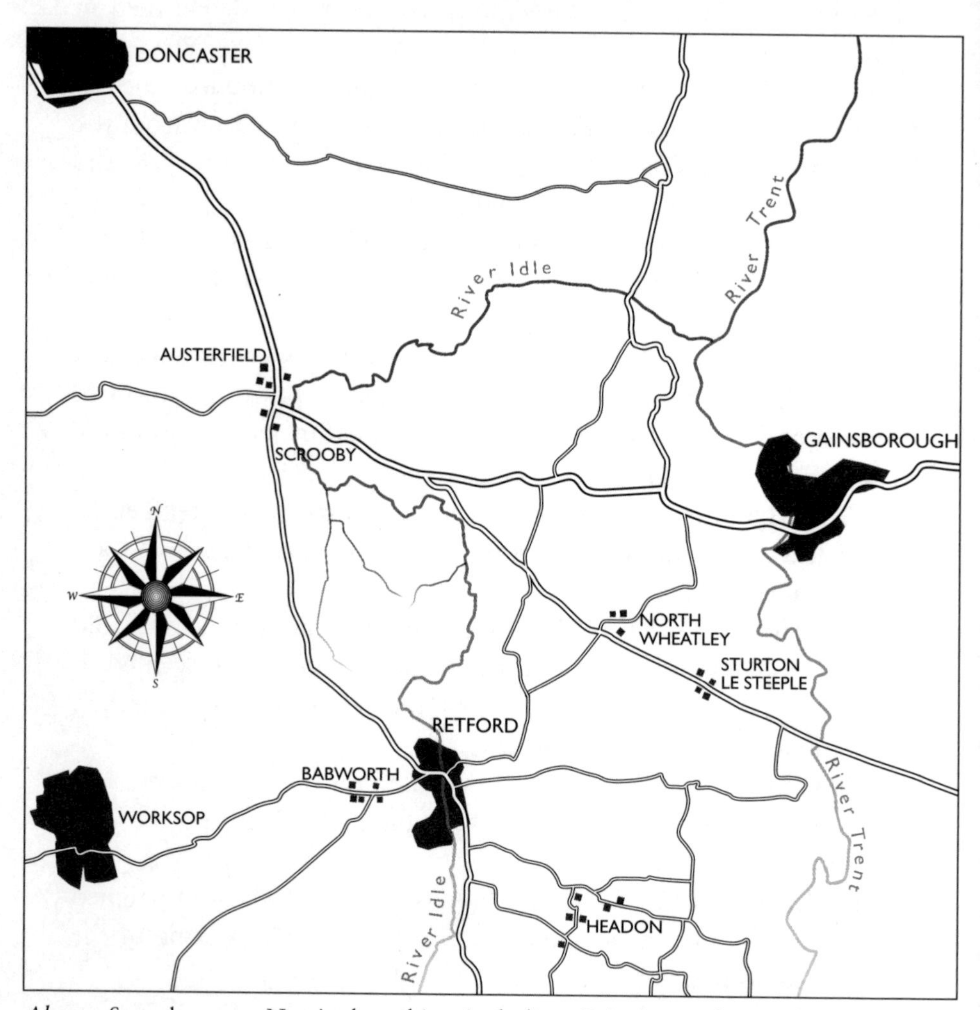

Above: Scrooby area, Nottinghamshire, including Gainsborough, Headon, Sturton le Steeple, North Wheatley, Babworth, Austerfield, Worksop and Doncaster, the tight little circle of communities which proved to be a powerhouse.

Opposite: The old world the Pilgrims left behind and their first new world, Holland.

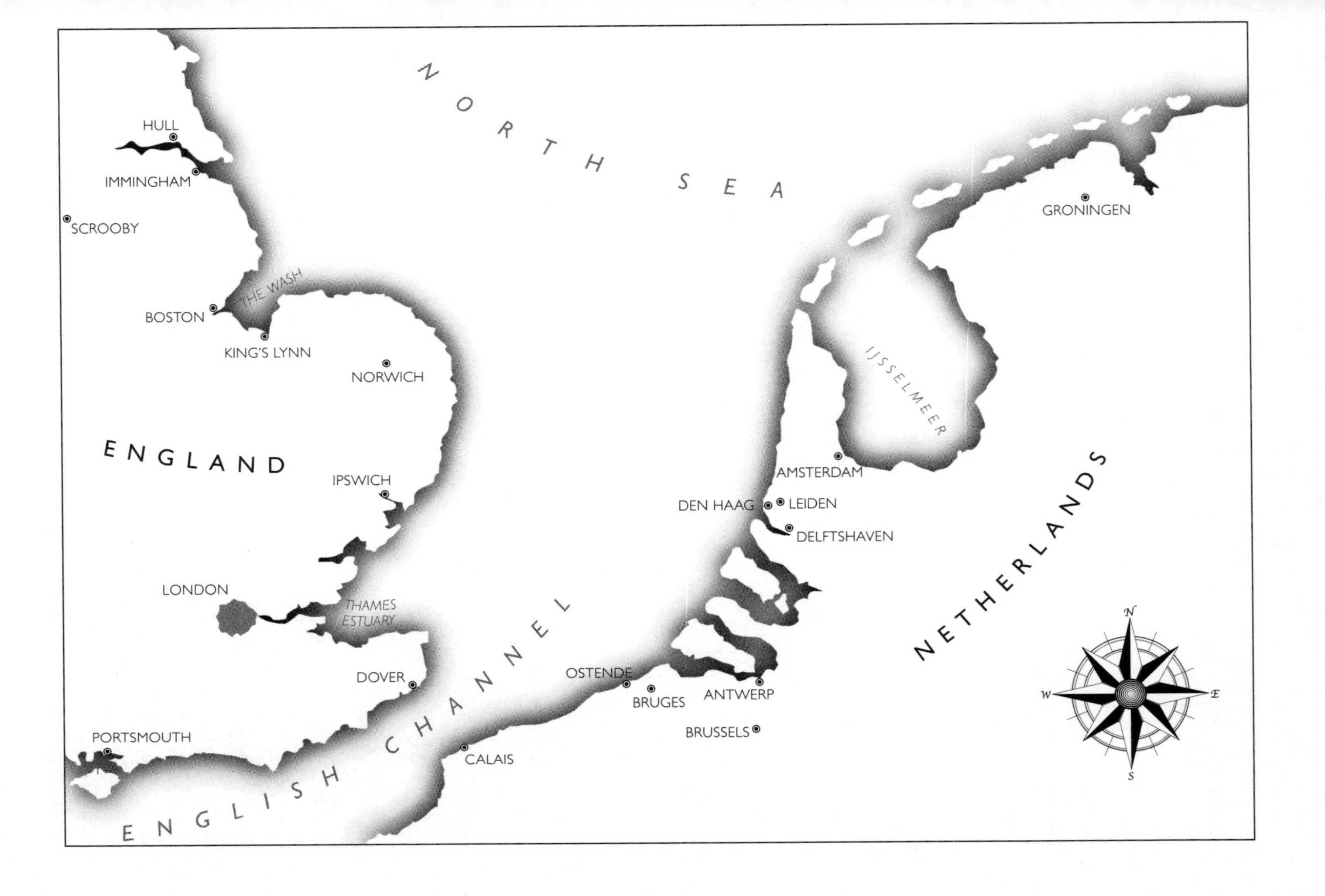
NORTH SEA
HULL
IMMINGHAM
SCROOBY
THE WASH
BOSTON
KING'S LYNN
NORWICH
ENGLAND
IPSWICH
LONDON
THAMES ESTUARY
DOVER
PORTSMOUTH
ENGLISH CHANNEL
CALAIS
OSTENDE
BRUGES
ANTWERP
BRUSSELS
DEN HAAG
LEIDEN
DELFTSHAVEN
AMSTERDAM
IJSSELMEER
GRONINGEN
NETHERLANDS
N
E
S
W

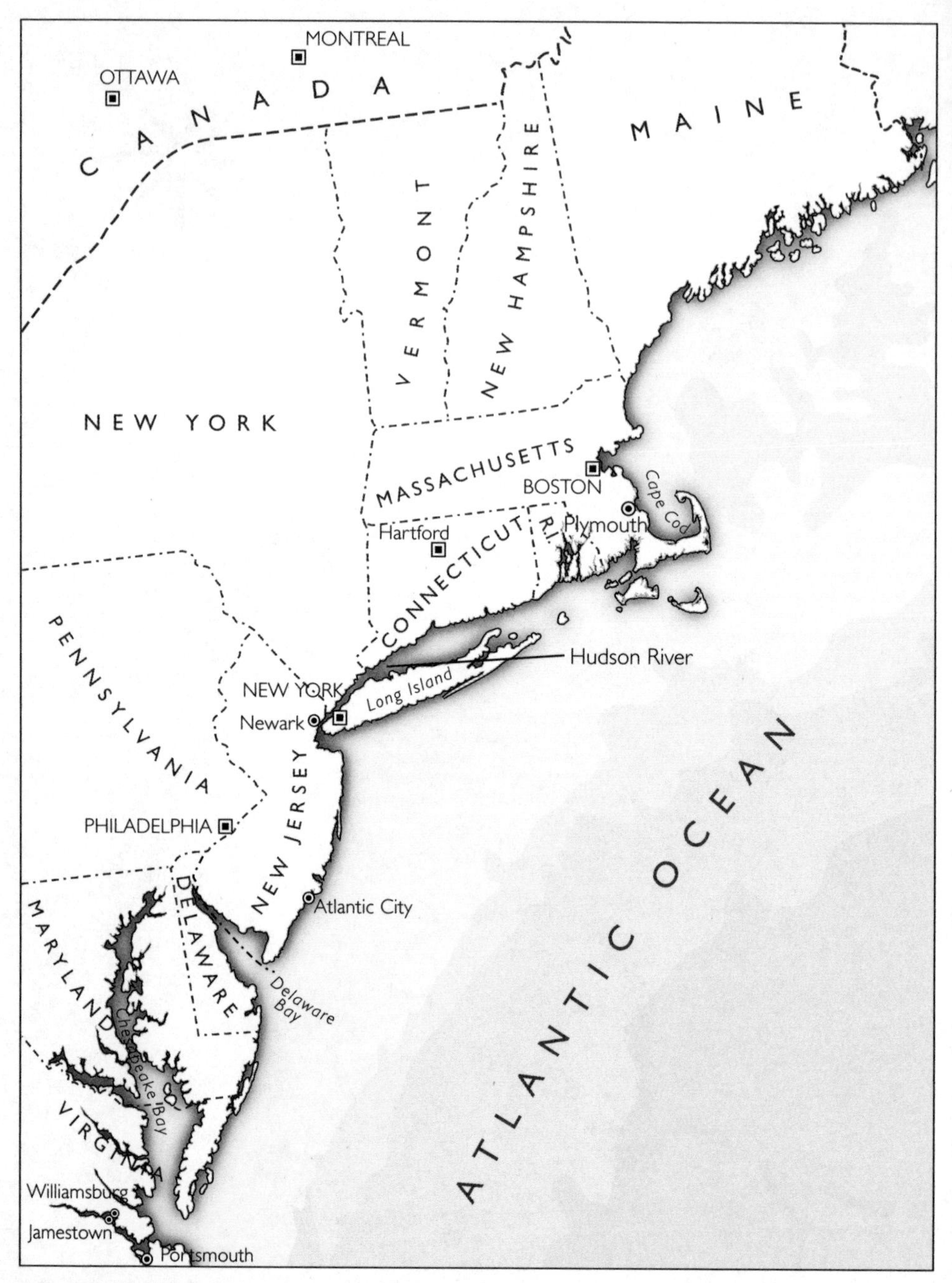

Above: The full sweep of the Atlantic seaboard: Plymouth, where the *Mayflower* went, the Hudson where it should have gone, and the nearest settlement, Jamestown, Virginia.
Opposite: Indian tribes, often hostile to one another, covered the whole area.

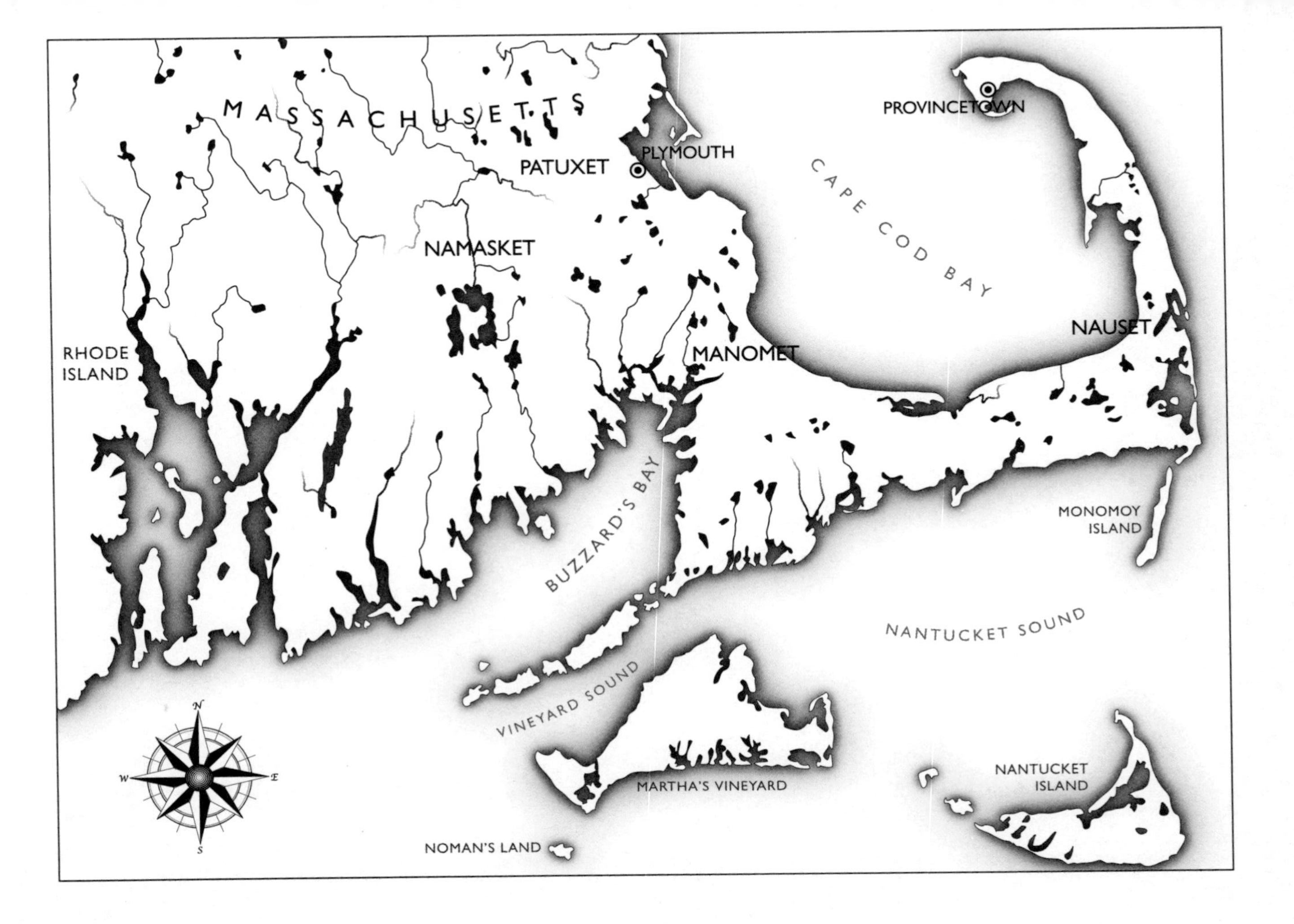
MASSACHUSETTS
PATUXET
PLYMOUTH
PROVINCETOWN
CAPE COD BAY
NAMASKET
RHODE ISLAND
MANOMET
NAUSET
BUZZARD'S BAY
MONOMOY ISLAND
NANTUCKET SOUND
VINEYARD SOUND
MARTHA'S VINEYARD
NANTUCKET ISLAND
NOMAN'S LAND
N
W
E
S

PART ONE

Old Worlds

PROLOGUE

Shoreline

An ordinary place. At low tide the brown mud dries and cracks into a mosaic of squares, making the mudflat look, absurdly, as if it has been tiled. The creek which wriggles through it towards the distant sea is not really a creek any more but a gully, almost a crevice, holding a little static water. It will fill again when the tide rises to it. The gully has sloping banks and the mud on top of these dries in a different way, so completely that the tiling is parched and bleached, making a piebald-coloured patchwork.

This is industrial landscape, as any cargo port must be: car parks, metal security fences, men in hard hats, elephantine lorries murmuring under their loads. Great metal arms fold out into the sea on solid supports to embrace ships' cargoes. Gantries wheel and turn silently, lifting loads and setting them down. Pyramids of coal, near a railway line where long freight trains clink and whisper as they lumber by, form one part of the backdrop. Vast, circular storage sheds, flanked by white office buildings in the geometrical modern style, form another. There is a permanent petrochemical smell in the air, borne on the wind.

The pathway to the gully, loose but slightly compacted shale, is the width of a lane and you do not see it until you are upon it. The walk down it to the shoreline is not long, perhaps twenty yards.

There is a clump of long, wild grass, unkempt as an old peasant's hair. The detritus of the consumer culture – a discarded cigarette packet, chocolate wrappers, bits of cardboard, fragments of cellophane – lie embedded in this grass; then there is a low, brick parapet and, just below, the mudflat arching down to the sea.

Was it *exactly* here that it all began?

The sounds of industry are flattened by the wind, this same wind which brushes the sea into rilles full across the mouth of the broad estuary beyond the metal arms. The sea sighs as it licks the rim of the mudflat in its endless, timeless rhythm. This is not a silent place but it is a quiet place.

There are, I suppose, paradoxes in all things touched by human beings but few more poignant or bewildering than *exactly* here: an anonymous and ordinary creek which is not a creek butting on to the banality of commerce. There was a plaque to mark the spot but it has been moved somewhere else and, anyway, nobody really knows where the spot was.

That morning in 1608 – might have been spring, might have been early summer – a group of around a hundred people waited. They were mostly ordinary, country folk.

The location, 'a large common a good way distant from any town',[1] had been chosen for the protection it offered. The nearest villages, Immingham and Killingholme, comprised just a few cottages and, anyway, Immingham was a couple of miles inland.[2]

Women and children rode in a boat in the creek, waiting.

The men walked the 40 miles from their homes in one English county, Nottinghamshire, to its neighbour Lincolnshire. What they were preparing to do was illegal without royal permission and they had none. As they walked, they were very vulnerable. Any little lad with sharp eyes tending sheep in a pasture might sound the alarm; any farm labourer sowing in the field might pause, wonder, go and tell his master; any crofter repairing a roof might glimpse them trekking their way across the flatland of Lincolnshire; any horseman riding by might come upon them.

Maybe they moved in groups, to attract less attention. Maybe they moved in one group, walked doggedly forward, drank with their cupped hands from freshwater streams, rested a moment or two under the boughs of old oak trees, gnawing hunks of bread they had brought. They may have had a serenity about them because, even in their vulnerability, they were sure their God was watching over them.

The women and children had come these 40 miles by river in a small sailing ship, known as a bark, which had been hired. The bark also carried the goods. The seamen had had to navigate the meres and waterways which meandered through the countryside to the estuary before they turned the bark towards the sea. They followed the shoreline towards the mudflat and the common. The bark got there a day early.

At the mouth of the estuary the water was so rough that it frightened the women. They, 'very sick, prevailed with the seaman to put into a creek hard by, where they lay on ground at low water'.[3] The women and children must have seen the mudflat drying as the tide slipped away, must have gazed across the grey waters towards the other side of the estuary a couple of miles away. To these people, whose horizons had been the area around their own communities, the estuary must have spread itself vast, hostile, forbidding.

Nobody knows when the men came in, that evening, in the hours of darkness or after dawn.

The women and children spent the night on the bark.

The ship to take them off was Dutch. It sailed into the estuary in the morning, but the tide had gone out, slipping down the mudflat and leaving the bark beached. It was some time before midday. From where he had dropped anchor in the estuary, the ship's captain saw this just as he saw the men 'ready, walking about the shore'.[4] He sent a rowing boat and, when it reached the shoreline, some of the men clambered into it. The boat was rowed back to the ship and the men went aboard. Just as it was preparing to return for more, the captain 'espied a great company' of armed troops, both horse and foot. Someone, somewhere, had sounded the alarm.

The captain swore. Transporting illegals now posed a direct danger to him, so, 'having the wind fair, weighed his anchor, hoisted sails and away'.[5]

The men left behind and the women and the children in the bark watched as the sails unfurled and the ship sailed out of the estuary and into the North Sea.

As the troops bore down on them some of the men dispersed and others stayed to help the women. It was heart-wrenching to see

> these poor women in this distress. What weeping, and crying on every side, some for their husbands that were carried away in the ship . . . others not knowing what should become of them, and their

> little ones. Others again melted in tears, seeing their poor little ones hanging about them crying for fear and quaking with cold.[6]

The Dutch ship receded, but on deck the situation was no less heart-rending. The men there were in 'great distress for their wives, and children', now being taken by the armed force and were faced with the realisation that, as they stood on the deck powerless, they themselves had only the clothes they wore and 'scarce a penny about them'.[7]

Within a comparatively few minutes the whole attempt at flight had broken up. Who knew where those who had fled were, or if they would even be seen again? Those guarding the bark were arrested and would clearly see the inside of a prison, perhaps for a long time, perhaps for life. The women and children would be taken into custody and if their men were on the Dutch ship they would not see them again.

The ship, receding further, was headed towards a great storm which battered it for fourteen days, sweeping it helplessly up to the Norwegian coast. Seven of those days were as dark as night and the storm so tremendous that the sailors cried out 'we sink, we sink'.

The men were still certain their God was watching over them, even when 'water ran into their mouths and ears'.[8]

Those who had fled, those who were arrested, those who were distraught and those who were nearly drowned would, together, help forge the matrix of a nation as mighty as any that had gone before it.

ONE

Noises in a Quiet Land

Always there are two concurrent stories. One, the foreground, is told incessantly and often in the most elaborate detail; the other, the background, is habitually not told at all.

The foreground is populated by notable people and notable events whose places in the long historical narrative are eternally fixed by deeds and dates. You probably know them. This is the domain of kings and conquerors, wives and mistresses, popes and prelates, dictators and diplomats, battles won and lost.

The background is a silent kingdom where the broad, constant flow of ordinary folk lived and died, generation after generation. They are strangers, held for ever in their anonymity. You might find their names in ancient, fragile, handwritten records or engraved into weathered, tilting headstones, but you will not find them anywhere else and you certainly do not know them.

The group at the mudflat were one such; having come from the small village of Scrooby in Nottinghamshire and its surrounding area, which would also have been anonymous except for a road, a manor house and regular stops by Royal Mail coaches. They were background people who had come to an ordinary place, waited there, and been scattered.

Here are some examples of the silent kingdom:

> As to the landless, we know even less about them and have little idea about their numbers.

> Of the houses of the working class in the first half of the sixteenth century we can say little. They are rarely described in contemporary documents and no structures have survived anywhere.

In Cheapside, London, alone there were fifty-two goldsmiths' shops, so full of treasure that all the shops of Rome, Milan, Florence and Venice could not together rival such magnificence. But of the teeming, squalid streets and lanes and alleys of the poor we hear nothing.[1]

Of the first real settlement in the United States at Jamestown, Virginia:

What . . . could induce the labouring classes of England to abandon their homes for the dangers of the Virginia voyage? The answer, today, cannot be taken direct from the men and women best capable of giving it. To us, the poorer social classes are dumb. They had few means to tell their thoughts to posterity, since they were largely illiterate and since the presses were mostly used for the purpose of their betters, which did not include making surveys of mass opinion.[2]

Of the place from where, in the fullness of time, the group would cross the Atlantic:

Such a subject as the life of ordinary people in Southampton in the early seventeenth century is the hardest of all to illustrate since [it] is so wide – what their homes were like, their customs and habits, their entertainments, their relations and attitudes towards their neighbours, their conditions of work. [It] is made more difficult because most of the surviving records were for legal and administrative purposes . . . Ordinary people who were good and happy do not figure much.[3]

Eventually, the group would – without seeking it, without realising it, without calculating it and certainly without intending it – achieve the almost impossible feat of moving themselves to the foreground.

The pathway to this begins some three hundred years before, in the Reformation, a handy catch-all to express the growing tension between Catholicism's grip on most of Europe and those seeking reform. There have always been deep disputes over whole tracts of the Reformation. One view was that the doctrine of the Catholic Church

> had remained pure. Saintly lives were yet frequent in all parts of Europe and the numerous beneficial medieval institutions of the Church continued their course uninterruptedly . . . Gradually, however, and largely owing to the variously hostile spirit of the civil powers, fostered and heightened by several elements of the new order, there grew up in many parts of Europe political and social conditions which . . . favoured the bold and unscrupulous.[4]

Just as many said (and say) precisely the opposite. John Wyclif did. He is widely regarded, in another catch-all phrase, as the Morning Star of the Reformation. A Yorkshireman, his date of birth is unclear but seems to have been between 1320 and 1330. Many details of his life have been lost, but he is known to have spoken of 'dominion founded on grace', meaning:

> the right to exercise authority in church and the right to own property. He maintained that these rights were given to men directly from God, and that they were not given or continued apart from sanctifying grace. Thus, a man in a state of mortal sin could not lawfully function as an official of church or state, nor could he lawfully own property. He argued that the Church had fallen into sin and that it ought to give up all its property and the clergy should live in complete poverty.[5]

To popes, accustomed to splendour and wielding absolute authority, this was revolution.

Wyclif did more than preach his own views: he took a practical step. In the early 1380s he led the movement to translate the Bible into English because he 'believed that if the common people' had it in 'their own language they would demand a reformation of the church'.[6] They would also be able to make up their own minds on how they wanted to worship.

In an age of authority, represented by the pope and, domestically, by hereditary kings and queens, this democratisation grew so dangerous it moved King Henry IV to decree, in 1401, that people preaching Wyclif's ideas were heretics and could be burnt. How much influence Wyclif *actually* had still presents itself as one of those deep disputes. A couple of views on that: his 'direct influence' on the Reformation's origins 'appear to be surprisingly slight',[7] but Wyclif's 'ideas spread to the Continent and helped prepare the way' for it.[8]

The core of the matter was that

> the Pope's laws interfered in many matters of Church and State and men talked of a need to limit the Pope's authority; but some of them needed the help of the Pope to manage the Church in their lands, and used the Pope's supreme power as a dispensing agent.
>
> Everyone wanted reform, or professed to want reform. How to reform and what to reform was not so clear. The energies of some reformers went to create new religious orders, or little groups of prayer and study.[9]

They have handy catch-all labels of their own: Protestantism (any western Christian church separate from the Catholic Church 'in accordance of the principles of the Reformation')[10] and Puritanism (simplifying and regulating worship because the Reformation was incomplete).

> The emergence of Puritanism in the second half of the sixteenth century was a response to the unique form the Reformation had taken in England. Yet its roots can be traced back to a tradition of reform in the Christian Church. The Reformation itself began on the Continent, when in 1517 Martin Luther nailed his Ninety-five Theses on indulgence to the door of the cathedral of Wittenberg protesting against what he deemed to be the corruption and ecclesiastical abuses in the Church of Rome.[11]

That particular notable date, 31 October 1517, serves as well as any for a beginning to the journey to the shoreline, although

> many students approach the Reformation in much the same way as medieval travellers approached the vast dark forests of southwest Germany – with a sense of hesitation and anxiety, in case what lay ahead should prove impenetrable . . . It is tempting for such students to ignore the *ideas* of the Reformation altogether, in order to concentrate on its social or political aspects.[12]

In December 1485, Ferdinand and Isabella of Spain had a daughter, Catherine. They immediately followed the contemporary custom of trying to find a political match for her because, in the ever-shifting foreground of European alliances and enmities, marriages were powerful cement. They found their match: Arthur, the eldest son of King Henry VII of England. Arthur was two, but that was as irrelevant as the fact that Catherine was three. An alliance had been cemented – she came as part of a treaty.

When Catherine was almost sixteen she travelled to England for the marriage. Her journey evidently took three months and the ship bringing her survived several storms, but she arrived safely at Plymouth on 2 October 1501. Here was, all unknown and unknowable, a meeting point between foreground and background because, 119 years later, the shoreline people would embark from one of these Plymouth quays, perhaps the same one . . .

Catherine and Arthur were married a month after her arrival, Arthur's younger brother Henry – then eleven – playing a prominent part at the ceremony. However, Arthur died six months later, possibly from lung disease. His death did not shift the foreground, but what to do? Young Henry had two assets, health and availability, and that gave the question its answer. Catherine was betrothed to him. It would prove, in all senses, a fateful step. By 1505, when Henry was old enough to marry her, the foreground had altered, taking with it the king's enthusiasm for an alliance with Spain. That forced Henry to wait until the king died, four years later, before he became Henry VIII, the marriage could take place and the fateful step was taken.

The England to which Henry VIII succeeded in the spring of 1509, two months before his eighteenth birthday, was still

> medieval in every important aspect. The King enjoyed jousting; the archer and the long-bow were objects of national pride and training . . . around possibly half the villages of England stretched the hedgeless open fields that had hardly changed, except in detail, for hundreds of years.[13]

The background: a population of perhaps 2½ million meant that England was essentially empty of people. Progress, in the broad sense of the word, can scarcely have existed from one generation to the next. The empty land was filled with woodland and forests; pastureland where most toiled simply to survive; untouched by time, small, isolated communities grouped round their spired churches and – sometimes – their moated manors.

The distribution of wealth, or rather the almost complete absence of it, was stark. In London, well into Henry VIII's reign, 8,588 people were earning up to £4 a year, giving them an estimated total wealth of around £18,000; 45 people had an annual income of more than £1,000, giving almost £78,000.[14]

To broaden that (the statistics are from somewhat later): in the county of Lincolnshire, figures were fixed for labour. Apprentices or servants in farming above sixteen and under twenty-four were to have 24*s* a year, plus meat and drink; those of ten and under sixteen, 10*s*. Mowers were to have 5*d* a day with meat and drink, 10*d* without. For cutting an acre of wheat or rye the fee was 14*s*, or by the day 3*d* with meat and drink, 8*d* without. Thrashing a quarter of wheat or rye 12*d*, barley, peas, beans and oats 5*d*; reaping an acre of beans or peas 6*d*; making hay by the day 2*d* with meat and drink, 5*d* without. And so it went.[15]

If a labourer earned 6*d* a day without meat and drink – he would have to provide his own – and there was demand for his work 180 days a year, he would get £4 10*s* a year. This enabled him and, if he had one, his family to survive, with most of the money going on food and drink, then in descending order, rent, fuel and clothing.

Accumulating enough capital to buy land was simply not a possibility for most of the population. When the time came and the shoreline group had finally crossed the Atlantic they found themselves standing on a *continent* of fertile land – with no landlords.

The foreground: Catherine could not produce a son and heir, something Henry needed for political and dynastic reasons. The agonies Catherine suffered remain poignant. In January 1510 she had a daughter who was either stillborn or died the same day. In January 1511 she had a son but he died on 22 February. In November 1513 she had a son, again either stillborn or died shortly after birth. This happened again in December 1514, although a daughter, Mary, was born in February 1516 and survived. Another daughter was either stillborn or died shortly after birth on 10 November 1518.

It is probable that Henry stopped sleeping with Catherine in about 1525. He had several affairs before and after that date and one of them resulted in Anne Boleyn becoming pregnant in December 1532. He resolved to marry her but needed the Pope to annul the marriage with Catherine. The Pope would not grant the annulment and Henry's response, after years of haggling, was to banish papal power from England. Once that was done and the primacy of the Church of England established, the Archbishop of Canterbury, Thomas Cranmer, would be able to take care of the annulment himself. This happened on 23 May 1533, and the Act of Supremacy the following year gave Henry full authority over the Church.

The pregnancy of December 1532 produced a girl, Elizabeth; a boy was stillborn or died shortly after birth in 1534, another in 1536. The problem of the male heir had recurred and Henry resolved to marry again. He was able, as people with absolute power can, to solve problems in the simplest and most direct way. Rather than divorce her, he had her beheaded (for alleged adultery).

Henry also dissolved the monasteries, which has been called the 'greatest act of plunder' since the Norman Conquest.[16] In 1536, there was open rebellion against this new order, known as the Pilgrimage of Grace. On 21 October, three noblemen met in the small, rural Nottinghamshire village of Scrooby, which was prevented from existing in its own anonymity by the road, the manor house and the Royal Mail.

The Pilgrimage was causing ferment in the nearby town of Pontefract (Pomfret) and something had to be done. The noblemen – it was likely they met in the manor house – sent a herald bearing a proclamation 'to be read amongst the Traitors and rebellious persons assembled at Pomfret, contrary to the King's laws'. Then they rode away, leaving Scrooby to drift back into its slumber.

Henry's third wife, Jane Seymour, produced the longed-for son and heir – Edward – in 1537, but Henry died when Edward was only nine. When Edward died in 1553, Mary came to the throne.

> Half Spanish, the daughter and confidante of Catherine of Aragon, sometimes treated by her father as a bastard, Mary grew up with an attachment to Rome so fervent as to be fanatical.[17]

She moved ruthlessly to restore Catholicism and appointed a Catholic to replace Archbishop Cranmer, a powerful figure who had shaped the Church of England, moving it firmly towards Protestantism, and who was burned at the stake in Oxford. Soon enough, she would be called Bloody Mary.

By now many Protestants had taken refuge abroad: there was a tradition of doing that. Physically, they were patient people, born of an age which – limited by the speed of a horse or a sailing ship – could not be hustled. They would wait for their chance to return to England and begin the process of the Reformation again, and that would take as long as it took. A central figure among the ordinary folk, William Bradford would write that

> besides those worthy martyrs and confessors which were burned in Queen Mary's days and otherwise tormented, many fled out of the land to the number of 800 and became several congregations, at Wesel [on the Rhine], Frankfort, Basel, Emden . . . Strasbourg, Geneva etc.[18]

Mary died in 1558, to be succeeded by Elizabeth. The nuances of this astonishing woman continue to tantalise. Nobody really knew what she thought, although she spoke a great deal; she took good care that they did not know. As the daughter of Anne Boleyn, she was a Protestant. She was a horsewoman and she liked a glass of beer, she used strong language and always had her wits about her, and yet she always remained regal.

Although she began to dismantle the Catholic structure Mary had put in place, she was certainly shrewd enough to grasp, and fast, what the Reformation meant politically and what it might mean for the stability of the realm. However subtle her politics, though, the numbers of people wanting to purify the Anglican Church of Papist elements continued to grow. They came to be known as Puritans, initially a term of abuse, but subsequently a matter of some pride. They denounced the wealth and ornate dress of some clergymen, and the sale of favours which made the Church 'a huge mess of old and stinking works'. Little groups

> flourished wherever religion was unsettled. And the religion of Elizabethan England was still, in a manner, unsettled . . . England chose a middle road . . . at least from 1567 there were a few groups or congregations who could not bear to worship in churches where surplices were used or men knelt to receive the sacrament, and who withdrew to illicit, secret, hunted meetings.
>
> The Reformation appealed to the open Bible. The Reformers had desired and planned that the simplest labourer in the fields might be able to read it. [T]he labourer was beginning to read for himself, and with potent consequences. England . . . was to test what happened when the . . . brazier and the feltmaker and the coachman went into the Bible to fetch their divinity for themselves.[19]

Background and foreground were moving towards each other. By 1571, a man called William Brewster was living in Scrooby. Ordinarily, such a man would have been lost within the broad, constant, silent flow – but there was the road, the manor house and the Royal Mail. Scrooby sat astride the Great North Road, one of England's four great spokes to and from London. Watling Street went to Chester and travellers to Ireland used that; the Dover Road went down to the Channel and the boats for the Continent; the road to Plymouth connected London to the West Country.

The Great North Road was like an umbilical cord connecting the capital, York and Edinburgh. Scrooby was a staging post for the Mail between a small place, Tuxford, and the town of Doncaster. Here are the ten posts in the area:[20]

	Miles from London
Darlington	241
Northallerton	225
Boroughbridge	206
Wetherby	194
Ferrybridge	177
Doncaster	162
Scrooby	152
Tuxford	137
Newark	124
Grantham	110

The road from Tuxford passed through tiny Torworth and, two-thirds of a mile further on, another tiny place, Ranskill. This was a crossroads with a track to the left for the hamlet of Blyth, to the right for the hamlet of Mattersey. Scrooby (Scrubey in those times) was 2 miles further on, before the road twisted right and moved to the town of Bawtry. Doncaster was some 9 miles away.

Because of the Great North Road, Brewster was in a position to hear the latest news and gossip as travellers came through. Villages of the same size even a few miles away were isolated from this.

Scrooby, an agricultural community, had a population of about 150 to 200. A yeoman class – small-scale freeholders – was establishing itself, with labourers working for them or the manor. Everything was intensely manual. Their dwellings would have been on plots from medieval times. The road was the village street running below the church. Ducks and geese wandered along it. Unsurfaced, it was prone to flooding and travellers had to pick a path through the puddles and standing water. A river, the Idle, wended a course through the flour mill, itself on a medieval site beside the manor house but with a diversionary channel in times of flood, complete with sluice gates. The old mill wheel must have creaked and there may well have been a smithy attached to the manor house, hammer blows echoing into the creaking of the wheel.[21]

Scrooby had originally been a Danish settlement and possibly meant 'farmstead or village of a man called Skropi', from Old

Scandinavian, the language of the Vikings, comprising Old Danish and Old Norse.[22] The Scandinavian invasions had been between the ninth and eleventh centuries and one enduring result was in the place-names scattered across the northern part of England. 'Anywhere ending in *by* is almost certainly of Danish origin, as in *Grimsby* and *Derby*. Another Viking place-name is *wick* as in Swainswick, Keswick and Chiswick. *Thorpe* (Danish) and *thwaite* (Norwegian) are also common Viking names, as is *toft* (meaning a plot of land), and *scale* (a temporary hut or shelter).'[23]

The surrounding area was arable and, because of the rivers, rich pastureland for grazing.

> There would have been sheep walks on the low range of hills between the Trent and the Great North Road and to the west of the road, but no massive flocks. North of a line from Gainsborough to Bawtry, that is, a few miles from Scrooby, the fenland ran up to the Isle of Axholme and to Hatfield, full of wild duck, goose, swan, waders and bitterns (butterbumps, the Pilgrims would have called them) and sometimes the sky would have darkened with flights of fowl. There were plenty of fat eels and there were deer in the woods.[24]

Scrooby appeared in Domesday Book as Scrobi, a *berewic* (outlying part of a manor) to the Archbishop of York's manor at Sudtone, now Sutton-cum-Lound. You can find fleeting mentions of Scrooby in the years to come, almost like fragments lifted from the flow of time – the archbishops had extensive hunting grounds and the 'franchise of free warren', which gave them exclusive rights to game. In 1258 the archbishop made grants and hay at Scrooby, and decreed that the poor should be given an annual pension of four marks.[25] In 1315, the archbishop allowed his bailiff of the day 74*s* 8*d* to buy flint and stone to build a chamber at the manor house.

John Leland, Henry VIII's antiquarian, set out to create a travelogue of the whole country. He went west from the town of Gainsborough and reached Mattersey, a hamlet on the track from the Ranskill crossroads. 'Thence I rode a mile, in low wash and somewhat fenny ground; and a mile further or more by higher ground, to Scrooby.' He described the town as mean in the old sense of the word: shabby, unimpressive. He did remark on two aspects, the church (for more about this see the next chapter) which he found not very large but well built out of neatly squared stones, and the moated manor house with its buildings built around courtyards. Those around the first were 'very ample and all built of timber' except for the front of the hall which was of brick, and he entered 'over cut-stone steps'. Then Leland rode on, as so many others did and would do, across a ford in the Idle and 'so betwixt the pales of two parks belonging to Scrooby' he reached Bawtry. The Idle could be navigated, linking Scrooby with nearby towns like Bawtry.

You can trace similar histories in a thousand English towns and villages. They *are* the background, and the little communities – insular, mostly isolated, unchanging in character, each generation tilling the same ground – sank very deep roots. Even though Scrooby was not isolated, the roots must have gone as deep. For any inhabitant to leave it permanently would represent a profound and astonishing decision.

Brewster lived at the manor. He was postmaster, a position of importance and responsibility, because by law he had to service the riders who passed along the road with Mail. The Great North Road was more than a spoke: it was an artery along which the lifeblood of the kingdom flowed. To maintain the flow, the postmaster was required to have three 'good and sufficient' horses constantly ready with saddles and bridles for them, and a supply of post bags for the riders. While the riders were at Scrooby, their welfare was his responsibility. He had to feed and house them in the manor, where he had been appointed bailiff and receiver in 1575.

The organisation of the postal network was taken with great seriousness and spawned its own bureaucracy. There were elaborate rules, for example, about what to do if 'the carriers come so thick, or in such number, that the Post's own supply of horses shall not be able to suffice'. And this: 'No man riding in Post, shall ride without a guide: which shall blow his horn, so oft as he meeteth company, or passeth through any town, or at least thrice every mile.' The objective was to deliver from London to Berwick in 42 hours during the summer and 60 in winter.[26]

> The post was expected to cover seven miles an hour during summer, and five in winter. Within one quarter of an hour of the arrival of a packet, the postmaster either had to carry it himself, or cause it to be carried to the next post. He was to provide three strong leather bags, well-lined with baize or cotton, in which to carry the packet. No packet should be entrusted to anyone except to an actual servant of the post. No private letters, or packets, nor any other kind of luggage should be delivered before delivering Her Majesty's packets. If any misdemeanours occurred, the postmaster himself would be held responsible.[27]

As well as Brewster's duties with the Mail, he collected the manorial fees and rents, and could act as a magistrate. This manor had once been the seat of the archbishops of York and was splendid enough for Henry VIII to have spent a night there. Cardinal Thomas Wolsey, the most important man in England after Henry, stayed several times – perhaps for periods of months – and liked it so much he planted a mulberry tree. The manor was surrounded by a moat and so had to be reached across a drawbridge. It had, or had had some years before, thirty-nine apartments and the great hall was big enough to accommodate six tables and nine benches as well as one cupboard. It had a chapel with a timber altar, a reading desk, two organs and a clock.

The money raised at the manor could have been substantial. A knight paid 'ten shillings for the use of a horse and a guide to Tuxford and seven shillings and tenpence for supper, a hot drink of spiced ale, bed and breakfast'. On the way back, he paid 'eight shillings for the use of a horse to Doncaster, two shillings for burned sack,[28] bread, beer, sugar and wine'.[29] Even allowing for the fact that this was long after the time of the labourers' wages already described, these prices were steep.

Brewster married Mary Simkinson at Scrooby. Née Smythe (or Smithe), she was a widow who had previously been married to a John Simkinson of Doncaster. In 1566 or 1567 the Brewsters had a son who, like his father, was called William. They would have another son, James.

In the foreground, the life of another Mary – Queen of Scots – was played out within the mosaic of European alliances. Mary was the granddaughter of Henry VIII's sister Margaret while Elizabeth was, in Roman Catholic eyes, the product of the illegal 'marriage' to Anne Boleyn. Mary, the Catholics insisted, was the rightful queen. After an inter-Scottish battle near Glasgow, Mary fled to England, putting herself at the mercy of Elizabeth. That was 1568 and she would be Elizabeth's prisoner for nineteen years. When Elizabeth finally decided what to do with her, it would impact directly on Brewster.

Young William Brewster was a bright lad and went to Cambridge University in 1580, arriving on 3 December. His father could clearly afford it. He entered Peterhouse, the oldest college (founded in 1281) as a Pensioner, meaning a student with lodgings, and was taught Latin and some Greek.

Universities, and university towns, are places where young men meet ideas. Straight away at Cambridge, Brewster encountered a radical group of academics and clergymen who were approaching religious extremism. They demanded even more reform of worship, and specifically even more freedom for people to interpret the scriptures as they wanted. These were dangerous demands but Brewster had met his big idea. It was Puritanism.

Many others met their big idea at Cambridge, too, as it was arguably the centre of gathering religious fervour. The town and university produced, in geographical terms, an astonishing concentration of influential people who were 'stirred by the fires'. They would take their profound beliefs and their theology with them when they left, expanding the concentration into an area of some 20 square miles, with Scrooby near its northern edge. This in turn produced a sense of communal strength, although perhaps dynamic is a better word. Seldom, if ever, can so many people from the background, and living in so many anonymous places, have had such an impact – however indirectly – on the world.

Brewster's big idea was delivered to him by one of the radicals, Robert Browne, who seems to have been a human volcano. A furious Puritan and prominent Separatist – they advocated a complete break with the Church of England – Browne thought, for example, that 'an idle person ceased to be a member of the church of God'.[30]

Browne, who gave his name to a movement, the Brownists, was offered a position as curate of the church next to Corpus Christi College in Cambridge, but proved too volcanic for the congregation there and did not stay long. He went freelance, preaching wherever and whatever he wanted in the town and surrounding area without the appropriate licence from the bishop. Browne's brother got a licence for him, and one for himself, but Browne burned them both.

The influence that Browne had on Brewster must have been profound. He was at an impressionable age. Perhaps he heard what he wanted to hear, perhaps what he heard converted him. Either way, he had found what was to guide him through the rest of his life, taking him from Scrooby into exile – in his case, Holland – and then, far into the next century, his final resting place in Massachusetts.

He left Cambridge between 1582 and 1583 (although one source suggests he might have been there only a few months) and there are conflicting views on whether he graduated. He went into service with Sir William Davison, the British Ambassador to Holland.

> After he had attained some learning . . . of the Latin tongue and some insight in the Greek, and spent some small time at Cambridge, . . . being first seasoned with the seeds of grace and virtue, he went to Court and served that religious and godly gentleman Mr Davison divers years when he was Secretary of State, who found him so discreet and faithful as he trusted him above all other that were about him, and only employed him in all matters of greatest trust and secrecy. [He] esteemed him rather as a son than a servant; and for his wisdom and godliness he would converse with him more like a friend and familiar than a master.[31]

Holland was ruled by Spain, and the Dutch wanted their freedom. They came to Elizabeth for diplomatic and financial support and, cannily, she demanded securities for the loans she gave. The Dutch offered two towns and a castle. The keys to one of the towns, Flushing, were presented to Davison who passed them on to Brewster for safe keeping. The first night he had them he slept with them under his pillow. He was presented with a gold chain and

Davison 'commanded him to wear it, when they arrived in England, as they rid through the country, till they came to the Court'.[32]

Brewster was now in the foreground, or rather Davison took him there. For years, Elizabeth had procrastinated about signing a death warrant for Mary. In 1586 she decided to do it but, for political reasons – all else aside, Mary had had close relations with Catholic France – needed to distance herself from the decision. Davison issued the warrant and subsequently Elizabeth claimed he had put it in among other papers she had had to sign that day, the implication being that she had signed it without reading it. In 1587 Mary was executed, Davison arrested and sent to the Tower.

Somehow Brewster continued to serve Davison – it is not clear for how long, possibly until 1588 – before returning to Scrooby to settle down. He was certainly back there by 1589 when his father became or had become ill. A complaint was made about the slowness of a messenger carrying a dispatch between Berwick and London. He had taken 83 hours to travel the 155 miles from Berwick to Newark, a great deal longer than he should have. The messenger made up some time on the stage from Doncaster to Scrooby, but he still took two hours to cover the 7 miles before he handed the dispatch over to Brewster.

In 1590, Brewster senior died. The supposition ought to be that son succeeded father as postmaster in the natural way, although there is an absence of documentation. The supposition is strengthened because somebody must run the manor house and Brewster senior had been living in it.

When Brewster junior was about twenty-six, a year or two after his return to Scrooby, he married Mary, surname unknown. Strenuous (and tenuous) efforts have been made to discover her family and there is even speculation that Brewster had had children before the arrival of the generally recognised first-born, Jonathan, in Scrooby on 12 August 1593 – the year a strong Act was passed against Puritans and Separatists, threatening the Punishment of Persons Obstinately Refusing to Come to Church.

> All persons above the age of sixteen, refusing to come . . . or persuading others to deny Her Majesty's authority in causes

> ecclesiastical, or dissuading them from coming . . . or being found present at any conventicle or meeting under pretence of religion, shall upon conviction be committed to prison without bail till they shall conform and come to church.[33]

The Act threatened 'perpetual banishment' and 'death without benefit of clergy' if ever transgressors dared return from the banishment. Three Separatist leaders were executed and one of them, John Penry, had evidently been a classmate of Brewster at Cambridge.

The tantalising nuances of Elizabeth allow several interpretations. 'Her religious settlement may have been a patchwork of compromise but the Church of England took root and earned respect and affection' is one.[34] Another has to be that even her skills could not contain the forces in play, notably the Separatists, an extremist group who wanted to break away from the Church completely because they felt it contained too much Catholicism and the Sabbath was not being observed properly.

In 1594, Brewster's brother James was appointed vicar of Scrooby's mother church, Sutton-cum-Lound. He had a reputation as a rebel in the established Church and selected his curates by taking good care that they shared his views. This created momentum for moving the congregations in the direction of Separatism.

James Brewster is a person from the background, and perhaps that's just as well because his was a fertile family. One genealogical table suggests there were nine Brewster children, of whom three were called James. They seemed to have lived in and around Scrooby and some may have held positions within the Church.

In time, William and Mary had a full family of their own. Five children followed Jonathan. One, described simply as a child, was probably born in Holland and died there shortly afterwards. The others have a beautiful, and slightly strange, cadence to their names: Patience (born *c.* 1600), Fear (*c.* 1606), Love (*c.* 1611) and Wrestling (either 1605 or 1614). They were a sturdy lot. They were going to need to be.

TWO

The Manor House

The cavalcade that daily travelled the Great North Road and rescued Scrooby from its anonymity has gone into the great silence. Only imagination can recreate it.[1] Most travellers would have gone on foot, pilgrims perhaps; pedlars who used it as an artery, leaving it for the rough tracks that led to tiny hamlets such as Blyth and Mattersey where they would try and sell their wares; groups of workmen – carpenters, stonemasons, tilers with their tool bags searching out employment; farmers driving cattle and poultry to market; runaways and the eternally hopeful tramping towards distant London.[2]

There were the horsemen: the messengers bearing official documents, riding urgently between staging posts, Brewster and his equivalents all up and down the artery with change of horses ready. The riders at full gallop must have been dramatic figures against a static backdrop, heads down, capes billowing, horses breathing hard. Others were also on horseback but proceeding at a more leisurely pace: the merchants going about their business; the titled and the wealthy with their servants and guards.

They must have touched Scrooby with a worldliness. They all saw, as those who pass through today see, St Wilfred's Church

named for a seventh-century archbishop of York. The church's early fifteenth-century square tower supports a tall spire which, with its four pinnacles, symbolises Christ's five wounds. Its bells called young William Brewster to worship. The south aisle, with its Tudor-style windows, dates from the sixteenth century. Near the churchyard the Old Vicarage, more a private dwelling, also dated from the sixteenth century, but with modern renovations and expansion it hardly resembles the little thatched-roof cottage of Brewster's day.[3]

The interior has the timelessness of any English country church, a sense of antiquity, continuity, solidity. It is in such places that the past seems close. They looked upon these thick walls just as anyone can now; and the beautifully carved rail and chair – the carving flowing easily, like handwriting across the darkened wood – were the same to William Brewster's gaze as they are to ours, although much else has changed. Two ornately carved chancel seats remain, however, and what may possibly have been a leper window. 'Of the bells in the tower, one is of recent casting, and one was put there in 1647, but the other two bear the dates 1411 and 1511.'

This is slightly deceptive, however, because the inside of the church is not as it was in 1610.

> It was thoroughly gutted and restored in 1864. Most parish churches have had a very serious make-over, usually in Victorian times, and there's a very good reason for this. The post-Reformation Church of England was bedevilled by absentee clergy. Often they put in a curate to take the services and this was true of Scrooby. The upshot was that the rector of the church was not around enough to see that the fabric was in order but when the Church started losing a good deal of ground to the Methodist movement in the early nineteenth century they decided the only way they could combat this was to have a fundamental change of plan and to put a resident clergyman into each parish.
>
> It would be true to say you have a church that would be more recognisable in 1608 from the exterior rather than the interior. It would probably have had oak pews and a screen separating church from chancel. It would have been symmetrical inside – meaning that there would have been a north aisle and a south aisle. The floor would almost certainly have been of earth. The medieval font (now transported to Chicago) was chucked out when the Victorians were redoing it. The Victorians liked perfection. If something was damaged in any way, they would quite readily replace it and with a perfect new example. There was no room in their thinking for anything else. The pulpit would have been oak.[4]

At Babworth, Richard Clyfton – another whose big idea was delivered to him by Robert Browne at Cambridge – had been Rector of All Saints' Church for more than ten years.[5] His preaching must have had plenty of Browne's purity and power because people began to travel to hear it, the Brewsters among them. Perhaps they rode. Perhaps they walked the tracks and meadows, guided by and drawing ever closer to the church's square spire. Babworth had only 96 inhabitants and was about 7 miles from Scrooby. In character, their churches were very similar. Clyfton was a 'grave and reverend preacher, who by his pains and diligence had done much good, and under God had been a means of the conversion of many'.[6]

In 1598 Brewster was 'cited' in an ecclesiastical court for 'irregular church attendance' at St Wilfred's, presumably because he was attending Babworth. The fact that his absence had been noted – by any local clergyman or informer working for the Archbishop of York – might have been dangerous for him and his lucrative position at the manor. He was not, however, the kind of man to be dissuaded.

In 1602, a twelve-year-old lad had joined the congregation. William Bradford, born in the village of Austerfield across the county boundary in south Yorkshire, had walked the 10 or 11 miles to Babworth, coming down the Great North Road through Scrooby, past the crossroads at Ranskill and then on through Barnby Moor. Nobody knows why he did this, but when he got there he met his big idea.

His father died a year later. He was brought up by grandparents and, after that, by uncles, but it would seem that Brewster became a surrogate father. The two men who would help to shape the mighty nation were now in place.

Others were not far away. In Gainsborough, which could only be reached from the Scrooby area by taking a ferry across the River Trent, there was a minister called John Smyth. His early life is obscure and tracing it no easy matter: the name is common in whichever direction you look, then and now. He was another who had been to Cambridge, then appointed a lecturer-preacher in the city of Lincoln in 1600, but was dismissed two years later as a 'facetious man' with 'strange doctrines'. He came to Gainsborough in 1602 or 1603, but

> the vicar from 1566 to 1602 was John Jackson, a literate man of mediocre abilities. He was succeeded in 1602 by Jerome Phillips, who remained there until 1608, and was followed by Henry Clifford. It was the poverty of Jackson's ministry which eased the way for the appointment of Smyth. Phillips himself was content to enjoy the income from his parish but performed no duties. It enabled Smyth to establish himself as the spiritual leader of the more devoted members of the congregation. Smyth was a man of greater intellectual status and influence than his critics sometimes allow.[7]

It may be that Smyth's guidance on 'certain ideological points' was sought by the people at Scrooby. Whatever, his position was made relatively easy and safe because Gainsborough's lord of the manor had a family history of Puritanism. His parents, staunch Puritans, held secret religious meetings in their home during the reign of Bloody Mary. His father had been imprisoned and, on release, fled abroad with his wife. She was still alive when Brewster took up the position of postmaster at Scrooby. Smyth had even preached to sixty or seventy people at Gainsborough.

Queen Elizabeth died in 1603 and was succeeded by James VI of Scotland who became James I of England as well.

> By 1603 . . . there were many of the new king's subjects who were far from happy with the Church to which they were forced to belong.
>
> Puritans were those whose life-styles were more influenced than others by Protestant principles and who were more concerned than others to reform the Church. In 1603 it is highly unlikely that there were many Puritans who wanted a disestablished Church, or even a state Church without bishops. Those who had advocated radical measures like these in the later years of Elizabeth's reign had been severely punished . . . There may, of course, have been Puritans who adopted a radical stance but one has to be satisfied with the conclusion that, if they existed, they were too prudent to show themselves to the authorities.[8]

This covered, no doubt, many little groups scattered here and there – including Scrooby – perfectly.

In 1604 James held a great conference at Hampton Court, which was attended by leading religious figures and reformers. Like the Reformation itself, the conference is open to differing interpretations and James may well have been sympathetic to the demands of the Puritans. Delicate territory. The Church establishment was entrenched and the landed gentry against reform. After Hampton Court, James felt a reform programme had been agreed and was annoyed that the Puritans kept on making their demands. In September 1604 a list of 141 rules was announced and James issued a proclamation that Puritan clergymen had to conform or lose their positions 'as being men unfit, for their obstinacy and contempt, to occupy such places'.

> It had now become abundantly clear to the Puritans that, not only were they unable to reform the Church of England from within, but also that there was no room at all for them. A few of the more redoubtable, like Clyfton at Babworth and Robinson at Norwich, were forced outside into schism and opposition. The rest bided their time.[9]

The Robinson was John Robinson, another Cambridge graduate and originally from Sturton-le-Steeple. In 1592 he had gone to Corpus Christi and graduated in 1595. He was elected a fellow, and became college dean in 1600. When he married in 1604 he had to resign the fellowship because the college did not allow married men to hold them. He took Holy Orders and went to St Andrew's church, Norwich, but was excommunicated under the 141 Rules, which he did not accept. He returned to Sturton-le-Steeple, moved back into the dynamic – and bided his time. He would not have to wait long. The dynamic itself was moving.

In 1607, Clyfton resigned his position at Babworth and joined the congregation at Gainsborough.

In 1605, Robert Southworth, Vicar of Headon – just to the east of Scrooby – had been deprived of his living (although whether for Puritanism is not clear). William Brewster offered him a position at

Scrooby as unlicensed curate. That year seventeen men and women were due to appear in court for going to Sturton-le-Steeple to hear Robinson preach on Whit Sunday. There is a sense of the pace quickening. The tightness of the area around Scrooby, of almost no geographical significance at all, would ultimately interconnect with events being played out immense distances away, although that would take time.

In 1605, while Southworth was being offered his position, a Captain George Weymouth went on an expedition for some English merchants to explore the commercial possibilities of Canada and New England. He sailed down the Maine coast to Massachusetts where he found Indians. He reasoned that the merchants at home would be 'interested' to see some and kidnapped a couple. 'We used little delay, but suddenly laid hands upon them . . . they were strong and so naked as our best hold was by their long hair on their heads.' He bribed another three. 'We gave them a can of peas and bread, which they carried to the shore to eat but one of them brought back our can presently and stayed aboard with the other two.' That Indian was Squanto,[10] a member of the Wampanoag tribe, whose territory stretched along a verdant shoreline and included two islands.

The pious people at Scrooby, many of whom probably had not travelled beyond the immediate area in their lives, would never have heard of such distant places and probably would not have been very interested if they had. Nor can they have imagined that one warm Thursday, beside a vast bay, five men would move towards them across a flatland of stubble bearing skins for trade and some fresh dried herrings. One of them was Squanto. The Scrooby people, clutching their muskets, had found a lifeline – but that was fifteen years away.

In 1606 King James had become anxious to secure a share of North America. Henry VIII had tried and failed, Queen Elizabeth had employed Sir Walter Ralegh and put settlers on Roanoke, North Carolina but that had failed. All that remained was the name Virginia, a tribute to the unmarried queen covering an area from Florida to New England. James seems to have been more determined. On 10 April he issued letters patent (Charters) to two groups of investors, the Virginia Company and the Plymouth Company.

The Virginia Company was given land between latitudes 34 and 41 (Wilmington, North Carolina, to Connecticut) and the Plymouth Company land between latitudes 38 and 45 (lower Delaware to Maine). In the overlap, either could establish colonies but not within 100 miles of each other.

That same year the Bishop of Durham – Tobias Matthew, who could sniff out Puritans like a hunting dog – was transferred to York, so that Scrooby fell within his range. At Durham he had

> acted as the political agent of the Crown, and had reported on the affairs of the northern shires and of Scotland. He curried royal favour by vigorously supporting the policies of Elizabeth and James. At Durham, he harassed recusants [people who defy authority] and other nonconformist groups. On his translation to York, the political and ecclesiastical activities grew apace, and he was determined to root out all heretical and schismatical practices in his diocese.[11]

The leading Puritans and Separatists were not passive. They met in Coventry at the home of one Isabel Wray, wife of Sir William Bowes – a knight who was sympathetic. Among those present were Clyfton, Robinson and Smyth. At this meeting, Robinson became a convinced Separatist and Smyth argued that separation from the Church of England was the only course. The overall feeling of the meeting was against taking such a course, however. Smyth understood that, in general, the Puritans would not support the Separatists and their radicalism. The Separatists would have to go it alone. 'Never a man to be afraid of the logic of his own thinking, Smyth renounced his Anglican orders'[12] and, already operating in sympathetic Gainsborough, was elected pastor.

Clyfton was already among the congregation there, and Brewster joined it, too, but to get to Gainsborough was a 9-mile journey there and a 9-mile journey back for both of them. That may have been decisive. Clyfton was fifty-three, ancient in those days. Some time around 1606 a little congregation started to meet in the chapel at Scrooby manor. Tradition has it that Brewster set it up, Clyfton becoming pastor and Robinson becoming teacher.[13] In effect, the three of them had left the Church of England.

One author[14] points out that 'it is almost impossible for us nowadays to realise the crass ignorance of the country peasantry in England' at that time. 'Clyfton, Brewster, Robinson and Smyth were all Cambridge men', and but for them the story of the *Mayflower* would not have happened.

Leaving the Church of England was drastic enough but it begged another question. How long could they stay in England? Bradford describes the prevalent climate. The Separatists

> could not continue long in any peacable condition but were hunted and persecuted on every side, so as their former afflictions were but as flea-bitings in comparison of these which now came upon them . . . Some were taken and clapped up in prison, others had their houses beset and watched day and night . . . The most were fain to flee and leave their houses and habitations, and the means of their livelihood.[15]

Bishop Matthew began his assault in March 1607 and nobody was safe. He calculated that 'once the lay and clerical leaders had been silenced, their congregations, like sheep without a shepherd, would be scattered'. The little group at Scrooby must have felt immediately vulnerable: the churchwardens at various communities in the area were 'all in their turn presented' in court 'for allowing Separatist preachers to use their pulpits. They were then dismissed with a warning.'[16]

The services on Sundays in Scrooby manor house must have been held against a constant fear that, at any instant, they might be betrayed. They cannot have known, even inadvertently, if idle gossip by any of the congregation had given them away; and the Great North Road made the situation worse. Strangers and officials were passing through all the time.

There was a possible problem with St Wilfred's in that the congregation there could not help noticing the absence of those worshipping at the manor, and word of this was bound to spread. However,[17] services at St Wilfred's were only every other Sunday, so Brewster's group could use the alternate Sundays as they wished and without suspicion. It is also possible that they attended St Wilfred's as a sort of cover. In any case the Brewster group may have been small, and included many from beyond the parish: so small, in fact, that they were hardly missed, anyway.

The pace quickened decisively now, moving towards a decision. On 30 September, Brewster resigned his position as postmaster, suggesting that the decision had been taken. Seeing

> themselves thus molested and that there was no hope of their continuance [in England], by joint consent they resolved to go into [Holland] where they heard [there] was freedom of religion for all men – and also how sundry from London and other parts . . . had been exiled and persecuted for the same cause . . . were gone there and lived in Amsterdam and in other places . . . So after they had continued together about a year, and kept their meetings every Sabbath, in one place or other . . . they resolved to get over into Holland . . . in the year 1607 and 1608.[18]

There was religious freedom in Holland and John Smyth had already decided to exploit this. He had taken the Gainsborough community to Amsterdam, perhaps early in 1607. If so, he might have acted as pathfinder for the Scrooby community. Either way, Smyth was over there and still temperamentally volcanic.

The Scrooby decision was possibly made in the early autumn, perhaps around mid-September. Their departure – more properly, their flight – is popularly stated as being September: a granite obelisk recording where they made the attempt says so, but if Brewster only resigned on 30 September, how was it possible? More likely, they left soon after this.

To stay at home posed a potential danger because this was an age of swift justice and brutal punishments. Under Elizabeth, for example, treason – which included failing to recognise her as head of the Church – involved the guilty man being dragged to the place of execution, hung until half-dead and then quartered alive. Anyone advocating a disestablished Church was severely dealt with. James was known to live in horror of witchcraft and had highly unpleasant things done to those convicted of it. What might he do to the Separatists?

To try and go abroad posed a direct danger because, without official permission, it was illegal. By statute, anyone had to have a licence to go, which was obviously out of the question for the Scrooby group. Smyth, evidently, had circumvented this by going quietly and he had made it to the other side of the North Sea without causing ripples. Pathfinder or not, Smyth had shown how it could be done. The Scrooby group prepared to follow.

How the decision was reached, or where, is not known. To have debated it with the whole congregation would have been a strategy with very high risks: any member of the congregation, reporting to the authorities, would have destroyed the plan. What seems more likely is one, or all three, of the triumvirate running and shaping the group – Brewster, Robinson and Clyfton – realised that flight was inevitable; they would have prudently and discreetly discussed it among themselves; the group would have included Bradford early on, and then approached other members of the congregation individually and sounded them out, again prudently and discreetly.

In rural Scrooby, the ordinary folk were being asked to abandon their homes, all their possessions except what they could carry, everything they had known all their lives, risk prison, and – if they evaded capture – take themselves and their families to a foreign country about which they knew little or nothing and certainly would not have spoken a word of the language. At the instant of their flight, any prospects of returning, even in the distant future, would effectively be gone. It is worth repeating: to leave permanently represented a profound and astonishing decision.

Speculation is tenuous at the best of times. There can be no doubt that in a pious age, when the only explanation for the world came from religion (or straightforward superstition), belief was not a matter of educated choice or preference, it was life itself. The differences between the various Protestant groups – a myriad of them – and the Catholic Church were great, but not greater than their similarities. But that's a different story.

This story centres on three or four dominant people leading a group of very determined, stubborn, devout, ordinary folk who had all had a choice forced upon them, or they had forced it upon themselves. The decision was the result of the choice:

> to go into a country . . . where they must learn a new language and get their livings they knew not how, it being a dear place, and subject to the miseries of war,[19] it was by many thought an adventure almost desperate, a case intolerable, and a misery worse than death – especially seeing they were not acquainted with trades, nor traffic (by which that country does subsist) but had only been used to a plain country life and the innocent trade of husbandry [farming].[20]

Once the decision had been taken – 'by joint consent', which is a powerful phrase in an autocratic age – the move had a logic of its own. They might be able to shape it, they might not. They cannot have known it, but whatever happened, they would worship as they wished. They were prepared to die for it, and many would.

The journey would be hard, but life was hard. Ask any labourer bending his back every daylight hour for a couple of coins, ask his wife in the hovel where their stillborn children had come and gone.

So, on one day or over many, they made their decision. They do not seem the kind to have entertained self-doubts, and God would protect them. They were sure *He* would never abandon them – so they went.

> There was a large company of them purposed to get passage at Boston in Lincolnshire, and for that end had hired a ship wholly to themselves and made agreement with the master to be ready at a certain day, and take them and their goods, at a convenient place, where they accordingly would all attend in readiness.[21]

How many went, or exactly who they were, is lost now. Sometime in September, Brewster had made contact with a sea captain, an Englishman. They were to make their way to the Lincolnshire port of Boston 60 miles away and, as discreetly as they could, board the ship from a place on the seaward side of the town, called Scotia Creek. This was at Fishtoft, where the creek enters the River Whitham.

Before they left Scrooby, they had to decide what to sell and what to take with them, and it would have to be done discreetly.

Malcolm Dolby explains that 'we do not know how many people owned houses but most people would have been tenants. They did not sell anything when they decided to leave because they did not have anything to sell.'

There was some suggestion there were intermediaries to launder money – not launder it in the modern sense of the word but to hold on to finances on their behalf. Someone in Hull held money in trust for one of the women, presumably as a result of her selling-up. There would have been an element of selling-up or at least a decision to leave things in the hands of family and trusted friends to deal with on their behalf.[22]

Their journey to Boston was made, according to one source,[23] in small boats travelling down the Idle from Scrooby 'past Bawtry Parish Church, where the original course of the river ran and where they picked up more passengers, into the Trent at Gainsborough and Torksey, still 50 miles distant from Boston, thence via the Fosse Dyke to Lincoln'.

That ancient city, dominated by the great Norman cathedral on a hill, still had medieval streets and a lingering sense of the Roman occupation. The Romans had built the Fosse Dyke, a canal between the Trent and the Witham: the Witham ran, and runs, right through Lincoln, 'where the High Street crosses the river, with a medieval house built on the bridge'.[24]

But did the group go this way? They could certainly have travelled by water from Gainsborough, following the incoming tide up the Trent, then the Fosse Dyke, then along the narrow waterway of the Witham through the very centre of Lincoln and, on the ebb tide, to and through Boston.[25]

It would have looked very different from Scrooby, but 'the need to avoid Lincoln itself and episcopal authority would have been more important than avoiding the generally sympathetic Puritan Boston townspeople'.[26]

Did they, instead, send the women and children by boat while the men walked? The women and children would have been relatively safe from arrest (arresting them could only bring problems). Did the men take a sweeping detour which kept them away from towns and villages until they reached the precise place for embarkation?

Travelling overland from Gainsborough would have taken them eastward to the Wolds in open country and then south along the Northdyke Causeway (today the A16) through the fens until it meets the fork in the road, north-east of Boston – left to Waynflete, right towards Boston. They would have turned left on to the Waynflete road then right into Rochford Tower Lane (past Rochford Tower itself, which still stands). They would have continued to Fishtoft and the boggy riverside. This whole journey from Gainsborough to the north-west outskirts of Boston could only have been achieved by passing through about three fenland villages on the causeway.

The 'roads' they used would have been rough tracks with some rubble repairs and wide: they were 'drover roads' to herd livestock to the markets. On foot in dry weather, they would have used the grass verges to avoid what the livestock had left. The roads became very muddy when they were wet and the quality varied from quite poor to very bad. Whether the men did this or were in the boats, the little flotilla probably passed underneath the bridge at Lincoln almost unnoticed, as the city was a major inland port and there would have been plenty of traffic. The flotilla would have kept on towards Boston. From a long way off they would have seen the spire of St Botolph's, 272ft high and referred to locally as 'the Stump'.

As they drew closer they could see more clearly the intricacy of the spire, and if they were doing this under cover of darkness its lantern would have been lit. They would have been in awe at the height and majesty of the tower.[27] The church stood near a rickety-looking wooden town bridge linking the cluster of buildings on one side to the market square on the other.

Boston was a port and market town, both of which had gradually declined since the town's heyday as an important destination of Hanseatic League traders.[28] It was famous for its annual May Fair (still celebrated today).

They would have slipped silently past wharves with wooden cranes and stacks of sacks and barrels, some outside and some in timber warehouses. They would have seen shipbuilding and glimpsed the great stone Gysors Hall counting house and perhaps the remains of the Hanseatic steelyard warehousing. Merchant ships of all sizes and nationalities were moored on both sides of the river.

Beyond the bridge, a narrow road came down from the market-place.[29] Timbered buildings, some of red brick, lined the far side of the road, facing the river. One was the Guildhall, a deep and ornate fifteenth-century building: an arched door from the road, an arched window either side, an almost cathedral-like arched window above. How many people in the houses noticed the flotilla? Did anyone glance from an upstairs window and see the boats borne on the current? Did anyone wonder what was happening? Did the group hear, as they passed, the locals and their dialect?[30] The flotilla continued through Boston and out into the open flatland of the fens again. The Witham began to broaden as it neared the sea, becoming The Haven. They slowed and moved into the side stream of Scotia Creek.[31] The hamlet of Fishtoft lay about a mile away over the flatland. They waited. It may have been a long time and at each moment they were vulnerable.

The ship to take them sailed up and moored, maybe some distance away, at where The Haven was deeper. Darkness had drawn in, burying Fishtoft. Probably they used the boats to reach the ship, hauling their possessions up onto the deck, but once they had done that the captain

> betrayed them, having beforehand complotted with the searchers and other officers so to do. [They] took them, and put them in open boats, and there rifled and ransacked them, searching them to their shirts for money, yea even the women further than became modest. [Then they] carried them back into the town and made them a spectacle and wonder to the multitude, which came flocking on all sides to behold them.[32]

Because Boston was something of a stronghold of Puritanism[33] the group had a crucial advantage, even though they were 'rifled and stripped of their money, books, and much other goods, and were presented to the magistrates'. Messengers were dispatched to the Privy Council (advisers to the king) to announce the capture and receive judgement about what to do with them. In the meantime they were imprisoned, although 'the magistrates used them courteously and showed them what favour they could but could not deliver them till order came from the Council table'. Quite how many went to prison is unclear – presumably the women and children did not. Of the men, it may well be that some were placed under guard, a system of parole.

After a month in prison most were freed and sent back home, but seven of the principal figures – among them Brewster, Clyfton, Robinson and Bradford (although being so young he was not held as long as the others) – remained locked up. Eventually they appeared before magistrates at the Boston Guildhall and were bound over to the assizes. After this, they were escorted down a narrow, winding staircase under a trapdoor in the court and through the barred doors of two cells. These cells were rudimentary, smelling of must, entombed in silence and no doubt cobwebbed. It may be that some of the group had been in the town gaol ('Little Ease') which stood, with the Ostrich Inn, between the Stump and the marketplace.

At Scrooby 'it was particularly distressing for Mary Brewster, who was left in charge of her young children, Jonathan a boy of fifteen, Patience aged about nine and Fear, not yet a year old. They had lost many valuable possessions, including a large part of Brewster's library, and were in very straitened circumstances.'[34]

Concurrent stories again: the principals were released when they went to the assizes, which implies leniency, and that depended on the inclinations of the court – but on 10 November, a man called Gervaise Neville appeared before a court in York charged with heresy and Separatism. He lived at Scrooby and may have been a member of Brewster's congregation. He would not take the oath and accused the Church itself of heresy. The court there had a different inclination: he was sent to prison.

On 1 December, Brewster himself was summoned to appear before the High Commission, to which the Church of England used to make everyone conform. The official citation read.

> Willelmum Bruster of Scroobie, aforesaid gentleman. Information is geven that he is a Barrownist [Brownist] or disobedient in matters of Religion etc. proces was served on him by the said Robt. Blanchard and he geave him his worde to appeare this day.

> He did not appear on the day he was summoned – the Commission imposed a fine of £20 to be paid to His Majesty's use and declared an attachement should be directed for his apprehension.

Another from Scrooby, Richard Jackson had been summoned to appear on the same day but he did not either. He was also ordered to pay £20 for his 'manifest contempt and disobedience' and was to be apprehended. Both men went into hiding: a report on 15 December said that one W. Blanchard, who was after them, certified that 'he can not finde them, nor understand where they are'.

The ordinary folk in the group were not in danger of arrest, but how did they survive the winter? They had sold up and then been robbed of what they had left at Scotia Creek. Perhaps they were able to stay with family and friends, ekeing out a subsistence doing whatever work they could on the farms around. Perhaps they were able to call in the 'laundered' money.

Brewster, Clyfton, Robinson and Bradford survived the winter, and resolved to try again. They would not wait long, either, as they could not afford to linger.

THREE

Going Dutch

In the spring, eight or ten weeks after the fiasco at Boston, the ordinary folk were waiting on the shoreline where, at low tide, the brown mud dries and cracks into a mosaic of squares, making the mudflat look as if it has been tiled; and the gully with sloping banks where the mud dries into a piebald-coloured patchwork.

The Scrooby group tried to leave again. This time they waited at Killingholme Creek,[1] 40 miles north of Boston, for the Dutch ship to come and take them off – but the bark that brought them had stuck on the mudflat, marooned by low tide. The countryside around was similar to Scrooby, rural and pastoral. Immingham, the little village which was 'just over there', had been inhabited as early as AD 100 and built up around AD 400 when the Anglo-Saxons 'crossed the North Sea and settled among the marches of the Humber estuary, where a small stream flowed into the river. From here they could fish, hunt wild birds and cut reeds, and just inland there were forests to provide timber. In medieval times there was a flourishing port.'[2] It was all very traditional: the anonymity of the background, generation after generation.

Long after the group had left, Scrooby was recorded as having just eleven houses grouped around a close, and at three people to a house that would have yielded a population of thirty-three. No doubt it was more or less the same in the spring of 1608. The fields around it had delightfully evocative names – Barmill Hill, Round Close, Crake Hill – and there was a Marsh Lane near the houses, a Green Garth Lane cutting across the big close.

No doubt, this particular day, the inhabitants were going about their business and, anyway, Killingholme Creek was too far away for them to see what was happening there, that's why the Scrooby group had chosen it. The Dutch ship sailed up at about noon the day after the women and children reached the creek. The captain saw some of the men were walking up and down on the shore – impatient? nervous? – and that everything seemed ready. He sent a boat to begin lifting the group. When the first of them had been brought back and were aboard the boat the captain prepared to get more, but then he saw

> a great company (both horse and foot), with bills and guns and other weapons (because the country was raised to take them). The Dutchman seeing that, swore the sacrament; and having the wind fair, weighed anchor, hoisted sails and away. But the poor men which were got aboard were in great distress for their wives and children, which they saw thus to be taken, and were left destitute of their help; and themselves also, not having a cloth to shift them with [change into] more than they had on their backs, and some scarce a penny about them, all they had being aboard the bark. It drew tears from their eye, and anything they had they would have given to be ashore again; but all in vain, there was no remedy, they must thus sadly part.[3]

Who had betrayed them, nobody knows, nor how it had been done. Perhaps they had been seen the day before as they made their way to the creek: strangers moving across country who were obviously not labourers or craftsmen with their tools looking for work must have been unusual; a barge full of women, children and possessions must have been equally unusual. Anyone could have sounded the alarm, but sounded it to whom?

From where the 'great company' came nobody knows. Grimsby is just to the south, but in the sixteenth century the harbour silted up and the town declined. Would there have been sufficient people and weaponry to form the 'great company'? Hull was the big town, but spread over the north bank of the River Humber, making the journey problematical. Whatever, the horsemen seem to have come by land.

> The rest of the men that were in greatest danger, made . . . to escape away before the troop could surprise them, those only staying that might be assistant unto the women. But pitiful it was to see the heavy

> case of these poor women in this distress; what crying, and weeping on every side, some for their husbands that were carried away in the ship . . . others not knowing what should become of them and their little ones; others again melted in tears, seeing their poor little ones hanging about them crying for fear and quaking with cold.[4]

The Dutch ship moved out into the North Sea, into a great storm which lasted for two weeks and carried the ships nearly to the coast of Norway. It was so dark the people on the ship saw 'neither sun, moon nor stars'.

Initially the sailors would have been concerned with refolding the sails and getting everything fastened down so they did not lose them. If you could reach a rope you held on to it as you moved. The idea was to try and ride out the storm – there was nothing else they could do. They would have to go wherever the wind and tide took them. A wooden ship was like a bobbin, moving up and down, up and down, veering from side to side and could have been turned around again and again in the swell.

It was an exceptional storm in that, ordinarily, such storms might last for six hours. At one point it raged so fiercely that, when the ship dipped, even the sailors gave up hope, shrieking and crying out. A trough between the waves could be 30ft or more, as if sudden walls of water encircled it and were preparing to crush it. The sailors recovered their nerve when the ship rose again. At one point, however – with water running into their 'mouths and ears' – the sailors called for salvation and cried out 'we sink, we sink'. But the storm passed, leaving a big, dead swell. The ship still moved up and down, but the people on it were not being thrown around any more.[5]

Paradoxically, the authorities seem to have had little or no idea what to do with those they had taken at the creek. They were shuffled from 'one place to another, and from one justice to another', but the central (and sexist) point could not be avoided: were so many women and innocent children to be thrown into prison when they were guilty of only following their husbands? Nor, of course, could they be sent home because, having sold up, they pointed out that they had no homes to go to. After they had been 'turmoiled' for some time the authorities were glad to see the back of them.

Brewster, Robinson and 'a few of the other principal members of the congregation stayed behind to comfort them and to afford what protection they could', although how much could only be problematical. This second setback, so soon after Boston, discouraged some who 'shrank at these first conflicts', but others joined the group with 'fresh courage'. Somehow, over a period of time, they all reached Holland, 'some at one time, and some at another; and some in one place, and some in another'. The group re-formed 'with no small rejoicing'.[6]

Brewster and Robinson would embark for Amsterdam when, and perhaps only when, all of the group who wanted to go had got there. In total, the group numbered between twenty and thirty.[7]

The tiny, furtive splinter groups making their way across when and where they could were still part of the silent kingdom; of their adventures we know nothing, nothing at all – with one exception. Bradford hints at 'perils' on land and sea to be overcome and recounts how (writing in the third person) 'a viper' – an officer on the ship taking him over – escorted him to the nearest local magistrate in Holland after another ('envious') passenger had betrayed him by pointing out he was fleeing England. The magistrate dismissed the case out of hand and Bradford proceeded to Amsterdam.

Was Brewster the engine driving it, organising it, shepherding them, making the arrangements and occupying himself with the details? Were there secret meetings in and around Scrooby? Were there women holding babies and pleading to stay? Were some of the determined, stubborn, devout men looking deep into themselves and finding confusion?[8]

A curiosity, too. When the Gainsborough and Scrooby congregations left, the Separatist movement left with them, and left so completely it was almost as if it had never been. Four men from Cambridge University had built it up and they took it with them.[9]

Holland had had a turbulent and uneasy past. A century and more before, the area known as the Low Countries – embracing present-day Belgium and Holland – had been assimilated by the dukes of Burgundy but, by one of those dynastic marriages we have already met, Philip II of Spain, a Catholic, inherited them. The Dutch, Calvinists – followers of the French Protestant theologian John Calvin – did not like that and drove the Spaniards out. This was the start of the Dutch Republic's golden age when, in 1572, some Calvinist seamen captured the town of Brielle to use as a base to fight the Spaniards. Other towns then rose.

England and France signed a treaty of alliance with Holland and, a year after the Scrooby group gathered in Amsterdam, Spain signed a Twelve Year Truce. 'The Dutch had been fighting for freedom and liberty of conscience and were prepared to extend both to everyone.'[10] The Dutch had a specific creed: 'every citizen should remain free in his religion, and no man be molested or questioned on the subject of divine worship'.[11]

Naturally, the rural folk of Scrooby were confronted with many new sights and experiences, walled and fortified towns guarded by armed men, different clothing, different customs and manners, and the 'strange and uncouth language'. They had reached, it seemed to them, a new world.[12] Amsterdam was much more than a city of refugees. The Dutch with their

> continually expanding and improving merchant fleet . . . exploited the whole known world and into Amsterdam flowed all kinds of merchandise from the timber and pitch of the Baltic to the spices and silks of the East Indies. Amsterdam's great days came when the Spaniards crippled the port of Antwerp. Jews driven by the Inquisition from Portugal had established Amsterdam as the world's diamond cutting and dealing centre. Flemings driven from Antwerp were both cloth merchants and financiers, and Jews, Flemings and Dutch but mostly Flemings pioneered national banks, chartered companies, a stock exchange and all the intricate machinery of large-scale capitalism. The Dutch Republic was the most solvent state in Europe, and its solid prosperity arose out of the tolerance it had extended to refugees from outside its own frontiers.[13]

This new world, however, was not as alien as it might have been. Holland was

> a logical choice for the Scrooby group when the decision to flee was taken. England had closer links to the Netherlands than any

> other country. In a declaration of 1585, Elizabeth called the Dutch England's 'most ancient and familiar neighbours'. To English dissenters, the Dutch republic was particularly attractive because it hosted a large English community, claimed an international reputation for religious tolerance, and was deeply committed to the Reformation.[14]

A tolerant society is not 'tidy', as people are doing their own things, and Amsterdam was like that. One description talks of it as a place of 'all sects, where all the pedlars of religion have leave to vend their toys'. Toleration produces tensions, because people do not have to do what other people want them to do. To those of absolutely rigid beliefs, where minutiae was the literal difference between heaven and hell, toleration produced tensions all of its own.

Amsterdam was a lively city. Every country's largest city has, and always has had, a worldliness about it, regardless of whether it is the capital or not (in Holland this was The Hague). In any sort of liberal culture, that big city becomes a sequence of windows on the world, teeming with immigrants mingled with the sights and smells of distant lands. If it is also a port it is an ever-open door to the world, with all manner of people passing through. If the Scrooby group wanted to lose themselves in the bustle of the city nobody would be troubling them to do anything else, but what impact would the worldliness have on them and, more particularly, their children?

Smyth had brought an estimated forty members of the Gainsborough congregation with him when he came in 1607. He worked as a physician and worshipped at the Ancient Church, a place with a strong attraction for Separatists. It had been established in England in 1587, but when its founder was hanged for Separatism it moved to Holland and was now led by a pastor called Francis Johnson and a teacher called Henry Ainsworth.

Right from the start, however, Smyth was cantankerous. He led his congregation away from the Ancient Church, because in his view the Separatists should not, in public worship, use English Bible translations. God could not have spoken English, since the language did not exist in Biblical times, and *therefore* the translations could not be purely God's word. Translation had to corrupt them.

What really happened is that 'all hell broke loose', with Smyth and his questioning, 'restless mind' at the epicentre. He began to examine the basic beliefs of the Separatist Church and decided it had to be reconstituted.[15] He affirmed that he had good cause to reconstitute the Church, its ministry and its baptism. He set up his own church in a bakery and 'preached directly from the original Greek and Hebrew, with his sermons often lasting hours. He prohibited all speakers from using any written or printed helps or any translations of the Bible.'[16] He banished all music, even singing psalms, and 'rejected infant baptism completely'. The tensions had arrived.

> To the Separatists the points raised by Smyth were very disturbing. The vaguely unreligious student of our own times finds the constant Calvinist bickering over delicate shades of theological colouring either boring or exasperating, but in the sixteenth century all educated men were intensely interested in theology, and once they had grasped and held what they thought was an aspect of Divine truth they were ready to go to the stake for it (and a great many did), because only by following the true path without the slightest deviation could they hope to find salvation and a life after death. No one really believed that there was no life after death. But Smyth was a bit much even for the sixteenth century; both Robinson and Brewster found his 'instability and wantonness of wit' something of a bore.[17]

The tension produced uproar. Smyth pronounced that no Separatists could be regarded as Christian because, as infants, they had been baptised and an infant could not 'make a covenant with the Lord'. In the logic of it, all had to be broken up and begun afresh with 'each member' baptised into the Christian faith. The logic faltered, however, because if none of them was now regarded as baptised how could any of them begin afresh? 'An unbaptised person could not very well baptise others.' Smyth solved this by baptising himself so he could baptise the others. It produced a 'shock wave' which 'swept through the Anglican as well as Separatist Churches, generated by a mixture of doubt and horror'.[18]

St Wilfrid's, Scrooby. The Pilgrim Fathers would feel an instant familiarity with this church. *(Courtesy Bassetlaw District Council)*

The Whitham flowing through Boston. It seems likely that the women passed this way on the attempted flight to Holland. *(Author's Collection)*

The Guildhall at Boston – the cells where some of the Pilgrim Fathers were held are underneath. *(Author's Collection)*

This seems the most likely candidate for the creek at Immingham where the women were marooned on the second attempt to get to Holland. *(Author's Collection)*

The beautiful *Mayflower* replica, safely in harbour, Plymouth, Massachusetts. *(Author's Collection)*

Provincetown harbour today, where the Mayflower moored, with the long spit of sandunes across the horizon. *(Author's Collection)*

Leyden Street, Plymouth, Massachusetts – the site of the original settlement. Brewster gardens are to the left. *(Author's Collection)*

The Town Brook flows through Brewster Gardens. Plymouth Plantation was to the right. *(Author's Collection)*

As the Scrooby community arrived, Amsterdam had three English churches: Smyth's, the Ancient, and the English Reformed. The latter was Presbyterian – governed by elders who all had the same rights – and composed of English merchants. The Scrooby community joined the Ancient and worshipped in their building in Lange Houtstraat, but they would find tensions there, between Johnson and his brother George, and Johnson and Ainsworth. This was about sex.

George had married a widow, Thomasine, but Johnson felt she dressed immodestly and that George was 'blinded, bewitched and besotted'[19] by her. Bradford was kinder, describing her as a 'grave matron', modest in her appearance and always helpful.

> She was a young widow when he married her, and had been a merchant's wife by whom she had a good estate, and was a godly woman, and because she wore such apparel as she had been formerly used to, which were neither excessive nor immodest. [Their] chiefest exceptions were against her waring of some whalebone in the bodice and sleeves of her gown, corked shoes and other such like things as the citizens of her rank then used to wear.

Bradford said Thomasine and George had been willing to 'reform their fashions'. He also described the Ancient Church:

> At Amsterdam before their division and breach they were about three hundred communicants. [They] had for their pastor three able and godly men for deacons, [and] one ancient widow for a deaconess, who did them service many years, though she was sixty years of age when she was chosen. She honored her place and was an ornament to the congregation. She usually sat in a convenient place in the congregation, with a little birchen rod in her hand, and kept little children in great awe from disturbing the congregation. She did frequently visit the sick and weak, especially women and, as there was need, called our maids and young women to watch and do them other helps as their necessity did require, and if they were poor she would gather relief for them of those that were able, or acquaint the deacons; and she was obeyed as a mother in Israel and an officer of Christ.[20]

No doubt Bradford was being diplomatic when he wrote that, just as Edward Arber was being undiplomatic when he wrote that '[the] Ancient Church was to be an object lesson to the whole World of what the Christian Church of the Future, in all its holiness and usefulness, was to be'. However, its story was 'nothing but a tissue of folly, wrongheadedness, and violence: of hypocrisy, wrangling, and immorality: so that its members became quite odious to the inhabitants of Amsterdam'.[21]

The tensions between Johnson and Ainsworth became so acute that Ainsworth led a small breakaway group in 1610, moving into a former synagogue a couple of doors down the street.

By then the Scrooby group had gone. After a period between nine months and a year, Robinson and the other elders sensed where the tension was leading. They feared the 'flames of contention' would engulf them, too, and launched a pre-emptive strike: they decided to leave Amsterdam. They had also glimpsed 'fair, and beautiful, cities flowing with abundance of all sorts of wealth and riches', but soon enough had had to confront the 'grim and grisly face of poverty coming upon them like an armed man', from which they could not fly.[22] It suggests the group was finding difficulty in making a living (although that will be contradicted in a moment). Perhaps they suffered normal 'cultural bewilderment'[23] at being plucked from Scrooby's slumbering meadowlands and transplanted into the midst of the bustle of a great commercial city. No doubt the tension within the Ancient Church was another factor. They decided to move on to the city of Leiden, some 25 miles to the south.

Clyfton would stay. He was a teacher with the Johnson group and too old to contemplate a further upheaval, especially now that he felt settled in Amsterdam.

> [He] was a grave and fatherly old man when he first came into Holland, having a great white beard; and pity it was such a reverend old man should be forced to leave his country and at those years to go into exile. But it was his lot; and he bore it patiently . . . Sound and orthodox he was, and so continued to his end.[24]

The Scrooby group acted properly. Robinson sent a petition to the city fathers asking permission to settle at Leiden. It read:

> To the Honorable and Court of the City of Leiden
>
> With due submission: John Robinson, minister of the Divine Word, and some of the members of the Christian Reformed religion, born in the Kingdom of Great Britain, to the number one hundred persons or thereabouts, men and women, represent that they are desirous of coming to live in this city, by the first day of May next and to have the freedom thereof in carrying on their trades without being a burden in the least to anyone. They therefore address themselves to your Honor humbly praying that your Honors will be pleased to grant them free consent to betake themselves as aforeside.

The British Ambassador in the Dutch Republic, Sir Ralph Winwood, protested and demanded extradition, but the Leiden authorities were not having any of it. Winwood then went over their heads to the States of Holland, the highest governing body. They queried the matter with the Leiden authorities, who were clearly not prepared to be pushed around by anybody, and replied that they had no information about the status of the Scrooby group – whether they had been banished, or were wanted – nor whether they were Brownists. The Leiden authorities made it clear that the group could certainly settle in the city. The town clerk, Jan van Hout, noted:

> The Court, in making a disposition of this present Request, declare that they do not refuse honest persons permission to come and have their residence in this city; provided that such persons behave themselves honestly, and submit to all the laws and ordinances here, and that, therefore, the coming of the petitioners will be agreeable and welcome.
>
> This was resolved [by the Burgomasters] in their session at the Town Hall this 12th day of February, 1609.
>
> In my presence and signed.
>
> J. van Hout.

Leiden, Holland's second city, had been liberated from the Spanish in 1574 after a long siege when it held out, despite starvation and the plague. These were tough people.

In many ways, Leiden was a microcosm of Holland: open, not closed. As they approached, the Scrooby community would have seen spires, among them Pieterskerk (St Peter's Church) just to the south-west of the city centre. The church stood in a clearing with more than half-a-dozen cobbled streets feeding into it. They would come to know this area intimately, as most of them settled there. Leiden was criss-crossed by canals, as two branches of the Rhine flowed through it. Its university, founded a year after the lifting of the siege, was 'deeply committed to the Reformation, but its dominant theology was a practical and nationally orientated humanism'.[25] The town had a homely, handsome feel, despite a population of about 35,000, and was famous for its textile industry, which offered potential employment.

> It was beautiful exceedingly, in its way. One of its French chroniclers described it thus: The city of Leyden is, without contradiction, one of the grandest, the comeliest, and the most charming, cities of the world. The cleanliness and breadth of its streets; the number of its canals provided with bridges, bordered on either side by lindens, which (during the summer heats) cast delightful shadows where the people make their promenade; the tidiness and elegance of its buildings; and its great number of public Places embellished likewise with lindens or elms; and the extreme neatness of the bricks with which the streets are paved.[26]

However, as Bradford pointed out, it was not on the sea and consequently did not afford the breadth of employment possibilities that a major port did. As a result it was not so beneficial for the group's ability to make a living. Now that they had arrived, they made the best of it, tackling 'such trades and employments as they best could', and consoling themselves with 'peace and their spiritual comfort' over material possessions.[27]

Brewster rented a house in Stincksteeg (Smelly Alley) and set up as an English teacher to students, particularly those from Denmark and Germany, but other members of the community found life harder.

Five months after they moved in, the States of Holland chartered a ship to do some exploring and claim any territory they found along the way. They hired an Englishman to undertake the voyage. On 12 September 1609 the ship went down a river as far as what is now Albany, New York. The river had no name but it soon would have. The explorer was called Hudson: Henry Hudson.

If the Scrooby community imagined they had escaped the tensions of the Reformation, they were wrong. At Leiden, these tensions reached right in to the university. Two of its theology professors were locked in an argument about how to interpret Calvinist Protestantism, and it was more fierce because it was compressed into one small, febrile place – the university.

Jacobus Arminius was in dispute with Francis Gomer, who happened to be the Dutch Calvinist leader. Arminius's followers set out their theory of salvation, rejecting the Calvinistic predestination and stating that men could have will without usurping the authority of God. This became *so* fierce – the state of man's soul was in play – that it provoked rioting, and would continue to provoke it despite the fact that Arminius, who had been ill for some time, died of tuberculosis on 19 October, his wife and nine children – the youngest only thirteen months – at his bedside.

In Holland, Separatists had an effective way of spreading their views: the printed word, on which there were no restrictions. During the first year at Leiden, Robinson – now regarded as a leading theologian – exploited this by publishing *A Justification of Separation*. The group would use this freedom again, and that would bring tensions of its own.

They resumed their lives in the background, and concentrated on survival. This background remains dark with only momentary fragments to illuminate it. On 13 December 1610

> William Pontus, fustian-worker [thick cotton cloth], bachelor from England . . . accompanied by William Brewster, Roger Wilson and Edward Southworth, his acquaintances, [married] Wybra Hanson, spinster, also from England, accompanied by Janie White, Ann Fuller and Mary Butler, her acquaintances.[28]

One estimate says that about half the group were in the textile industry, while others found work as 'masons, carpenters, tobacco sellers and much more'.[29] In fact, a couple of the group were 'among Leiden's first tobacco-pipe makers'.[30] As well as teaching students Brewster was also a ribbon-maker.

Perhaps as many as two-thirds of the group lived around the Pieterskerk. Where did they worship initially? No record survives, although in 1611 four members, including John Robinson, 'bought an old house and garden, with adjacent enclosed grounds, in the Kloksteeg [Bell Alley]'.[31] It was known as The Green Close, and became the group's centre. Robinson lived on the first floor, while the ground floor provided a meeting place for worship and business.[32] Some dozen small houses were built on the vacant land for the poorer members.

Bradford bought a house there, after he had sold the land he had inherited in Austerfield, and moved in with his bride, which may be a clue, however generalised, about how the group had been able to sell up. They could, it seems, get money out of the country.

Some of the Scrooby group – which ought now to be more accurately called the Leiden group – did well enough to become *Poorters*, citizens of Leiden. This was a civic status, not one involving nationality, so they remained English, but the status was not granted to just anybody. You had to be proposed. Bradford became a *Poorter* in 1612 and Jonathan Brewster in 1617.

In December 1613 Bradford, by now twenty-three, married Dorothy May, sixteen, originally from Wisbech, Cambridgeshire, and whose family were in the Ancient Church congregation. It was, according to Dutch custom, a civil service.[33]

The Scrooby group tended to marry among themselves, or compatriots. If they did marry 'out' it would be to someone who had 'religious ties with the English Separatists. These marriages indicate the strong ethnic identification . . . at least among the first generation.'[34] At these betrothals, the bridegroom's employment was often noted, and this gives some of the fragments.

Some of the group had gone into the textile industry, from hatmakers to Brewster's ribbons, but most handled coarse woollen fabric, and were largely unskilled and low paid. It was the sort of simple, menial work a man reared in England's meadowlands would be able to do. Bradford, however, served an apprenticeship in silk and eventually set up his own business, making corduroy, although that apprenticeship was difficult as he set about the 'Learning and Serving of a Frenchman at the Working of Silks'.

In sum, once properly settled the community 'came to raise a competent and comfortable living, but with hard and continual labour'.[35] It was, after all, what they expected life to be and what life was – in Scrooby, Leiden and everywhere else.

Meanwhile, Squanto of the Wampanoag tribe had been living in England with Sir Ferdinando Gorges, a leading pioneer in the New World (he eventually founded Maine) and a major player in the Plymouth Company. In 1611, an English ship, under one Edward Harlow, sailed into the harbour of Cape Cod, Massachusetts, from where Squanto had been kidnapped by George Weymouth. Harlow now kidnapped several more Wampanoag. A folklore of fear and injustice was being created among the Indians and, when European settlers came, they would not forget.

Gorges saw Squanto's potential, taught him to speak English and intended to use him as guide and interpreter on future expeditions. In 1614 Gorges did just that. Squanto went with Captain John Smith, who would trade with the Indians and map the coastline. This map could be little more than a record of the shape of the coastline and its prominent features. The Prince of Wales would give these features names; an inlet with an island he called Plimouth. Once Smith had finished he sailed back to England, but left another ship, under Thomas Hunt, at Cape Cod to continue trading. Apart from the Wampanoag and a sub-tribe, the Patuxets, the small but vigorous Nauset tribe also lived in the area. Hunt followed the familiar European custom, if you can use such a legitimate word about something utterly illegitimate, of increasing his profits by kidnapping Indians and selling them as slaves. He lured twenty Nausets and seven Patuxets on to the ship, had them seized and bound, then sailed for the slave market of Malaga in Spain. Squanto, it seems, was one of them – who would have been interpreting. Once in Malaga, Hunt offered the Indians at £20 a man; some friars bought them – including Squanto – and taught them Christianity.

Back in Holland, the Leiden group had found their rhythm of life.

> [They] continued many years in a comfortable condition enjoying much sweet and delightful society and spiritual comfort together in the ways of God, under the able ministry and prudent government of Mr. John Robinson, and Mr. William Brewster who was an assistant unto him in the place of an Elder [Clyfton, who had stayed at Amsterdam].
>
> . . . many came unto them from divers parts of England, so as they grew a great congregation. And if at any time any differences arose or offenses broke out (as . . . some time there will, even amongst the best of men) they were ever so met with [confronted], and nipped in the bud betimes [early] or otherwise so well composed as still love, peace, and communion was continued. Or else the church purged off those that were incurable, and incorrigible when, after much patience used, no other means would serve, which seldom came to pass.[36]

If this reads like propoganda, it was. Who were the incurable and incorrigible? Did they represent potentially fatal tensions within the community? Was the community really able to live in love, peace and communion without rumours, gossip, intrigue, short tempers, complaints, internal politicking and all the other failings people seem to have?

They held three services a week, one on Thursday evenings and two on Sundays, when the formal service lasted from 8 a.m. to midday, the less formal in the afternoon with 'lay preaching, with previously selected male members speaking from Scripture texts assigned by the pastor'.[37] But the women remain in the background. The betrothal records might have been illuminating, but they never give the woman's employment. Some of them became midwives. Others[38] may have worked at or near their homes weaving, a cottage industry, and one in which Dutch women were involved.

To them all, life meant toil. The houses they lived in were small, probably a couple of rooms. Here they had to maintain a home, raise their children and, perhaps, do their weaving. Even in the middle of so many tensions and changes, a woman's position remained unaltered. If, at the outset, her husband had decided to stay in Scrooby rather than flee, no doubt she would have lived a different life at the superficial level – tending animals rather than cloth – but the core of it would still have been mercilessly hard work.

In 1615, various merchants including Gorges put up money for an expedition to exploit New England's fishing grounds. Ships came back laden with fish and several kinds of fur (beaver, otter, martin, black fox, sable). This was profitable enough for the venture to be repeated each summer, with modest trading posts set up to buy the furs. Plimouth was temporarily renamed Thievish Harbour when some Indians stole from the trading post there.[39]

In 1616, Clyfton died in Amsterdam. He was sixty-three and his death caused the Scrooby community 'great grief, not only because it reminded them of the happiness and struggles of days gone by, but because he had died a lonely and disappointed man'.[40]

At Leiden, meanwhile, Robinson had enrolled as a theological student at the university and was persuaded to 'enter the Arminius controversy on the side of the Calvinists. The action of Robinson would almost certainly be supported by Brewster and his Church. They would see the invitation given to Robinson as a tribute, not only to his debating skill and to his growing reputation as a theologian, but also to the developing status of the Scrooby Church in the eyes of the citizens of Leiden.'[41] Robinson was

> a man learned and of solid judgement, and of a quick and sharp wit, so was he also of tender conscience, and very sincere in all his ways; a hater of hypocrisy and dissimulation, and would be very plain with his best friends. He was very courteous, affable and sociable in his conversation . . . towards his own people especially. He was an acute and expert disputant, very quick and ready, and had much bickering with the Arminians, who stood more in fear of him than any at the university.[42]

The Arminian–Calvinist tension produced one of the riots, and the city magistrates 'even had to make barricades on both sides of the town hall to protect themselves'.

By the end of 1616 or the beginning of 1617, Brewster decided to exploit the freedom of the word as Robinson had done. Brewster was helped by three men, firstly Thomas Brewer – 'a gentleman of wealth and property from the Droitwich area of Worcestershire. He had been educated at King's School, Worcester, and apprenticed to a London printer. He owned a house in the Kloksteeg, not far from Brewster's home.'[43] They employed John Reynolds, a printer from England, and then Edward Winslow, also a printer and a Gloucestershire man who had joined the group from London. (In the summer of 1617, Reynolds married Prudence Grindon in the presence of Mary Brewster and son Jonathan, who was a ribbon-maker.)

The printed word might have been subject to tight control in England, but in Leiden Brewster could print what he wanted and smuggle copies over. There is confusion about how many books Brewster produced,[44] although the first three bear this imprint:

Lugundi Batavorum
Apud Guiljelmum Brewsterum
In vico Chorali

In Leiden
by William Brewster
in Choir Alley.

They were in Latin and uncontroversial, possibly a cover for the ones to follow: these would propagate the Separatists' views and attack King James and his bishops. Brewster and Brewer were subtle. Each year they would print one major, non-controversial book which occupied the press most of the time. If the house was raided, that's what would be found. The controversial material – polemical pamphlets – was printed much faster.

That summer, Isaac and Mary Allerton were witnesses to the betrothal of Edward Winslow and Elizabeth Barker. This suggests that the Leiden group, even grown to three hundred, was still homogeneous and had managed to isolate itself from the influences around them enough to maintain that homogeneity. It had not. When they began to understand this they also understood that they faced a choice as stark and profound as the one that had confronted them at Scrooby. Their decision would be the same.

FOUR

Going Home

In about 1617, the Leiden group began to comprehend what must be done. Perhaps it was a gradual thing, because increasingly the children were becoming the concern, although Bradford uses strange phraseology. Many of them 'that were of best dispositions and gracious inclinations', and who had learnt to be so after all the hardships, became 'decrepit in their early youth, the vigor of nature being consumed in the very bud as it were'. Of more concern even than that, many were being subsumed by 'the great licentiousness' of Dutch youth and the 'manifold temptations'. They were being 'drawn away by evil examples into extravagant and dangerous courses'. This process of assimilation was surely viewed with mounting horror by a group so pious and devout – Bradford writes of its causing great grief. Some, he added, 'became soldiers, others took upon them far voyages by sea, and others some worse courses tending to dissoluteness and the danger of their souls'.

The community faced destruction by time itself, and saw its members progressively degenerate into corruption. Clearly much more had been going on than love, peace and communion. The next generation, which ought to have been preparing itself to carry the sacred flame forward, had discovered the world beyond Reformation rigidity and seemed to like it.

The dangers of staying in Holland had already been demonstrated by Smyth, who wanted to lead his congregation into a merger with a group in Amsterdam called the Mennonites, who believed that only believing adults should be baptised. Some of Smyth's congregation were unhappy about this and made their way back to England (and formed the first Baptist church there). What remained of the congregation melted away. The dangers foreseen by Bradford would eventually be realised, because those who did not go from Leiden, then or in the future, returned to England, settled in other Dutch cities or merged with other churches.

The discussions about leaving are enveloped in the same darkness as the decision to leave Scrooby, the women just as silent. The leaders took the initiative again. They reviewed the dangers facing them and at the same time gazed intently at the future. Bradford uses clearer phraseology here, describing how 'in the agitation of their thoughts, and much discourse of things hereabouts, at length they began to incline to . . . removal to some other place'. It was not done for the novelty of finding something new, he stressed, nor under 'giddy humour' but for entirely rational reasons.

Leiden really had proved a hard place to earn a living. Many that came, and many that might have wanted to come, could not cope with it, and some were so alarmed at the prospect that they preferred prison in England. Bradford claims, however, that overall the group bore the hardships stoically, but they had to consider a further factor. They were ageing prematurely because of the hardships: 'continual labours, with other crosses and sorrows.' Gazing ahead only a few years, the group was in danger of scattering or sinking under the weight of their burdens.

The intermarriage within the group was continuing and children were being born, but for how long? There was a fear that the children would become Dutch through a process of entire absorption,[1] 'so the argument swung to and fro. Many solemn days of prayer and mortification were observed both in public and in private. Eventually a majority decided that they must leave Holland.'[2]

There was something else, too, which had to be weighed in the equation. They could not found heaven on earth in Holland, but they might do, as Bradford said, in a remote part of the world even 'though they should be put even as stepping stones unto others for the performing of so great a work'.

If they felt they had to move on, they faced another choice: where would they go? Or rather, which remote part of the world? There was talk of Guiana in South America. It must have seemed tempting as a location, not least because it had been written about by Walter Ralegh and they would have some idea of what they were going to –

but that area was in the Spanish sphere of influence and therefore too dangerous. The community turned its gaze north of Guiana and some voices were raised for Virginia, where, as Bradford would write, 'the English had already made entrance, and beginning'. What anyone in Leiden could know of the real situation in Virginia is unknown. However:

> The place they had their thoughts on was some of those vast, and unpeopled countries of America, which are fruitful and fit for habitation, being devoid of all civil inhabitants; where there are only . . . brutish men which range up and down, little otherwise than the wild beasts of the same. This proposition being made public, and coming to the scanning of all, it raised many variable opinions amongst men, and caused many fears, and doubts among themselves.[3]

Leaving England for Holland, trading one flat land for another, was a step that might or might not involve finality. England was not far away if they ever wanted or were able to return. At 3,000 miles, America would be finality – if they got there: the perils of a long sea crossing were self-evident, especially for the old and 'the weak bodies of women. The change of air, diet, and drinking water would infect their bodies with sore sickness and grevious diseases.'[4] Small wonder the community suffered fears and doubts. Holland was a civilised country and even so it had been a struggle, no matter that it was a neighbour, civilised and wealthy. America would be raw and potentially deadly. Any who survived the journey would face the constant presence of the Indians:

> the savage people who are cruel, barbarous and most treacherous, being most furious in their rage and merciless where they overcome. [They are not] content only to kill and take away life but delight to torment men in the most bloody manner. [That might be] flaying some alive with the shells of fishes, cutting off the members and joints of others by piecemeal; and, broiling on the coals, eat the collops [slices of meat] of their flesh in their sight whilst they live; with other cruelties horrible to be related.[5]

It was enough to 'move the very bowels of men' – Bradford does not elaborate on what effect it had on the women, especially the mothers – but there was a financial aspect, too. Some objected that such a venture would require a lot of money, both for the voyage and buying all that they would need when they got there. The decision was made in spite of all this, and it was for America.

A curious thing happened. It became 'in fact, on its mundane side, a colonial adventure, to be provided for and conducted after the manner then usual with such undertakings.[6] It was not left to [them] to discover for themselves the way in which their Colony must be formed. There had been others in the field before them.' The attraction afforded by their imaginations and their sense of adventure was followed by more sober judgements about what the colonies were really worth. Smith, the cartographer, had said that any colonists would not find, as the Romans had done in their empire, any country to pillage. Whatever you got you would have to work for it. The consequence of this was a 'business-like spirit. The principles of colonisation had already been reduced to system.'

The Virginia Company, by then, held extensive rights and had the settlement at Jamestown, although the Anglican Church was established there and making sure both its doctrines and practices were in force. The settlement was on marshy, malarial ground and suffering prolonged drought. Jamestown was decimated.

For a couple of years, the Virginia Company had been offering large grants of land to colonists called Hundreds or Particular Plantations. The settlers could govern themselves, dispense justice and carry on trade with the Indians.

The problem was to find people prepared to go to North America, and here all at once were the Leiden group. In the autumn of 1617 they sent two emissaries – Robert Cushman (a Doncaster man who had married John Robinson's sister) and John Carver – to London to talk to the Virginia Company.

Carver and Cushman took with them a carefully worded document, put together by Brewster and Robinson, for the Privy Council requesting a patent for land in America. It was designed to convince anyone challenging it – the king, the Church of England, the Virginia Company – that the Leiden group were not rebellious breakaways. They wanted 'the privileges granted to the general Company as a whole' to be 'transmitted to themselves, so far as the limited area assigned to them was concerned'.

In effect this gave them self-government but left them under the nominal protection of Jamestown and Virginia. The document was set out in seven meaty, numbered paragraphs but nothing could conceal the fact that it was a 'disingenuous set of Articles, in which they stressed the civil authority of the King and of the bishops, but were more ambivalent about their religious authority'.[7] It finished with a flourish:

> 7. Lastly, we desire to give unto all Superiors due honour, to preserve the unity of the Spirit with all that fear GOD, to have peace with all men what in us lieth, and wherein we err to be instructed by any.
>
> (signed) *Subscribed per JOHN ROBINSON and WILLIAM BREWSTER.*

The message did not deceive the Privy Council which wanted a great deal of clarification. Robinson and Brewster provided it, 'protesting with that air of naivete and injured innocence' that they sometimes adopted.[8]

> And though it be grevious unto us that such unjust insinuations are made against us, yet we are most glad of the occasion of making our just purgation [cleansing oneself of accusation] unto so honourable personages.

Robinson and Brewster set out how their church functioned in terms of doctrinal difference from the Established Church but, by the tone of the letter, minimised the differences. Brewster, perhaps sensing that the pressures were mounting to leave Leiden, used his connections. He wrote to Sir Edwin Sandys, a Puritan involved with the Virginia Company. Brewster had had the manor house at Scrooby from Sandys's father; and had met Sandys himself while he was serving with Sir William Davison. Sandys must have replied because in December 1617 Brewster and Robinson sent a response which was a thunderous self-justification.

First. We verily believe and trust the Lord is with us; unto whom, and whose service, we have given ourselves in many trials, and that he will graciously prosper our indeavour, according to the simplicity (pure-mindedness) of our hearts therein.

Secondly. We are well weaned from the delicate milk of our mother country and [are] inured to the difficulties of a strange and hard land which yet, in great part, we have by patience overcome.

Thirdly. The people are for the body of them industrious and frugal, we think we may safely say, as any company (society) of people in the world.

Fourthly. We are knit together as a body in a most strict and sacred Bond and Covenant of the Lord, of the violation whereof we make great conscience and by virtue whereof we do hold ourselves straightly tied to all care of each other's good, and of the whole, by every one and so mutually.

Lastly. It is not with us as with other men whom small things can discourage or small discontentments cause to wish themselves at home again. We know our entertainment [maintaining ourselves] in England, and in Holland. We shall much prejudice both our arts and means by removal. If we should be driven to return [from Virginia], we should not hope to recover our present helps and comforts, neither indeed look even for ourselves to attain unto the like in any other place, during our lives, which are now drawing towards their periods.

These Motives we have been bold to tender unto you, which you in your wisdom also impart to any other our worshipful friends of the Council [for Virginia] with you of all whose godly disposition and loving [care] towards our despised persons, we are most glad; and shall not fail by all good means to continue and increase the same.

We will not be further troublesome, but with the renewed remembrance of our humble duties to your Worship – and so far as in modesty we may be bold, to any other of our wellwishers of the Council with you – we take our leaves committing your persons and counsels to the guidance and direction of the Almighty.

Yours much bounden in all duty,
JOHN ROBINSON WILLIAM BREWSTER
Leyden December 15th anno 1617[9]

The Virginia Company, seeing profit no doubt, had encouraged the group to believe that King James would grant them religious freedom in America. The reality was different. Sir Robert Naunton, Secretary of State, championed their cause to James, and a certain amount of pressure was applied to the Archbishop of Canterbury. It was all fruitless. Significantly, however, they did obtain a concession. James would not 'connive at them, and not molest them provided they carried themselves peaceably' but he would not go further, and certainly would not authorise them.

It was an uneasy compromise. It may have been the product of its own pressure, because Jamestown was in such trouble and in no position, as a colony, to add to the wealth of the kingdom. However, if James prevented a further colony such a move would not add to the wealth of the kingdom, and if he left a vacuum Spain and Portugal might fill it. Beyond such mundane calculations, perhaps another lay: to James, these were troublemakers and they would make a lot less trouble 3,000 miles away in the wild land of brutish inhabitants. At one point, however, he did ask how the community intended to make a living and was told by fishing. He replied 'so God have my soul, 'tis an honest trade, 'twas the Apostles own calling'.

Fragments from Leiden suggest the community was still trying to be a bastion against the scattering. Edward Winslow and Elizabeth Barker were married on 6 May 1618, as already seen. Patience Brewster, one of William's daughters, was a witness to the betrothal of Thomas Smith, a wool-comber, and Anna Crackstone on 12 December. Bradford's son John was born in the house he had bought so soon after the group first arrived.

In Spain, Squanto was still living with the friars, but somehow he gained his freedom and worked a passage to England, despite whatever distrust of the English he must have harboured after his kidnapping. He joined an expedition to Newfoundland on a ship out of Bristol, as interpreter.

Captain Thomas Dermer, who had worked for Ferdinando Gorges, happened to be in Newfoundland and came across him. Dermer wrote to Gorges explaining that 'his Indian' had been found, and asked for instructions. Dermer brought Squanto back to England where, before the next expedition, Gorges lodged him with the treasurer of the Newfoundland Company, who had set up the first chartered settlement there. That next expedition had two objectives: to make peace with the Indians after the Hunt debacle and restart trade. Squanto would be invaluable in both.

In the foreground, a major attempt was made to resolve the running sore between Calvinists and Arminians at the Synod of Dort, a gathering of – among others – Dutch, Swiss, German and English theologians in the town of Dordrecht. Apart from the Dutch, twenty-six delegates came from eight countries. John Hales, chaplain to British Ambassador Sir Dudley Carleton, attended as an observer. The Synod began on 13 November 1618. That same month a new Dutch law was passed prohibiting seditious printing.

In the background, the talking within the community went on and (it seems) a final decision had been made by the spring of 1619, whatever the noises were coming out of London. A further pressure to leave was added on 8 April when the twelve years of truce between Holland and Spain ended. If Spain resumed hostilities there would inevitably be a bloody war and, if Spain won, Holland would have Roman Catholicism imposed upon it. Both possibilities can have brought only dread to the group.

Also in the background, there were more fragments. One of the oldest members of the community, James Chilton, was assaulted and badly wounded[10] by some youths who accused him of harbouring Arminians. Meanwhile, on 19 April Bradford sold his house on the north side of Achtergracht.

The Gorges–Dermer expedition reached New England. During May it sailed into Cape Cod Bay and Dermer went ashore at Patuxet,

Squanto's village. Epidemics had killed everyone. Squanto was the only survivor, and would linger with the Wampanoag tribe 'as a kind of ghost'.[11]

On 8 May, Cushman wrote back to Leiden with the news that an expedition under Francis Blackwell had run into serious trouble at New England – it had happened that winter, but evidently Cushman had only just heard. Blackwell was Elder of the Ancient Church in Amsterdam and had decided to go to Virginia. He had split the Church in Amsterdam, been arrested in London while trying to arrange the crossing and secured his release by betraying one of his fellows. Cushman wrote that the ship had

> had northwest winds which carried them to the southward, beyond their course . . . the Master of the ship and six mariners dying. It seemed they could not find the [Chesapeake] Bay till after long seeking and beating about.
>
> Master Blackwell is dead . . . yea, there are dead 130 persons. It is said there were in all 180 persons in the ship so as they were packed together like herrings. They had amongst them the flux [dysentery] and also want of fresh water so as it is rather wondered at that so many are alive.
>
> Heavy news it is, and I would be glad to hear how far it will discourage you. I see none here discouraged much but rather desire to learn to beware by other men's harms, and to amend that wherein they have failed.[12]

The Synod at Dort reached its judgement on 9 May and the Calvinists won. In July, the States General passed a law 'prohibiting both dissident religious gatherings in private homes and the collection of alms to support ministers, orphans, and the poor outside the Dutch Reformed Church'.[13] Although this law was aimed at the Arminians and was never used against the Leiden group, it could have been.

Cushman and Brewster were to go to London to see what they could get from the Virginia Company: a curious journey, because Brewster was liable to be arrested when his feet touched English soil and his printing press had been busy producing a very controversial book called *Perth Assembly*. Its publication was imminent and would be potentially very, very dangerous to Brewster. He and Cushman found the Virginia Company in turmoil, divided into factions and bankrupt. They made little progress and Cushman reported this back, adding that Brewster was unwell, and that it was not certain whether he would return to Leiden or go to the north of England. This was a euphemism designed to relay news that Brewster had gone into hiding.

However, on 19 June a patent came through from the Virginia Company. 'Sir Edwin Sandys was now its treasurer. They had been advised not to take out the Patent in their own name, but in the name of John Wincop and his associates. Wincop was the Tutor and Chaplain to the household of the Earl of Lincoln. He intended to go with [them] to America but unfortunately died before they sailed.'[14] Ironically, the group could not make use of the patent because what they needed most was money, and money was what the Virginia Company did not have.

In the summer, David Calderwood's *Perth Assembly* appeared. It was a strong attack on King James and the Scottish Presbyterian Church by a non-conformist Scot. Calderwood had been imprisoned for publishing seditious material, but he remained unrepentant. The manuscript was smuggled over to Holland from Scotland, Brewster set it in type and printed it and it was smuggled back in the false bottoms of some barrels of French wine. The king was not amused and immediately unleashed a manhunt to find its author and whoever had printed it.

In July, Ambassador Carleton reported to Naunton that he had information the book had been printed by 'a certain English Brownist of Leyden [*sic*] as are most of the Puritan books sent over, of late days, into England'.[15] Carleton said that Brewster

> hath been, for some years, an inhabitant and printer at Leyden but is now within these three weeks removed from thence, and gone back to dwell in London where he may be found out, and examined, not only of his book *De Regimine Ecclesiæ* but likewise of *Perth Assembly* of which, if he was not the Printer himself, he assuredly knows both the Printer and the Author.

All this is uncertain – dates, times, motives, precise movements – but Brewster must have travelled to London knowing the publication was imminent.

Naunton wrote from London to Carleton on 3 August:

> I am told William Brewster is come again for Leiden where I doubt not but your Lordship will lay for him, if he come thither, as I will likewise do here, where I have already committed some of his complices, and am commanded to make search for the rest.

Carleton responded that as far as he was aware Brewster had not come back and added he felt he would not be returning. Brewster had left his Leiden house and taken his family with him. King James was still not amused. On 23 August Naunton wrote to Carleton:

> My good Lord. His Majesty doth so much resent those Puritan pamphlets which are there [at Leiden] imprinted underhand by the practises of BREWSTER and his complices in those parts, and in Scotland and here – divers of whom, as we are informed, have made very lately an escape from hence and are slipped over . . . to Leyden with him. [His Majesty] hath commanded me again, over and beside what I wrote unto you in my former [letter], to require your Lordship . . . to deal roundly with the States [General], as in his name, for the apprehension of him the said BREWSTER as they tender His Majesty's friendship.

On 27 August, Calderwood sailed to Holland and would secretly worship with the group.

Brewster was in hiding, although in September he told the Leiden city council that because of the law about seditious material he and Brewer had stopped printing, with the suggestion that this had happened the previous December, just after the new law came into force. Since *Perth Assembly* appeared that summer the implication was clear. Brewster had not done it.

The Dutch authorities were in a dilemma of the most delicate kind over Brewster and the publication. They could scarcely surrender their religious tolerance and seize him at the behest of a foreign ruler, whatever the new law said. King James might demand that Carleton deal firmly with the Dutch authorities, and ordinarily they would not have tolerated such behaviour, but their relationship with England carried real significance. In the political balance, the Dutch had to weigh-up Spain and add England as a counterweight. To hold the balance between inconvenient individual rights and the realpolitik of avoiding Spanish rule demanded compromise.

To the pragmatic Dutch this was no bother at all. They prohibited Brewster from using his printing press while they seized the type, books and pamphlets; students at the university – Brewster was a tutor there – created a diversion by shouting *Privilege!*, allowing Brewster to slip away.

On 10 September, Carleton wrote to London that Brewster and Brewer had been arrested, and this despite Brewster's being ill and in bed. Carleton had to write again explaining that the Leiden bailiff, a 'dull, drunken fellow', had got the wrong man: whoever it was – it was not Brewster.

The compromise was that the Leiden council 'tried their utmost to co-operate with the English authorities without endangering the lives of the two culprits'.[16] Brewster went into hiding at the village of Leiderdorp, near Leiden. If the Dutch had been reluctant to comb Leiden for him they were scarcely likely to look further afield. They did have Brewer however, who as a student of letters at Leiden University enjoyed special rights and was put in the university prison, where he had support from other students and the staff. Brewer denied any role in *Perth Assembly* and the university refused to surrender him.

The type from the printing press was taken to the university for safe keeping and Carleton wrote that 'certain experienced printers, which have viewed the letters [of type], affirm that all and every one of the books [with] which he is charged . . . were printed by them'.

The rector of the university discreetly sent people, one a friend of Robinson, to try and persuade Brewer to go to England, and eventually he agreed, but only with the most stringent guarantees. King James would grant him safe passage and regard him and his possessions (the printing press) without prejudice. Brewer would have the right to return to Holland and the king would meet the cost. James was 'beside himself with anger'[17] but had to agree. Brewer went and was questioned fruitlessly for two months. About Brewster and the printing press he said nothing.

During these days and months Brewster became a shadowy figure – Naunton had already written to Carleton expressing regret that 'Brewster's person hath escaped you'. It may be that he, too, was in England and, living under cover, was trying to make the arrangements for the voyage to Virginia. He called himself Master Williamson. He may have spent some of the time in Scrooby, but more likely he melted into the teeming streets and alleys of Aldgate in east London where many Dutch immigrants as well as merchant adventurers lived.

The group were now approached by a Dutch concern, the New Netherlands Company, who said they could settle along the Hudson river – Holland had claimed the land there. The group was guaranteed naval protection for the crossing, would be provided with cattle and could worship as they wished. It was the only offer they had.

Negotiations were opened. The New Netherlands Company was not the only one to scent opportunity. Thomas Weston, then about thirty-six and originally from Staffordshire, was a dubious entrepreneur whose 'self-serving interests and sometimes illegal and sometimes immoral business deals' would bring a great deal of trouble with them.[18] He had joined the Ironmongers' Company in London and sent an agent to Holland to trade, including for the cloth made by the group. He had sensed early on that the Pilgrims wanted to leave Leiden for America and saw a chance to make money. He had been involved in trying to set up the Virginia Company deal despite being arrested for a customs offence, which was unrelated.

Now he saw his chance. He travelled to Leiden and began lengthy discussions. Weston was a salesman. He talked them out of any involvement with the New Netherlands Company or with the bankrupt Virginia Company. Instead, he talked them into an involvement with himself. He explained that a group of London merchants and financiers would put the money up for them to go to America. Brewster, worldly and wise, might well have seen Weston for what he was but, of course, Brewster was hiding somewhere in England. The community reached agreement with Weston and this was duly drawn up. They had been tempted and were unable to resist.

Weston proposed a joint stock company with the London merchants supplying the money and the group supplying the labour. Shares were in units of £10 and each person over the age of sixteen received one. They could also invest in the venture. All profits were to stay in joint stock for seven years, after which they could keep their houses, land and property, but the profits from fishing and trading were to be divided among the shareholders. Weston returned to London to raise the money and seventy merchants joined him in what became known as the Merchant Adventurers.

Carver went from Leiden to London to work with Cushman making the preparations. They were to handle the money, arrange the shipping and buy provisions but not to exceed their remit.

However, around this time they heard from Weston and others that 'sundry Honorable Lords had obtained a large grant from the King for the more northerly parts of America, derived out of the Virginia Patent, and wholly secluded from their government, and to be called by another name, viz. New England'. The destination – nothing to do with the Dutch – would be on the Hudson.[19] Weston saw money again, to be made out of the abundant fishing, and tried to persuade the group that the Hudson was where they should go. There were other attractions – plenty of hunting, too, and from the religious point of view, the Anglican Church was not represented there. The whole thing, however, proved divisive.

> Some of those that should have gone . . . fell off and would not go; other merchants, and friends that had offered to adventure their moneys, withdrew and pretended many excuses, some disliking they were not to Guiana. Others again would adventure nothing, except they went to Virginia. Some again (and those that were most relied on) fell in utter dislike with Virginia, and would do nothing if they went hither. In the midst of these distractions, they of Leiden, who had put off their estates and laid out their moneys, were brought into a great strait, fearing what issue these things would come to, but at length the generality was swayed to this latter opinion.[20]

Clearly members of the group felt they were fully entitled to voice their opinions, and reserved the right to go or not go. The 'generality' meant that, once the opinions had been expressed and argued through, the majority were 'swayed'.

Weston saw a chance and in midsummer renegotiated the original Leiden agreement, setting out terms much more favourable to himself. This new document was of ten Articles but with two main changes. After seven years, the 'houses, lands, goods and chattels, be equally divided betwixt the adventurers, and planters' – the London money men *and* the group rather than, as in the original, just to the group; and the group was forbidden from having '2 days in a week for their own private employment, for the more comfort of themselves and their families'. This was as serious as the new seven-year stipulation, because the two days would have given them time to do all manner of things for themselves, and in setting up a Colony from nothing there would have been an endless amount to do.

Cushman agreed, because he felt he had no choice. If he had not, 'all was likely to be dashed, and the opportunity lost [so] they presumed to conclude with the merchants on those terms, in some things contrary to their order'. Cushman had no authority to negotiate or sign anything like this without referring it back to Leiden.

When word reached Leiden, the group was outraged. They considered it betrayal; they were deeply offended at being presented with something that had already happened, and annoyed because they felt it had been foisted on them on the grounds that if it had not been agreed the whole venture might be delayed. Robinson wrote to Carver saying he felt Cushman was not fit to handle such negotiations or to

> deal for other men, by reason of his singularity and too great indifference for any conditions, and, to speak truly, we have had nothing from him except terms and presumptions.[21]

Cushman considered resignation, but that risked everything collapsing, leaving the group horribly exposed – they had sold up – but also leaving the central problem of finding a place unresolved. On 10 June 1620, however, Cushman wrote a strong response from London, addressing it to Carver. This is an extract:

> Loving friend. I have received from you some letters full of [dis]affection and complaints: and what it is you would have of me, I know not. Your crying out 'Negligence! Negligence! Negligence!' I marvel why so negligent a man was used in the business. Yet, know you! that all that I have power to do here, shall not be one hour behind, I warrant you!
>
> You have reference to Mister Weston to help us with money, more than his Adventure: when he protesteth, But for his promise, he would not have done anything. He saith, We take a heady course, and is offended that our provisions [preparations] are made so far off, as also that he was not made acquainted with our quantity of things: and saith, That in now being in three places too far remote [Leiden, London and Southampton] we will, with going up and down, and wrangling and expostulating pass over the summer before we will go.
>
> And to speak the truth there is fallen already amongst us a flat schism; and we are readier to go to dispute, than to set forward a voyage.[22]

Robinson could only write to the Merchant Adventurers complaining about the changes, and pointing out that Cushman had had no authority to agree them. Among so many continuing tensions, there was another. The Merchant Adventurers began to recruit others who would go and this was done without regard to religion. They would be called Strangers.

The Adventurers appointed a Christopher Martin, a Puritan, as treasurer 'and ordered him to buy provisions, which he did – but without anyone's consent, help or permission, and he later refused to say how he spent all the money'.[23] It was a chaotic and frantic time. Martin, Carver and Cushman were acting independently, and simply purchasing the provisions they thought would be needed.

The idea was to sail over to the Hudson in two ships from Southampton, where a total of sixty-seven Strangers would join up with the group. The group bought a 60-ton Dutch vessel, the *Speedwell*, and had it fitted out. This would take them to Southampton and then accommodate some of the party for the crossing. Once on the Hudson the *Speedwell* would be used as a workhorse for fishing and trade. The Adventurers hired a 180-ton vessel, the *Mayflower*, to take the majority of the party and most of the stores on the Atlantic crossing.

But who from Leiden was to go? The aged and the infirm would not, and then there was the cost to consider. Moreover, as we have seen, Ainsworth's Church at Amsterdam had made a disastrous foray into the New World in 1618, and of 180 people, only 50 survived. Such knowledge must have been a powerful disincentive to waverers.

Is that why certain families split up, some staying, some going? Or was this for the most pragmatic of reasons – those staying to follow once a Colony had been established? Did real fear run through? How much dissent over the choice of the Hudson was there and what happened to it? There are partial answers:

> We came to this resolution, that it was best for one part of the Church to go at first, and the other to stay, viz. the youngest and strongest part to go. Secondly, they that went should freely offer themselves. Thirdly, if the major part went, the pastor to go with them; if not, the Elder only. Fourthly, if the Lord should frown upon our proceedings, then those that went to return and the brethren that remained still there [in Leiden] to assist and be helpful to them, but if God should be pleased to favour them that went, then they also should endeavour to help over such as were poor and ancient, and willing to come. These things being agreed, the major part stayed and the pastor with them.[24]

The separations – friend from friend, family member from family member – were heart-rending. Bradford and his wife Dorothy, who had been married in Leiden, left their two-year-old son John behind. Mary Brewster took her two youngest, Love and Wrestling, but left the other three, Jonathan, Patience and Fear. Isaac Allerton took his pregnant wife and three small children, a complete family. How many from Leiden went cannot be definitely stated. Caleb Johnson reckons twenty-two men, thirteen women and seventeen children, with children defined as under twenty-one. There was no real shape to any of it. The families did what they decided was best for themselves. It is worth noting that phrase, because deliberately empowering the individual and respecting their decisions must have been rare, if known at all, among ordinary folk in the early seventeenth century.

Many must have had mixed feelings about the leaving of Leiden. They had lived in the town for a decade, and the Bradfords, the Winslows, the Allertons, the Fullers had married there. Robinson would stay behind to minister to the remainder of the community and follow as soon as possible. Brewster would stand in for him on the other side of the Atlantic but, being unordained, could not administer the two ordinances: baptism and the Lord's Supper. Meanwhile, the *Speedwell* awaited them at Delftshaven, a port some 24 miles south of Leiden.

The *Mayflower* under her captain Christopher Jones, had been used to carry cloth to the west coast ports of France, bringing back wine and cognac. She was known as a sweet ship for that reason, in comparison to less savoury cargoes. She had delivered a cargo of wine to London in January 1620, and was cleared from London to La Rochelle on 6 March to fetch more wine. She had returned with it by 15 May, after which 'it is likely she lay idle, or was being overhauled and painted, until chartered' by the community before 19 July.[25] It is possible that she was moored at Leigh-on-Sea and from there picked up people who were joining the group: some may have gathered in Billericay; it is also possible that Jones had already picked up the London people at Rotherhithe. On 19 July the *Mayflower* sailed into Southampton with about seventy passengers on board.

The *Mayflower*'s first mate, John Clark, came from a Rotherhithe family. He was baptised and married in the parish church, whose rector had been to Holland to study Dutch Protestantism. Separatists had been holding meetings at nearby Southwark. These facts have led to speculation that, at the least, the crew would have understood what motivated the voyage.

On 20 July the Leiden group gathered at Robinson's home in the Kloksteeg so that he could preach a farewell message. It was a day of 'solemn humiliation'.[26] Robinson chose Ezra 8:21. 'And there at the river, by Ahava [the Hebrew for love], I proclaimed a fast, that we might humble ourselves before our God, and seek of him a right way for us, and for our children, and for all our substance.' Bradford caught the mood. They spent a 'good part of the day very profitably' – presumably attending to all the final details – and 'the rest of the time . . . pouring out prayers with great fervency mixed with an abundance of tears'. They had a farewell feast that night, goose and pudding, at Robinson's.

> Our pastor's house being large . . . we refreshed ourselves after our tears with singing of Psalms, making joyful melody in our hearts as well as with the voice, there being many of the congregation very expert in music; and indeed it was the sweetest melody that ever mine ears heard.[27]

Next morning they left on a canal boat, working across past The Hague to Delftshaven and some, or most, of the congregation went with them for the farewell.

> As Leiden receded into the distance, with its familiar red-tiled roofs, its lofty spires, and its great windmill with white sails slowly turning in the morning breeze, Pilgrim hearts and minds doubtless flooded with tender memories.[28]

Bradford insists that they 'knew they were pilgrims' and 'looked not much' on the material world, even Leiden. This is one of the earliest usages of the word pilgrim applied to the people on the *Mayflower*, and Bradford spelt it with a lower case p. It occurs in the Letter to the Hebrews, and means someone travelling to a foreign land.

The journey would have been slow, but when they reached Delftshaven they found the *Speedwell* ready and waiting. They spent the rest of the day loading. Perhaps they gathered that evening at the Old Church of the Dutch Reformed Church for a final service. Because so many were there – some had even come down from Amsterdam – a large place was needed. They did not sleep much that night.

> The next day (the wind being fair) they went aboard, and their friends with them, where truly doleful was the sight of that sad

> and mournful parting, to see what sighs and sobs and prayers did sound amongst them, what tears did gush from every eye, and pithy speeches pierced each heart, that sundry of the Dutch strangers that stood on the quay as spectators could not refrain from tears.[29]

Winslow, who like Bradford was to sail on the *Speedwell*, captured the same mood. Pastor Robinson said prayers and

> a flood of tears was poured out. [Those who were not sailing] accompanied us to the ship, but were not able to speak to one another for the abundance of sorrow to part; but we only going aboard . . . we gave them a volley of small shot, and three pieces of ordinance.

It may be that Robinson led prayers on the deck, but the tide was right and time short. Pastor Robinson sank to his knees and then the whole congregation followed. With 'watery cheeks' Robinson commended them to the Lord and the Lord's blessing. They rose and began embracing, and more tears were shed. The wind took the *Speedwell* and now Delftshaven drifted into the distance as Leiden had done.

Pastor Robinson never did get to America, and never again saw those who were waving to him from the deck. Young John Bradford – was he there, in the arms of whoever was charged with caring for him? – never saw his mother again, and did not see his father for seven years. When he did, he found he had had a stepmother for four years.

The *Speedwell*, with around fifty passengers, moved down the River Maas, which broadened until it reached the Hook of Holland where the North Sea spread before it. The weather was benign, the wind constant. As the little ship moved past the Hook it was travelling nicely.

Dermer had made a further expedition with Squanto to Wampanoag country, but during this he and his crew were attacked by another tribe, the Nausets of Cape Cod, and Dermer was taken hostage. He was sure they would have killed him if Squanto had not pleaded so hard for his life. They travelled on, to Martha's Vineyard, and met more Indians there. One of them knew Dermer worked for Gorges, this same Gorges who had once kept him prisoner. The Indian was afraid that Dermer might try it again. He and the others launched an attack just as Dermer and a party of men were going ashore from a boat.

All in the party were killed except Dermer and the man who had stayed on the boat to guard it. Dermer, badly wounded, managed to get back into it, but the Indians would have 'cut off his head' if the other man, sword drawn, had not been able to save him. They escaped and reached Virginia where Dermer died, perhaps of his wounds, perhaps of something he caught, perhaps both.

This was the country the *Speedwell* and the *Mayflower* were preparing to sail straight towards.

PART TWO

New Worlds

FIVE

Stormy Weather

On Wednesday 26 July 1620 the *Speedwell* sailed into Southampton harbour after a voyage estimated at four days from Delftshaven. As she came in, the passengers saw the *Mayflower* for the first time. She was moored at the West Quay, a narrow promontory of land along the shore of the River Itchen, just above Southampton Water.

Southampton was a pragmatic choice as a place to gather and start the journey from; it was 'suitable for the Atlantic voyage with plenty of experience among its merchants and sailors of the crossing to Newfoundland, Virginia and the American coast and of the necessities required for it, yet fairly near to London if reference to the government or the Company was needed'.[1]

If the *Speedwell* had had to go to London it would have meant a journey up the Thames Estuary and back down again, and tactically Southampton was relatively quiet with 'fewer royal officers to bother about the shipload of exiles from Holland'.[2] It was an ancient town and consequently the exact opposite of the place to which they would be going. Dating from Roman times, it was first built on a bend in the River Itchen and rebuilt on the other side in about AD 650 as the Saxon town of Hamwic.[3] The castle had been sold in 1618 and was now in ruins, but the keep survived as an imposing sight on the top of the mound.[4]

> The town was not as rich as it had been in the late medieval period but was still a much-visited port, particularly for privateers, and was pretty prosperous. The population was probably around 4,000. Big ships were being built there still, three including the *Speedwell* of 60 tons in 1606 for instance,[5] and in 1635 a visitor noted the shipbuilding area. The town was heavily

involved in the Newfoundland fisheries at this time as well and 153 merchants exported goods from the port in 1619.

Long before, it had received Italian trading vessels laden with all sorts of riches, and the traders on these vessels bought the local wool and particularly cloth. They dealt in luxuries, not staple foods.[6] Southampton had prospered, but now that trade was going through London the town had difficulty in maintaining the thirteenth-century walls, which still enclosed it. One problem was money, another that the inhabitants took its stones to repair their own houses.[7] The walls had become obsolete because powerful cannons were now available and a siege gun could have blasted a gaping hole in the wall.[8]

The *Speedwell* anchored at the West Quay, and the first to come aboard were 'a quartet of trouble':[9] Carver, Cushman, Christopher Martin and Weston, who had been acting independently. That had created rancour, confusion, waste and overlap.

Carver claimed he had been buying provisions in Southampton, and as a consequence had no idea what Cushman had been buying in London. Cushman accused Martin of having spent £700 'upon what I know not'. The Strangers had appointed Martin as their agent, who had been buying provisions in Kent. Indignant, he would not explain what he had spent, but accused Cushman of betraying the whole venture to the Adventurers, whom he called bloodsuckers, by signing the revised agreement.

At this delicate juncture, Weston arrived with the revised document and demanded that the leaders sign it 'to have the conditions confirmed'. They refused. He was not pleased. They told him

> he knew right well that these were not according to their first agreement, neither could they yield to them without the consent of the rest that were behind [in Leiden]. And indeed they had special charge when they came away from the chief of those that were behind not to do it. At which he was much offended and told them they must look to stand on their own legs, so he returned in displeasure and this was the first ground of discontent between them.[10]

The group, now joined by the Strangers, spent nearly two weeks in Southampton and, sadly, it must have been a very anxious time for all of them, particularly the leaders.

> Almost certainly the emigrants would have slept on their ships but shopped daily for cheap fresh provisions to cook on board to conserve their precious stores which, of course, had to be kept in expensive casks and crates. The women must have shopped for various articles such as needles, ribbons, or perhaps a pan or a plate which they would have realised that they had forgotten to pack. Southampton, after all, was intended to be their last stopping place in the Old World.

Southampton was no doubt a typical town of its time:

> Every resident must have been known to everyone else at least by sight, though there was also a floating population of sailors and those attracted in by the prosperity of the town. Those born in town could usually depend on kindly treatment from the authorities if poor or ill and sometimes even if they had misbehaved, but the life of the poor newcomer was precarious and often short since the Mayor and Aldermen did their best to send them out of the town.
>
> There was much closer contact between neighbours than today, who would be met when fetching water from the nearest public pump (few houses had wells and this was probably not very good water for drinking) or when shopping at the only available shops, at compulsory attendance at the Parish Church, or arguing about casting rubbish into the streets, and when being entertained with drinking and supper in each other's houses or in the nearby beerhouse.
>
> Long hours were worked but there were still many holidays or saints' days still surviving the Reformation, and the people amused themselves heartily and even violently. Watching bull baiting, travelling players or dancing bears, town ceremonies or the ducking of a scold, practising archery at the Town Butts or playing bowls on the town bowling green and elsewhere,

> gambling and playing cards, and of course drinking – these were some of the amusements of the people. Added to this would be the pastime (since human nature does not change) of watching the ships come and go from the quayside, the *Mayflower* and the *Speedwell* among them.[11]

One new member joined the emigrants in Southampton, John Alden, a tall, blond, and very strong young man of twenty, who was hired as a cooper to look after the indispensable water, beer and other stores in barrels and boxes. His birthplace is not known, but it was probably Southampton, as at least one Alden family can be traced back two centuries there, and an arrow maker called John Alden was a resident there between 1587 and 1620. He is recorded in court in early summer 1620 claiming £20 from Hugh and Ellen Russell (for unpaid work?). There is speculation, after a final reference to him on 6 August, that he might have died between then and 15 August, when the *Mayflower* sailed. There is further speculation that, if son John felt he could never recover the debt, he might as well take his chance on the *Mayflower*; the Southampton Town Minutes also record that in July the town was ordered to press-gang a hundred people for the Royal Navy, and John – only twenty, single and with such a useful occupation as cooper – would be a prime candidate. If that is correct the *Mayflower* presented a very attractive option, as the Navy was a place of brutal discipline.[12]

The *Speedwell* was a problem. It had needed expensive work done on it because it listed badly and was taking in water. But before he left, Weston said he was not contributing a penny, 'so they were forced to sell off some of their provisions to stop this gap . . . some 3 or 4 score firkins of butter [a firkin = 56lb] which commodity they might best spare having provided too large a quantity of that kind'.[13]

A letter was written to the Merchant Adventurers on 3 August signed by the leaders of the Leiden group to make plain their feelings, stressing that Cushman had signed 'without our commission, or knowledge; and though he might propound good ends to himself yet it no way justifies his doing it'. The letter added that 'our main difference is in the 5 and 9 articles, concerning the dividing, or holding of house and lands – the enjoying whereof some of yourselves well know was one special motive, amongst many other, to provoke us to go'. The letter complained that they had only seen a 'private copy' of the new agreement before reaching Southampton, 'upon sight whereof we manifested utter dislike, but had [sold] off our estates and were ready to come, and therefore was too late to reject the voyage'.

It offered a gesture of conciliation:

> Yet since you conceive yourselves wronged, as well as we, we thought meet to add a branch to the end of our 9 article, as will almost heal that wound of itself . . . promising you again in the behalf of the whole company that if large profits should not arise within the 7 years, that we will continue together longer with you. This we hope is sufficient to satisfy any in this case, especially friends.

The letter ended:

> We are in such a strait at present as we are forced to sell away £60 worth of our provisions to clear the [port] and withal to put ourselves upon great extremities, scarce having any butter, no oil, not a sole to mend a shoe, not every man a sword to his side, wanting many muskets, much armour, etc. And yet we are willing to expose ourselves to such eminent dangers as are like to ensue, and trust to the good providence of God . . . Thus saluting all of you in love, and beseeching the Lord to give a blessing to our endeavour, and keep all our hearts in bonds of peace and love, we take leave . . .

Where was Brewster? He might have slipped on to the *Speedwell* at Delftshaven, but Southampton seems much more likely: as far as anybody knows, he was already in England.

> Although Brewster's name, as a matter of policy, did not appear in the later stages of the negotiations [to secure a patent] it was a matter of simple logic that he would emigrate with his Church, and try to escape the due processes of law. Where then were the King's agents? The list of passengers would be scrutinised, but Brewster's name did not appear on them.[14]

One possibility is that he was travelling under the name he had adopted, Master Williamson. In Holland it was common to use the father's name to form your own, and William Brewster's father was also William, giving Williamson. Dutch officials would have understood but English officials, at Southampton or elsewhere, would have taken the name 'at its face value'.[15] And Brewster's papers would all be quite properly in the name of Williamson since they would have been issued in Holland.

How tight or lax scrutiny at Southampton might have been is not clear. The two boats, one at either side of the promontory, would hardly have been guarded day and night and even if they had, a gaggle of people were loading provisions, hauling this and that, shouting to each other, coming and going. Under cover of darkness, Brewster could have slipped aboard either ship, and surely did. The reunion with his wife and two children must have been discreetly handled. An open show of delight might stir suspicion.

When the *Speedwell* was considered seaworthy, and departure imminent, everyone gathered on the *Mayflower*'s deck. Brewster felt confident enough to address everyone, reading out a farewell letter from Robinson. It was a long letter, and perhaps an emotional one full of religious flourishes – under repentance and God's pardon, 'great shall be [a man's] security and peace in all dangers, sweet his comfort in all distresses, with happy deliverance from all evil, whether in life or in death'.

It was also full of practical common sense and so important that it demands to be quoted extensively.

> And as men are careful not to have a new house shaken with any violence before it be well settled and the parts firmly knit, so be you, I beseech you brethren, much more careful that the house of God which you are, and are to be, be not shaken with unnecessary novelties or other oppositions at the first settling thereof.
>
> Lastly, whereas you become a body politic – using amongst yourselves civil government and are not furnished with any persons of special eminency above the rest, to be chosen by you into office of government – let your wisdom and godliness appear, not only in choosing such persons as do entirely love and will

> promote the common good, but also in yielding unto them all due honour and obedience in their lawful administrations: not beholding in them the ordinariness of their persons, but God's ordinance for your good; not being like the foolish multitude . . . But you know better things, that the image of the Lord's power and authority which the magistrate beareth is honourable, in how mean [ordinary] persons [what]soever. And this duty you . . . ought the more conscionably to perform because you are at least for the present to have only them for your ordinary governors, which yourselves shall make choice of for that work.

In the age of hierarchies, this was both an outline of what we might call democracy and guidance in how to put it to practical effect. It would have astonishing consequences which, arguably, are still felt today.

How many ordinary Englishmen before this moment had ever had the freedom to choose who they would put into office to wield enormous, perhaps absolute, authority over them? Those they chose would – again in the practical world – not be a lowly elected stratum of government but the government itself. Whatever any patent said, whatever any royal decree set down, whatever laws and instructions might come from England to the distant Colony, it would in every practical way be self-governing.

They stood on the deck listening, perhaps murmuring approval, perhaps nodding, perhaps some holding hands; no doubt the children fidgeted, restless and uncomprehending. No doubt the seagulls cawed and soared; perhaps a breeze stroked the water into little waves which lapped against the flanks of the boats. Every adult knew, even if only at the most personal and private level, they had given a total commitment to an enterprise that was profoundly dangerous – not just the crossing, but the raw and brutish land that awaited them where, with their bare hands, they would have to found their heaven. However dogged, however fatalistic, however much they felt under the protection of their God, they *must* have felt a decisive moment, and probably the decisive moment of their lives, was at hand.

The chronology of when Robinson's letter was read out, or how soon after the reading they set sail, is not clear. It was read when 'all things' were 'now ready and all business despatched', which strongly suggests it represented the centrepiece of the departure, and that soon they would be on their way. That could have been 5 August, the day they sailed.

The whole group was divided between the two ships. Each had a governor and two or three assistants to maintain order in their communal living arrangements and supervise the handing out of stores. Martin was governor of the *Mayflower*, which has fed speculation that the Strangers went with him, and the Leiden group were on the *Speedwell* under Cushman, although the division seems to have been a hundred people on the former and twenty on the latter, suggesting the Leiden group had been split between the two ships.

The *Mayflower* slipped away from the West Quay, followed by the *Speedwell*, which was captained by Reynolds.[16] They moved out towards the English Channel down Southampton Water, into the Solent and round the Isle of Wight. With three masts and six sails, the *Mayflower* no doubt looked as impressive as sailing ships did when the wind was with them and sails were stretching. The *Speedwell* had evidently been given new, taller masts and increased sails to stay with the *Mayflower* – she was only a third of the size.

The *Mayflower* is still an elusive vessel. Contemporary accounts do not even give her name, and there are no plans that reveal her dimensions. One authority[17] prefaces his approximate calculations by saying, 'it is safe to assume' she conformed to 'the period type of ships of her size and occupation'. A ship of her 'type and tonnage was built for roominess and carrying capacity; high-pooped, deep-bellied, able and seaworthy'. She measured, in all, about 128ft in length, 'quite a sizable ship, after all, to swing around in a tight place'. She 'held her width well forward and aft, however, giving her plenty of deck-room'. The deck was around 113ft long.

However cramped she was with so many passengers, their provisions and the crew, the *Mayflower* was big enough if the *Speedwell* rode behind sharing the burden, but about three days out they realised that the *Speedwell* was in no condition to make the journey, so both ships turned towards the port of Dartmouth, arriving on 13 August. From there, Cushman wrote to a friend. It was a vast outpouring, filled with invective, self-justification and self-pity. The tone was not helped by the fact that he had been violently seasick.

He began by saying that 'an infirmity of body hath seized me, which will not in all likelihood leave me till death. What to call it I know not but it is a bundle of lead as it were crushing my heart more, and more, these 14 days, as that although I do the actions of a living man yet I am but as dead.'

This was only getting into his stride. He went on to say that the *Speedwell*

> will not cease leaking, else I think we had been halfway at Virginia. Our voyage hither hath been as full of crosses, as ourselves have been of crookedness. We put in here to trim her, and I think . . . if we had stayed at sea but 3 or 4 hours more she would have sunk right down. And though she was twice trimmed at [Southampton], yet now she is as open and leaky as a siever; and there was a board a man might have pulled off with his fingers 2 foot long, where the water came in . . . we lay at [South]Hampton 7 days in fair weather waiting for her, and now we lie here waiting for her in as fair a wind as can blow and so have done there 4 days, and are like to lie 4 more, and by that time the wind will happily turn as it did [at Southampton]. Our victuals will be half eaten up I think before we go from the coast of England, and if our voyage last long we shall not have a month's victuals when we come in the country.

Cushman now turned to what clearly was more than an irritant: Martin, Weston and the renegotiated agreement. Cushman was fully into his stride:

> Near £700 has been bestowed at [Southampton], upon what I know not. Mr Martin saith he neither can nor will give any account of it, and if he be called upon for accounts he crieth out of unthankfulness for his pains and care . . . We are suspicious of him . . . Also he so insulteth our poor people, with such scorn and contempt as if they were not good enough to wipe his shoes. It would break your heart to see his dealing, and the mourning of

our people. They complain to me and alas I can do nothing for them. If I speak to him he flies in my face . . . mutinous, and saith no complaints shall be heard or received but by himself, and saith they are . . . waspish discontented people, and I do ill to hear them. There are others that would lose all they had put in, or make satisfaction for what they have had, that they might depart, but he will not hear them, nor suffer them to go ashore lest they should run away. The sailors are also so offended at his ignorant boldness, in meddling and controlling in things he knows not what belongs to . . . some threaten to mischief him, others say they will leave the ship, and go their way . . .

As for Mr Weston . . . he will hate us ten times more than ever he loved us for not confirming the conditions.

He now mounted his self-defence, and – audaciously, no doubt – tried to shift the blame towards Pastor Robinson:

. . . but now some pinches [hardships] have taken [the group], they begin to revile the truth, and say Mr Robinson was in the fault who charged them never to consent to those conditions, nor choose me into office . . . but he and they will rue too late, they may now see, and all be ashamed when it is too late, that they were so ignorant, yea and so inordinate in their courses.

He saved a final blast for Martin, calling him in effect a liar. Martin evidently told him the merchants were

bloodsuckers, and I know not what: simple man, he indeed never made any conditions with the merchants, nor ever spake with them; but did all that money fly to [Southampton] or was it his own? Who will go and lay out money so rashly and lavishly as he did and never know how he comes by it, or on what conditions. I told him of the alteration long ago, and he was content; but now he domineers and said I betrayed him into the hands of slaves. He is not beholden to them, he can set out 2 ships himself to a voyage: when, good man? He hath but £50 in, and if he should give up his accounts he would not have a penny left him, as I am

> persuaded. Friend, if ever we make a Plantation God works a miracle; especially considering how scant we shall be of victuals, and most of all ununited among ourselves, and devoid of good tutors, and regiment. Violence will break all. Where is the meek and humble spirit of Moses?

How near to the truth all this is remains problematical, not least because Cushman seems to have been working his way through his own agenda and perhaps, facing the danger of the voyage, wanted the letter to represent his side of events if the worst happened and he was in no further position to do it for himself. The reference to being disunited may be suggesting that there were tensions here and the Strangers and the Leiden group were distinct factions, or it may be that the option of harmony within each faction was to some extent illusory, the way it has to be in any collection of human beings – especially if they are prepared to risk all.

With the Leiden faction, it might have been because, living in the freedom of Holland and having tasted the intoxication of being involved in the decision to go to America, they felt they had the right to their opinion, the right to express it and the right for it to be heard. They might just have been a cantankerous lot anyway . . .

The *Speedwell* was 'searched and mended' very thoroughly, from stem to stern, and some leaks found. They were plugged and the men working on her 'conceived . . . that she was sufficient' and could 'proceed without either fear or danger'.[18] The two ships left Dartmouth on about 23 August, but when they had covered some 100 leagues (300 miles) beyond Land's End, Reynolds realised that the *Speedwell* was 'so leaky' that he dared not go further. The pumping they were doing was scarcely keeping pace with the water coming in. He and Captain Jones decided to turn for land again. They headed towards their third port of call, Plymouth. They must have made slow progress because they did not get there until 7 September.

Plymouth has a natural harbour on a big inlet, reached by a waterway known as Plymouth Sound, flanked by land on either side.

> [The ships] would have sailed in under the Hoe, past Fisher's Nose and with the new fort on top which Francis Drake had built.

> It had superseded the medieval fort above the narrows of the harbour entrance, which had reverted to a military store. In front of it, a stubby pier projected in front of the Barbican, or watergate, where a winch operated a chain which could be lifted to keep out enemy ships. Beside the pier new stone steps led down to the water's edge. Just north was the causey, a stone causeway running out over the mud to low-water mark, and beyond that the new quay of 1570. Facing this quay were new, brightly-painted, Elizabethan houses, their upper storeys leaning forward. Narrow little streets led off this quay.[19]

How near the *Speedwell* actually was to sinking raised suspicions, especially after being declared seaworthy so emphatically after the repairs at Dartmouth. Cushman was emphatic that the ship leaked like a sieve, but others believed Reynolds and his crew now realised how dangerous the journey would be, and in an age of superstition, might even have felt it was cursed. If they needed a reason to abandon the whole expedition, a leaky ship would provide it; not forgetting that the ships had been hired, and presumably paid for, for a whole year. So they came into Plymouth, where Catherine had come from Spain a century and more before to marry Henry VII's eldest son, Arthur, which would have so many direct and indirect consequences – including, on this 6 September, for the emigrants.

In 1620, the population of Plymouth and its neighbouring smaller settlement of East Stonehouse was around 6,000.[20] The town was largely centred on the west and north-west shores of Sutton Pool, the tidal harbour to the north of the mouth of the Plym. It had grown in importance from the middle of the thirteenth century, and by the seventeenth was consolidated as a trading and strategic naval port.[21] Because the very name Plymouth carries such resonance within our story, it is worth examining this last port of call before the New World.

> There was a little development beginning around the harbour. The Friary Quay would be the main facility to the north-east and some new housing had been built in the vicinity. There were possibly quays developing at Coxside, to the east, and there would have

been an established rope-making concern at Teat's Hill opposite the new quay built to service the sixteenth-century privateering trade.

The town was still largely confined to the medieval street layout, focused on the waterfront Southside Street, Woolster Street and Vauxhall Street and as far as Old Town Street to the north-west. New Street may have been recently laid out or more likely redeveloped and paved on the back of sixteenth-century prosperity. Other infilling had taken or was taking place.

Approaching Plymouth by sea, St Nicholas' Island, newly fortified (and to become better known as Drake's Island) would have been the landmark to the west. Ships may well have lain at anchor in the lee of it, at the entrance to Millbay, as yet undeveloped – though the town's (now derelict) Tide Mills were here.

The Cattewater, the mouth of the Plym, was another anchorage. It was protected by the natural limestone promontory of How Stert. Henrician gun platforms and occasional blockhouses guarded the Hoe foreshore.

The tower of St Andrew's Church, to the north of the town, and the new Hoe Fort (Drake's Fort of 1595) at the east end of the Hoe would be dominant; both utilising Plymouth limestone which can appear very white, especially in sunlight. The medieval (*c.* 1400) Castle Quadrate was still standing and in use on the rising land just west of the harbour entrance. It had its own quay. A building called the Fish House stood on a part of the natural rock outcrop that ran east–west across the entrance to Sutton Pool – this may have had associations with local fishing (pilchards?) or possibly Plymouth interests in the Newfoundland fisheries. The harbour entrance was therefore a tricky, narrow one – it had been guarded by a chain during the previous century.

Houses would be fairly densely constructed in a mixture of traditional timber frame, but there would also be newer, substantial stone-built merchants' homes (like Yogge's House that still stands near the church). If houses had been built with gardens, these were often built on.

Stone-built stores and warehouses dominated close to the waterfront, though often incorporating houses on the same site – they were not all open quays as now.[22]

Nobody knows where the *Mayflower* and *Speedwell* moored. The main quays were the Barbican Pier, the Southside (later Barbican) Quay, Smart's Quay, New Quay, Hawkin's (Jenning's) or Custom House Quay, Gaye's or Guy's Quay, Foxhole (later Vauxhall Quay) and Friary Quay/Weeke's Quay.

The two ships may have simply anchored in the Pool itself, or even in the Cattewater, with the passengers and crew coming ashore by small boat. At low tide, ships around the harbour would sit on the mud and any assessment of and repair to the *Speedwell* would have been carried out in those conditions.

The developed quays had stone walls. There were probably at least two cranes there, although their exact positioning is unknown. Whether they were hand-winched or winched by a man/mule-powered wheel is also unknown.[23]

The passengers would have heard distinctive west country dialect.[24] These would have mingled with many other foreign accents, because Plymouth was a port.

They had the *Speedwell* thoroughly examined and, as at Dartmouth, no special leak could be found. One explanation was that the ship had been 'over-masted' – too much sail – and when she was on the open seas the structure would open up, letting water in. That led to an overall conclusion: the whole ship was weak.

The stay at Plymouth lasted fourteen days and during it the settlers had to decide what to do. They decided to leave the *Speedwell* and transfer everything to the *Mayflower*, even though 'it was grevious and caused great discouragement'. The original arrangement had been ninety passengers on the *Mayflower* and thirty on the *Speedwell*. There was also the matter of Reynolds's integrity, because after the *Speedwell* was sold and masts and sails returned to their normal dimensions she sailed often and, according to Bradford, was profitable. Bradford claimed that Reynolds had shown 'cunning and deceit' because, fearing they did not have enough food, he had no wish to make the voyage at all and had found this method of freeing himself and his crew. Bradford further claimed that some of them had confessed to this afterwards.

The decision to switch everything to the *Mayflower* had a direct impact on the number of people who could go, but this seems to have resolved itself naturally. Some simply dropped out, like Cushman – ill, of course – taking his family with him. Cushman's 'heart and courage was gone' and it was gone from others, too: Thomas Blossom and William King, who, like Cushman, had been horribly seasick. They all knew that North Atlantic crossings were for spring and summer, not winter, and the delays had already pushed their voyage into autumn. Another factor, to stay at all, might have been a difficult decision, 'since under the laws operating at this time, anyone likely to become a charge on the parish through poverty could be summarily sent off to his or her place of birth' – the 'last thing' the Leiden group wanted.[25]

One report suggests that they met Captain Smith, the voyager of 1614 who had called the area New England, mapped it and written a book about it. Smith offered to lead and advise the trip, but this was refused, although the settlers took copies of the map and book. Smith would later say that their 'humorous ignorance caused them far more than a year to endure a wonderful deal of misery with infinite patience . . . thinking to find things better than I advised them'.[26]

Plymouth was a good place to be. The town was steeped in the traditions of Protestantism and had been able to appoint its own vicars for generations. From around 1608 these had been people known to be Puritans. In fact, Plymouth is generally regarded as a largely Puritan town by the time of James I (1603), or at least as having strong leanings that way.[27] Plymouth was a good place to be for other reasons. Its merchants had been the first to trade across the Atlantic, and it may be that while the group were waiting to sail they heard the folklore of the explorations. It was a rich one, and salty old sea dogs could have embellished a wonderful tale or two. Sir Richard Grenville and his fleet had sailed from Plymouth in 1585 to create the (failed) colony of Roanoke, North Carolina.

Ships from Plymouth had been working the Newfoundland Cod Banks since the sixteenth century, which may partly explain the rise of 'Devon-based merchants, masters and seamen in the sixteenth-century circumnavigations and explorations, and early American colonisation voyages'. As the *Mayflower* passengers waited, some eight Plymouth boats were fishing off New England and forty or fifty off Newfoundland; the season stretched from March to

September. This fishing necessitated temporary settlements on the land, but these were not proper colonies and the people probably stayed a couple of years at most.

Plymouth was accustomed to provisioning ships for Atlantic crossings, and the *Mayflower* and *Speedwell* were, in a sense, just another couple of unremarkable ships destined for New England. The town would not have regarded their arrival and departure as in any way abnormal, and certainly the passengers were not going into the complete unknown. Plymouth's mariners would have regarded a sailing in September, however, as 'ill considered' just when the fishing boats were coming back, via Portuguese and Spanish ports.[28]

While they were at Plymouth the Strangers may have sampled some of Plymouth's roaring taverns, although the Leiden group would surely have disapproved. They were, however, well looked after, because when they left they spoke of 'having been kindly entertained and courteously used by divers friends there dwelling'.[29]

Where did the passengers stay? Some may have been lodged in merchants' houses, especially the more senior members. 'Island House, a surviving contemporary building, bears a plaque to this effect. It is possible other lodgings were found by the poorer townsfolk. Perhaps stores and warehouses were also pressed into use. Perhaps some of the passengers remained aboard.'[30] Certainly, they may have spent their final night at Island House, in the Barbican district.

The *Mayflower*'s full complement of passengers was 104, including 3 pregnant women – 2 children would be born on board. The crew is estimated to have been between 25 and 30 and the 104 total includes 5 of them: 3 who had been hired to settle at the new Colony, 2 to live there for a year – one of whom was William Trevore, a labourer of unknown age. The crew total includes a mariner to take charge of the shallop, an open boat with oars and sail which was stowed on the *Mayflower*, and was to be used as a general workhorse at the Colony. John Allerton, the brother of Isaac, was intended to return and escort the next party from Leiden. Then there was John Alden from either Southampton or Harwich . . .

Of the original Scrooby group, only the Brewsters and the Bradfords were going. About both passengers and crew not much is known and any documentation is presumed lost forever, but there are fragments about the leading characters.

THE LEIDEN COMMUNITY

Isaac Allerton: about thirty-four, a tailor from London who went with his wife Mary and three children.
Bradford: aged thirty, and his wife Dorothy.
Brewster: about fifty-three, his wife Mary and children Love and Wrestling.
John Carver: age unknown, and his wife Catherine.
James Chilton: aged about fifty-seven, a tailor from Canterbury and his wife, name unknown. He was the oldest.
Samuel Fuller: aged forty, silk-maker and physician, travelled alone.
John Howland: aged between twenty-one and twenty-five, from Huntingdonshire, also travelled alone.
Myles Standish: age traditionally given as thirty-six, and his wife Rose, age unknown. He has been described as a 'one-man army. We can infer that he was short, had reddish hair and a ruddy complexion and that he was an experienced soldier and leader of men.'[31] He was fiery, 'hot-headed and unafraid'.[32] He would take in hand the defence of the Colony.
William White: age unknown, and his wife Susanna, also age unknown. White would die in either 1620 or 1621 and his widow marry Edward Winslow in the very first civil wedding to be carried out in what can be described neatly enough as the legal world of the English.

THE STRANGERS

Alden: the cooper.
John Billington: age unknown, travelled with his wife Ellen, also age unknown, and their two children. A tempestuous family, primed by devilment. Billington would be the first man hanged at the Colony, for murder.
Francis Eaton: age twenty-five, with his wife Sarah, age unknown, and their son Samuel, still a 'sucking child' during the voyage.

Stephen Hopkins: age unknown, was in a unique position; of the passengers, only he had made the voyage before – to Jamestown. He travelled with his wife Elizabeth, age also unknown, and four children.

Richard Warren: age unknown, a London merchant.

There is a silent postscript, revealing how servants were regarded. Carver's maidservant is known only as Dorothy, and even that has only recently been discovered.[33] There is a sad postscript, too, because among the 104 there were numbered 4 children called More – Ellen (eight), Jasper (seven), Richard (six) and Mary (four). Their mother Katherine had gone through a marriage of convenience with a Samuel More, her cousin. The four children were supposedly a product of that, but in fact she was having a torrid love affair with a Jacob Blakeway. More realised that the children looked nothing like him and an acrimonious divorce followed, and she rejected the children.

> At first, Samuel entrusted Katherine's four children to various of his tenants, but apparently the enraged Katherine continued to abuse them. So he was compelled to send them further away, and to provide for their education and maintenence 'in a place remote from these partes where these great blotts and blemishes may fall upon them.' Accordingly, they were handed over to John Carver and Robert Cushman to transport them.[34]

These children were in practical terms orphans. They were divided among three families. Richard and Mary, the two youngest, were given into the care of Brewster. After the seven years of the covenant they would have an allocation of 50 acres of land – Richard would live into the 1690s and be one of the last surviving *Mayflower* passengers.

The crew included four mates and a master gunner. The first officer was John Clarke, another who had been to the New World before, and the doctor, Giles Heale.

They were ready. On 6 September, a Wednesday, the wind was from the east-north-east, or rather a small gale blew. The ship moved out of Sutton Harbour into Plymouth Sound, the long, broad promontory of Rame Head looking around Cawsand Bay to their right. Once they had rounded that they were into the English Channel where it broadens towards the Atlantic. They were suddenly faced with the ocean.

The *Mayflower* has itself been the subject of intensive research, not least because neither picture nor drawings of it survive. The name was not at all unusual; in 1620 the Plymouth records show three – but not the one which made this voyage because, while it was at Plymouth, it landed no cargo. On 23 May 1620 it was back from a second crossing that year to France, bearing brandy. Weston chartered her. Captain Jones, who was also part-owner, may well have handled her business affairs and may have based her at Rotherhithe.

Jones would have had a cabin on the half-deck, with the rest of the crew finding accommodation where they could. If the passengers had the largest cabin and the deck, it would have given each of them the space of about the size of a modern single bed. Their sleeping arrangements are unknown, and have been the subject of much conjecture with one view that families slept together. Probably whole families huddled in their blankets on their straw mattresses, perhaps even on deck. Cooking was a problem too. There was a little brick oven, the presumption is that this, again, was done by whole families. They must all have been cold and very wet, with seawater and perhaps rainwater dripping and dribbling down through all the decks.

How frightened were the children, especially at night? How were they comforted? What strange, unending orchestra of sounds played to them: timbers groaning and complaining, the breeze hissing through the rigging, the constant lapping of water against the ship's hull, the seamen calling roughly to each other?

> The food and drink were . . . monotonous. Beer was their normal drink. Bacon, salted meat, dried fish, cheese and pulses [edible seeds] comprised their main diet. The more wealthy passengers had brought such things as sugar, raisins and citrus fruits . . . while Brewster, Bradford and one or two of the other leaders had brought a quantity of brandy and gin.[35]

As the ship creaked into the Atlantic they had a 'prosperous wind' for several days and that raised hopes of a quick crossing, although some could not avoid seasickness.

The mechanics of controlling the *Mayflower* demanded skill. 'The secret of a sailing ship is rhythm, operating through the rigging to the sails, spars [masts] and hull, blending smoothly to give the ship a hatful of wind. Shortness, width and a high superstructure in proportion make a ship like the *Mayflower* difficult to manoeuvre and fatiguing to steer.'[36]

Once they had reached the Atlantic and Land's End had drifted into the distance, Smith had to make sure the *Mayflower* moved clear of the Bay of Biscay and the risk of getting sucked towards the rocks on the Finisterre coast, then make a choice of route. He could go by the trade winds, head south and turn, as Columbus had once done. He could head north towards Greenland and let the Arctic current take the ship: shorter but more dangerous because the seas would be rougher, and in a few days it would be October – almost winter. We do not know which way they went and, as with so much, the probability is that we never will.

Judging by the weather the ship encountered it may well have been the northern route. The favourable conditions did not endure. They ran into crosswinds and 'fierce' storms which 'shrewdly shook' the ship, and the upper part leaked. Worse, a main beam bent and cracked – something so serious that part of the group met the captain and some of his officers to debate whether to go on or turn back. This provoked a 'difference of opinion' among the seamen who were drawn between losing their wages if they turned back and risking their lives if they went on. Jones acted as arbiter, but because the ship was basically robust and 'firm under water' they decided to continue. There is a hint of mystery here, however, because to repair the main beam they were able to use a 'great iron screw' the group had brought from Holland to re-erect the beam. When that had been accomplished, 'the carpenter and master affirmed that with a post under it, set firm in the lower deck, and other ways bound he would make it sufficient'.[37]

The voyage brought tensions beyond the danger, tedium and cramped accommodation. One sailor, 'a proud and very profane young man', taunted the passengers 'in their sickness', and cursed them every day, saying he 'hoped to help to cast half of them overboard' before the ship reached the New World. If anyone admonished this sailor he would 'curse and swear most bitterly'. By a strange irony, about halfway over (in Bradford's estimation) the sailor fell ill with a 'grevious disease' and died in a 'desperate manner'. He was the first to be buried at sea.

There is no chronology to the voyage and no way of knowing when this happened; nor when they encountered storms where the winds were 'so fierce, and the seas so high, as they could not bear a knot of sail. But were forced to hull for divers days together.' With the sails down, the ship would have been battered whichever way wind and waves took it, wallowing and rolling, dipping and rising. It was all anybody could do to cling on to anything that gave a hold. They might have been back on the North Sea out of Immingham, being borne up towards the Norwegian coast. In October, somewhere in the midst of this,[38] Hopkins's wife Elizabeth gave birth to a baby boy, called, aptly, Oceanus.

On calmer days Brewster might have organised daily services on the deck – prayers, psalms, Bible-reading – the congregation gathered round him, his voice trying to reach out above the waves; and the congregation moving uneasily and probably queasily with the movements of the ship.

> The ship was wet – Upham[39] thought there could not have been a dry bone on board – and cold. She was cramped, too, badly ventilated, unlit below decks, none too lavishly provisioned, reeking of vomit and bilge.
>
> Packed in as they were, every operation took a long time: cooking their own meals in twos and threes and fours, the smoke from their little braziers blowing into their faces, keeping an eye on the children . . . trying to make themselves comfortable enough to snatch an hour or two of sleep below decks, where it was not always possible even to stretch out – these framed their days. Days of wrestling with private terrors, with personal sickness, and discomfort (how did the women and girls manage when they had their periods, for example?).[40]

Another young man, John Howland from Huntingdonshire, showed how dangerous the voyage was. The ship 'lay at hull in a mighty storm' and as it rolled Howland was thrown into the sea but he grabbed a topsail halyard – rope for raising or lowering sail – and held on though he was a long way under the water. They hauled him above the waterline and, with a boathook, lifted him back on to the deck. He lived until 1673.

Only one passenger died, William Butten. He was a servant of Samuel Fuller, described as 'a youth' whose origins are unknown. The cause of death is also unknown, but it happened when they were approaching the coast and three days before they made landfall. Captain Jones would have known they were nearing the coast the previous day 'by the change in the colour of the sea water and by the general appearance of the western clouds', and 'it is more than likely he had already caught the pungent, earthy smell of the land in the offshore breeze. Landsmen may not appreciate that to a mariner approaching the coast after long days at sea, a wind from off the land is as laden with the message of the earth and growing things as ever the sea breeze is of things salty to the nose of the landlubber.'[41]

They made landfall at dawn. That landfall, after their 'long beating at sea', was judged to be Cape Cod and 'they were not a little joyful'.[42] It was 9 November 1620 and they had been at sea for sixty-five days.

Mapmaker Smith wrote that 'being pestered [overcrowded] nine weeks in this leaking unwholesome ship, lying wet in their cabins, most of them grew very weak, and weary of the sea'.[43]

The land they could see comforted them just as much as the leaving of the Atlantic did, a good-looking land with woods running down to the sea. It looked much as it does today, because 'except for the straightening-out of the Back Side [of Cape Cod] through the washing-away of outjutting points from time to time, and the filling-in of the harbors and bends with the débris, neither the history of modern surveys nor a comparison with ancient landmarks and records shows that any far-fetched and radical changes in the coastline have taken place'.[44]

It is possible to work out with a high degree of probability what happened after landfall. At daybreak – 6.30 a.m. – they were not yet close enough in to the shore to be certain exactly where they were. It may be that Captain Jones knew, because he knew he was close to the 42nd parallel of latitude, and if he followed that it would take the *Mayflower* to Cape Cod. Jones would have known, too, that 'he was pretty well in toward the Cape before daylight on the ninth, whether he confided to his passengers or not', although at daybreak itself 'it is extremely doubtful if he would let his ship get into much less than seventy-five fathoms [1 fathom = 6ft] before it was light enough to see'.[45] That might place the ship some 9 miles offshore from Eastham and East Orleans.

The passengers could now see land, the land some of them would know for the rest of their lives. It might have been a 'golden sunrise of a beautiful November morning'. The emotion of the passengers must have been one of relief. Whatever the future would bring them here, they were at least alive to face it.

Anyone on deck would have seen Cape Cod's landmark, the Highland of Truro, because it is visible from 15 miles in clear daylight, its 'bold clay bluffs . . . rising nearly one hundred and fifty feet sheer from the sea'.[46] To the south, they would have seen the high banks of the Back Side, rising nearly a hundred feet. These distinctive landmarks told those who would been before – Master's Mates Clark and Coppin – that they were looking at Cape Cod, shaped like a vast arm crooked out to sea, almost a shield.

They were now some 5½ miles from South Wellfleet beach. There followed some deliberation among the passengers and Jones because, however tempting the safe reaches behind the shield, they ought to have been in the Hudson river a very long way away. They may have discussed it for an hour or so, because time was now a pressing factor. They were running short of provisions – fresh water and firewood, for example – and scurvy was breaking out. It was decided to continue down to the Hudson. The weather was fine, the wind helpful; they tacked and set off.

How many yearned to go ashore here and now, and put the Atlantic for ever behind them? How many cared any more about contracts and niceties and the Hudson? How much or how little were they involved in the discussion? Were the women, so tormented by so much, involved at all or did they wait in their cubby holes, nursing the children, until the decision had been made? Did anybody tell them what was happening?

The *Mayflower* began to tack southwards at 9 a.m., the breeze coming from the north. She was covering perhaps 4 miles an hour until around 1 p.m. when the wind changed to the east, slowing her to 3 miles an hour. As she went soundings 'were undoubtedly frequently done, because at the slow gait she was going through the water, the hand-lead could be used by an experienced hand' without affecting her speed. At somewhere around 3 p.m. they would have reached Pollock Rip at the far side of Monomoy Island, lying just to the south of the Cape. These are the Shoals – 'that barrier of shifting, barely submerged sandbars' which almost blocks the entrance to Nantucket Sound.[47]

'They fell among dangerous shoals, and roaring breakers, and they were so far entangled therewith.'[48] The ship had reached the Shoals, and was in danger of foundering. A storm seemed to be brewing and the decision was taken to turn back towards Cape Cod. Did Jones insist that going on presented too much of a danger? Was there another discussion at all? Had the passengers simply had enough? Was the sight of goodly, wooded land just back there too tempting? At the top of Cape Cod, inside the shield, was a natural harbour called Provincetown. They decided to anchor there.

Many years later, one necessary question was posed. The truth of the answer is unknown, but here was another suspicious mystery to take its place alongside the motives of the *Speedwell*'s crew. Nathaniel Morton, writing in *New England's Memorial* (Boston, 1669), suggested they had turned back from the Hudson partly because of the storm and partly because of the 'fraudulence and contrivance' of Jones. The Dutch, Morton claimed, intended to establish their own Plantation on the Hudson and had bought Jones off. Using the storm as a pretext, he had dump his passengers somewhere round Cape Cod.

This seems doubtful, because the danger posed by the Shoals cannot be disputed, but the statement leads to a further question: were the passengers, in retrospect, justifying their decision to land where they did rather than at the Hudson? They had no patent north of the 41st parallel,[49] which by coincidence began just south of the Shoals. Blaming Jones would be a good cover.

Sunset was at 4.35 p.m., darkness by 5 p.m. Jones turned the *Mayflower* away and, running as hard as he could, might have sailed 6 miles from the Shoals by darkness. 'With night shutting down on him fast, with no chart to hint at what might lie ahead, with no moon till after midnight to lighten his path, and with his recent vivid illustration of how suddenly a ship might run into shoal water in this locality fresh in his mind, the logical thing to do would be to heave her to for the night.'[50]

Next morning, at 6 a.m., Jones would have daylight again, and as he prepared to sail by 6.30 he would have been able to see the coastline at Chatham. He probably had a favourable wind as he ran the *Mayflower* up the coast, and that night, when he heaved to again, he might have reached Race Point at the northern tip of Cape Cod. He was safely into deep water and somewhere around the wide mouth of Cape Cod Bay.

By 5 a.m. the next day he would have been able to make out Race Point. By dawn, as the ship drew into the Bay and prepared to tuck itself into the safe little harbour, a further decision had to be made. It would be a momentous one.

SIX

The Compact

They had no right to be where they were and who knew what trouble that might make for them? They had no right to make laws or elect leaders. That was the legal position, but in realpolitik it represented no more than niceties. The nearest English community was more than 500 miles away in Virginia, and England 3,000 miles back across the Atlantic. The settlers, surveying the shoreline as the *Mayflower* rode at anchor in Cape Cod Bay, were on their own and they knew they were on their own.

Just over there was an unknown land, possibly teeming with hordes of brutish Indians concealed among the trees. Who could tell what else was there? Nor could the settlers be united in spirit and purpose, because some had come to establish their particular heaven on earth and others had come to make money.

A few of the Strangers behaved like the entrepreneurs they were (or wished to become). They understood very well the importance of the geographical position – not the isolation of it, although that must have been a factor, but that being in the wrong place made any previous arrangements invalid. In short, they maintained it gave them the freedom to do whatever they liked once they got ashore.

They had shown their discontent by making 'mutinous' speeches: 'none had power to command them, the patent they had being for Virginia, and not for New England, which belonged to another government with which the Virginia Company had nothing to do'.[1]

This had to be resolved, and it would be done in a subtle, far-reaching way. A meeting of all the settlers was arranged, to draw up a binding agreement and sign it. The subtlety lay in that they were doing it as volunteers, and by themselves for themselves. 'Such an act by them done', William Bradford concluded, '(their condition considered), might be as firm as any Patent, and in some respects more sure'.

Who decided? And who called them all together? Brewster?

> This day before we came to harbour, observing some not well affected to unity and concord but gave some appearance of faction, it was thought good there should be an association and agreement that we should combine . . . in one body and to submit to such government and governors as we should by common consent agree to make and choose.[2]

The men would have met on the deck, perhaps after morning prayers. Maybe they would not have done so until after breakfast. On the deck there must have been further strong arguments, because the immediate prospect of absolute freedom, something no ordinary Englishman could have imagined, had to be intoxicating and possibly slightly disconcerting. On one side were the disciplined Leiden group, long accustomed to the hierarchy of their Church to give their lives meaning and structure, and on the other a random group who by definition were not disciplined but ambitious individuals.

If both groups gazed across to the shoreline they saw 'oaks, pines, juniper, sassafras, and other sweet wood'[3] and it was all theirs. So was everything else.

Cape Cod appeared 'a good harbour and pleasant bay, circled round, except in the entrance, which is about four miles over from land to land . . . It is a harbour wherein 1,000 sail of ships may safely ride'.[4]

Did somebody make a great speech to rival the Gettysburg Address, carrying the day by force of argument and logic? Was that Brewster? Bradford? Did they yearn for Robinson's eloquence – Robinson still in Holland, Robinson they would never see again. Did the logic need no eloquence because all knew that anarchy could be lethal for everyone? Did somebody, in this extraordinary forum of strong desires and stronger emotions, find the phrases to say they had come to a threshold, could cross it within hours but faced the rest of their years without laws unless they made decisions now? Were the phrases spoken with just enough pitch to be heard above the waters of the Bay lapping against the ship, and a light morning breeze breathing through the rigging over their heads?

Did someone read out – again – Robinson's farewell, beginning:

> whereas you become a body politic – using amongst yourselves civil government and are not furnished with any persons of special eminency above the rest, to be chosen by you into office of government – let your wisdom and godliness appear not only in choosing such persons as do entirely love and will promote the common good but also in yielding unto them all due honour and obedience in their lawful administrations: not beholding in them the ordinariness of their persons, but God's ordinance for your good; not being like the foolish multitude.

Or was it all done quietly, on the nod? Something extraordinary did happen. An agreement was drawn up which represented both a matrix and an insurance policy – the latter because it proclaimed that they were loyal subjects of King James. It was called the *Mayflower* Compact.

> In the Name of God, Amen. We whose names are underwritten, the loyal subjects of our dread sovereign Lord, King James, by the grace of God, of Great Britain, France and Ireland, King, Defender of the Faith, etc,
>
> Having undertaken, for the glory of God, and advancement of the Christian faith and honour of our King and Country, a voyage to plant the first Colony in the northern parts of Virginia, do by these presents solemnly and mutually in the presence of God, and one of another, covenant and combine ourselves together into a civil body politic, for our better ordering and preservation and furtherance of the ends aforesaid; and by virtue hereof to enact, constitute and frame such just and equal laws, ordinances, acts, constitutions and offices, from time to time, as shall be thought most meet and convenient for the general good of the Colony: unto which we promise all due submission and obedience. In witness whereof we have hereunder subscribed our names at Cape Cod the 11 of November, in the year of the reign of our sovereign Lord, King James of England, France and Ireland the eighteenth, and of Scotland the fifty-fourth. Ano. Dom. 1620.

John Carver	William White	Edward Fuller	Gilbert Winslow
William Bradford	Richard Warren	John Turner	Edmond Margeson
Edward Winslow	John Howland	Francis Eaton	Peter Brown
William Brewster	Stephen Hopkins	James Chilton	Richard Britteridge
Isaac Allerton	Edward Tilly	John Crackston	George Soule
Myles Standish	John Tilly	John Billington	Richard Clarke
John Alden	Francis Cooke	Moses Fletcher	Richard Gardiner
Samuel Fuller	Thomas Rogers	John Goodman	John Allerton
Christopher Martin	Thomas Tinker	Degory Priest	Thomas English
William Mullins	John Rigdale	Thomas Williams	Edward Doty
			Edward Leister

The Strangers were John Alden, John Billington, Peter Brown, Richard Britteridge, Richard Clarke, Edward Doty, Francis Eaton, Richard Gardiner, Stephen Hopkins, Edward Leister, Edmond Margeson, Christopher Martin, William Mullins, John Rigdale, George Soule, Richard Warren, William White and Gilbert Winslow. Virtually all of them had signed, and four servants too: Howland (with the Carver family), Soule (with the Winslow family) and Doty and Leister (both with the Hopkins family); the mutiny was over.

Significantly, Standish was the first of the non-Leiden group to sign, although[5] it is necessary to proceed with great caution about many aspects of the list. For simplicity I am taking the document at face value. The complications are explored in the footnote.

Standish had fought the Spaniards in Holland, been to Leiden and 'was well known to Pastor Robinson', who would 'express his affection for him' in subsequent letters.[6] A trained soldier preparing to take charge of the Colony's defences, Standish would have regarded any hint of anarchy with disdain and deep disapproval. Was he central to getting the Strangers to sign?

Various people did not sign, but with good reasons. Robert Carter was possibly too young – his age has been estimated at from fifteen to twenty-five. Others may have been too young also: William Holbeck, age unknown (with the White family), John Langmore, age unknown (with the Martin family), Solomon Prower (the stepson of Christopher Martin and Mary Prower), aged between thirteen and twenty-one, Elias Story, age unknown (with the Winslow family), Edward Thompson, age unknown (and nothing else known about him), William Trevore, age unknown (a labourer hired to work for a year), Roger Wilder, age unknown (with the Carver family). Given all this, the extent of the unanamity is striking. The unintended consequences of the Compact, serving as a matrix, would be profound.

No women signed. The men – even the servants – are coming from background to foreground, but their womenfolk, who had endured and contributed so much, remained where they can barely be seen and never heard.

Nobody knows if the Compact had been drawn up in advance, as seems likely, and was read out as a discussion document or simply presented, but each man had to sign. A table would have been needed, with the Compact laid out for the signing of each. Did they lean or was there a chair? Probably a chair because 'writing was a laborious undertaking in those days'[7] and each man may have taken a minute or two to do it. It might well have been 9 a.m. before the last man – Leister – had signed.

A further decision remained. Who would hold authority? They decided, or rather 'confirmed',[8] John Carver as governor for that year.

It was another profound moment. Were several candidates debated? Had the Leiden leaders made up their minds in advance? Can it have been coincidence that Carver was the first to sign the Compact? Was his appointment done on a simple show of hands?

However it was done, Carver became not only their first governor, but the 'first colonial governor in the entire New World to be named by the colonists themselves in a free election'.[9] Carver's age is unknown and his origins are obscure. There is a suggestion he came from Yorkshire and a further one[10] that he was married twice, both times in Leiden, with the presumption that his first wife died there.

> [Carver] had many claims to the position . . . He was probably one of the original company, and was a man of substance who had sunk most of his considerable fortune into the enterprise, probably more than any other planter. He had been the leading spirit in the emigration from Leiden, and was employed in the London negotiations because of his knowledge of the world.

Although he upbraided Cushman for negligence, he also strove to keep the peace between him and the others. Apart from Brewster he was probably the eldest of the company, and his wife's younger sister was John Robinson's wife.[11]

The *Mayflower* need not have been stationary while this was going on, but moving slowly in. By 8 a.m. she could have been approaching Provincetown Harbour and an hour later, the signing done, the harbour would be opening up in plain sight. There was a problem, however: 'We could not come near the shore by three quarters of an English mile, because of shallow water.'[12]

Jones would find 'nothing but soft mud and poor holding ground in the middle of the Harbor, with shoals and flats all along the northerly and westerly sides under the mainland [until] he finally stands back on to the hard bottom under the lee of the Point'. At 10 a.m. 'just as four bells chimes out from the ship's belfry on the break of the half-deck, Master Christopher Jones shoots his ship into the wind and lets go his anchor in twelve fathoms of water, about an eighth of a mile inside of Long Point; and the *Mayflower* of London . . . swings to her moorings in the New World'.[13]

The coast beckoned and beguiled, a spit of land now only a mile away to the north. It was virgin territory, never permanently settled by the Wampanoag and only occasionally visited by Vikings and pirates.[14] They would need an hour to get the longboat over the side and prepare and arm those who would go ashore – fifteen or sixteen – where, however beguiling the land itself after what the ocean had done to them, 'they had no friends to welcome them nor inns to entertain or refresh their weather-beaten bodies, no houses or much less town to repair to, to seek for succor'.[15]

When the men had stowed muskets and axes on the longboat and were ready, they began to row. The logical place to aim for was what is now the southern end of Provincetown – the town – because deep water went nearer the shore there than anywhere else and the terrain was clear so there was nowhere for Indians to hide. When the longboat reached shallower water the men had to clamber over the side and wade 'a bow shot or two in going a-land'.[16]

It might have been midday. Bradford says that when they did reach the shore they 'fell upon their knees and blessed the God of Heaven, who had brought them over the vast, furious ocean, and delivered them from all the perils and miseries thereof, again to set their feet on the firm and stable earth, their proper element'. A priority was wood, because all they had had was gone, but they also wanted a feel of the land and whoever might be living there.

> They found it to be a small neck of land. On this side where we lay is the bay, and the further side the sea, the ground or earth, sand hills, much like the downs in Holland but much better; the crust of the earth a spit's depth [spit = spade depth], excellent black earth . . . the wood for the most part open and without underwood . . . At night our people returned, but found not any person nor habitation, and laden their boat with juniper, which smelled very sweet and strong, and of which we burned the most part of the time we lay there.[17]

The next day was a Sunday. They rested and prayed. On the Monday they took the shallop ashore for repairs. It had been used on the voyage as sleeping quarters, and to fit had had to be cut to size. Evidently it had also opened up with the people sleeping in it. It needed repairs and caulking (waterproofing) before they could use it as the shoreline workhorse. This proved time-consuming and took more than two weeks.

There was no question of establishing the Plantation at Provincetown, because the long wade to the shore meant they could not unload their provisions easily, and wading through freezing waters caused many colds and coughs. That Monday, however, several passengers went ashore to 'refresh themselves and our women to wash, as they had great need'.[18]

They were impatient. What they did on the Tuesday is unrecorded, although

> every day we saw whales playing hard by us [and] if we had instruments and means to take them we might have made a very rich return. [Jones] and his mate, and others experienced in fishing,

> professed we might have made three or four thousand pounds worth of oil . . . Cod we assayed but found none, there is a good store no doubt in their season. Neither got we fish all the time we lay there, but some few little ones on the shore. We found great mussels, and very fat and full of sea pearl but we could not eat them . . . they made us all sick that did eat, as well sailors as passengers; they caused us to cast and sour [vomit and diarrhoea].[19]

They wanted to explore, but the carpenter was only just beginning the job of repairing the shallop – there would be complaints about how slowly he worked – so on the Wednesday a party of sixteen armed men under Standish went ashore in the longboat to see what they could find. It was pre-agreed they would spend no more than two nights away. Everyone had a sword, a musket and corslet.[20]

Without the shallop, whatever wood or food they found would have to be carried on their backs. What really enticed them, however, was that as the *Mayflower* sailed into the harbour they thought they had seen a river, which meant fresh water. When they were ashore they arranged themselves in single file and set off, keeping close to the sea. After about a mile they saw 'five or six people with a dog coming towards them'[21] – the party thought initially it might be Jones and some of the crew, who were also ashore. But it was not. It was some Indians, who ran into some woodland, whistling the dog after them. The party followed, keeping their eyes open for an ambush, chased them out of the woodland but could not catch them. This was the first contact, itself momentous. It was also the first of many meetings in what would prove to be a strange relationship.

The Indians looked on the settlers 'with apprehension and great curiosity'. The *Mayflower* 'was much larger than [their] biggest canoe', although they were not unfamiliar with large ships before the *Mayflower* came. Explorers had passed this way, the Vikings 'frequently' and then 'European fishermen from Spain, Portugal, France, and Ireland fished for codfish' off the coast years before the *Mayflower*.[22]

The settlers followed the Indians by their footprints for about 10 miles and noticed that the Indians were using the same route they had used for their outward journey. At one point, a sort of crossroads, the Indians had run up a hill either to try and shake the party off or verify that the party was following them. As night fell the party set up camp, some fetching wood and lighting a fire while three others acted as sentinels. At dawn they set off again and were able to follow the Indians' tracks again as far as 'the head of a long creek'. After that the Indians moved into more woodland, the party following and thinking that, by now, they must be near the Indians' dwellings. However,

> we marched through boughs and bushes, and under hills and valleys, which tore our very armour in pieces and yet could meet with none of them, nor their houses, nor any fresh water, which we greatly desired, and stood in need of . . . We had brought neither beer nor water with us, and our victuals was only biscuit and Holland cheese, and a little bottle of aquavitae,[23] so as we were sore a-thirst. About ten o'clock, we came into a deep valley, full of brush . . . and long grass, through which we found little paths or tracks, and there we saw a deer, and found springs of fresh water, of which we were heartily glad, and sat us down and drunk our first New England water with as much delight as ever we drunk drink in all our lives.[24]

They kept on heading south and eventually made a fire by the shore so that the *Mayflower* could see where they had reached. Then they continued towards where they thought the river would be.

The geographical importance of a river was self-evident, apart from a constant source of fresh water. Virtually every European town was built on one. A river offered navigation and ease of transport; and more immediately it might allow the longboat to get to the shore to begin the unloading.

In another valley they found a 'fine clear pond of fresh water, being about a musket shot broad, and twice as long'. It seemed suddenly like a land approximating to milk and honey: small vines grew there, deer hunted there, fowl were to be had, there was an abundance of sassafras.[25] A little bit further on they found a huge cleared area – about 50 acres – which they thought the Indians had once used for planting corn and which, the party felt, could be ploughed.

Where was the river? There was a discussion about that and some thought it best to go down to the sea and walk across the sands to find it. By now, wearing armour and carrying heavy weapons across this sand, the party was becoming exhausted and strung back, so they made a halt and waited until everybody had caught up. Then they continued and found a small pathway leading to

> certain heaps of sand, one . . . covered with old mats, and had a wooden thing like a mortar . . . on the top of it, and an earthen pot laid in a little hole at the end . . . We, musing what it might be, digged and found a bow, and, as we thought, arrows, but they were rotten. We supposed there were many other things but because we deemed them graves we put the bow in again and made it up as it was, and left the rest untouched . . . We thought it would be odious unto them to ransack their sepulchers [tombs]. We went on further and found new stubble, of which they had gotten corn this year, and many walnut trees full of nuts, and great store of strawberries, and some vines. Passing thus a field or two . . . we came to another . . . and there we found an house had been, and four or five old planks laid together. Also we found a great kettle, which had been some ship's kettle and brought out of Europe.[26]

This discovery may have been ominous. Had the Indians murdered the crew of a ship to get the kettle? The party found a mound of sand, obviously man-made, and dug it up. Within they found a 'little old basket' full of Indian corn. They dug further and found a 'fine great new basket' full of this year's corn – 'some yellow, and some red, and others mixed with blue'. This basket was 'round, and narrow at the top'. It held about three or four bushels (1 bushel = 64 US pints) and two men could just about lift it.

While two or three of them were digging and lifting, the others stood sentry in a ring. Then they were 'in suspense' over what to do with the kettle and the corn. They had a long discussion: their Christian values were at stake. To take the kettle and corn was straightforward theft, so they reached a compromise with themselves. They would take the kettle loaded with corn and as much extra corn as they could carry, and if at some later time they met the Indian owners, they would 'give them the kettle again, and satisfy them for their corn'.[27]

The story of the settlers exploring the hinterland is, almost inevitably, dominated by their own accounts and one-sided, however objective the accounts tried to be. There was another side, that of the Indians. This is what it looked like from the hinterland:[28]

> The first concerns of the new arrivals were finding something to eat and a place to settle. After anchoring off Cape Cod . . . a small party was sent ashore to explore. Pilgrims in every sense of the word, they promptly stumbled into a Nauset[29] graveyard where they found baskets of corn which had been left as gifts for the deceased. The gathering of this unexpected bounty was interrupted by the angry Nauset warriors, and the hapless Pilgrims beat a hasty retreat back to their boat with little to show for their efforts.

They had a staff, or maybe cut a branch down, and put it through the handle of the kettle, hoisted it onto two men's shoulders and set off. Others filled their pockets, but were already so laden with armour that they could not carry much. The rest they reburied. As they made their way they came upon 'the remainder of an old fort, or palisade' which they thought must have been built by 'some Christians' near where they anticipated the river would be; and the river was there, dividing itself into two arms by a high bank, 'but whether it be fresh water or only an indraught of the sea we had no time to discover'.

They found a couple of canoes and resolved to investigate further when the shallop was available. Then they returned to the fresh-water pond for the night, made a large fire and took it in turns to stand guard. It rained hard. Next morning they dried their muskets and set off back towards Provincetown and the *Mayflower* – and got lost. They came upon a bough of a tree held taut by rope and under it some acorns. While Hopkins was explaining that it was an

Indian trap to catch deer, Bradford came up to have a look and 'as he went about, it gave a sudden jerk up, and he was immediately caught by the leg'. Perhaps it made them all laugh, except Bradford himself. No doubt they cut him free quickly enough, although they admired the craftsmanship of the trap and the rope.

Eventually they emerged from these woods and saw three bucks. As the party walked, they flushed out 'three couple of partridges' which took to the wing. When they reached a creek they saw 'great flocks of wild geese and ducks' which, naturally enough, were frightened.

As the party returned, they were moving through woods, on sand and sometimes in water up to their knees. They saw the *Mayflower* and fired their muskets so the crew would know where they were. The longboat came to fetch them, and so did Jones, Carver and 'many of our people' who were already on the shore.[30]

The travel to and from the ship was proving a serious problem, because it could be done only at high water. It meant wading, sometimes up to the knees but other times midway up the thigh. Some made the journey because they had tasks to fulfil, some because they wanted to be on land and there was the constant risk of catching serious colds.

The shallop was seaworthy on 28 November, although evidently not yet completely finished, and a second more major expedition was mounted involving it, the longboat and twenty-four passengers. Captain Jones wanted to lead the expedition, taking nine of his sailors whom he thought would be the most effective. It was to be for four days and would penetrate further than the settlers on foot with their armour had been able to do.

Now the real test began. They left in weather so rough and a crosswind so strong that it would seem they headed for the nearest shore or were virtually carried there. They waded ashore. In this wind, the shallop 'could not keep the water' and was forced to lie up there overnight. It was snowing. Some of the party marched 6 or 7 miles further, on the understanding that the shallop would come to them next day. The wind blew throughout the day and at night the temperature dropped below freezing.

The following day at about 11 a.m. the shallop reached them and they sailed down to the river they had found. They named the place Cold Harbour. It was not deep enough for ships but might, they thought, be good enough for smaller craft. They marched along the broader of the two branches, the shallop following, but at length, 'as night grew on, and our men were tired with marching up and down the steep hills, and deep valleys, which lay half a foot thick with snow' they pitched camp under a few pine trees. They had shot three plump geese and six ducks which they ate with 'soldiers' stomachs'. They had had little else all day.

The prize was fresh water, and they assumed they would find that at the head of the river. But their resolution did not hold 'because many liked not the hilliness of the soil, and badness of the harbour, so we turned towards the other creek . . . that we might go over and look for the rest of the corn that we left behind when we were here before'.[31] They named this Cornhill. They dug up the corn and a little further away found a bottle of oil. At another place they found more corn and a bag of beans. In total, they had 10 bushels. It was hard going: the ground was not only covered in snow but frozen underneath. Because they had not brought tools, they had to use their short swords and cutlasses to prise open the earth and then lever it up.

Jones had had enough – bad weather coming in – but some of the party wanted to explore further and, specifically, find out where the Indians lived. The motives must have been twofold: protection – if the Indians were hostile and the settlers knew where they were they could stay away from them – and self-interest. The Indians had survived for countless generations in these conditions and the settlers could learn from them.

Jones took off the weaker members and the remainder, some eighteen, stayed the night. Next morning they followed what they thought were Indian pathways, penetrating 5 or 6 miles into the woods. Finding nothing they resolved to go back to the creek and try to dig up more corn. They saw a canoe on the river, and a flock of geese. Someone shot a brace and they rowed over in the canoe to fetch them. Later they came across what seemed to be a graveyard, although it was larger than any they had found so far. They wondered what it was and decided to dig. They had found the

Indian habitation and under mats a bow, brooches, bowls, trays, dishes. They came to a new mat and

> under that two bundles, the one bigger, the other less. We opened the greater and found in it a great quantity of fine and perfect red powder, and in it the bones and skull of a man. The skull had fine yellow hair still on it, and some of the flesh unconsumed. There was bound up with it a knife, a packneedle, and two or three old iron things. It was bound up in a sailor's canvas cassock and a pair of cloth breeches. The red powder was a kind of embalmment. We opened the less bundle . . . and found of the same powder in it, and the bones and head of a little child [with], about the legs and other parts of it, bound strings and bracelets of fine white beads. There was also by it a little bow, about three quarters long, and some other odd knacks. We brought sundry of the prettiest things away with us, and covered the corpse up again.[32]

They debated whether the adult might have been an Indian lord or king, although some said Indians only had black hair. They even wondered if it was a Christian of 'some special note' who had died among them and they had 'buried him to honour him'. Others in the party expressed a different opinion, that the Indians had killed him and had buried him like this 'in triumph over him'.

A couple of sailors, who had just come on to the shore, saw two houses which seemed to have been occupied until recently. They went in but took fright and made for the main party. There, seven or eight men joined them and they all went back. The 'houses' were 'made with young long sapling trees', bent and both ends stuck into the ground. The houses were round, 'like unto an arbour, and covered down to the ground with thick and well-wrought mats'. The settlers had discovered tee-pees.

> In the houses we found wooden bowls, trays and dishes, earthen pots, handbaskets made of crab shells wrought together; also an English . . . bucket . . . We also found two or three deers' heads, one whereof had been newly killed . . . It was still fresh . . . There was also a company of deer's feet stuck up in the houses, harts'

> horns, and eagles' claws . . . also two or three baskets full of parched acorns, pieces of fish, and a piece of broiled herring . . . There was thrust into a hollow tree two or three pieces of venison but we thought it fitter for the dogs than for us.[33]

They got down to the shallop to catch the last of the tide. Before the expedition, they had intended to bring along beads and other things to leave, both as a sign of peace and an indication that they wanted to open trade – but they had not brought the beads or any other offerings. One way and another, they had had to leave for the expedition in too much haste.

While they had been away Suzanna White had given birth to a son, Peregrine, on the *Mayflower*.

With winter drawing in and Captain Jones anxious to sail for England, a decision had to be made about the place for the Colony. Some thought the creek would do: the land there was certainly fertile enough to grow corn, as the Indians had proved. There were also the fishing possibilities of Cape Cod, a place of very un-English perspectives.

> In fair weather we saw [whales] swim and play about us. There was once one when the sun shone came and lay above water for a good while as if she had been dead, within half a musket shot of the ship – at which two [passengers or crew] were prepared to shoot to see whether she would stir or no. He that gave fire first, his musket flew into pieces, both stock and barrel, yet thanks be to God neither he nor any other man was hurt with it, though many were thereabout . . . The whale . . . gave a snuff and away.[34]

On 4 December, Edward Thomson died, cause unknown. The Billington family, however, were very much alive – as they would keep on proving. Francis Billington, aged about fourteen, had in his father's absence obtained some gunpowder and was fooling around with it. He fired a loaded fowling-piece (a gun for shooting fowl) near a little half-full barrel of powder – but mercifully it did not ignite. Some thought that if it had, the ship might have been very badly damaged.

On Wednesday the 6th the third expedition set off with ten men who had volunteered to go on it. Carver went, and Standish, Bradford and Hopkins, both the ship's mates, the gunner, some seamen and servants. It was a viciously cold day. It seems they went in the shallop, but when they got clear of the *Mayflower* it took an age to get round a sandy point about a furlong away. Seasickness or cold struck at two of the party – Edward Tilley had cold, they thought, but the gunner was 'also sick unto death'. The thought of profitable trade made the latter keep on . . .

Once they cleared the sandbank they got the sail up and 'within an hour or two' were near the shore, sailing into calmer waters. They were making good progress, although the weather remained bitterly cold. The water froze their clothes and 'made them many times like coats of iron'. They sailed on for about 20 miles and 'at length we met with a tongue of land, being flat off from the shore, with a sandy point. We bore up to gain the point and found there a fair . . . road.'[35] They decided to investigate this further the following day, but approaching the shore, they saw ten or twelve Indians 'very busy about a black thing'. They could not tell what it was. The Indians saw them and made off and as they went they seemed to be carrying something with them. The shallop landed a couple of leagues from them.

They pitched camp, posted sentinels and saw the smoke from the Indians' fire 4 or 5 miles away. Next morning they continued to investigate and found two freshwater brooks – the first they had seen – and narrow enough to stride over them. They also found a 'great fish, called a grampus, dead on the sands'. The people in the shallop found two more, similarly dead, 'cast up at high water, and could not get off for the frost and ice. Some were five or six paces long and about two inches thick of fat.'

They explored inland and found more evidence of Indian occupation, then, meeting up with the shallop, they pitched camp again. They constructed a little barricade of logs and branches the height of a man, and those most weary quickly fell asleep. Around midnight, however, they heard 'a great and hideous cry'. The sentinels were shouting 'Arm! Arm!' They sprang to their feet and fired their muskets. The noise ceased. The party reflected that it must have been foxes or wolves. One of the party said he had heard a noise like that in Newfoundland.[36]

They stirred around 5 a.m. and two or three fired their muskets again, this time to make sure they were in working order. After prayer they prepared themselves for breakfast and the journey of the day, but before that they took their 'things' – including their guns – down near where the shallop was and laid them on the shore. It was still dark, or perhaps softening into dawn, and their campfire still burned. At that moment the Indians attacked. One of the party came back running hard shouting 'they are men – Indians! Indians!' Arrows flew. Some men from the party sprinted towards their muskets. As they sprinted, the Indians made 'dreadful' cries which sounded like, *woath woach ha ha hach woach* – so loud that the party thought they must be confronting thirty or forty Indians and some, in the darkness, thought more. Standish had a flintlock musket at the ready and fired it, another man fired his. That was enough time for two more men to load and, from the other side of the barricade, fire.

The shallop and its possible capture was an immediate concern and the men at the camp expected those at the shallop to defend it. They shouted across to ask them what the situation was and how it was going. The answer echoed back, *everyone is well, keep your courage*. From the shallop three shots rang out. A 'lusty man' who appeared to be their leader – the party thought him courageous – had positioned himself 'within half a musket shot of us' and was firing arrows. They saw him fire three and each was 'avoided': the target of the first arrow simply stooped and it flew over him. Someone pointed a gun straight at this leader, he 'gave an extraordinary cry' and the Indians ran off.

None of the party had been injured, although, with the arrows coming at them from all directions, there had been some near misses. More than that, they had hung their coats on the barricade and had not had time to put them on when the attack began. They now found these coats 'shot through and through'. Leaving six men to guard the shallop, the party followed the retreating Indians, but returned after loosing off a couple of musket shots.

They compiled a rough sort of inventory, picking up and counting eighteen arrows which, mostly, had fallen into the leaves on the ground. From this they concluded that there must have been many more arrows they did not find. (They gave the eighteen to Jones to take back to England.) The varieties of tips that had been used were brass, harts' horn and eagles' claws. They named the place The First Encounter.

The Indians lived as much in the background as the villagers at Scrooby had done. From the settlers' side they loomed from the woods in unknown numbers as marauding savages, making their noises, firing their arrows and running away. From the Indians' side an invasion was under way and it was being carried out by people with devilish weapons like muskets and who knew what other magical powers? These people in their strange costumes inevitably brought with them the reputation of those who had preceded them, the kidnappers, the exploiters, the slave-traders.

> When the *Mayflower* appeared in Cape Cod Bay and dropped her anchor in the harbor at Provincetown, the Indians were carefully watching her every move. It was apparent to them that these newcomers were not just fishermen or traders, as there were women and children in the company. Several well-armed parties seemed to be searching for an appropriate place to build a village. Their movements and the implications of their actions were discussed in council.

The Indian version of the 'first encounter' was quickly brought to the attention of the chiefs.[37]

The settlers embarked in the shallop searching for a harbour. Coppin, who had been here before, assured them he knew of a good harbour and that they could reach it before nightfall, but after an hour or two snow and rain began to fall. In the middle of the afternoon the wind got up, gouging the sea until it became so angry that the hinges of the rudder broke. They could not steer with it. Two men seized oars and ploughed them into the waves, struggling to hold the shallop steady and give it some direction. Everyone on board knew they were now in great danger. It was about to become mortal.

Coppin called out, *Keep your spirits up – I see the harbour!* but darkness was drawing in and the storm was worse. A strong wind blew and they hoisted what sail they could, but the wind was so strong it broke the mast into three pieces and swept the sail over the side. Coppin may well have mistaken the 'apparent gaps between Gurnet Point and Saquish Head for the harbour entrance. His course took them right over Brown's Bank and, in the tumbling seas over its shallows, the press of sail carried away the mast. The men leapt to the oars and they held on to the north, only to find in the dusk and the rain the vicious line of breakers on Saquish Neck dead ahead of them.'[38]

If you are men turn the boat round or we're finished! Coppin shouted to those rowing. The rowers responded and when they had wrestled it round he shouted, *Keep your spirits up! Row hard!* He was sure they could ride in to the shore safely, and the tide was running hard with them. It carried them round Saquish Head to a place where they saw land before them, surrounded by many rocks. The shallop beached on sandy ground.

Coppin said he had been mistaken and had never seen the place before. The party was uncertain what to do. Some, afraid of the Indians, felt it would be safer to spend the night on the shallop. Others were wet and cold beyond endurance and went ashore. They had difficulty lighting a fire, but eventually managed it. Seeing the warmth, the people on the shallop came ashore, too. It seemed a torment without end: some time after midnight the wind changed direction and a hard frost set in. The battered little group, huddled around the makeshift campfire listening to the wind singing and shrieking, did not know that they were safe from the Indians because they were on an island. They did not know that on the far side of the bay – over there, in the darkness – a peaceful, welcoming brook ran its gentle course into the sea.

They did not know that they had come home.

SEVEN

Noises in Another Quiet Land

The America to which the settlers awoke on Saturday 9 December – a sunny day, a clear sky – was a lot emptier than the England they had left behind, never mind that they had not known they were on an island or that there was a welcoming creek across the bay or that they were on the rim of a continent.

It may have seemed to them that the Wampanoag were everywhere, but they were not. The Wampanoag had been devastated by three epidemics which had swept across New England, and the abandoned sites the settlers had already come upon were the direct consequence. These epidemics, probably brought by Europeans sailing the coast of Maine and exploring the land, may have been some form of plague.

The Saturday was bathed in sunshine and the settlers realised they were on an island. They named it after John Clark, the *Mayflower*'s first mate, who had reputedly been the first man ashore. They dried their clothes, checked their weapons and explored the island, but found nobody on it. Next day they prepared to keep the Sabbath as they habitually did, by resting.

On the Monday they addressed their immediate preoccupation of finding a place for the Plantation. They 'sounded' the bay and found it good for shipping. They sailed the shallop over to the mainland and went ashore finding various cornfields and not just the main brook but other smaller, running brooks. It looked a good place – the cleared ground for corn was one factor – and, if it was not ideal, no matter. In the depths of this winter a quick choice had become a necessity. They reacted as they always did, with their specific blend of fatalism and optimism. The place already had a name, Plymouth: it was called that (Plimouth) on Smith's 1614 map, and since Plymouth was their last port before the crossing they left the name alone.

They returned to the *Mayflower* with this good news, although Bradford learned that his young wife Dorothy had fallen overboard and drowned while he had been away. The background envelops it. In Bradford's detailed account of the whole adventure, he makes no mention of his wife's death never mind how he took it. Perhaps the fatalism covered the grief, perhaps the fact that life was so vulnerable and short created helplessness and acceptance. Did he feel remorse that he had brought her here? Did he even think like that? Her family was originally from Wisbech. Her maiden name was May. She had left her five-year-old son John in Leiden. She was probably twenty-three. Beyond that, she is for ever now a stranger. We do not even know what she looked like.

Before Friday 15 December, when the ship weighed anchor and turned south towards the place for the Plantation, James Chilton, Jasper Moore and Edward Thompson had died of scurvy, a vicious disease that haunted travellers on the oceans. (Scurvy is caused by a vitamin C deficiency which breaks down the protein collagen, leading eventually to haemorrhaging in the body's cells.[1])

The *Mayflower* reached to within two leagues of the land when a headwind stopped it. On the Saturday the wind was fair and they completed the final leg of their great journey, although half an hour later the wind changed direction and would have taken them back up towards Provincetown. The myth was born. The first ashore stepped on a rock, subsequently named Plymouth Rock. We shall be returning to this moment. The land looked good and there seemed to be two islands in the bay[2] covered in 'oaks, pines, walnut, beech, sassafras, vines' and some trees they did not recognise. Their optimism increased. There was an abundance of fowl, and they reasoned plenty of fish in season, too. They soon tasted cod, turbot and herring, the biggest mussels they had ever seen, crab and lobster.

That Sunday they rested again, staying on the *Mayflower*, and next day went on land. They pushed ahead on foot 7 or 8 miles along the coast, but saw no Indians or traces of them. However, they did find four or five small brooks of very sweet fresh water. Here, too, there were many kinds of trees and herbs. The vegetation was lush and the clay soil promising for pottery. The walking had exhausted them and they returned to the *Mayflower* for the night.

On the Tuesday they explored further, some on land, Jones and others in the shallop. He sailed some 3 miles up a creek, to be called the Jones river. Everyone spent the night on the *Mayflower* again, and they knew it was time for a decision about where to site the Plantation. This had now resolved itself into three choices, Clark's Island, the Jones river and Plymouth.

Clark's Island offered sanctuary from the Indians, because it would be harder for them to attack, especially by surprise, and easier to defend. Indians in canoes were unobstructed targets with nowhere to hide. As a permanent home, however, it lacked adequate fresh water and fertile soil.

The settlers who had seen the Jones river site (today, Kingston) initially liked it a great deal, but there were practical reasons for rejection. It was 'far from our fishing, our principal profit, and so encompassed with woods that we should be in much danger of the savages'. They would have to clear a great deal of ground, a very difficult task because there were comparatively so few settlers.

Plymouth remained. It had land already cleared, and obviously fertile because the Indians had planted it with corn some three or four years earlier, as the settlers estimated. It had the brook, providing as much fresh water as they needed and big enough to harbour not only their shallop but others they might build. Fish would come to the brook, too. It had a 'great hill' and on that they could construct a platform for their cannons. It would command the whole area and give a view of the whole bay – even perhaps as far as Cape Cod. The disadvantages were twofold. The wood they would need to build the whole Colony – never mind the platform – was a quarter of a mile away and would have to be carried. There was, though, plenty of it. And they did not know if any Indians lived in the vicinity.

The brook scoured the sand at its mouth, enabling a boat to come close in regardless of the tide, and 'a big granite boulder, dropped by the ice cap centuries before, enabled the lively to leap ashore dry-shod and would make the basis of a simple wooden jetty'.[3]

The decision was made 'by most voices' – *Plymouth*. This was the Wednesday. However impatient the settlers were to get ashore and start building houses for shelter, and however desperate the women and children were to get off the *Mayflower* onto *terra firma*, a storm raged the following day. The shallop could not initially reach the shore to provision the people who had stayed there overnight, leaving them soaked and very cold. They had nothing to eat, either. At around 11 a.m. the shallop did go, but the wind was too strong for it to get back, this wind which forced the *Mayflower* to ride with her three anchors down. The storm continued into the Friday, when the morning gave birth to a stillborn boy.

Mary Allerton's age is not known, but since the eldest of her three children – Bartholomew – was estimated to be about eight, it is a reasonable assumption that she was in her mid-to-late twenties. The background darkens over her as it does over Dorothy Bradford. What had Allerton been through, pregnant and with the three children to look after on such an interminable voyage on this lurching, creaking, smelly wooden ship, constantly battered by what winter brought? Did she accept the death fatalistically? Did that fatalism soften the grief because, lacking any conception of modern medicine, beyond taking sensible precautions it was all chance? Did the others console her that it was all the will of God, and His will must not be questioned?

On the Saturday they finally made it ashore, felling and carrying timber for the first house, which would be communal. On the Sunday, with twenty-four settlers ashore, they thought they heard Indians and prepared to confront them, but none came. That day Solomon Prower died.

They spent Christmas Day busily because, according to their beliefs, they did not celebrate it. Some felled timber, others sawing it, splitting it, carrying it. Towards nightfall they thought they heard Indians again and readied their muskets, but again none came. On the *Mayflower* they drank water, but Captain Jones allowed them some beer – on shore they had none at all. The Colony was a week old.

The weather continued to torment them, because on the Tuesday the shallop could not reach shore; however, it relented the next day and they were back at work. The day after that they took a further democratic, or rather communal, step. Apart from the first house, many men went to work on the platform for the cannons. Security was crucial both individually and collectively.

By now, they had decided on the ground plan for the Plantation. It would have two rows of houses on either side of a street and, that afternoon, they prepared to measure the ground and stake it out. Because the timber had to be carried, the fewer the number of houses the better, at least for the time being. Single men were allocated to join families 'as they thought fit' – presumably a single man could pick which family. That brought the total number of families down to nineteen.

Larger families were given bigger plots, on the basis of a ½ pole wide by 3 poles long per person. Since a pole was 16.5ft, each person's calculated space was 6.25 × 49.5ft. This may seem an arbitrary figure – it included both house and garden – but it had been reached pragmatically, because a stockade would have to be constructed round the whole Colony and the longer that stretched, the more difficult it was to erect. Many of the settlers were tired. Many were weak with colds (perhaps even 'flu) after the wading at Cape Cod and being literally frozen to the bone on the expeditions ashore.

The fact that they had not seen any Indians did not mean the Indians were not there. The settlers lived each moment with the possibility that the Indians, masters at concealing themselves in this terrain, were poised to annihilate them.

The position of each plot along the central road was decided by lots. At that moment they all became landowners. Contemporary accounts make nothing of this, no doubt because the granting and division of land was the only thing to do and the only way to do it; and in another sense, as far as they were concerned, nobody owned the land so they could decide what to do with it themselves – something unimaginable in England for several centuries. No doubt, too, the struggle for survival overrode all future ambitions, land included. If this little band of essentially marooned people had wished, they could have allocated themselves a larger area than England herself measured. King James would not have liked it, but he was in London – not Plymouth, Massachusetts . . .

There would then be nineteen houses, and here was another problem: the settlers sensed that they must employ realpolitik again, because nineteen houses would preserve as much individuality as possible and yet form a community. However, it was agreed that every man would build his own house, 'thinking by that course men would make more haste than working in common'. This produced a paradox, because the common house – about 20ft square – was nearly finished: only the roof remained to be built. Progress on that was hampered by frost and continuing bad weather, restricting the working week to half, but even so, 'some would make mortar and some gather thatch so that, in four days, half of it was thatched'.[4]

They were continually tormented by the weather during the Friday and Saturday – storms and rain – and now they saw columns of smoke from Indian fires which they estimated were 6 or 7 miles away. On the Sunday they rested. It was the last day of December. They were in no position to look back, but if they had they would have seen a crowded calendar.

NOVEMBER	
Saturday 11	Sign the Compact, go ashore
Sunday 12	Rest
Monday 13	Shallop taken ashore to be repaired
Tuesday 14	----------
Wednesday 15	First expedition
Thursday 16	First expedition
Friday 17	First expedition
Saturday 18	----------
Sunday 19	Rest
Monday 20	----------
Tuesday 21	----------
Wednesday 22	----------
Thursday 23	----------
Friday 24	----------
Saturday 25	----------
Sunday 26	Rest
Monday 27	----------
Tuesday 28	Second expedition
Wednesday 29	Second expedition
Thursday 30	Second expedition

DECEMBER

Friday 1	---------
Saturday 2	---------
Sunday 3	Rest
Monday 4	Edward Thompson dies
Tuesday 5	Billington's gunpowder 'plot'!
Wednesday 6	Third expedition/Jasper, a servant of Carver, dies
Thursday 7	Third expedition/Dorothy Bradford drowns
Friday 8	Third expedition – shallop at Clark's Island/James Chilton dies
Saturday 9	Third expedition explores Clark's Island
Sunday 10	Rest
Monday 11	Third expedition sounds the harbour
Tuesday 12	---------
Wednesday 13	---------
Thursday 14	---------
Friday 15	*Mayflower* sails for Plymouth harbour
Saturday 16	Arrives
Sunday 17	Rest
Monday 18	Probe on foot along the coast
Tuesday 19	Probe on foot and with the shallop
Wednesday 20	Decision where to build the Colony
Thursday 21	Storm – nobody ashore/ Richard Britteridge dies
Friday 22	Continuing storm/Mary Allerton gives birth to a stillborn boy
Saturday 23	Ashore, felling timber
Sunday 24	Rest/Solomon Martin dies
Monday 25	Felling timber
Tuesday 26	Weather too bad to go ashore
Wednesday 27	Felling timber
Thursday 28	Measuring the ground, allotting the housing plots
Friday 29	Heavy rain, cold, stormy
Saturday 30	Heavy rain, cold, stormy

They moved into January, the first new year of the Colony. Using the *Mayflower* as a home base was now proving a problem, because it lay 1½ miles into the bay and getting the shallop to and from it occupied valuable time. They worked on, although during the Wednesday they saw more smoke from Indian fires. Next day Standish and a little party resolved to find these Indians. They went to where the fires had been, but found nobody there. On the way back they shot an eagle for supper and, in the eating of it, could hardly distinguish it from mutton.

On 5 January, the Friday, a sailor found a live herring on the shore. Captain Jones had it for his supper, but that was not the point. It raised the prospect of more fish. So far, lacking small hooks to do any fishing, all they had had was a single cod. Next day Christopher Martin was 'very sick and to our judgement no hope of life'.[5] Carver, on land, was called 'to speak with him about his accounts' – his will – and Carver got there the following morning. Martin was dead within twenty-four hours. Mary Martin had lost her son Solomon, from a previous marriage, and now her husband in just over two weeks.

On the Monday the weather cleared and they were able to work while Captain Jones (and presumably some of his mariners) went exploring for fish in the shallop, but he ran into a storm and was in some danger for a time. When they came back they brought three big seals and an excellent cod. They assured the settlers that they would have plenty of cod soon. This same day Billington and one other – a ship's mate – went off exploring. Billington had climbed a tree on a hill the week before and seen what he thought was a 'great sea'. He had resolved to go and find out. It was 3 miles away and when they reached it they found

> a great water, divided into two great lakes, the bigger of them five or six miles in circuit, and in it an island of a cable [608ft] length square, the other three miles in compass. In their estimation they are fine fresh water, full of fish and fowl. A brook issues from it, and it will be an excellent help for us in time. They found seven or eight Indian houses, but not lately inhabited. When they saw the houses they were in fear.[6]

That was natural enough, because they were only two men with one musket between them. By now, too, the seemingly all-pervading presence of the Indians and their physical absence must have been almost sinister. The settlers did not yet know about the epidemics.

A crisis was coming, or rather returning. The settlers lacked fruit and vegetables and scurvy struck again. On Thursday 11 January, Bradford collapsed as he worked. He was 'vehemently taken' with pain and they thought he would die immediately. Evidently he had particularly suffered with the cold on the last expedition. However, he recovered a little towards nightfall.

In his delirium, Bradford wanted 'but a small cann of beere' – alcohol was not only a sort of anaesthetic but anyone risking a drink of stored water, unboiled, often found it contaminated. Bradford's request opened up a tension between the settlers and the *Mayflower* crew, who had kept all the beer on the ship. Bradford's request was answered by the crew: *even if you were our own father, you could not have any*.

The crew were by no means immune, beer or no beer, and about half of them would die before the *Mayflower* finally set sail for England again. That included officers and the 'lustiest' men: among them the boatswain (as we shall see in a moment), gunner, three quartermasters and the cook. Eventually Jones relented and told the governor he should send for beer for the sick even if there would be only water left for the journey home.

Tension opened up between crew members, too, however rough and ready they were. In this misery those who had been 'boon companions in drinking and jollity in time of their health and welfare began now to desert one another'.[7] As some fell ill the others, fearing infection, said they would not 'hazard their lives for them' by going to the cabins where they lay – 'if they died let them die'. The passengers still on board showed them 'what mercy they could, which made some of their hearts relent'. The boatswain, evidently a proud young man, 'would often curse and scoff at the passengers but when he grew weak they had compassion on him and helped him'. He was so moved he said he did not deserve this after the abuse he had heaped upon them. 'O, you, I now see, show your love like Christians indeed one to another, but we let one another lie, and die like dogs.'[8] Another lay 'cursing his wife', calling out that if it had not been for her he would never have come on this terrible voyage. He also cursed his fellows, claiming, *I did this and that for you, I spent money on you*, but now they were 'weary of him, and did not help him'. Another gave a companion all he had 'to help him in his weakness'. This companion

> went and got a little spice and made him a mess of meat once, or twice; and because [the companion] died not so soon as he expected, [the man] went amongst his fellows and swore the rogue would cozen [deceive] him. He would see him choked before he made him any more meat, and yet the poor fellow died before morning.[9]

This was the background as the crisis on land deepened. The day after Bradford was struck down, heavy rain fell at noon, so heavy it stopped work. Four men had been dispatched to gather and cut thatch in the morning about 1½ miles from the Colony. Having done that all morning, two of them, John Goodman (of whom little is known) and Peter Brown went off with their dogs – a spaniel and 'a great mastiff bitch' to find more, instructing the other two to bind what had already been cut and then follow.

When they followed they could not find Goodman or Brown anywhere, although they 'hallowed and shouted as loud as they could'. They made their way back to the Plantation and told the story. A search party went out but could not find them either.

Next day a stronger party – ten or twelve men – tried again. The feeling was that the Indians must have taken or killed them. This party ranged for 7 or 8 miles and still found nothing. They returned dispirited, and everyone else felt so too. That night Goodman and Brown came in and told *their* tale. They had come to a lake and at the water's edge found a big deer.

> The dogs chased him and they followed so far as they lost themselves and could not find the way back. They wandered all that afternoon being wet, and at night it did freeze and snow. They were slenderly appareled and had no weapons but each one his sickle, nor any victuals. They ranged up and down and could find none of the savages' habitations. When it drew to night . . . they

> could find neither harbor nor meat but, in frost and snow, were forced to make the earth their bed, and the element their covering.[10]

As if this was not enough they thought they heard two lions roaring for a long time, then a third. This third lion sounded dangerously near and they prepared to climb a tree for safety – although up there they would be completely exposed to the cold. They decided to stay at the base of the tree, ready to climb it at any instant. They could barely restrain the mastiff from setting off towards the noises. All night they walked up and down under the tree to ward off the cold. At dawn they moved on, passing lakes, brooks and woods and found fine, level land 5 miles long which the Indians had cleared by burning. They reached the Colony by night, 'being ready to faint with travel and want of victuals, and almost famished with cold. John Goodman was fain [left with no alternative] to have his shoes cut off his feet they were so swelled with cold.'[11]

The common house was now full of beds, side by side, with Carver and Bradford lying ill in two of them. The gunpowder was in there and each man had his musket loaded. At about 6 a.m. on the Sunday, a spark from something 'flew into the thatch' and instantly set it alight. Carver and Bradford, however ill they were, got up and got out fast. The roof-beams survived, singed no doubt.

Nobody was hurt. Those on the *Mayflower*, however, assumed the Plantation was under attack by marauding Indians and there had been considerable loss of life, because so many settlers were on land by now, a number augmented by those who had gone to celebrate the Sabbath. The critical mass of the expedition had shifted, more settlers now on the land than the ship. The *Mayflower* people had to wait three-quarters of an hour before the tide turned and they could get ashore to help – help that was not needed.

Monday was too wet for work, and too wet for anyone on the *Mayflower* to come ashore. After that the weather held for the next three days and on the Friday they resolved to add a common shed to the common house. Some of their provisions were already on shore and if Indians were watching they saw 'a lot of baggage' and understood that the settlers had come to stay.[12] They understood, too, that 'there would be great changes in the way we would live'.

Rain after midday the following Monday hampered the settlers again:

> This day in the evening, John Goodman went abroad to use his lame feet that were pitifully ill with the cold he had got. Having [the] spaniel with him, a little way from the Plantation two great wolves ran after the dog. [It] ran to him and hid betwixt his legs for succor. He had nothing in his hand but took up a stick and threw at one wolf and hit him, and they presently ran both away, but came again.[13]

Goodman seized a wooden stake but the wolves sat 'on their tails grinning at him' for a while then, when they were ready, loped off.

On the Saturday they finished the common shed, rested on the Sunday and, under good weather, worked on the houses on the Monday. In the afternoon they 'carried up our hogsheads of meal to our common storehouse'.[14] They were, in a very real sense, putting down roots.

On the Monday of the following week the shallop and longboat began to ferry their goods to the shore, from where they could be carried to the shed. That day Rose, wife of Standish and age unknown, died. No cause of death was given and in a sense she joins the death of Mary Allerton's stillborn son and Dorothy Bradford's death in the darkness of the background and the silences of the quiet land. Whatever Rose Standish's life had been, there is almost no point of reference except the group of settlers she lived among, and the timber houses going up in two rows beside a harbour in a distant land of which, across two hard and frozen months, she had glimpsed the merest fragment.

Sleet and frost kept them from working for the next two days, although on the second Captain Jones and others saw two Indians who made off before anyone could try to talk to them. The implications of this were delicate, because the Indians had to be regarded as both a danger and a potential source of advantages. The settlers might *have* to fall back on the Indians' skills and knowledge to help them get through this agony of a winter; they might be able to trade with the Indians, getting some of the food they needed and provisions in general. They had no hope of growing anything for months and resupplying them would have to be done from a range of 3,000 miles. That could not even begin until the *Mayflower* had recrossed the Atlantic to England. Before that, nobody would have any idea where they were. They *ought* to have been somewhere beside the Hudson river . . .

Maybe Standish, the military man, had already tried to find the Indians: 'meet with them' was the phrase used at the time, but it is ambiguous because it could mean have a meeting with them or simply find them. He surely understood that, regardless of the material advantages such as sourcing food, knowing your enemy – disposition, weaponry, numbers, morale – was information any commander treasured.

There is no contemporary suggestion they would try to convert the Indians, at least not yet. They refer to them repeatedly as savages and leave it at that, as if the description is a statement of fact and all-encompassing. The Leiden people among the settlers would come to that all in good time, speaking of 'the real and glorious progress of the Gospel among those poor Indians of America, and those reverend and learned ministers which are principally employed in preaching the Gospel to them in their own language'.[15]

What did the Indians themselves think? It is extremely difficult to know and the nearest we can get is re-creation. For example, a recent academic exercise[16] involved a Wampanoag (called 'Fast Turtle') answering questions *as if* he had been there in 1620, and it is about as near as we are going to get. On religion, he said the Leiden people had 'very strong beliefs. They were very serious and sanctimonious and felt that the Wampanoags should practise the Puritan's religion, Christianity, and observe their rules of conduct.' The Leiden people were not, and would not be, in a position to embark on anything like this for a long time but, and this was to be repeated all over Europe's colonial conquests for the next 200 years and more, whenever the deeply religious came upon virgin human material, they could not resist converting them.

Eight of the settlers died in January. They were now into February, another bitter month. The weather on the first Sunday was so bad that it made them fear for the *Mayflower*, unballasted by the goods now in the shed. The wind gusted more strongly than they had experienced before – strong enough to damage the walls of the houses.[17] It was so cold they could do little work and the roof of the communal house caught fire again 'by a spark that kindled in the roof, but no great harm was done'.[18] That same day, Captain Jones killed five geese and distributed them among the sick. He also came upon a deer from which the Indians had taken the horns and which was being devoured by a wolf.

The fragments become more sparse. Friday 16 February was like so many others, fair but frosty and racked by a northerly wind. After midday, one settler was out trying to shoot fowl at a creek 1½ miles away. He had set up a stand in the reeds. A dozen Indians went by in the direction of the Plantation. He lay down, it seems, to conceal himself and as he lay he heard the sound of many more. He waited until they had gone by and then ran back as fast as he could to sound the alarm. People working in the woods were called back and took up their arms.

The Indians did not come. It can only have added to the eerie feeling that the Plantation was surrounded – or about to be at any moment – by an uncounted, ephemeral horde of tribesmen who would practise their savagery even on the women and children; a horde who had unseen eyes watching, waiting; a horde who were always coming but never did.

The settlers, armed and poised now that the alarm had been given, could not see even a single Indian. The Indians, however, did light a big fire near where they had passed the man shooting fowl. Standish and Francis Cooke, who had been at work in the woods, left their tools to go and investigate, but when they went back the Indians had made off with them.

It all had a disquieting effect. The settlers decided to be more vigilant in setting up watches, and they would make sure the cannons were constantly ready for use, despite the damp weather. Next day the settlers called a meeting to establish military orders and formally reconfirmed Standish as the man in charge of defence. While they were doing this they saw a couple of Indians on a hilltop 400 yards away – or less – gesturing for the settlers to come. In turn, the settlers gestured for the Indians to come. It became a stand-off, broken when Standish and Hopkins crossed the brook and went towards them ostentatiously bearing a single musket. In full view of the Indians they laid this down on the ground as a sign of peace and an indication that they wanted to talk. The Indians did not; Standish and Hopkins heard the sound of a lot more behind the hill and the encounter came to nothing. Evidently the meeting about security was not resumed, or if it was it came to no definite conclusions, because it would be discussed again some weeks later.

The Plantation was making progress in self-defence. On 21 February, Jones came ashore with his sailors bringing a small-bore cannon, and all hands helped to drag it up the hill to the platform. Then they dragged another, which was already on the shore. These two were mounted. They would have an immediate and dual psychological impact, reassuring the settlers and deterring the Indians.

Jones brought a 'very fat goose to eat with us, and we had a fat crane, and a mallard, and a dried neat's tongue [neat is a bovine animal], and so we were very kindly and friendly together'.[19]

Even now, the background had not become foreground. About half the expedition had died, 'especially in January and February, being the depth of winter, and wanting houses and other comforts; being infected with scurvy and other diseases, which this long voyage and their inaccomodate conditions had brought upon them'.[20] The death rate was sometimes '2 or 3 of a day' and of the '100 and odd persons scarce fifty remained'.

At one point only six or seven fit men remained, but they

> spared no pains day and night, but with an abundance of toil and hazard to their own health fetched them wood, made them fires, dressed them meat, made their beds, washed their loathsome clothes, clothed and unclothed them. In a word, did all the homely, and necessary offices for them, which dainty and queasy stomachs cannot endure to hear named.[21]

One of them was Brewster, the other Standish. Even they, untouched by illness, could not do more than alleviate the distressed. On 21 February, William White, William Mullins and 'two more' died. Mary Allerton, who had given birth to the stillborn boy, went too.

Was she able, in those last few moments in a rough wooden house, to cry out, *what will happen to my children here?*

Because it was imperative that the Indians did not know the real situation – how weak the Colony was in manpower – the dead were buried at night at a place called Cole's Hill, which was about as far as the living could carry them. They were put into unmarked graves to conceal how many had died, and it is also possible the settlers, in their desperation, leant the men who were ill against trees, their muskets on rests in front of them.

The women remain silent, and the men said nothing about the women. There is no record of when the women were allowed ashore, or what they were able to do when they got there. The contemporary accounts speak quite naturally about the men exploring, cutting wood and thatch, hauling cannon, shooting game, fighting the Indians, getting lost. Were the women consulted about the location of the Colony and the allocation of the nineteen houses? In those houses, single men were billeted. Were the women consulted about which single man joined their family? How did the women make the wooden houses into homes? When did they make love, and where did they do that if they had children? How long and hard were their days? Did they cry, perhaps often? Did they feel any sense of homecoming, or was this a continuation of England, the man earning and protecting and deciding, the woman following in a lifetime of obedience? How religious were the women?

Regardless of how tight the background holds them, we might – we surely can – see the children. As children do, they would be out playing whenever they could, by the brook, hide-and-seek among the logs, and their mothers scolding them if they moved too far away: *the Indians will get you*. The Indians remained a presence which did not have to manifest itself physically to intimidate. They were seen and unseen, everywhere and nowhere, and you never knew, never knew. It was time for the settlers to meet them.

EIGHT

Among the Indians

Twenty years before, the Wampanoag had numbered around 12,000. By this winter only 2,000 survived on the mainland and 3,000 on the islands.[1] As many as ten villages had been depopulated and lay abandoned on the mainland. The settlers, coming upon them by chance as they explored, may not have understood the reason; but they had died of diseases brought by Europeans, and the mortality rate at Patuxet had evidently been total.

The Wampanoag name means eastern people, with their territory stretching roughly from north of Boston to Narragansett Bay, Rhode Island, including the islands of Martha's Vineyard and Nantucket. They were divided into numerous sub-tribes and lived by farming, hunting and fishing.

The fierce Nausets lived on Cape Cod, although their number had been ravaged from 1,500 to around 500. Because Cape Cod was such a prominent landmark, the Europeans had been coming for a long time and, as we have seen, 'riding the Gulf Stream home from the Caribbean were often tempted to increase profits by the last minute addition of some human cargo. The Nauset soon learned from sad experience that the white men from these strange ships frequently came ashore, not for trade, but to steal food and capture slaves.'[2]

The Wampanoags' 'villages were concentrated near the coast during the summer to take advantage of the fishing and seafood', but, the harvest gathered, they 'moved inland and separated into winter hunting camps of extended families'. Before the epidemics the population was such that the 'hunting territories were usually defined to avoid conflict. Ownership passed from father to son.' The Wampanoag were a confederacy, with lesser sachems (leaders) under a Grand Sachem.[3]

Like the Nauset, they had experience of Europeans, although contact is perhaps a better word. This began during the sixteenth century as fishing and trading vessels roamed the New England coast as well as, presumably, the Gulf Stream riders.

The Wampanoag watched as the settlers chose 'of all places' the 'site of the now-deserted Wampanoag village of Patuxtet. There they sat for the next few months in crude shelters – cold, sick and slowly starving to death. The Wampanoag were aware of the English but chose to avoid contact with them for the time being.'[4]

Into March 1621, the settlers continued their work. On 3 March 'the wind was south, the morning misty, but towards noon warm and fair weather; the birds sang in the woods most pleasantly; at one o'clock it thundered, which was the first we heard in that country; it was strong and great claps but short . . . after an hour it rained very sadly till midnight'.[5] The birdsong may have represented hope that the worst of the winter was over – but before that happened another thirteen would die.

In contemporary and subsequent accounts, these things were mentioned sparingly, fleetingly and with an economy of emotion. The emphasis lay on God – and hope.

> This poor handful of men [were] far already diminished. They saw no Indians all the winter long, but such as at first sight always ran away . . . This blessed people was as a little flock of kids [and] there were many nations of Indians left . . . as kennels of wolves in every corner of the country. And yet the little flock suffered no damage by those rapid wolves! We may and should say, *this is the Lord's doing, 'tis marvellous in our eyes.*
>
> It was afterwards by [the Indians] confessed that upon the arrival of the English in these parts, the Indians employed their sorcerers, whom they call *Powaws* . . . to curse them, and let loose their demons upon them, to shipwreck them, to distract them, to poison them, or any way to ruin them. All the noted *Powaws* in the country spent three days together in diabolical conjurations to obtain the assistances of the devils against the English . . . but the devils at length acknowledged . . . that they could not hinder those people becoming owners and masters of the country.[6]

On 7 March, seeds were sown, and this must have represented hope. That day a party of six – Carver and five others – made a mini-expedition to the great ponds, which seemed to offer plentiful fishing. Along the way they noticed signs of deer, although they did not see any animals themselves. They did see fowl, including one which was 'milk-white' and had a very black head.

On 16 March, the settlers were continuing the discussion of the military orders from the month before – perhaps in the communal house – but the Indians interrupted it again. They appeared in the distance and the men seized their muskets. The Indians did not come and the meeting resumed. It was interrupted again in a moment of genuine and enduring drama. A tall, straight Indian with a shock of black hair trailing down his back strode towards the Plantation and continued into it. He was naked except for some leather around his waist with a fringe about 9in long – to protect his modesty. He carried a bow and two arrows, one headed, the other unheaded. Consternation. He was alone. He strode past the houses and on to where the discussion was taking place, but some of the settlers 'intercepted' him outside and would not let him go in. He spoke to them in English – *Welcome!* – and explained that he had learnt the language, although in broken form, from the Englishman who had fished at Monhegan, the island off the coast of Maine a hundred or more miles away. You could sail it, he said, in a single day if you had a strong wind or walk it in five.

He was called Samoset. He was 'free in speech' within the constrictions of his knowledge of the language. He explained that he was a *sagamore* (a subordinate chief) of an Algonquin tribe in southern Maine. He could and did name the ships' captains who had come to fish. The settlers questioned him extensively. He was the first Indian they had met in any proper sense, and the fact that he could speak English at all was an extraordinary bonus. He had been in the area for eight months and knew what was going on.

The settlers had the moment they had been looking for, one with delicate implications. The danger the Indians posed could be evaluated if Samoset provided their disposition, weaponry, numbers and morale. This had to be balanced against the many potential advantages: peace, food and trade. He said the branch of the

Wampanoag tribe he was with was sixty strong and the Nausets more numerous. It was the Nausets that the expeditions from the *Mayflower*, when it was anchored in Provincetown Harbour, had encountered, and it was they who had stolen the tools Standish and Cooke left behind on 16 February. Standish must have listened even more intently as Samoset explained that the Indians in general were 'much incensed and provoked against the English'. About eight months before, they had encountered a voyage financed by the Plymouth Merchants and Sir Ferdinando Gorges. They had killed three Englishmen and two more only just got away by fleeing to Monhegan Island. This was a consequence, it seemed, of Hunt's behaviour in 1614, this Hunt who had tricked twenty Indians from here and seven Nausets, kidnapped them and sold them into slavery.

As the settlers went ashore for that first expedition from the *Mayflower* any Indian seeing them can only have had one thought: Hunt. Samoset talked. He described the countryside and their various regions. He spoke of the *sagamores* and said how many men they had.

The wind began to rise and Samoset had a horseman's coat thrown over his shoulders. He asked for beer but the settlers gave him water. It may be that they had no beer to give him, it may be that what they had they were guarding for themselves (understandably, illness still ravaged them); it may be that they feared how he might react to alcohol. They did give him some biscuit, cheese, pudding, and a piece of mallard. He enjoyed this and explained that he was acquainted with English food. He said that the Plantation stood at a place called Patuxet, but all the inhabitants had died in an epidemic about four years ago, and so the settlers could simply take it for themselves. Nobody else would be able to lay claim to it.

They talked all afternoon and would have been happy for him to have left before nightfall but, for whatever reason, he did not want to go. This made them uneasy. They thought it would be safer to have him out of the way on the *Mayflower* and he was content with this. He was taken down to the shallop, but the wind was too high, so instead they lodged him in the house of Stephen Hopkins – in the middle of the Colony – and watched him.

Next morning they gave him a knife, a bracelet and a ring. Before he left he said he would come back and bring some of the Wampanoag with whatever beaver skins they had to trade. They told him that the Indians would be required to leave their bows and arrows a quarter of a mile away. He came back on the Sunday accompanied by five Indians wearing deerskins except the leader who had a wild cat's skin on his arm. They also wore leather above and below their waists.

They reminded the settlers of English gypsies in complexion, with little or no hair on their faces, but their hair down to their shoulders, 'some trussed up like a feather, broad-wise, like a fan, another a fox tail hanging out . . . Some had their faces painted black from the forehead to the chin, four or five fingers broad, others after other fashions, as they liked.'[7]

The Indians duly laid down their bows and arrows and brought the stolen tools. The settlers gave them 'entertainment as we thought was fitting them' including food, which they ate hungrily and then they danced and sang 'like antics'. The leader had a 'thing like a bow-case' attached to his waist. It contained corn powder, which could be added to water. They had brought three or four beaver skins but the settlers would not trade on this, the Sabbath, and asked them to bring more. They said they would leave these skins and come back in a night or two, but the settlers were not happy with that. They wanted the Indians to go, although Samoset was either ill or pretended to be and stayed on until the Wednesday.

The settlers gave each Indian some trifles, especially the leader, and went with them to where they had left the bows and arrows. This was a tense moment of sudden mistrust. A couple of the Indians wondered what was going to happen and began to slink off but the others called them back. They picked up their arrows and the encounter broke up with assurances of goodwill.

The weather on the Monday and Tuesday was good enough to allow more seed planting, and on the Wednesday they sent Samoset away with 'an hat, a pair of stocking and shoes, a shirt, and a piece of cloth to tie about his waist'. That same day they had a meeting 'to conclude of laws and orders for ourselves', the one twice interrupted by the Indians. Now it happened again. The meeting had been in progress about an hour when they saw two or three Indians on a hilltop who 'made semblance of daring us'. Standish and one other advanced towards them with muskets, another two unarmed men following. The Indians struck a defiant pose, but when Standish got near them they ran off.

On the Thursday, fair and warm, they met again over law and order and were interrupted a fourth time because Samoset came back bringing with him a companion – Squanto, who had had such an improbable and amazing life since Weymouth had kidnapped him in 1605. At that moment the long interconnecting strands were joined.

Samoset and Squanto were accompanied by three others bearing a few skins to trade and some freshly caught red herrings – dried but not salted. They explained (though evidently Squanto's English was not fluent) that the great chief Massasoit was nearby with his brother and all their men. After an hour Massasoit and the men appeared on the hilltop and there followed another uneasy stand-off: the settlers unwilling to send Governor Carver to parley, the Indians reluctant to come to the Plantation.

Squanto acted as middleman. He went to Massasoit who decreed that the settlers should send one emissary. They chose Edward Winslow, who was instructed to make it clear that the settlers wanted peace and trade. They sent with him gifts of 'a pair of knives and a copper chain with a jewel' for Massasoit and a knife and 'a jewel to hang in his ear' for Masassoit's brother. They also sent 'a pot of strong water, a good quantity of biscuit and some butter'. Massasoit was delighted.

Winslow made a speech, assuring Massasoit that 'King James saluted him with words of love and peace . . . and that our governor desired to see him and truck with him, and to confirm a peace with him as his next neighbour'.

Massasoit listened attentively, although Squanto may not have been able to translate it very well. Then Massasoit got down to the serious business of eating and drinking. Once he had satisfied himself he gave what was left to the tribesmen and began to cast a covetous eye on Winslow's sword and armour, intimating that he wanted to buy it. Winslow was not selling and made that plain.

Massasoit and twenty men set off towards the Plantation, leaving Winslow 'in the custody' of his brother. When they neared the brook they laid down their bows and arrows. Standish and Williamson waited at the brook for them with half a dozen men holding muskets.[8] This was, however, the opposite of a stand-off: one went over from this side, one went over from the other in a symbolic exchange. Massasoit was escorted to a partially finished house where the settlers placed a green rug and three or four cushions. Carver arrived straight after, with a drummer and trumpeter soon following as well as some musketeers. After salutations, Carver kissed Massasoit's hand and Massasoit reciprocated. They sat down. Carver called for some strong water – perhaps brandy – and toasted Massasoit who in turn 'drunk a great draught'. That made him sweat for a long time afterwards. Carver called for a little fresh meat, which Massasoit ate, again giving the rest to his men. Massasoit had 'in his bosom hanging in a string, a great long knife'. He was intrigued by the trumpet and some of his men tried to blow it – with mixed, and perhaps hilarious, results. Maybe that set the tone.

They negotiated the peace treaty which, at first reading, seemed to favour the settlers. It gave them security at a time when they were in no position to threaten that of the Indians, but in fact was equitable.

1. That neither Massasoit nor any of his should injure or do hurt to any of our people.
2. And if any of his did hurt to any of ours, he should send the offender, that we might punish him.
3. That if any of our tools were taken away when our people are at work, he should cause them to be restored, and if ours did any harm to any of his, we would do the like to them.
4. If any did unjustly war against him, we would aid him; if any did war against us, he us.
5. He should send to his neighbour confederates, to certify them of this, that they might not wrong us, but might be likewise comprised in the conditions of peace.
6. That when their men came to us, they should leave their bows and arrows behind them, as we should do our pieces when we came to them.

This was applauded (whether literally is not clear), although Massasoit sat next to Carver and 'trembled for fear'. Nobody seemed to understand why. Massasoit said that within eight or nine days they would come to the far side of the brook and plant corn there. They would also stay there all summer. Massasoit was

> a very lusty man, in his best years, an able body, grave of countenance and spare of speech; in his attire little or nothing differing from the rest of his followers, only in a great chain of white bone beads about his neck . . . at it behind his neck hangs a little tobacco which he gave us to [smoke]. His face was painted with a sad red-like murrey [dark red], and oiled both head and face that he looked greasily. All his followers likewise were in their faces in part or in whole painted, some black, some red, some yellow, and some white, some with crosses . . . Some had skins on them, and some naked, all strong, tall.[9]

The treaty concluded, Carver took Massasoit back to the brook and they embraced. Eventually Massasoit's brother came, but was fearful of their weaponry 'and made signs of dislike'. They entertained him. Two tribesmen wanted to stay all night, but the settlers would not have that, although they relented for Samoset and Squanto, who did stay. Massasoit and the tribesmen spent the night in the woods half a mile from the Plantation, where they had been joined by their women and children.

Despite the peace treaty, the settlers took what to them must have seemed sensible precautions. They kept a 'good watch' that night, although no danger of any kind manifested itself. They did feel, however, the peace treaty was sincere and that Massasoit wanted it to work. They reasoned this because whenever one or two settlers had been far from the settlement working or shooting fowl the Indians could easily have harmed them, but had not.

There were also inter-tribal politics. The Wampanoags were at war with the Narragansetts to the south and Clause 4 of the treaty – in effect, a mutual defence pact – strengthened Massasoit's position. The feeling was that the settlers' weaponry (especially, perhaps, the cannons on the platform) had made a profound impression on Massasoit, and he knew they would make the same impression on the Narragansetts. In realpolitik, that was as good a reason as any for believing that the treaty would hold.

Next day some of the Indians came back, the settlers assumed for food. In fact they said Massasoit would like to see them. Standish and Allerton went 'venturously' to him and were warmly welcomed. Massasoit gave them 'three or four groundnuts and some tobacco'. Carver asked for Massasoit's kettle and, when it was brought to him, filled it with peas – something else which delighted Massasoit.

On the Friday, Samoset and Squanto were still at the Colony, Squanto – as would subsequently become clear – working out his own agenda. At midday he went off to catch eels and at night returned with 'as many as he could well lift in one hand'. The settlers were glad of them ('fat and sweet') and impressed that Squanto could catch them by hand – 'without any instrument'. That same day they finally finished the meeting about law and order, including military orders, and chose the governor for the year, re-electing Carver. It was 24 March and to the Pilgrims the 25th was New Year's day.[10]

Realpolitik was never very far away. The settlers decided to send an expedition to visit Massasoit, partly to continue the tone of friendship, partly to know where the tribe lived and how many men they really had. Stephen Hopkins and Winslow were to go. Squanto's abilities as an interpreter, however limited, had opened up these possibilities.

They would take a red cotton horseman's coat 'laced with a light lace' as a present so that 'both they and their message might be more acceptable'. This was offered not out of fear, the delegation would say, and added that although the Indians were welcome to visit the settlement, as they had been doing, 'not knowing how our corn might prosper, we could no longer give them such entertainment as we had done'. Massasoit or 'any special friend' of his would, however, be welcome and Carver sent a copper chain. If Massasoit sent messengers they should bring the chain and then the settlers would know they were bona fide. Carver also sent word that the settlers wanted to square matters over the buried corn which they had taken when they first arrived and 'the owners thereof were fled for fear of us'. The settlers would reimburse them with a similar amount of corn, English meal or anything else they wanted. Carver also requested an exchange of corn so that, as a trial, theirs could be planted to see which of the two the soil liked best. This two-man delegation would leave on 10 June.

On the last day of March the shallop took the remaining settlers off the *Mayflower*. This had been a natural progression, the building of houses proceeding steadily, the Indians posing no immediate threat and, anyway, it was spring. The ship had provided safety for them, and its presence riding at anchor in the Bay must have been a source of reassurance as much as the cannons on the platform. Captain Jones's views on the passengers is not known: whether he felt a moral responsibility to protect his passengers, whether he was not keen on recrossing the Atlantic in winter with a depleted crew, or for how long his contract with the merchants ran – it had been 'hired at London' – but his was a commercial operation and each day he rode at anchor was another day lost.

Squanto was by now a pivotal figure, and he knew that. He showed the settlers how to plant Indian corn, 'dress and tend' it. He explained that unless they caught fish and used it as fertiliser the corn would not grow. English seed was also sown – wheat and peas – but it did not fare well. Squanto gave other hints about provisioning themselves. He would make himself indispensable.

Winslow, looking back (in a letter written the following December), would describe the situation:

> You shall understand that in this little time that a few of us have been here, we have built seven dwelling-houses, and four for the use of the Plantation, and have made preparation for divers others. We set some twenty acres of Indian corn and sowed some six acres of barley and peas, and according to the manner of the Indians we manured our ground with herrings or rather shads,[11] which we have in great abundance, and take with great ease at our doors. Our corn did prove well, and God be praised we had a good increase of Indian corn, and our barley indifferent good but our peas not worth the gathering . . . We feared they were too late sown, they came up very well and blossomed, but the sun parched them in the blossom.[12]

The *Mayflower* set sail for England on 5 April, without cargo or passengers. That not one of the settlers sailed with her can be interpreted as 'a sign of the new confidence'[13] that Plymouth was, or was likely to become, a going concern despite the loss of life. Only about fifty settlers remained. She took just a month to get back to the Thames, arriving on 6 May.

During April, Carver died at the age of fifty-four. They were planting seed when he 'came out of the field very sick, it being a hot day. He complained greatly of his head and lay down, and within a few hours his senses failed, so as he never spoke more till he died, which was within a few days after . . . He was buried in the best manner they could, with some volleys of shot by all that bore arms; and his wife being a weak woman, died within 5 or 6 weeks after him.'[14] Bradford was chosen as Carver's successor soon after, but because he had not fully recovered from the illness that had nearly killed him, Isaac Allerton became his assistant.

The younger generation assumed leading positions. Bradford (aged thirty-one) had been in from the beginning. He had spent his youth with Brewster at Scrooby. Allerton (thirty-four) had been in from Leiden, where he had come down from Amsterdam to join the community. They, with Standish (thirty-six) and Edward Winslow (twenty-five), were 'to lead the Colony through its formative years'[15] and 'though they still had the benefit of Elder Brewster's advice he was from now on the elder statesman, the religious teacher and not the civic leader'.

The Plantation was taking shape. It must have seemed that they had a real future; that, here on a hillside overlooking an ocean, their construction of heaven on earth had begun.

PART THREE

Our Worlds

PROLOGUE

Shoreline

An ordinary place. As the days melted into weeks, and the weeks melted into months, it must have become a familiar place, too: the Plantation being built on cleared land which sloped down to an ocean of chilled blue, and the ocean itself a magnificent, forbidding panorama, enormous as a horizon.

From virtually anywhere within the Plantation they could see it, and the waves which lapped and licked and gurgled onto the rocks at the shoreline must have constantly whispered to them, *you are on your own, you are completely isolated, you are very vulnerable – but nobody can tell you what to do.*

These days, it is difficult to see the sturdy people in their boots and coats going down The Street with the ocean spread before them, the backdrop to all their days; difficult to picture them – wistfully perhaps – scanning the horizon for the ships which came so rarely; difficult to understand *how* they understood that home was so far, far away, and never to be seen again. When the waves whispered to them about isolation, it was true: they were isolated.

Each must have reached an accommodation with themselves: this Plantation, taking its shape as the trees were felled and cut into planks for the houses, is home now and for ever. They did not, of course, imagine they were helping to found a new nation. They were Englishmen living beyond the reach of England, that was all.

And still, they must have felt that their God had brought them here, and would bless them here, and would never leave them.

The first ordinary place, Immingham – overlooking the iced blue of the North Sea, and a similar panorama – was a transit station, no more; and the modern docks have buried the bleakness of what it was like that distant day while they waited to go.

The second ordinary place, Provincetown – the same ocean of chilled blue, another similar panorama – was no longer a transit station; and the modern place it is now has buried the bleakness of what it was like that distant day while they waded ashore.

This third ordinary place, Plymouth, was their haven before the building of heaven; but the modern town and its parks and carparks have buried the sense of what, daily, they saw from the slope of The Street down to the shoreline and beyond. The water still brushes over rocks, but these ones have been carefully laid to prevent erosion and maintain a certain genteel decorum for the waterfront. It is as different as that.

The generations after 1620 built their town on the place where the Plantation was, and now no sense of it remains except in the street names and the general contour of the sloping land.

The Town Brook still runs, clear and fresh, along the flank of where the Plantation was, but now it is a neat little park with a bridge and signs about not feeding the ducks.

Just for a moment you can see in your mind's eye a maiden or two tramping through the snow of that first desperate winter to fill their buckets, see them hold the buckets by their handles in the water at an angle, let the clear, fresh water fill them; walk slowly back up the slope, trying not to spill any, talking quietly.

These days, there are souvenir shops milking history as hard as they can. Outside one, a couple of lifesize dummies in period costume speak in mechanical voices and look as if they need a ventriloquist to get hold of them or, failing that, a strangler. T-shirts they have, and trinkets you do not want to take home they have.

This ordinary place guards its secrets, whatever the guide books and plaques and tourist maps and signs proclaim. Somehow this makes you more curious about how it grew from that to this.

The *Mayflower* – well, *Mayflower II* – is just over there on the far side of Plymouth Rock, moored to a jetty. It is a strangely fascinating shape, clumsy and sleek all at the same moment, squat and tall, bigger yet smaller than you thought. Mariners in traditional costume are placed strategically around it – salty old sea dog stuff – giving little explanatory talks to the groups of tourists who come by, and answering questions. There is a common feeling among these tourists: incredulity that so many passengers and crew could have spent sixty-seven days on the high seas in a cramped ship like this, all angles and ladders and decks, with no creature comforts; a common feeling that this ship is small, like *small*.

The *Mayflower* is a copy, of course, and a copy of the best guesses of the experts who built it in 1956, because neither plans nor drawings survive, so nobody knows – any more than they know where the fragmented group stood gazing at the North Sea waiting for the Dutch ship to take them off, or where the waders came ashore at Provincetown, holding, as they would have done, their muskets high to keep their powder dry.

But they *did* wait somewhere, they *did* wade somewhere, they *did* step ashore somewhere. It leads to a question: what was the place like then? All else aside, it was their normality; and, as we shall see in a moment, they behaved quite normally. It is time on the long voyage to see how it grew from that to this.

NINE

Thanksgiving

The first wedding was on 12 May, between Winslow and Susanna White, widow of William. Winslow had been a widower for only six weeks, and Susanna for twelve. She had a five-year-old son, Resolved, and Peregrine who had been born on the *Mayflower* at Cape Cod. The marriage was probably one of survival for both bride and groom.

The service was conducted in the Dutch custom by a magistrate (thus making inheritance between the couple legal). The Leiden group did not regard the marriage ceremony as a religious one and consequently the civil ceremony took place before Bradford. Perhaps the wedding was symbolic as well as practical. It implied that they were committed to creating a normal life – and, by virtue of that, they had come to stay.

That sense of permanence was reinforced on 1 June when John Peirce obtained a second patent – the original had been issued by the Virginia Company to him, in 1619 – from the Council for New England which in essence made the Colony at Plymouth legal. The original, of course, had been for a settlement on the Hudson river. Neither Peirce nor the other Merchant Adventurers financing the whole thing knew that the *Mayflower* had set them down at Plymouth until the ship got back to England in May. Even though they were 3,000 miles away, the colonists at Plymouth understood that, overall, they needed authorisation from England to remain where they were. Peirce, with a lot of money at stake, understood that, too. This second one, known as the Peirce Patent, bestowed legality.

On 10 June the two-man delegation and Squanto set off to take up Massasoit's invitation. Squanto said they would reach the town of Nemasket – one of Massasoit's – that night to rest. Winslow and Hopkins assumed Nemasket would not be too far away because its inhabitants 'flocked' to the Plantation on any excuse, but it turned out to be 15 miles away. As they walked towards it a group of ten or twelve Indians – men, women and children – pestered them then followed them to the town, which they reached at 3 p.m. The Indians entertained Winslow and Hopkins as best they could, giving them a bread they called *maizium* and the 'spawn of shads [marine fish], which then they got in abundance, insomuch as they gave us spoons to eat them. With these they boiled musty acorns, but of the shads we ate heartily.'[1]

The Indians asked either Winslow or Hopkins to shoot a crow – evidently crows had been damaging their corn – and were full of admiration when the shot rang out and the deed was done. After that Squanto said they should move on because 8 miles away they would find better food. They got there at sunset and found some men from Nemasket fishing on a weir they had constructed in a river to catch bass. These Indians had plenty of bass and exchanged some for food from Winslow and Hopkins. They slept in the open and remarked that, although the Indians spent the whole summer there, they had not bothered to build any dwellings.

Where exactly were they going? It is likely the Indian route they were on – the Nemasket Path – was well-trodden and they had found it. The Path led inland from Plymouth to an area veined by streams and ponds which the Indians called the place of fish. Because the settlers were unfamiliar with the Eastern Algonqian language they may have understood the name to be a town near a 'wading place' – a ford on a small river. Here the Nemasket Path connected with trails leading north, west and south. In fact, several Indian towns were situated nearby. Which of these the little party went to remains quite unknown.[2]

Next day they left, six Indians going with them, and had gone about 6 miles along the river bank when they reached a shallow crossing place. The Indians told them to 'put off our breeches' because they would have to wade across. Two elderly Indians were over on the far side. Winslow estimated one man was sixty, a tremendous age. These two, seeing the party crossing, ran swiftly and 'low in the grass' towards them. Using their voices they charged the party with their bows and 'demanded what we were, supposing us to be enemies, and thinking to take advantage on us in the water'. Once the two understood that the party was friendly they welcomed them with the food that they had. Winslow or Hopkins gave them a small bracelet of beads.

Only these two men were still alive: it pointed to the sheer scale of the epidemics. Later the party would find that 'thousands of them died. They not being able to bury one another, their skulls, and bones were found in many places lying still above ground.'[3]

The party pressed on, the weather hot, and found the countryside verdant. It reminded them of England, with plenty of small rivers, although the Indians would only drink the water at a springhead. When they came to any small brook the Indians offered to carry them over and, in case Winslow or Hopkins was tired, carry their muskets. The Indians also said that if they would like to take their clothes off, they would carry those, too. They would also find many towns and fertile soil in clearings on both sides of the main river but the people were all gone. The river flowed into the sea at Narragansett Bay, 'where the Frenchmen so much use'.

Walking through weeds more than head high, they noted how much good wood there was: oak, walnut, fir, beech and very big chestnut. Although the landscape was wild and overgrown it was not so dense that a man might not ride a horse through.

One of the Indians saw another in the distance and the Englishmen asked if he was afraid. *If he and others with him are Narragansett*, the man replied, *we will not trust them.* Winslow and Hopkins hoisted their muskets and said, *do not be afraid.* The Indian came up, was friendly, and 'had only two women with him'. The baskets they carried were empty, but they brought water in their bottles and everyone drank together.

'After, we met another man with two other women, which had been at a rendez-vous by the salt water, and their baskets were full of roasted crab fishes, and other dried shell fish, of which they gave us, and we ate and drank with them; and gave each of the women a string of beads, and departed.'[4]

They reached one of the towns Massasoit ruled and ate oysters and other fish. Then they continued to Pokanoket, but Massasoit was not there. A message was sent to him and they waited. One of the two Englishmen was about to load his musket but, seeing this, 'the women and children . . . through fear ran away, and could not be pacified till he laid it down again'.

Massasoit arrived and took them into his 'house' where they relayed what the Governor had said, then put the coat on him and the chain round his neck. 'He was not a little proud to behold himself, and the men also to see their king so bravely attired.' They would endure a difficult evening and night. Massasoit agreed to the Governor's requests and made a great speech naming each place where his writ ran, which the Englishmen estimated at thirty. At each name the tribesmen shouted the equivalent of *yes*, and however delightful this performance was to them, the Englishmen found it very tedious. Afterwards he lit some tobacco and began to talk about King James, 'marvelling that he would live without a wife'. (James had married Anne of Denmark in 1590 but she died in March 1619). Massasoit did not give them any food, because evidently he did not have any.

They all lay down for the night. The bed was made from planks about a foot from the ground with a thin mat over them, the Englishmen at one end, Massasoit and his wife at the other. Worse, two of his 'chief men' joined them, so that by morning 'we were worse weary of our lodging than our journey'.

The following day the sub-chiefs came in with their tribesmen, and 'we challenged them to shoot with them for skins' – presumably a competition between the muskets and the bows and arrows, with skins the prize for the winners. The Indians were not having any of it, but they did want to see either Winslow or Hopkins shoot at a mark. This was done with hail-shot and the Indians were amazed to see the target, whatever it was, so full of holes.

Massasoit appeared with two fish he had shot. They resembled English bream but were three times bigger and 'better meat'. They were boiled and at least forty people wanted a share. This was the only meal the Englishmen had in two nights and a day. If one of them had not brought a partridge they would have had nothing except their small share of the bream. That was the Thursday. Massasoit wanted them to stay, but they decided they would go back to Plymouth to spend the Sabbath there. They feared they would be 'light-headed for want of sleep . . . what with bad lodging, the savages' barbarous singing (they used to sing themselves asleep), lice and fleas within and mosquitoes without, we could hardly sleep all the time of our being there'.[5]

On the Friday morning before the sun rose they left, although Massasoit was 'both grieved and ashamed, that he could no better entertain us'. Massasoit kept Squanto, who would engage in some trade for the settlers, but appointed another – Tokamahamon, a member of the Wampanoag tribe – to replace him. He proved to be faithful. They stopped at the same town on the way back and

> were again refreshed with a little fish, and bought about a handful of meal of their parched corn, which was very precious at that time of the year, and a small string of dried shell-fish, as big as oysters. The latter we gave to the six savages that accompanied us, keeping the meal for ourselves. When we drank we ate each a spoonful of it with a pipe of tobacco, instead of other victuals.[6]

They took a 5-mile detour to go to a house where they thought there might be food, but it was unoccupied. By nightfall they had reached the weir where they had slept on the way to Massasoit, but again found no food. An Indian shot a shad in the water and 'a small squirrel as big as a rat, called a neuxis'. He gave them half of both.

They wrote a letter to Plymouth and sent Tokamahamon with it, asking for food to be sent to Nemasket. As it proved, this was unnecessary, because although only two Indians remained with them they caught a lot more fish and everyone ate well, keeping some for breakfast.

> About two o'clock in the morning arose a great storm of wind, rain, lightning and thunder in such violent manner that we could not keep in our fire, and had the savages not roasted fish when we were asleep we had set forward fasting . . . the rain still continued with great violence, even the whole day through, till we came within two miles of home.
>
> Being wet and weary, at length we came to Nemasket. There we refreshed ourselves, giving gifts as had showed us any kindness.

> Amongst others one of the six that came with us from Pokanoket, having before this on the way unkindly forsaken us, marveled we gave him nothing, and told us what he had done for us. We also told him of some discourtesies he offered us, whereby he deserved nothing, yet we gave him a small trifle whereupon he offered us tobacco.[7]

The two Englishmen felt this was stolen and, if it was, would not accept it under any circumstances. They explained to the assembled company that if they did their God would be angry with them. The Indians wanted them to stay the night and were full of wonder when they said they would press on back to Plymouth 'but God be praised, safe home that night, though wet, weary, and surbated [sore feet through walking]'.

Around this time, John Billington got lost in the woods and 'wandered up and down some 5 days living on berries, and what he could find'. Eventually he came across Indians at Manomet, but they took him to the Nausets. Governor Bradford made enquiries among the Indians and Massasoit sent word saying where Billington was. Bradford dispatched a party of ten men in the shallop, accompanied by Squanto and Tokamahamon, to get him back. They set off in fine weather, but soon they ran into a storm 'of wind and rain, with much lightning and thunder, insomuch that a spout arose not far from us'. It did not last long and that night they harboured at a place called Cummaquid, approximately midway between Plymouth and Provincetown. They had, evidently, hoped to find Billington there. They 'anchored in the middest of the bay', presumably for security reasons.[8]

In the morning they saw Indians looking for lobsters. They sent Squanto and Tokamahamon to explain why the party had come and that the Indians should not be afraid: the Englishmen would not hurt them. The Indians said Billington was well but at Nauset. They invited the party to eat with them 'which as soon as our boat floated we did'. Six went ashore. The Indians' chief came and Winslow found him 'a man not exceeding twenty-six years of age, but very personable, gentle, courteous, and fair conditioned, indeed not like the savage save for his attire'.

The harmony was about to be broken. A woman, 'whom we judged to be no less than an hundred years old, which came to see us because she never saw English, yet could not behold us without breaking forth into great passion, weeping and crying excessively'. They asked why and listened to her story. She had had three sons and Hunt had tricked them. They had gone onto his ship to trade with him, and he had kidnapped them, taking them to Spain. As it would seem, they never came back because she was 'deprived of the comfort of her children in her old age'. The party apologised, explained that Hunt was a bad man and condemned him while assuring her they would not 'offer them any injury' even if it would get them 'all the skins in the country'. They gave the old woman some small trifles and that mollified her a bit.

After dinner they set off in the shallop for Nauset, taking the chief and two of the tribe with them, but when they arrived 'the day and tide were almost spent', and they could not get the shallop close in. The chief and his men did go ashore with Squanto to tell the Nauset why they had come. The Indians wanted them to bring the shallop in, but the party did not trust them and, literally, wanted to keep their distance. They only let two Indians into the shallop. The subject of the corn which had been taken in the early expedition was dealt with. The Nausets were promised restitution, and the party invited one of them to come to Plymouth – they called it Patuxet to him – for satisfaction or they would bring him corn. He said he would come to them.

After sunset, a train of a hundred Indians brought Billington, 'behung with beads'. Half the Indians came to the shallop with him, the other half stood off holding their bows and arrows.

The party heard disturbing news from the Nausets. The Narragansetts had 'spoiled' some of Massasoit's men and taken him prisoner. Without Massasoit's guarantee, the peace treaty was worthless, and Massasoit was not in a position to guarantee anything. The party's first thought was that the Colony was highly vulnerable because ten of the fittest men, who would have been central to its defence, were in the shallop. It left the Colony weakly guarded.

They would get back as quickly as they could, 'yet the wind being contrary, having scarce any fresh water left, and at least 16 leagues home, we put in again for the shore'. They met more Indians and were led a great way in the darkness searching for fresh water, but they could not find any. 'In the meantime the women joined hand in hand, singing and dancing before the shallop, the men also showing all the kindness they could.'[9] They reached Plymouth the following day. Whether Billington showed any contrition for what he had put the others through – and taking them away from the settlement at what might have been a moment of supreme danger – is not recorded, but it seems unlikely because the Billington family (possibly they came from Lincolnshire) were trouble or, as Bradford put it[10] 'one of the profanest families amongst them'.

There were four Billingtons: John and his wife Ellen, and sons John and Francis. John, who had got lost and just been found, was sixteen. His mother would be fined for slander and put 'in the stocks and publicly whipped'. John the father had been sentenced to be bound – hog tied – in March, giving him the dubious distinction of committing the first offence in New England.

> [He] came on board at London, and is this month convented [arraigned] before the whole company for the contempt of his captain's lawful command with opprobrious speeches, for which he is adjudged to have his neck and heels tied together; but upon humbling himself and craving pardon, and it being the first offense, he is forgiven.[11]

Billington went on to become the first settler to be executed for murder. Bradford said he would live and die a knave, and he did. Francis Billington, as we have seen, almost blew up the *Mayflower* in December in Provincetown Harbour.

Massasoit had been taken by the Narragansett. The tensions which the arrival of the settlers created were opening up. The chief of a Wampanoag sub-tribe called Corbitant, formerly under Massasoit, had travelled to Nemasket to try and 'draw the hearts of Massasoit's subjects from him'. He spoke with disdain of the English and stormed at the peace treaty, accusing Squanto of complicity, as well as Tokamahamon, and Hobomok, another Indian who had come to live at Plymouth. Hobomok was 'a proper lusty man, and a man of account for his valour amongst the Indians'.[12]

Squanto and Hobomok travelled discreetly to Nemasket, but not discreetly enough. Word reached Corbitant, who had the house where they were staying surrounded. A quarrel broke out and Squanto was captured. Ominously, Corbitant proclaimed that if Squanto should be killed, the English would have lost their tongue. Hobomok tried some sort of intervention, but Corbitant 'held a knife at his breast'. Hobomok was strong enough to break free and sprinted out of Nemasket. He kept on running until he was back at Plymouth, sweating profusely.

He explained the situation to Bradford and added that Squanto, he felt, was dead. Bradford saw clearly that the credibility of the Colony and its chances of any lasting peace were at stake. He took counsel. If the settlers did not respond, who would trust them again? Who would do business with them? Who would bring them any 'intelligence'? Would the Indians they had befriended turn on them?

The settlers' response was a party of ten or fourteen well-armed men under Standish. The party would 'fall upon' Corbitant's men

> in the night and if they found Squanto was killed, to cut off Corbitant's head, but not to hurt any but those that had a hand in it. Hobomok was asked if he would go and be their guide, and bring them there before day.[13]

Hobomok agreed and they set off, but

> the day proved very wet. When we supposed we were within three or four miles of Nemasket, we went out of the way and stayed there until night [so] we would not be discovered. There we consulted what to do, and thinking best to beset the house at midnight, each was appointed his task by the captain, all men encouraging one another to the upmost of their power.
>
> By night our guide lost his way, which much discouraged our men, being we were wet and weary of arms, but one of our men having been before at Nemasket brought us into the way again.[14]

They ate whatever they had in their knapsacks and then discarded them and anything else which might obstruct them in fighting. Then they moved on the house where they thought Corbitant was. Some burst in and demanded to know if he was there, but the Indians were so terrified they could not speak. The Indians were told not to 'stir', because if Corbitant was not there the party would not 'meddle' with them. They explained to the Indians that they had come to avenge the death of Squanto, but gave an assurance that they would not hurt the women and children. Even so, a few Indians 'pressed out at a private door and escaped, but with some wounds'.

The Indians said Squanto was alive and Corbitant and his followers had returned to their own territory. In fact, Squanto and Tokamahamon were in a house nearby. The party was offered some tobacco and some of what the Indians had to eat. 'In this hurly-burly, we discharged two pieces at random, which much terrified all the inhabitants, except [Squanto] and Tokamahamon, who though they knew not our end in coming, yet assured them of our honesty.'[15] Squanto and Tokamahamon heard the shots and calmed the Indians around them. The party now surrounded and entered another house where they thought Corbitant was. The young Indians in it, who knew of the settlers 'care' of women, shouted '*Neen squaes*, that is to say, I am a woman: the women also hanging upon Hobomok, calling him *towam*, that is, friend'.[16]

The Indians were ordered to make a fire so there would be enough light to search the house properly. Hobomok climbed on top of it, and called out to Squanto and Tokamahamon, who 'came unto us accompanied by others, some armed and others naked. Those that had bows and arrows we took them away, promising them again when it was day. The house we took for our better safeguard, but released those we had taken.' This house must have been on the edge of the town, because next morning the party marched into the middle. They made it clear that although Corbitant had got away this time, no place would be secure for him if he kept on threatening the settlers. They went further. They promised severe consequences if Massasoit was not returned from Narragansett to his former position; and if Corbitant 'make any insurrection against Massasoit – or Squanto, Tokamahamon and Hobomok for that matter – that would be avenged and Corbitant overthrown. As for those who were wounded, we were sorry for it, though themselves procured it in not staying in the house at our command; yet if they would return home with us, our surgeon should heal them.'[17] One wounded man and one wounded woman went with them. The party was back at Plymouth the day after it had left.

As a consequence of this expedition, Corbitant used Massasoit to mediate peace, although he was 'shy to come near . . . a long while after'.[18]

Sometimes silence can be eloquent. The contemporary accounts place the Billington rescue in June and give contradictory dates for the two forays into Indian country, but about the day-to-day life of the Colony, on which they had been so detailed so recently, they say nothing. The silence has placed this in the background; perhaps because its growth and functioning had become normal, however hard.

There is no mention of how the building work was progressing, or the tilling of land, or the crops; no sense that the settlement was becoming *deeper*; no feeling of how much or how little they ate, the difficulties and setbacks that inevitably there must have been. Instead, on 18 June the second offence at the Plantation – John Billington had, of course, led the way – took place in bizarre circumstances. It was

> the first duel fought in New England, upon a challenge of single combat with sword and dagger between Edward Doty and Edward Leister, servants of Mr Hopkins. Both being wounded, the one in the hand, the other in the thigh, they are adjuged by the whole company to have their head and feet tied together and so to lie for twenty-four hours without meat or drink, which is begun to be inflicted, but within an hour, because of their great pains, at their own and their master's humble request, upon promise of better carriage, they are released by the Governor.[19]

There is silence again until 18 September when they mounted an expedition to the Massachusetts tribe, ten men in the shallop, Squanto as guide-interpreter and two other Indians. It had the customary objectives: to have a look at the territory, make peace and trade.

They set off at midnight to catch the tide and sailed north until they reached what would become Boston Harbour, where 'being late we anchored and lay in the shallop, not having seen any of the people'. They went ashore next morning and found lobsters which the Indians had caught. Standish posted two lookouts on the cliff to guard the shallop and the rest went in search of the inhabitants. They came across a woman going to collect the lobsters and she told them where the Massachusetts were. Squanto went ahead on foot while they returned to sail the shallop there.

The chief proved to be under Massasoit, but 'the people were much afraid of the Tarrantines, a people to the eastward which used to come in harvest time, and take away their corn, and many times kill their persons'.[20] The chief even told them he kept constantly on the move to evade the Tarrantines. The party explained that other chiefs had acknowledged King James and if they did they would be under English protection. They went across the bay to meet the Massachusetts queen – the chief squaw – and as they went they noticed that the bay had at least fifty islands. It was so broad that they did not reach the other side until night and slept on the shallop as it rode at anchor.

They explored inland next day and found an abandoned settlement 'where corn had been newly gathered'. They found a house surrounded by a high palisade and trenches with a deceased Massachusetts leader inside and a similar house on the top of the hill where he had been killed.

They met some women the following day whom they assumed had earlier fled them in such terror that in one place they 'had left some of their corn covered with a mat, and nobody with it'. The women began to relax when they realised they would not be harmed, and they boiled cod for them. Eventually a man came 'shaking and trembling for fear' but he relaxed, too. Squanto, however, said the settlers should 'rifle' the women and take whatever was of value because 'they are bad people and have often threatened you'. The settlers pointed out that they did not behave like that, although if anyone tried anything on them they would be dealt with far worse than they wanted.

They went back to the shallop and the women 'sold their coats from their backs' – made from beaver skins – so they were naked. They covered themselves with branches. The settlers regarded the episode with 'great shamefacedness', as befits the prudish or the devoutly religious. The party had a good quantity of skins and said they would return.

At Plymouth they reported that the place they had been to would have made a better place for the Colony and wished they had been able to choose it in the first place, but there was no question of moving now.

At last there was a glimpse of the background. The settlers began to gather in

> the small harvest they had, and to fit up their houses and dwellings against winter, being all well recovered in health and strength; and had all things in good plenty . . . As some were employed in affairs abroad others were exercised in fishing, about cod and bass and other fish of which they took good store, of which every family had their portion. All summer there was no want, and now began to come in store of fowl as winter approached . . . and besides waterfowl there was great store of wild turkeys, of which they took many, as well as venison etc. Besides they had about a peck of meal a week per person [a peck = about 10lb, of perhaps oatmeal], or now since harvest, Indian corn to that proportion.[21]

Eleven houses had been finished, and in October Bradford declared three days of thanksgiving for the harvest. The wild turkeys would provide part of the food. Bradford sent four men fowling, so that 'we might after a more special manner rejoice together'. They bagged enough in one day to feed the settlement for a week. Massasoit was invited and arrived with ninety tribesmen who promptly went off and killed five deer. Settlers and Indians feasted for three days. It was the first Thanksgiving.[22]

In November word came from the Indians on Cape Cod that a ship was in the bay and they thought it French. The settlers were anticipating that other ships would come to them from England, but not so soon after the *Mayflower* had left – they had no way of knowing the *Mayflower* had recrossed the Atlantic in a month. As this ship sailed down the bay and neared them, Bradford ordered one of the cannons to be fired, a signal summoning everyone back to the Colony from whatever work they were doing. They prepared to defend it 'every man' and 'yea, boy that could handle a gun'.

The ship was called the *Fortune*, English and with thirty-five passengers including Cushman and his fourteen-year-old son Thomas; Brewster's son Jonathan; and John Winslow to join his brothers Edward and Gilbert. Twelve of the passengers were from Leiden, the rest Adventurers. One, Martha Ford, gave birth to a son on her first night ashore.

The arrival of the *Fortune* ought to have been much more than an umbilical cord to what remained of the Leiden community and England herself. In one sense it was, but in another, more important sense it was not, because the *Fortune* ought to have brought provisions. Instead the ship brought them thirty-five more people to feed and no food.

And a story unfolded: many of the thirty-five were 'lusty young men, and many of them wild enough',[23] but when the *Fortune* sailed into Cape Cod they saw 'nothing but a naked and barren place'. They began to ask themselves two questions: what will happen to us? What if the *Mayflower* settlers are dead? These young men became so alarmed they contemplated seizing the ship's sails to prevent it suddenly leaving them abandoned. The captain addressed them, calmed them and said that he hoped the ship had enough food to continue down the coast to Virginia if that proved necessary, and he would share the food with them. The potential mutiny was quelled.

The newcomers, however lusty, had nothing with them:

> not so much as a biscuit cake or any other victuals for them, neither had they any bedding, but some sorry things in their cabins, nor pot, or pan to dress any meat in; nor over-many clothes . . . the Plantation was glad of this addition of strength but could have wished that many of them had been in better condition.[24]

Weston had sent a strong letter addressed to Carver with the ship, not knowing of course that he was dead. Weston complained about some of the passengers who had boarded the *Mayflower* at Southampton, complained that they had kept the ship too long and complained that it had been sent back empty instead of brimming with cargo. He did, however, say that he had obtained the Peirce Charter and Plymouth was now legal, as we have seen.

The settlers understood that if they wanted to remain at Plymouth they would have to have it sanctioned by the English government – the original sanction, under which they had sailed, was valid for the Virginia Company's area, far to the south, of course. When the *Mayflower* returned to England, bringing news of where the settlers actually were, Weston and John Peirce obtained the new Charter. The settlers could stay, and Cushman urged them to accept it.

The Charter was more favourable to those from London investing in the colony than those living and working in it: the investors would be given land, the workers were given the promise that the terms of the Charter would be reviewed after seven years, possibly on more favourable terms to them.

In Weston's letter he suggested that their failure to return the *Mayflower* quickly – and return her full – was 'I believe more weakness of judgement than weakness of hands'[25] and added 'a quarter of the time you spent in discoursing, arguing and consulting would have [achieved] much more'. Bradford must have been enraged that Weston, snug in England, was suggesting they had squandered their time arguing when they had been engaged in a mortal struggle to get through the winter. In answer to the letter he said:

> You greatly blame us for keeping the ship so long in the country, and then to send her away empty. She lay 5 weeks at Cape Cod; whilst with many a weary step (after a long journey) . . . we sought out (in the foul weather) a place of habitation. Then we went in so tedious a time to make provisions to shelter us, and our goods, about which labour many of our arms and legs can tell us to this day. We were not negligent . . . it pleased God to visit us then with death daily and with so general a disease that the living were scarce able to bury the dead, and the well not in any measure sufficient to tend the sick. And now to be so greatly blamed for not freighting the ship doth indeed go near us, and much discourage us. But, you say, you know we will pretend weakness, and do you think we had not cause? . . . They which

> told you we spent so much time in discoursing and consulting etc, their hearts can tell their tongues [that] they lie.[26]

The assumption must be that when the *Mayflower* finally reached England, and the people who had put the money up were faced with no profit, an explanation was demanded, and either Captain Jones or members of the crew, or all of them, had taken the safe way out: they had blamed the settlers for wasting time talking. Weston was now told by the settlers that, if another ship did not come with provisions, famine was unavoidable, and added that Cushman, who was sailing back with the *Fortune*, would confirm this.

The *Fortune* was laden with beaver and otter skins and cedar wood, a cargo valued at £500. She was gone within two weeks.

The newcomers were allocated households to join and then Bradford and Allerton drew up an inventory of the total food store. Once they had that they divided it into the number of people and calculated that they could perhaps hold out for six months at half rations – until the fish were abundant again. Bradford and Allerton realised that any rationing below that in the winter might be catastrophic.

Soon after, the Colony did move on to half rations, and although there was general unhappiness about it, they bore it stoically and hoped a resupply ship would be coming from England once the *Fortune* got there and revealed their true plight. How many worked all down these difficult days with an eye to the sea, hoping to see sail in the distance? How many tried to calculate how long the *Fortune* would take to recross and another ship be dispatched? How many women found ways to stretch and stretch their rations? Was anybody given priority – the children or the working men who needed their strength? Did anybody cry themselves to sleep with hunger?

The Narragansett now made their move. Observing intently but from a safe distance, they could not have helped noticing that although thirty-five people were brought ashore from the *Fortune* no weapons or supplies came with them. The conclusion was of a Colony made vulnerable: more mouths. The Narragansett sent a 'bundle of arrows' tied round with a great rattlesnake skin.[27] The messenger who brought it asked to see Squanto, and when he was told Squanto was not there he seemed relieved – he must have feared being taken prisoner when the meaning of the bundle was revealed. He wanted to leave immediately, but Bradford and Allerton decided to put him in custody. Standish ordered two men – one was Winslow – to watch over him, treat him well and if possible try to find out what was going on.

'At first, fear so possessed him that he could scarce say anything.'[28] As the Indian became more 'familiar', a convoluted story emerged: in the summer the Narragansett chief had sent a messenger to sue for peace, but this messenger went back, provocatively and falsely, persuading the chief to war.

Winslow told Bradford and Standish, and a fine example of justice (or the settlers' conception of it) followed. They decided that it was 'against the Law of Arms' here just as it would have been in Europe 'to lay violent hands on any such' and freed the Indian. He was offered meat but refused it. He had only one thought: to leave.

When Squanto came back he explained that the bundle was a challenge. Bradford took counsel and sent the bundle back with gunpowder and bullets in it, meaning: *if you want war come and get it*. The Narragansetts refused to accept the bundle, or rather their chief – fearing it had some magical, deadly properties – would not touch the powder or shot. He would not even 'suffer it to stay in his house or country'. The bundle was moved around and finally came back to the Colony.

The settlers resolved to build a defensive wall. Winslow, however, in a letter dated 11 December set out Plymouth's attractions, a whole litany of them – hotter than England in summer, colder in winter but 'the air is very clear and not foggy'. He declared that 'men might live as contented here as in any part of the world'. He described the abundance of fish and fowl, fresh summer cod and lobster, and in September we 'can take a hogshead of eels in a night, with small labour', and this before he reached the grapes which tasted strong, the fruits and vegetables, the 'plums of three sorts'. The letter had descended into a cross between a recruitment drive and a holiday brochure. If you come

> be careful to have a very good bread-room to put your biscuits in, let your cask for beer and water be iron-bound . . . Let not your

Tourist guide on the riverbank to a moment in history. *(Author's Collection)*

The obelisk at Fishtoft outside Boston, marking the (supposed) place of embarkation *(Author's Collection)*

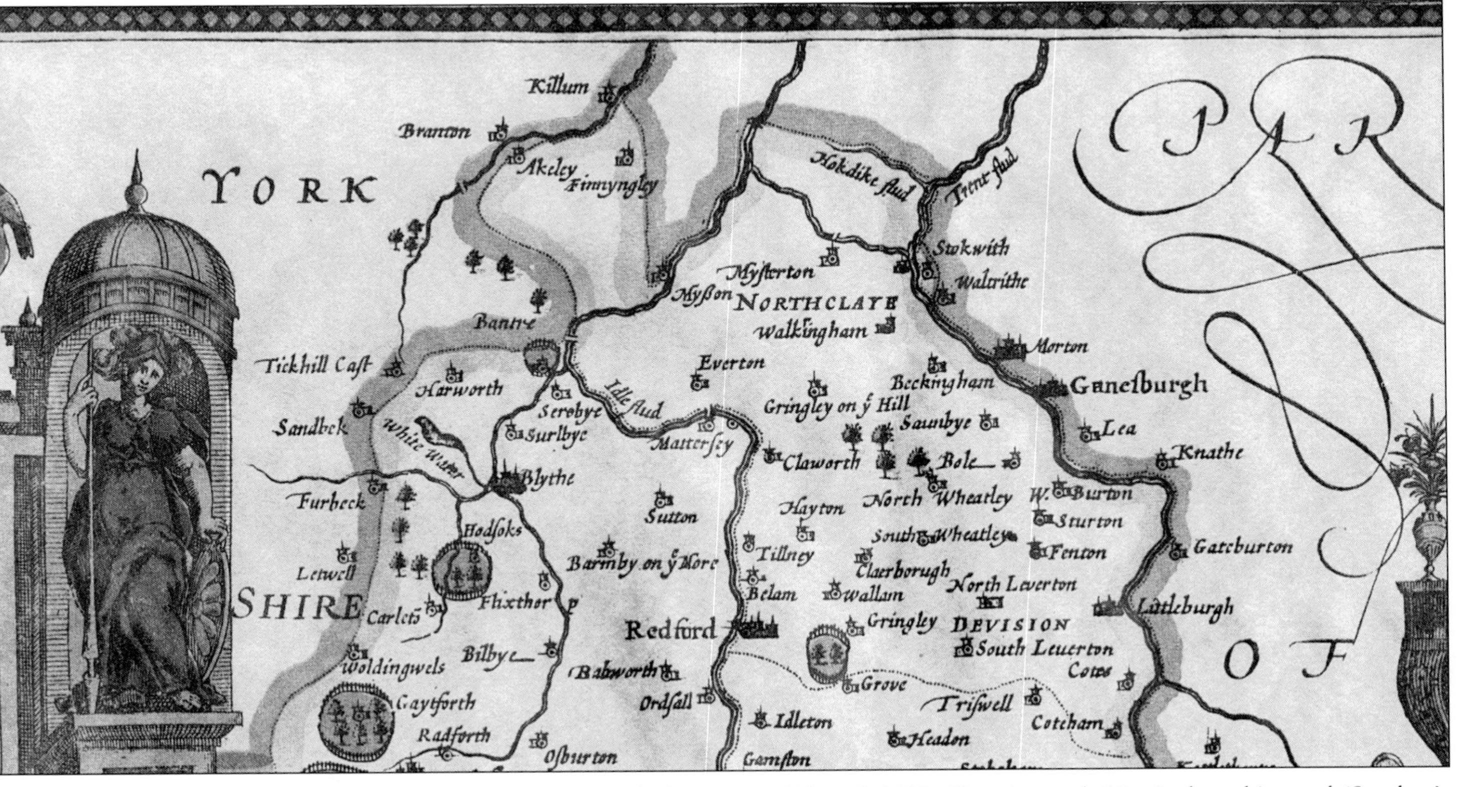

Master mapmaker John Speede drew England very precisely between 1610 and 1623. Here is north Nottinghamshire and 'Scrobye'. *(Author's Collection)*

Speede's map of the Lincolnshire coast, including Immingham. *(Author's Collection)*

An engraving by Edward Corbould of the embarkation of the Pilgrim Fathers, presumably from Holland.

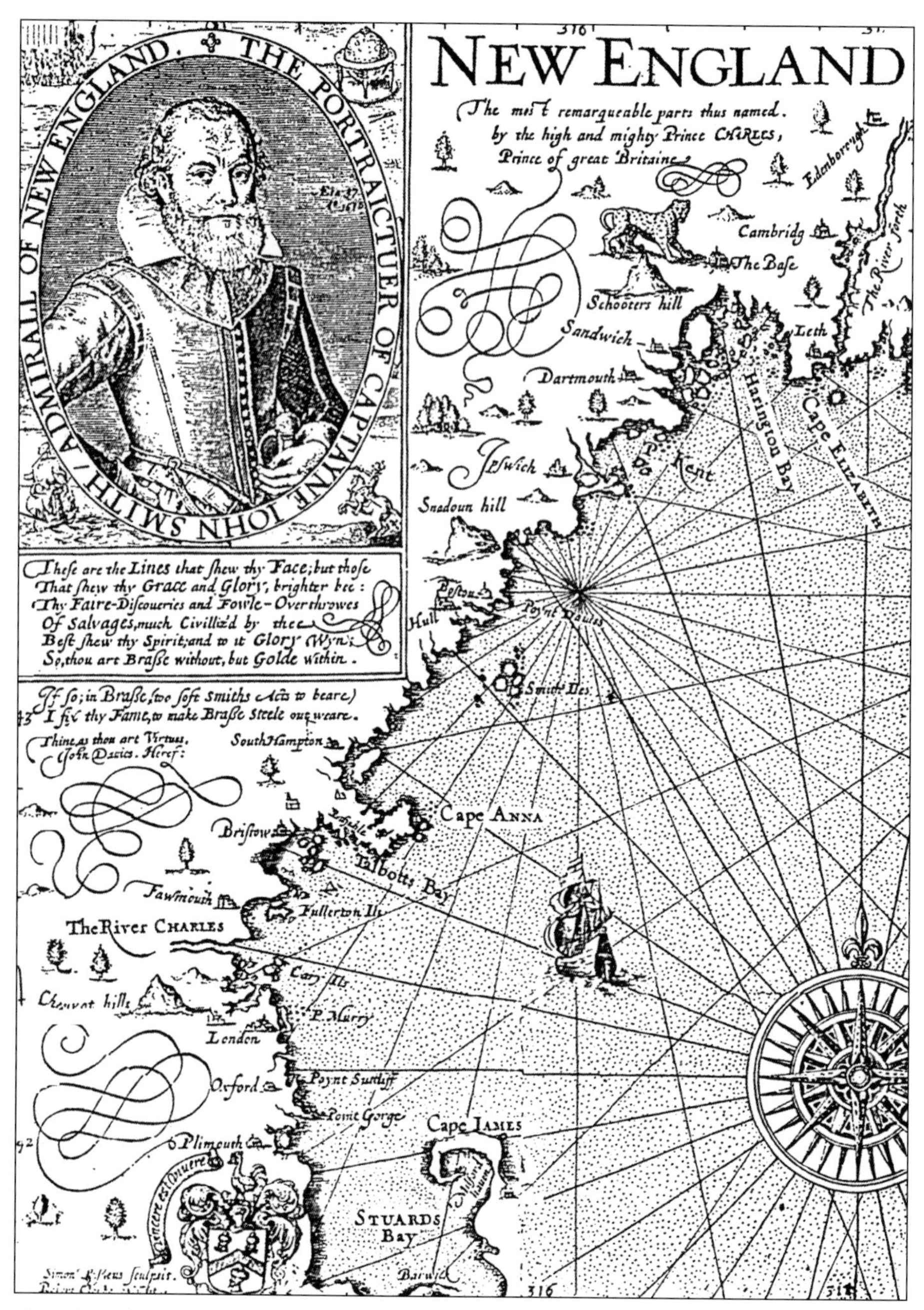

Captain John Smith explored the New England coastline in 1614 and drew this map. Plymouth can be seen bottom left, just above the coat of arms.

The Pilgrim Monument at Provincetown in 1910, showing what the terrain was like before the area was built up. *(Collection of the Pilgrim Monument and Provincetown Museum)*

The little spring in the clearing – almost certainly where the Pilgrim Fathers first drank fresh water in the New World. *(Author's Collection)*

Plymouth Rock in its resting place beside the shoreline at Plymouth, Massachusetts. *(Author's Collection)*

> meat be dry-salted, none can do it better than the sailors. Let your meal be so hard trod in your cask that you shall need an adz [tool for cutting away the surface of wood] or hatchet to work it out with. Trust not too much on us for corn at this time . . . By reason of the last company that came depending wholly on us, we shall have little enough till harvest . . . Bring good store of clothes and bedding with you. Bring every man a musket or fowling-piece, let your piece be long in the barrel, and fear not the weight of it . . . most of our shooting is from stands. Bring juice of lemons, and take it fasting, it is of good use; for hot waters, aniseed water is the best, but use it sparingly. If you bring anything for comfort in the country, butter or sallet [salad] oil, or both is very good. Our Indian corn, even the coarsest, maketh as pleasant meat as rice . . . bring paper, and linseed oil for your windows, and cotton yarn for your lamps. Let your shot be most for big fowls, and bring store of powder and shot.[29]

Astonishingly, Winslow rounds off his account of the year 1621 with a joke, or rather something 'of mirth than of weight'. On Christmas Day, Bradford called everyone out to work, but most of the newcomers said it went against their conscience. Bradford retorted that if they made it a matter of conscience he would accept that 'till they were better informed'. The Leiden people, of course, did not celebrate Christmas or other Christian holidays, as they held they were either made up by men or the Catholic Church.[30] Bradford 'led away' the rest to their work. When they came back at midday they found the refuseniks 'in the street at play openly, some pitching the bar, and some at stool ball,[31] and such like sports'. So Bradford[32]

> went to them and took away their implements and told them that was against his conscience that they should play and others work. If they made the keeping of it a matter of devotion, let them keep [to] their houses . . . There should be no gaming or reveling in the streets. Since which time nothing hath been attempted that way, at least openly.

They had survived the first year.

TEN

Roots

As they toiled, the little Plantation assumed a permanent shape. By March 1622 the wooden fence around it had been completed and each house was fenced off from the main street. That gave them their own plot of land for growing, with the obvious incentive to maximise what it could yield. Self-sufficiency meant survival in both the short and long terms.

The Colony remained vulnerable, embattled and precarious. The Leiden people gradually 'subdued' the Strangers,[1] so that all would be enacting the attempt at heaven on earth, but there was a problem. The very rigidity of beliefs, shared with only the remainder of the congregation in Holland, made them both insular and unattractive to the sort of new blood they would need: there was not enough of them to be self-sustaining. Nor was the economic base of the Colony broad enough to allow large-scale expansion.

Then there were the Indians. As the Plantation was on poor soil and the settlers were having problems catching enough fish, they needed to resume trade. In the spring they contacted the Massachusetts and prepared to visit them at the end of March, but Hobomok feared[1]

> they were joined with the Narragansetts and might betray them if they were not careful. He intimated also some jealousy of Squanto, by what he gathered from some private whisperings between him and other Indians. But they resolved to proceed and sent out their shallop with 10 of their chief men about the beginning of April, Squanto and Hobomok with them, in regard of the jealousy between them.[2]

Very soon an Indian – a member of Squanto's family – came running. He was frightened. His face had been wounded and there was still blood on it. He said that the Narragansetts and Corbitant were at the town of Nemasket and maybe headed towards the Plantation, Massasoit with them: the strategy was to attack while Standish's party was gone to trade. Bradford questioned him. The attack appeared so imminent, and the messenger so frightened that he kept looking over his shoulder. Bradford ordered the three cannons to be fired so Standish would hear them and return fast. As the cannons sounded, the settlers already had their guns in their hands. Standish heard and turned back. As the shallop neared the shore the men on it were ready to fight, too.

When the situation was explained, Hobomok did not believe it. Even so, a watch would be kept all that night. All quiet. Hobomok's wife was sent to Pokanoket and Massasoit's main residence there, but she found no preparations for aggression and, when she explained the panic at the Plantation, Massasoit assured her no aggression had been or was contemplated. He promised he was still abiding by the terms of the treaty between them, and if he was coming to the Plantation he would do so only in the way the treaty specified. Standish resumed his trip and made good trade.

The position and motives of Squanto now came into question. Some of the settlers suspected he 'sought and played his own game, by putting the Indians in fear – drawing gifts from them [and] making them believe he could stir up war against whom he would, and make peace for whom he would'. He convinced the other Indians that the settlers kept the 'plague buried in the ground, and could send it amongst whom they would'. This terrified the Indians, and forced them to depend on him. They were turning more towards him than Massasoit. When Massasoit understood this, amid understandable envy he sought Squanto's death, and that in turn forced Squanto to stay close to the settlers 'and never durst go from them till he died'.

The settlers exploited the division between Squanto and Hobomok. Bradford 'countenanced' the one, Standish the other, 'by which they had better intelligence' and made both the Indians more diligent.[3]

The Colony was drifting towards a food crisis when a boat appeared in the harbour towards the end of May, and – again – the settlers thought it might be French. It was a shallop from a ship, the *Sparrow*, which Weston and others had hired to fish the coast of Maine. It brought seven more settlers (Adventurers, as it seems, sent by Weston) but – again – no provisions. A letter from Weston asked that they be fed, or rather 'we pray you lend or sell them some seed corn and if you have the salt remaining of the last year, that you will let them have it for their present use and we will pay you for it'.[4] All this was 'cold comfort to fill . . . hungry bellies'. Weston's attempts to keep his earlier promises were dismissed as a 'slender performance'. Weston's letter ended with a strange choice of words: 'I find the general so backward, and your friends at Leiden so cold, that I fear you must stand on your legs, and trust (as they say) to God and yourselves.'

The 'general' presumably meant the Colony and the settlers, who Weston thought were idling their time away, as he had written before; the 'friends at Leiden so cold' presumably meant that the settlers had not sent enough money back to transport what remained at Leiden and Robinson to the Colony, and Weston was not going to pay it himself. They were in all senses on their own, although the absence of Robinson was felt in the most profound way. Brewster held the position of Ruling Elder, but that did not entitle him to administer the sacraments, only Robinson.[5]

The *Sparrow* was at Damariscove, a fishing base off the Maine coast where English and other ships gathered. Winslow went there in the shallop to try and get what food he could. The captains of the ships were sympathetic but, naturally, only had enough for their own needs. They gave Winslow what they could spare and 'would not take any bills for the same'. When Winslow got back to the Plantation he found it 'much weaker than when I had left it'. For the first time, there was no bread. Nor was the fishing any better.

It must have been terribly tantalising, because 'though our bay and creeks were full of bass, and other fish' the settlers did not have a strong net for encircling fish and 'for the most part' the fish broke through. The sea teemed with cod but the settlers had no equipment to catch them, either. What saved them was that there were sorts of fish that could be caught by hand.[6]

Massasoit was proving less friendly, and the Indians 'began again to cast forth many insulting speeches, glorying in our weakness and giving out how easy it would be ere long to cut us off. Now also

Massasoit seemed to frown on us.'[7] As a precaution, the settlers turned their attention to the hill within the Plantation – the Mount (or Burial Hill) – and decided to build a fort on it, 'from whence a few might easily secure the town from any assault the Indians can make'. The work began eagerly, because it promised permanent security and had another advantage: it needed so few to man it, and the rest could be released for work on the land.

The fort, to be constructed on the gun platform already there, would be of heavy oak timber with a flat roof enclosed by a parapet. It would take ten months to build, and describing it the following September, Emmanuel Altham, newly arrived, wrote home that

> this town is in such a manner that it makes a great street between the houses, and at the upper end of the town there is a strong fort, both by nature and art, with six pieces of reasonable good artillery mounted thereon; in which fort is continual watch, so that no Indian can come near thereabouts but he is presently seen. This town is paled round with pale of eight foot long, or thereabouts, and in the pale are three great gates.

In June, two ships came into the harbour – the *Charity* and the *Swan* – and brought a fresh sense of crisis. Weston, who had hired these ships, was the cause. The *Charity*, the bigger ship, was to continue down the coast to Virginia with its cargo of paying customers. Fifty or sixty men got off at the Plantation and would simply stay until the *Charity* returned. Then they would be shipped up to Massachusetts Bay to find a suitable place to form a Colony of their own. In the meantime Weston had left them in Plymouth. The *Charity* also brought letters, one from Weston. It was a savage document:

> As for myself I have sold my adventure, and debts unto them [the Adventurers]. So as I am quit of you, and you of me, for that matter, etc. Now though I have nothing to pretend as an adventurer amongst you, yet I will advise you a little for your good, if you can apprehend it. I perceive, and know as well as another, the dispositions of your adventurers, whom the hope of gain hath drawn on to this they have done; and yet I fear that hope

will not draw them much further. Besides, most of them are against the sending of them of Leiden, for whose cause this business was first begun . . .

So that my advice is (you may follow it if you please) that you forthwith break off your joint stock, which you have warrant to do both in law and conscience . . .

I desired divers of the adventurers, as Mr Peirce, Mr Greene [Richard Greene, Weston's brother-in-law?] and others, if they had anything to send you, either victuals or letters . . . by these ships, and marveling they sent not so much as a letter, I asked our passengers what letters they had . . . With some difficulty one of them told me he had one, which was delivered to him with great charge of secrecy, and for more security to buy a pair of shoes and sew it between the soles for fear of intercepting. I, taking the letter, wondering what might be in it, broke it open, and found this treacherous letter subscribed by the hands of Mr Pickering. [This] letter, had it come to your hands without answer, might have caused the hurt if not the ruin of us all [because] assuredly if you had followed their instructions, and showed us that unkindness which they advise you unto – to hold us in distrust as enemies, etc. – it might have been an occasion to have set us together by the ears, to the destruction of us all . . . I do believe that in such case [the Adventurers], knowing what business hath been between us, not only my brother but others also would have been violent and heady against you, etc. I meant to have settled the people [on the *Charity*] . . . with or near you . . . for their as [well as] your more security and defense, as help on all occasions. But I find the Adventurers so jealous and suspicious that I have altered my resolution and given order to my brother and those with him to do as they and himself shall find fit.

The letter which Weston had found concealed in the sole of a shoe was written by Pickering and Greene and addressed to 'Mr Bradford and Mr Brewster etc.'. The following is an extract:

The company hath bought out Mr Weston, and are very glad they are freed of him, he being judged a man that thought himself above the general . . .

> Mr Weston will not permit letters to be sent in his ships, nor anything for your good, or ours, of which there is some reason in respect of himself, etc. His brother Andrew whom he doth send as principal in one of these ships, is a heady young man, and violent, and set against you there. [He is] plotting with Mr Weston their own ends, which tend to your and our undoing in respect of our estates there . . . By credible testimony we are informed his purpose is to come to your Colony, pretending he comes for and from the Adventurers, and will seek to get what you have in readiness into his ships as if they came from the company, and possessing all will be so much profit to himself. And further to inform themselves what special places or things you have . . . that they may . . . deprive you.

There was a brief postscript:

> I pray conceal both the writing and delivery of this letter, but make the best use of it. We hope to set forth a ship ourselves within this month.

Weston continued in his savage tone, adding his comments about this letter from Pickering and Greene.

> To answer in every particular is needless and tedious. My own conscience, and all our people can – and I think will – testify that my end in sending the ship *Sparrow* was your good, etc. Now I will not deny but there are many of our people [who are] rude fellows . . . I am so far from sending rude fellows, to deprive you either by fraud or violence of what is yours, as I have charged the master of the ship *Sparrow* not only to leave you with . . . bread but also a good quantity of fish, etc.
>
> . . . Deal plainly with us, and we will seek our residence elsewhere. If you are as friendly as we have thought you to be, give us the entertainment of friends, and we will take nothing from you, neither meat, drink, nor lodging, but what we will in one kind or another pay you for.

Bradford concluded bitterly that all the Colony's hopes 'in regard of Mr Weston were laid in the dust and all his promised help turned into an empty advice'.

There was also a letter from Cushman, and it had taken so long to have any word from him that Bradford wondered what had been going on. Bradford deduced that Weston was censoring the delivery of letters and this one only got through because it was presented as from a wife to her husband at the Colony. Cushman was now able to describe the return journey of the *Mayflower*:

> Beloved Sir: I heartily salute you, with trust of your health, and many thanks for . . . your love. By God's providence we got well home the 17 of February being robbed by the Frenchmen by the way, carried by them into France . . . were kept there 15 days and lost all that we had that was worth taking, but thanks be to God, we escaped with our lives and ship . . . I purpose by God's grace to see you shortly, I hope in June next, or before.
>
> Mr Weston hath quite broken off from our company, through some discontents that arose betwixt him and some of our adventurers, and hath sold all his adventures, and hath now sent 3 small ships for his particular Plantation.
>
> The people which they carry are no men for us, wherefore I pray you entertain them not, neither exchange man for man with them except it be some of your worst. He hath taken a patent for himself. If they offer to buy anything of you, let it be such as you can spare, and let them give the worth of it. If they borrow anything of you, let them leave a good pawn, etc. It is like [likely] he will plant to the southward of the Cape.
>
> Mr William Trevore [seaman hired to stay for a year] hath lavishly told but what he knew, or imagined of Capawack, Mohegan and the Narragansetts. I fear these people will hardly deal so well with the savages as they should. I pray you therefore signify to Squanto that they are a distinct body from us, and we have nothing to do with them, neither must be blamed for their faults.
>
> We are about to recover our losses in France. Our friends at Leiden are well, and will come to you as many as can this time. I hope all will turn to the best, wherefore I pray you be not dis-

> couraged, but gather up yourself to go through these difficulties cheerfully and with courage in that place wherein God hath set you.
>
> Yours, Robert Cushman

Peirce wrote on the back of this letter. The following is an extract:

> Worthy Sir: As for Mr Weston's company, I think them so base in condition (for the most part) as in all appearance not fit for an honest man's company. I wish they prove otherwise . . .
>
> Your loving friend, John Peirce

The Colony now had even more extra mouths to feed and the new-comers were rude men. The settlers were already very hungry, but the new arrivals wasted what little corn was left by sparing 'not day and night to steal the same, it being then eatable, and pleasant to taste, though green'.[8] They pretended to be helping the settlers, but did not and returned the 'love we showed them with secret backbitings, revilings etc'. They stayed most of the summer. If they were caught stealing they were whipped, but it did not seem to deter them.

News came from one of the English captains fishing off Maine that there had been a massacre at Jamestown. It had happened on 22 March, described as fatal Friday. Jamestown had expanded and many settlers were living a long way from the town. The Indians attacked at 8 a.m. killing approximately 400 people. The effect on Plymouth can only have been profound.

John Pory, who was visiting the Plantation, sent an amazing letter to the treasurer of the Virginia Company of London. He spoke of the 'wholesomeness of the place (as the Governor told me) that for the space of one whole year, or the two wherein they had been there, died not one man, woman or child'. It was accom-panied by these ringing words: 'much plenty of fish and fowl every day in the year, as I know no place in the world can match it'. He spoke of the eels coming forth in abundance in March; in April and May 'come another kind of fish which they call herring . . . in infinite shoals'. And so it went, on through the whole year, with an abundance of fowl and fruit available, too. How then had the Colony been so close to starvation?

At the end of August two ships came into the harbour, the *Sparrow*, having completed her fishing expedition, and the *Discovery* under Captain Jones. Both were headed for Virginia. 'Of captain Jones we furnished ourselves with such provisions as we most needed, and he could best spare . . . and had not the Almighty, in his All-ordering Providence, directed him to us it would have gone worse with us than ever it had been, or after was.'[9] All the Colony had left was a small store of corn for the following year. From Jones they bought a 'store of English beads (which were then good trade) and some knives', but Jones would sell only at dear rates.

The *Charity* returned from Virginia and took the newcomers – or rather those who were fit; the others remained – to their new settlement at Wessagusset (today Weymouth, Massachusetts). It was less than 30 miles away, but the settlers must have been relieved to see them go.

The newcomers suggested a joint expedition involving the shallop and the *Swan* to trade around Cape Cod. A party from the Plantation under Standish was due to go towards the end of September, but he fell ill and Bradford took charge of it, Squanto acting as guide. They could not get through the flats and breakers to the south of Cape Cod and so put into Chatham. There they bought some corn.

> In this place Squanto fell sick of an Indian fever, bleeding much at the nose (which the Indians take for a sympton of death) and within a few days died there, desiring the Governor to pray for him, that he might go to the Englishmen's God in heaven, and bequeathed sundry of this things to sundry of his English friends as remembrances of his love.[10]

In a sense, Squanto's death marked the end of the beginning for the Colony. Whatever personal motives he had had, Squanto welcomed the settlers, guided them, advised them and, crucially, showed them how to sow Indian corn. Without that even these dogged people, these background people, would surely have gone under. The contrast with the new settlement at Wessagusset is very revealing. Here, Bradford's prose is beautifully eloquent about what happened 30 miles away:

> It may be thought strange that these people should fall to [such] extremities in so short a time, being left competently provided when the ship [the *Charity*] left them . . . Much [corn] they got of the Indians. [They] spent excessively whilst they had or could get it, and it may be, wasted part away among the Indians . . . And after they began to come into wants, many sold away their clothes, and bed coverings. Others (so base were they) became servants to the Indians, and would cut them wood and fetch them water for a capful of corn. Others fell to plain stealing, both night and day from the Indians, of which they grievously complained. In the end . . . some starved and died with cold and hunger. One in gathering shellfish was so weak as he stuck fast in the mud, and was found dead in the place. At last most of them left their dwellings. [They] scattered up and down in the woods and by the watersides, where they could find ground nuts and clams, here 6 and there ten. They became [the] scorn of the Indians and they [the Indians] began greatly to insult over them, in a most insolent manner. Insomuch that many times as they . . . had set on a pot with ground nuts, or shellfish, when it was ready the Indians would come and eat it up; and when night came, whereas some of them had a sorry blanket or such like . . . the Indians would take it and let the other lie all night in the cold. Yea in the end they were fain to hang one of their men whom they could not reclaim from stealing to give the Indians content.

Massasoit was ill. Winslow, with a London gentleman called John Hamden – who had spent the winter at Plymouth and wanted to see the countryside – and Hobomok were sent to him. On the way they were told that Massasoit was dead and buried that very day. They kept on and found him alive but very ill and blind. Winslow had a 'confection of many comfortable conserves' – a mixture of fruit – and 'on the point of my knife I gave him some, which I could scarce get through his teeth. When it was dissolved in his mouth he swallowed the juice of it' – the first thing he had swallowed in two days. He had a swollen tongue and his mouth was 'exceedingly furred'. Winslow cleaned it, gave him something to drink and his sight began to come back. Later Winslow made a broth of crushed corn, strawberry leaves and sassafras root, had it boiled, strained it through his handkerchief and gave him that. He enjoyed it.

Winslow took a shot at a couple of ducks 'some six score paces off' and killed one. It was extraordinarily fat and Winslow knew it would not be good for Massasoit's stomach. Massasoit ate it, however, and was violently sick. His nose began to bleed and they all feared he would die. Instead he had a good night's sleep and recovered. Quietly, Massasoit told Hobomok that the Massachusetts tribe were planning to destroy the newcomers' settlement, and the Plantation.

Eventually Standish and an armed party of eight men were dispatched. When they got to the Massachusetts, Standish reacted with brutality. He killed the leader with his own knife, whose point was needle-sharp, and others were hanged. Standish brought the leader's head back to the Plantation and it was put on a pike beside the fort. There would be no more trouble with the Indians for a generation.[11]

Soon after this, Thomas Weston arrived with some fishermen – he was disguised as a blacksmith and was under an assumed name. He had heard of 'the ruin and dissolution of his Colony'. He took a shallop and a couple of men to have a look but ran into a storm, lacked the skill to cope and the shallop went down in the bay between the Merrimack river and Piscataqua, an area to the north of Massachusetts and the south of New Hampshire. Presumably he and the other two swam to the shore:

> And afterwards fell into the hands of the Indians, who pillaged him of all he saved from the sea, and stripped him out of all his clothes to his shirt. At last he got to Piscataqua, and borrowed a suit of clothes, and got means to come to Plymouth. A strange alteration there was in him to such as had seen and known him in his former flourishing condition.
>
> After many passages, and much discourse (former things boiling in his mind) . . . he desired to borrow some beaver [skins]. [He] told them he had hope of a ship and supply to come to him, and then they should have anything for it they stood in need of. They gave little credit to his supply but pitied his case . . . They told him he saw their wants, and they knew not when they should

> have any supply, [and] also how the case stood between them and their adventurers he well knew. They had not much beaver and, if they should let him have it, it were enough to make a mutiny among the people, seeing there was no other means to procure them food which they so much wanted, and clothes also.[12]

In spite of all this they agreed to help him, although they stipulated that it must be done in secret to prevent any chance of mutiny. They let him have 100 beaver skins and he took them to the fishing fleet. It was enough to re-establish him, but he did not change. He proved 'a bitter enemy unto them on all occasions, and never repaid them anything'.[13] In the summer of 1623, a ship called the *Plantation* arrived, and two weeks later another, the *Anne*, and ten days after that a third, the *Little James*, which had endured a storm-ridden crossing. The latter two brought eighty-seven new settlers, twenty-nine of them from Leiden. One was a woman of 'about four score years'. The Brewster children Patience and Fear were on it, and two brides: the younger sister of Standish's wife who had died just after the *Mayflower* arrived. She would marry Standish. The other was a Mrs Alice Southworth, the widow of a silk worker from Sturton-le-Steeple, who would marry Governor Bradford.

Morton recorded:

> These passengers, seeing the low and poor condition of those that were here before them, were much daunted and dismayed, and, according to their divers humors, were diversely affected. Some wished themselves in England again; others fell on weeping, fancying their own misery in what they saw in others; others pitying the distress they saw their friends had been long in and still were under. In a word, all were full of sadness . . . They were in a very low condition, both in respect of food and clothing at that time.[14]

Significantly, perhaps, sixty of the passengers had had their passages paid for by the Adventurers, and that meant they had to pay their way by working for the common good,[15] but some thirty others, who had paid to come over, were free to do what they wanted. They were given plots of land, but not citizenship.

ELEVEN

Descent

John Smith, the mapmaker, described the Plantation in his 1623 book, *General History of Virginia, New England and Summer Islands*. It suggests a settled community, whatever the privations:

> At New-Plimoth there is about 180 persons, some cattle and goats, but many swine and poultry, 32 dwelling houses, whereof 7 were burnt the last winter, and the value of five hundred pounds in other goods; the Town is impaled about half a mile in compass. In the town upon a high Mount they have a fort well built with wood, loam and stone, where is planted their Ordnance: Also a fair Watch-tower, partly framed, for the Sentinel. The place it seems is healthful because in these last three years, notwithstanding their great want of most necessities, there hath not one died of the first planters. They have made a saltwork, and with that salt preserve the fish they take, and this year hath filled [fraughted in the original] a ship of 180 tons.
>
> The Governor is one Master William Bradford; their Captain Myles Standish, a bred soldier in Holland; the chief men for their assistance is Master Isaac Allerton, and divers others as occasion serveth; their preachers are Master William Brewster and Master John Lynford.
>
> The most of them live together as one family or household, yet every man followeth his trade and profession both by sea and land, and all for a general stock out of which they all have their maintenance, until there be a dividend betwixt the planters and the Adventurers.

Despite this settled appearance, it may be that the thirty free men created, or exacerbated, a fundamental tension within the Colony:

should it be a commune or based on private enterprise? Initially, with survival the imperative, they had had to function as a commune and under authoritarian leadership. That is how they erected the perimeter fence in a month. However, the allocation of plots for each family house, with the implication that they would become owners, contradict this. A commune would have erected a large communal dwelling.

The problem of food remained paramount, and the settlers began to think of ways to improve their corn crop. After lengthy debates at a general meeting, when evidently all options were examined, Governor Bradford – having taken advice from the elders – decided that they would abandon the communal approach. He assigned a parcel of land to each family, the size of it determined by how many people were in the family. Any boys and youths without a family were assigned one.

> At length after much debate of things, the Governor (with the advice of the chiefest amongst them) gave way that they should set corn every man for his own particular, and in that regard trust to themselves; in all other things to go on in the general way as before . . . This had very good success . . . it made all hands very industrious, so as much more corn was planted than otherwise would have been by any means . . . The women now went willingly into the field, and took their little ones with them to set corn [whereas] before would allege weakness and inability.
>
> The experience [of] the taking away of property, and bringing in community to a commonwealth would make them happy, and flourishing; as if they were wiser than God . . . was found to breed much confusion, and discontent, and retard much employment. The young men that were most able fit for labor and service did repine that they should spend their time, and strength, to work for other men's wives, and children, without any recompense.[1]

The division of land was for present use, and did not represent an inheritance – it worked. The allocation was carefully recorded and divided according to when the settlers had come, with those from the *Mayflower* getting better ground. The *Mayflower* plots were on the south side of the brook towards the bay and 16 acres 'besides Hobomok's ground which lieth between John Howland's and Hopkins's'. Those from the *Fortune* received plots totalling 15 acres east towards the sea and 19 acres 'beyond the first brook to the wood westward'. Those from the *Anne* received plots 'to the sea eastward . . . beyond the Brook to Strawberry Hill', 13 acres 'butting against the swamp and the reed-pond', more in a corner by the pond, some on the far side of the town towards the Eel river. Allerton got 7 acres, Brewster 6, Bradford and Billington 3, the rest 2 or 1.

Unfortunately, they had a six-week drought which threatened to destroy the corn. Then clouds gathered and the next morning 'soft, sweet and moderate showers of rain'[3] began to fall. It was hard to say which it revived quicker, the corn or the spirits of the settlers. The idea of the settlers taking responsibility for their own corn proved such a success that in future hunger was no longer a concern.

Another factor was livestock. Emmanuel Altham, writing to his brother Sir Edward Altham, says 'here is belonging to the town six goats, about fifty hogs and pigs, also divers hens'. This is the first reference to livestock, and how they got there is unknown. However, in 1604, the following year, the *Charity* arrived again, bearing Edward Winslow – who had returned to England – and, in Bradford's words, three heifers and a bull, the 'first beginning of any cattle of that kind in the land'.

The little Colony, still precarious, had assumed a life and character of its own and each passing day took it further away from England. Perhaps it was just as well. King James had had visions of becoming Europe's peacemaker. He married his daughter Elizabeth to a Protestant, Frederick V of Bohemia, in 1614 and hoped to marry his son Charles to the Catholic King of Spain's daughter. His plan provoked outrage in England, so Charles's marriage did not happen. James died in 1625 and Charles succeeded him and married another Catholic, Henrietta Maria. The new king was an Arminian – against predetermination by God – and Arminians said they were the only real Church of England. They called the rest 'puritains' and 'drove the conforming majority into opposition'.[4]

In the background, by 1627 the Colony had a herd of seventeen cattle. That year, everything changed. Isaac Allerton had been dispatched to England to sort out finances with the Adventurers. Allerton agreed that the Colony would buy the Adventurers out for £1,800, to be paid at £200 a year. The first instalment was due in September the following year. In fact, eight men in the Colony and four Adventurers who wanted to stay involved took responsibility for the whole debt 'in return for certain monopolies',[5] such as buying and selling fur. Effectively, the population of the Plantation now owned it, and would do so legally when the debt was paid.

Possibly because these men – known as Undertakers for what they had undertaken – now had a heavy and vested interest in the Colony making money, a general division of property and land was agreed. Bradford and '4 or 5 special men' were given the houses they lived in and every other household was valued. Land was given at 20 acres per person, 'five in breadth and four in length'. The common ownership of livestock ended; it, too, was divided.

The first lot went to Francis Cooke, his wife and eleven others: '4 black heifers and two she goats'. The second lot went to Isaac Allerton, his wife and eleven others: 'the Great Black cow came in the *Anne* to which they must keep the lesser of the two steers, and two she goats'. And so it went for twelve lots. The last of them read: 'to this lot fell the great white-backed cow which was brought over with the first on the *Anne*, to which cow the keeping of the bull was joined for these persons to provide for. Here also two she goats.'

The character of the Colony had formed itself. As Streeton points out, the Colony had been self-governing, had with the Compact given itself a version of democracy which England would not have for 'several centuries', and if the original Leiden group had planned a 'church-state'[6] the number and pressure of the inhabitants who were not Separatists had made that impossible. There was, however, one problem which could not be overcome. The Plantation was in the wrong place.

If it appeared settled to John Smith, it appeared no less so to Isaac de Rasieres, who was Secretary of the Dutch Colony of New Amsterdam – which ultimately became New York. De Rasieres, in a letter written in 1628, described what he had seen when he visited the Plantation in, it seems, late 1627. His account is both valuable and a classic. It is worth quoting at length:

> New Plymouth lies in a large bay to the north of Cape Cod . . . east and west from the said point of the cape, which can be easily seen in clear weather. Directly before the . . . town lies a sand-bank, about twenty paces broad, whereon the sea breaks violently with an easterly and east-northeasterly wind. On the north side there lies a small island where one must run close along, in order to come before the town.

Bradford told de Rasieres the bay was so full of fish that when the population wanted some, two or three people went out in a small boat and could catch enough for everyone for a day in a couple of hours:

> At the south side of the town there flows down a small river of fresh water, very rapid, but shallow, which takes its rise from several lakes in the land above, and there empties into the sea; where in April and the beginning of May, there come so many shad from the sea which want to ascend that river, that it is quite surprising. This river the English have shut in with planks, and in the middle with a little door, which slides up and down, and at the sides with trellis work, through which the water has its course, but which they can also close with slides.
>
> At the mouth they have constructed it with planks, like an eelpot, with wings, where in the middle is also a sliding door, and with trellis work at the sides, so that between the two dams there is a square pool into which the fish aforesaid come swimming in such shoals, in order to get up above, where they deposit their spawn, that at one tide there are 10,000 to 12,000 fish in it, which they shut off in the rear at the ebb, and close up the trellises above, so that no more water comes in; then the water runs out through the lower trellises, and they draw out the fish with baskets, each according to the land he cultivates, and carry them to it, depositing in each hill three or four fishes, and in these they plant their maize, which grows as luxuriantly therein as though it were the best manure in the world.

They had learned this, of course, from the Indians. De Rasieres then goes on to describe the physical appearance of the Plantation which, he estimated, contained about fifty families:

> New Plymouth lies on the slope of a hill stretching east towards the sea-coast, with a broad street about a cannon shot of 800 feet long, leading down the hill, with a crossing in the middle . . . The houses are constructed of clapboards, with gardens also enclosed behind and at the sides with clapboards, so that their houses and courtyards are arranged in very good order, with a stockade against sudden attack; and at the ends of the streets there are three wooden gates. In the center, on the cross street, stands the Governor's house, before which is a square stockade upon which four patereros [small cannon] are mounted, so as to enfilade [cover] the streets. Upon the hill they have a large square house, with a flat roof, built of thick sawn planks stayed with oak beams, upon the top of which they have six cannon, which shoot iron balls of four and five pounds, and command the surrounding country.
>
> The lower part they use for their church, where they preach on Sundays and the usual holidays. They assemble by beat of drum, each with his musket or firelock, in front of the captain's door; they have their cloaks on, and place themselves in order, three abreast, and are led by sergeant without beat of drum. Behind comes the Governor, in a long robe; beside him on the right hand, comes the preacher with his cloak on, and on the left hand, the captain with his side-arms and cloak on, and with a small cane in his hand; and so they march in good order, and each sets his arms down near him. Thus they are constantly on their guard night and day.

They could not isolate themselves, and although Bradford secured a new patent in 1630, so that the Colony could make its own laws provided they were not in conflict with English law,[7] external forces were coming in to play. As the population expanded they began to move out and establish small towns; and, more than that, other migrants were coming – from the same Boston in Lincolnshire where the Scrooby group had been in prison.

Local historian John Cammack says that 'Boston's population was a little under 3,000: it is estimated that about 10% – over 250 – sailed in the 1630s to Boston, Massachusetts, and that included many of its principal citizens.' They provided governors or deputy governors sixty times in the Colony's first sixty-two years.

This Boston migration brought with it the divisions of England. They were Puritans, who of course wanted to 'purify' the Church of England from within, rather than the Separatists at the Plantation who 'felt that their only option was to separate' from it.

Cammack points out that the Plantation people will 'always have the worldwide reputation as the romantic founders of America. Their image remains untainted unlike the Puritans who followed them 10 years later.' However, they did not found the first English settlement on the North American mainland. Jamestown, Virginia was founded in 1607, and the men there are described by Alistair Cooke[8] as 'commanded by a few sea captains and relatives of the backers, but most of them were ordinary sailors, footloose bachelors, adventurers, poor farmers, slum people, the odd gentleman, and some convicts'.

The Leiden group were quite different. Taking their women and children, 'their intention was to leave England for good'. The new Plymouth was the first English settlement where all were committed to stay for life but, as Cooke says, they were not the people who would 'secure Puritan New England. Left to themselves, they . . . would probably have remained the lonely inhabitants of a trading station and fishing stations. The men were still in England – the Bostonians – who would make the radical departure, first from the Church of England and then from the government of England.'

Boston had a harbour and the Bay Colony there would soon be the power centre of the New World, extending its influence down to the Plymouth Colony. Founded by John Winthrop of Suffolk, who has been described as 'the first great American', he constructed 'the most remarkable of the English colonies and the establishment of a truly new society in the New World'. Between 1629 and 1640, King Charles ruled without Parliament in what was known as the Eleven Years' Tyranny, and in that period as many as 20,000 Puritans may have fled to Massachusetts Bay. Crucially, the newcomers seem to have brought goods that were not being made in the New World, while the Colony was abundant enough to welcome them without undue strain.[9] With its poor soil and difficulty of access – for ships loading and unloading – Plymouth could never grow to rival Boston and worse, as the towns around came to life, it began to weaken.

The 1630s were a time of transatlantic movement. The English founded Maryland in 1635 and three years later Swedes were found in Delaware Bay, on what the Dutch claimed was their territory. Roger Williams, a preacher who had met *his* big idea in Cambridge – absolute separation of Church and state – was too much even for Bradford and was banished. He went on to found Rhode Island.

By now, the expansion of the Massachusetts Bay Colony was bringing the towns around Plymouth to life. In the 1630s, men from Massachusetts founded Sandwich, Barnstable and Yarmouth on Cape Cod. Others forged inland and founded Taunton. London adventurers established a settlement at Scitutate, midway between Boston and Plymouth.

The 1630s were also a time of dissipation for the Plantation itself, created paradoxically by the fact that it was now standing on its feet, functioning properly and could have been considered comfortably off. The paradox was that it 'began to spread with the demand for more land to be tilled'.[10] A new charter, in 1630, reflected this by giving the Colony much more land and some leading figures moved out to farm it. Standish and others – including John Alden and Brewster's son – founded Duxbury and set up their own church there. The dissipation was so pronounced that simply meeting in the Plantation and deciding what to do would not suffice, so a broader agreement was drawn up, superseded later by a general court, consisting of five men from the Plantation and two from each town within the Colony.

In 1642 the debts were paid, but by then the English Civil War had begun, bringing with it a second Reformation. Charles I had tried to suppress Puritanism. Oliver Cromwell, whose parents were Puritans, did not become a religious man until he was nearing thirty. A brilliant military commander, he defeated Charles's forces and came to regard himself as the enforcer of the Reformation, although legislation extended tolerance to the full spectrum of Protestant groups, however minor.[11]

The Civil War staunched the flow of immigrants. That meant Plymouth could not earn money from feeding them while they found their feet. Prices collapsed.

On top of this, Brewster died in 1643:

> His sickness was not long, and til the last day thereof he did not wholly keep [to] his bed. His speech continued til somewhat more than half a day, and then failed him, and about 9 or 10 o'clock that evening he died, without any pangs at all. A few hours before, he drew his breath short, and some few minutes before his last, he drew his breath long, as a man fallen into a sound sleep, without any pangs or gaspings, and so sweetly departed this life, unto a better.[12]

The Colony had a 'long argument with a new minister about the rites of baptism, drunkenness was appearing and sexual offences and deviations'.[13]

A year later after Brewster's death, so many people had left the Plantation that the church seriously considered moving somewhere else, but it stayed. 'And thus was this poor church left, like an ancient mother, grown old and forsaken of her children (though not in her affections) yet in regard of their bodily presence . . . her ancient members being worn away by death . . . and she like a widow left only to trust in God. Thus she that had made many rich, became herself poor.'

The Civil War produced, psychologically and physically, a sense that all the colonists in the New World were on their own and four colonies – Massachusetts, Plymouth, Connecticut and New Haven – signed Articles of Confederation. Bradford quotes the wonderful introduction and it is worth reproducing in full:

> Whereas we all came into these parts of America, with one and the same end, and aim; namely to advance the kingdom of our Lord Jesus Christ, and to enjoy the Liberties of the Gospel, in purity with peace. And whereas in our settling (by a wise Providence of God) we are further dispersed upon the sea coasts, and rivers, than was at first intended, so that we cannot according to our desires, with conveniency communicate in one government, and jurisdiction. And whereas we live encompassed with people of several nations, and strange languages, which hereafter may prove injurious to us, and our posterity; and forasmuch as the natives have formerly committed sundry insolencies, and outrages upon

several plantations of the English; and have of late combined themselves against us; and seeing by reason of those distractions in England (which they have heard of) and by which they know we are hindered, from that humble way of seeking advice, or reaping those comfortable fruits of protection, which at other times we might well expect; we therefore do conceive it our bounden duty, without delay to enter into a present consociation amongst ourselves for mutual help and strength in all our future concernments. That as in nation, and religion, so in other respects we be, and continue one according to the tenor, and true meaning of the ensuing articles.[14]

There were twelve articles, allowing each Colony to retain its own jurisdiction but giving them all mutual defence, and 'for the managing and concluding of all affairs proper' each of the four would elect two Commissioners 'which shall bring full power from their several courts . . . to hear, examine, weigh and determine all affairs of war, or peace, leagues, aids, charges, and numbers of men for war, divisions of spoils . . . receiving of more Confederates, or plantations into combination, with any of the Confederates, and all things of like nature, which are the proper consequences of such a Confederation, for amity, offense, and defense'.[15]

Plymouth was settling into the background. Standish of the fiery temperament died in 1656, at Duxbury on the other side of Plymouth Bay. A year later Bradford himself had passed away. He was sixty-seven. He had shaped the Colony and borne its burdens; and ultimately been repaid. The fur trade had been good to him; he had silver and Venetian glass on his table, an extensive library and a 300-acre farm, with orchards and gardens.[16]

Charles II was restored to the throne in 1660 and Plymouth sent off a declaration of loyalty, but the Colony refused a royal charter in case a governor was imposed on it. Charles busied himself with colonising New England further; there would be an Indian war when Massasoit died in 1661 – Massasoit's son Philip did not like the English; there would be the tricky matter of Plymouth being drawn into the Dominion of New England and therefore under the royal governor, albeit at Boston; there would be the problem of

James II fleeing England as William of Orange arrived, and Plymouth decided it wanted a royal charter. Meanwhile, the big boys of New York and the Massachusetts Bay Colony cast covetous eyes on Plymouth.

In 1685 the Colony divided itself into three counties, Plymouth, Barnstable and Bristol, and by then it comprised seventeen towns. Plymouth finally merged with the Massachusetts Bay Colony in 1691, and by then its people would have 'become totally absorbed' into the Bay Colony's 'worldly surroundings and culture'.[17] On 7 October 1691 a new Massachusetts charter, incorporating the three counties which the Plymouth Colony embraced, was signed in London. Early the next year the court at Massachusetts issued orders obliging the Plymouth counties to send representatives to the Massachusetts Assembly. The old Colony melted into the general story of America.

TWELVE

Common Ground

Myths stalk the land, and probably always will. It seems to be a necessary condition for nationhood. There is a striking line in one of John Le Carré's novels[1] about a country needing something *real*. 'Know what that is, boy? Illusions. Kings and Queens. The Kennedys, de Gaulle, Napoleon.'

The myths have to be simple, to reassure and to give identity. In that sense they are as important as historical facts and possess a different power: they do not exist by themselves – as, say, a battle or a coronation does – but answer a need. In the context of the *Mayflower* and the Compact today, the myths will lead to a sequence of paradoxes.

We have already met one, Thanksgiving. Originally a Dutch tradition, the Leiden settlers adopted it (the Dutch celebrated it to thank God for keeping the Spaniards at bay). The settlers held Thanksgiving after their first harvest but did not call it that and did not do so on an annual basis afterwards.[2] More likely they held a day of fasting and prayer, in keeping with their character. They did at least have turkey.

The first Thanksgiving in the Massachusetts Bay Colony was in 1630 and the first for the United States in 1777; it stopped in the early nineteenth century but Abraham Lincoln reinstated it in 1863 and Roosevelt cemented it as the fourth Thursday in November in 1941.

Here is another paradox. Apart from the Introduction, you have rarely read the phrase Pilgrim Fathers, although it has a very great resonance as well as being highly evocative. It is true that Bradford used the words 'they knew they were pilgrims' to describe their departure from Holland, but he did not use it again (except in a poem). They certainly did not call themselves Pilgrim Fathers but used a variety of other names: Saints, Strangers, Old Comers and

Old Planters, Planters, and later Forefathers.[3] The myth simplifies this to *only* the Pilgrim Fathers, a term used much later.

The reality is that nobody can agree on who the Pilgrim Fathers actually were. For ease, you could say all the passengers on the *Mayflower*, but that would include the Strangers who went for commercial reasons. They were not pilgrims and would have been shocked to be regarded as such. One authority[4] has mused that even if you confine it to the people who had been at Leiden you encounter problems: William Ring from Leiden was due to go on the *Speedwell*, did not and returned to Holland. Would he be a Pilgrim Father? John Alden, who was not from Leiden, did go on the *Mayflower*. More than that, what about the Leiden people who followed in 1630? The only answer is to say that the myth is enough.

Here is a further paradox. There is something comforting in the notion of paternal people in tall hats, held by deep convictions, riding the ferocity of an ocean and creating with their bare hands a country of great liberty; and sometimes it is presented so; but they were bigots – interesting, brave, decent, dogged, resourceful, held by their convictions – but bigots all the same. What they wanted was the obverse of freedom: their particular form of bigotry would reign absolute behind the palisade they would build. You only have to look at Bradford's petulant and narrow reaction to the non-religious part of the community when they wanted to celebrate Christmas and play ball games. Nor can we reasonably say that, given the chance, they would not have imposed it everywhere. There seems no doubt that sooner or later they either converted the non-religious or obliged them to conform. In 1624 the Revd John Lydford – a recent settler who inclined towards the Church of England – had enraged the community by baptising a baby with the sign of the cross. He may even have been plotting to take over the Plantation with an Adventurer, John Oldham. Both were expelled.

The *Mayflower* Compact does not fall into the category of paradox, because, despite the almost academic controversy about who signed it and in what order, there clearly was a document freely signed so that people could govern themselves. This must have been an extraordinary mental step, because none of the people signing can ever have experienced such a state of living, and perhaps never imagined it either. The rulers of England, absolute and all-powerful and never elected, had held sway since before the Saxons. No passenger on the *Mayflower*, nor any of their ancestors, had ever known what – within perhaps an hour of signing – would be reality when they waded ashore. They would make and enforce their own laws without, in practical terms, reference to anyone else.

What seems even more important is that the original consensus held and self-government functioned. The background people made it work. You can read a great deal into that and, at its fundamental, it is the same message on the Statue of Liberty further south, where the *Mayflower* ought to have gone: *send me your huddled masses, yearning to be free*. The flotsam and jetsam rejected by one society can make something mighty when they are released, like prisoners from a prison. I write these words when the United States is spending as much on defence as the next fifteen countries put together. As Alistair Cooke said, looking over Ellis Island where they tramped through with their little bundles: 'It's amazing how many of them made it – and are still making it.'

The Compact has its own mythology, but what – if anything – does it mean today and what happened to it since its signing in 1620?

In his majestic survey of United States history,[5] Hugh Brogan says the Compact was 'unconsciously but exactly followed' first in New England and then more broadly, in the frontier states of Texas, California, Iowa and Oregon. The model proved sturdy, giving generations of settlers a feeling that they were safe under the law and they 'conditioned American political assumptions'.

I want to broaden and deepen that.

'In the beginning, all the world was like America.' Professor Robert Bliss is quoting the English philosopher John Locke (1623–1704), who wrote about civil government, and I have used the words to open the way for the broadening and deepening. Professor Bliss is the Dean of Pierre Laclede Honors College at the University of Missouri-St Louis, taught American studies at Lancaster University in England and is an expert on the history of New England.

Like America? He means that once upon a time, there were no rules or structures anywhere. Professor Bliss points out that another

English philosopher, Thomas Hobbes (1588–1679), thought that such conditions would

> produce bloodshed, mayhem, violence and so on. Locke, who refers to the American experience when he was talking about his compact theories, thought that human beings can get together and peacefully sort this out.
>
> Most interpretations of the *Mayflower* Compact get it more or less wrong, although never entirely wrong, by stressing only its religious aims, its 'democratic' aims, or its contributions to the growth of 'American democracy' and/or 'American constitutionalism.' It may now be pointless to argue that these views are wrong – they are very deeply embedded, after all – but it may be useful to point out some other matters which can place the Compact in a seventeenth-century context. That, after all, is the context in which those compacters lived and breathed.
>
> The sociology of compacting is interesting, and was very interesting to near contemporaries – humble and more exalted, Puritan and non-Puritan, ordinary and more intellectual. I have no evidence that Hobbes was influenced by New England covenanting or compacting [their meaning is essentially the same], but he was certainly influenced by the chaos in Virginia.
>
> Examining Locke's 'in the beginning all the world was like America,' and what he might have meant, can help us figure the Pilgrims out, too. I taught at Lancaster University for 27 years, and each year had some luck with likening this compacting sociology seventeenth-century style to the practical problems Lancaster students faced – as strangers to one another, more or less equals to one another, and certainly previously free of one another – in organizing their living arrangements in their residential kitchens of 6, or 10, or in one college 20.
>
> In the situation many colonists found themselves in, compacting quite simply made sense. [It made sense when] the Plymouth people, on shipboard, drew up and signed the Compact, but it was not only done by them. In every New England town I have looked at, whether in Massachusetts, which had a charter and didn't need this to happen, or in say Exeter, New Hampshire

which was outside the charter, all these people did sit down and at the very least they fashioned a church covenant. I think more often than not – although I can't know this, it's my educated guess – they had a secular covenant.

If you move a whole social order from one place to another – aristocrats, gentry, yeomen, and servants, men and women and children, and so on – compacting seems an unlikely development because the means of keeping order are embedded in the transported social structure. So, for instance, in Virginia compacting was RARE partly because 90 per cent of the early migrants were young servants and 10 per cent were older masters.

It was likewise pretty much in Barbados and the Leeward Islands. Things could, and did, go wrong with this, and we find examples of what might be called pseudo-covenanting, but that came under the political and economic stresses of the English civil war, perhaps when the master class began to think it might need some local assent to stay in place.

Conversely, if you had a migration where the migrants were pretty much equal to one another and pretty much previously free of one another, then deciding on quite simple things – where does my house go? where does your house go? – becomes rather difficult: *who do you think you are, anyway, telling me that my house is over there in the swamp while yours is over here on the meadow?*

You have to have someone to adjudicate on that and a million other things. Throughout the colonists' letters, and often sermons and speeches during the seventeenth century and beyond, there is this vast and howling wilderness. That's how they refer to the Americas. We now know that it wasn't quite so howling and it wasn't quite so vast but they didn't know that. There is nothing laid on. They had to decide where the lane was going to be, where the fences were going to be, where the stream was to be forded and maybe eventually a bridge.

Hobbes confronted this state of nature and posited that fear and simple self-preservation would lead me, for instance, to say, *you'd better run the show because otherwise we will all be dead in a fairly nasty, brutish, and short time*. Locke was a little more sanguine because he had a somewhat sunnier idea about human nature. I think the Pilgrims and Puritans of New England did, too, at least if the human nature in question looked to them to be religiously safe, sage, and orthodox. So they tended to make covenant, most famously in the *Mayflower* Compact but also in a very great many towns and churches in New Haven, Connecticut, Rhode Island, Plymouth, and Massachusetts.

That kind of basic social agreement – as in, *well, we had better get on with this, and the best way to do it is to agree to do it* – was not easy to come to, and for many of the migrants it seemed frankly second best to some kind of command line structure, but it tended to be a common denominator solution to a set of quite practical difficulties. I think they found it pretty intoxicating.

(Daniel J. Boorstin argues[6] that the 'lawmakers' of the Massachusetts Bay Colony 'to the extent their knowledge allowed and with only minor exceptions, actually followed English example. Their colonial situation made them wary of trying to create institutions according to their own notions, and alert to the need of adapting old institutions to new conditions.')

There is a further fascinating aspect. Professor Bliss continues:

As in the Chesapeake[7] and West Indian colonies, this was not fool-proof or event-proof. Under the spur of dissent and challenges to clerical authority, Massachusetts quickly defined an orthodoxy. To be included in it, people had to qualify and, outside of it, people could be told what to do and believe, or what not to do and not believe. They were not parties to the compact.

In this regard, the *Mayflower* Compact certainly did NOT include all on shipboard – women and children, common sailors and perhaps others. That needs to be considered even though it would have been nearly impossible [in that era] for them to be included. So a compact is two things: a way to establish a governing ethos and a structure within the charmed circle of consent – those who sign up and are allowed to sign up; and to give government to those outside the charmed circle who are not even allowed to say whether they consent or not.

> This is very important, because freedom and equality have been hotly contested ground throughout American history. We can say 'covenanting' or 'compacting' became important parts of the American tradition – for example the federal and state constitutions at the time of the Revolution – but, all the way through that tradition up to the present, who is 'in' and who is 'out' of the charmed circle have been very serious questions: serious enough at some times that we have shed each other's blood over them.
>
> The compacts, in a sense, stand by themselves. They were written down and they were signed – people put their signatures. That says something very illuminating about the migration, that they were literate: unusually literate. That again created problems of authority. You didn't have a small minority of people who could read telling a large majority of illiterates what the Bible says. What can you do: establish effective means of coercion or is it more *politik* to sit down and have a few years' argument and come up with an agreement?

Nobody had years to spare, and certainly not the passengers on the *Mayflower* eyeing Provincetown Harbour a couple of hundred yards away, or less.

These days, Provincetown is a chic place of sexual liberation. You can see men holding hands quite openly, which would have had an impact on such as Bradford and Brewster. It is an expensive place which attracts artists and authors. The roads are cramped and mildly chaotic and they might belong to an English town on the genteel south coast. You can lose yourself among the antique shops and the places selling art which does not quite look like art.

There is the Pilgrim Monument on a hilltop, an obelisk 252ft high (and 116 steps, not counting ramps, if you want to walk up). Plans for building it were set out in 1901 by J. Henry Sears of the Pilgrim Club of Brewster, Massachusetts. He said: 'here in this harbor was the first landing made, the first prayers said, the Compact – that immortal charter of civil liberty – drawn and signed. Here the first white child saw the light and breathed New England air. Here in this soil lie buried the first of the Pilgrims to succumb to the hardships of their journey. Here on Cape Cod the Pilgrims drank their first draught of sweet New England water; here they met their earliest adventures while exploring the country to find a place of permanent settlement.'[8] The obelisk was completed in 1910. At 252ft (and 7.5in) you cannot miss it, and you are not intended to. It says, *yes, we know all about Plimoth/Plymouth but it began here.* As Laurel Guadazno of the Museum says: 'A group of Cape Codders got tired of Plymouth getting all the attention as the landing place of the *Mayflower* Pilgrims. They wanted the tower to be tall because at that time all traffic was on the ocean and if you went between Boston and New York, or points further south than New York, you had to come around the tip of the Cape. And it is up on the highest hill in town, which is itself about 100 feet up. They knew you would have to see the tower. Mariners say you can see it twenty miles out to sea . . .'

The Provincetown Museum, next to the Monument, is a busy, bustling, friendly place[9] full of artefacts charting the town's history. 'It has exhibits on famous people who lived in town, whaling because this was the third largest whaling port after Nantucket and New Bedford. You can almost think of it as an attic. These are things that Provincetown people wanted saved', Mrs Guadazno says. 'We have nothing from the *Mayflower* – nobody does. There's a place in Plymouth called Pilgrim Hall and they used to say they had a chair which belonged to Bradford, or one of them. As it turns out, when the wood was analysed it was made from trees that never grew in England. There is nothing.'

So the Museum has re-created exhibits about the Pilgrims, including an evocative video.

> We have about 80,000 visitors a year. Many of them just want to climb the Pilgrim Monument. We have done surveys and the visitors are from all over the world. It's incredible. The majority are from the Massachusetts area because they can drive down for a weekend but we have put out guest books and they are from all over. We've had our information translated into Russian because we've had so many Russians. Why so many? Who knows? People come to Boston, they make a little trip down to the Cape and

> often they don't know what they're getting into or where they're coming. They see the tower and they come to visit. Most Americans don't know the Pilgrim Fathers landed here. It's not taught in our schools. People frequently come up to us and say, *how come they didn't teach us this?*

Professor Bliss supplies part of the answer when he talks about

> a move afoot to bring documents back into the classroom. There's a large Federally funded project in West Virginia which is dealing with schoolteachers from grades 4 through 12, which is 9 years old through 18. I am the consultant for the colonial revolutionary period. One of the things I had to bring to the students' attention is the covenants – not just the *Mayflower* Compact but the Boston, the Charleston, the Exeter–New Hampshire and so forth. They are wonderful teaching devices, they are good documents and they are very interesting documents. Most American children are aware of the *Mayflower* in a misty sort of way. It's one of those things where people say, *oh, yes, I know something about that* without knowing very much at all.

On Cape Cod, because of conservation orders preventing building (President Kennedy, of Hyannisport down the coast, was a moving force) the pines and oaks which the Pilgrims knew are coming back and the area is beginning to look as they might have seen it. In Colonial times the area was a wood-based economy and swathes were cut down, but finally it is returning to its natural state. And what the Pilgrims did see were sand dunes flowing quickly into woodland, bushes and undergrowth – blueberry bushes and so on – of a density that a man could lose himself in 50 yards. 'It's difficult to push your way through because it's low and brushy and shrubby. And there are lots of marshes, so your feet would be constantly wet.'

There are well-marked Pilgrim trails and while the woodland is not overtly hostile, Indians could conceal themselves in the density easily; nor could the Pilgrims move without making a noise, and making themselves vulnerable. Every moment in the woods must have been nervous and uncertain, every footfall on a dry twig a giveaway, every fluttering of wings by a startled bird a moment of alarm, not least to hungry and thirsty men.

Nobody knows where the little pond is which gave them their first water, although Mrs Guadazno insists one candidate fits the description perfectly and, by deduction, is in the sort of place it would have been. It is no more than a small grassy clearing in the woodland a mile or two south of Provincetown: the water gurgles into a pond so low that you would have to sink onto your knees and stoop with cupped hands to get any; but there it is, cool, fresh water. *Because* there is nothing here except the woodland, the grass and the pool – nothing man-made – it is very easy to see them coming upon it, standing shoulder to shoulder on the grass, the first of them maybe taking his hat off and sinking to his knees, cupped hands outstretched.

From Provincetown to the town of Plymouth is a pleasant drive, and short by North American standards: a meandering, undulating country road with pleasant houses and gardens on either side, shops, restaurants flaunting seafood, motels. If you have ever seen a film of suburban America you have been there.

It must have seemed a long way to the Pilgrims, on foot in the woodland; a long way in their rowing boat or their shallop, too, when the calm of the Bay became angry with storms. The whole country, its contours and dimensions and scale, were concealed from them by the woodlands; and even the small part of it they were coming to know seemed big.

At Plymouth, there is a small segment of parkland: grass, some trees and a portico along the path by this. The stone is under the portico, so low that you have to gaze down, and it is protected by wrought-iron fencing. The stone is called Plymouth Rock

There is a descriptive signboard nearby, charting the story of the Rock, and it has many familiar caveats. Nobody can truly know if this is *the* Rock which was identified, in 1741, as the one on which the first of the *Mayflower* group stepped as they prepared to make Plymouth their permanent home: what would have been the most famous first-footing of all. The man who identified it was 95-year-old Thomas Faunce, the son of a first-comer to Plymouth. That was John, who came over on the *Anne* in 1623.

The story goes that Thomas was driven in an open wagon to the place where the Rock was and said that eight of the original passengers had assured him this was it. The signboard is more equivocal, saying that the Rock has been moved several times and bits of it have broken off. For example, in 1774 an attempt was made to haul it to the town square using oxen, but that only succeeded in splitting it. The top half was eventually taken to the town and the bottom half left where it lay. The two were rejoined in 1880.

The Rock may be regarded as a stepping stone, if you can put it like that, in two distinct directions: as maybe where the very first footfall fell or as the myth of that. Authenticity has a strength of its own, but in this case the mythology is very, very strong, too. You can watch young Americans come to it and see how much of the Anglo-Saxon diffidence and awkwardness they have inherited when they are confronted by a profundity like this. They fool around as they take their pictures, they make their little jokes. Now watch their eyes and you can see them saying to themselves, *this is where it really did begin.*

Plimoth Plantation, a couple of miles from the Rock, is a further paradox. It is both an unashamed re-creation and in the wrong place but it looks, feels, sounds and smells *right.*

The town of Plymouth is nothing like that because it can no longer be. The exact place of the original Plantation is a street lined with modern houses, and no sense of palisade, fort on the hill or timbered dwellings remains; and even what you are looking at is slightly deceptive because Leyden Street is widely held to be the Plantation's location, but, as the *Plymouth Guide*[10] notes, 'the Pilgrims' first houses were on First St not Leyden St: Plots allocated to the early settlers sloped to Town Brook.' The Brook still runs, but through a manicured park.

Plimoth Plantation resembles a theme park. The entrance, from a broad car park, has steps and a pathway leading to a modern building which sells tickets, has an extensive souvenir shop (you would be amazed at the ingenuity of attaching *Mayflower* association to such a variety of objects – or maybe you would not), and a cafeteria.

Beyond the building a path rises to The Crafts Center where artisans use seventeenth-century tools to make seventeenth-century household objects. That somehow prepares the visitor for the Pilgrim Village a little walk further on.

As I reached towards it, a man and two women in period costume worked in a field. They were doing this methodically, the man hoeing, the women on the ground weeding or sowing. You were, all at once, in 1627, the year selected for the Village. By then there is enough documentary evidence to make the reconstruction authentic and the whole Plymouth Colony was still contained within it.

You go into the Village through a gate in the palisade, a fence of vertical planks about 10ft tall, each shaped into an arrowhead at its tip to cut into any Indian (or anybody else) trying to clamber over. The planks are rough-cut, as they would have been, because the palisade needed to be erected quickly.

The fort with its cannon is a strong, almost squat building of heavy planking on the hill overlooking the cluster of houses, some thatched. They face each other across what is known as The Street, and they are arranged owner by owner as they were. You can go inside them. They are cramped, dark and basic.

That is a word that keeps coming back: the original Pilgrims had only what they had been able to bring or what they could make. It is very easy to forget that of all the myriad things you need to live, eat and run a household – sheets, pillows, curtains, rope, cloth, pins, needles, buttons, pots, pans, knives, spoons, ladles, plates, candles, matches, shoes, clothing, laces, thimbles, scissors, needles, soap; before you think about garden implements: hoes, rakes, trowels, sacks, bags, buckets; before you think about tools: hinges, nails, bolts, hammers, chisels, cramps, vices; before you think about defence: guns, gunpowder, bullets – if they had not brought it and could not make it they would have to do without.

They must have shared a great deal, but that can only have eased the basic hardship a little. Each house is but a single room, the bed against one wall and screened off by a curtain, a table in the middle with perhaps a solitary chair for the master of the house, the open fire in a corner with a cauldron suspended above it; perhaps a single shelf. Standing on the rough unmade floors, you feel a sense of 1627; feel the unbearable heat of summer's fetid night air, hear the winds of winter off the ocean moaning and screaming at the wooden cladding.

The staff wear period costumes and, just like in the field, the work they do – in their tiny gardens, or working on the houses – is exactly as it would have been. Each has the identity of an original Pilgrim and each is encouraged to speak in the accent of where their character came from in England. They use seventeenth-century vocabulary, of course. You might think this is American artificiality at its worst. Wrong. It is American artificiality at its best, and as well as anybody anywhere does it.

In one house, a man explains to a young school party about bread-making. They look a bit bored, the way kids on trips can be, but then something wonderful happens. He relates the bread of 1627 to the bread they eat, and draws them in like that, and he's holding a chunk from 1627 explaining the similarities and differences, and the kids are all attention, eyes almost sparkling.

I stopped a young woman in a bright blue costume and asked a modern-day question: do the staff get to choose their own costumes? 'No,' she said, in a near-olde-English accent and fixing me with a direct gaze, 'Master Allerton gets them and we have the ones we are given.' I wondered how close to the original site the Village was, but she said 'it is a young village. My husband started work on it seven years ago, in 1620.' She did not blush, feel awkward or look away.

Down the path beside the Eel River Pond there is Hobomok's homesite, with his winter and summer dwellings and a vegetable garden.[11] Wampanoag women are here, and a mother cooks lunch for her two children on an open fire: a fish gruel served in crude bowls from a big, simmering pot. The children liked it a lot.

The contrast between this family living in a clearing and the Village with its two rows of houses was striking enough, but, more than that, there was a sense that the very beginnings of an immense future were being carved out up there; down here nothing was happening except what had always happened.

In the cafeteria, I took a coffee and asked the young lady serving if they accepted English money. She looked mildly incredulous that anyone would ask if they could pay with some unknown *foreign* coins. 'No – American.'

'Well,' I said, 'you certainly used to.'

She did not get it, nor did she know why I was smiling; the spell of the proximity was broken.

It is very difficult for an Englishman to stand in Plimoth Plantation in what was a corner of England and see it all with a steady eye. It is difficult because England is so full of history. I live in a village where manorial rights on the green were transferred to the local council by King Henry IV on 13 February 1448, which would have been a long time ago even to the Pilgrims. The past is part of the backdrop to everyday life. I jog in the mornings across a field where there was a Saxon settlement – its contours can only be discerned from the air and I had no idea it was there until someone told me recently. Not far away are Roman remains, but Roman remains are everywhere. In this context 1620 and 1627 take their place in the long, unbroken vista of what the English did and where they did it.

But what relevance does this have now, not so much the Plantation but the Compact and the other covenants, those movable legacies which could be used, adapted or ignored all across the continent?[12] According to Professor Bliss:

> What happens is the compacts are made and they become a very important part of American rhetoric, for example, at the time of the Revolution in the 1760s and 1770s. People like John Adams[13] derive from these compacts and charters a kind of ancient contract with the English Crown that the Crown is reneging on. The documents allow the revolutionaries the nice trick of saying that they are really trying to conserve things and the people who are trying to effect change are over there in London. There's an element of truth in that, too, of course. You have this contractualism which then makes it (almost!) a foregone conclusion that the new 13 republics of the American revolution, the new American states, will have written constitutions; and they will be in the nature of contracts amongst the citizens. The United States constitution is an historical outgrowth of that. The constitution is 'we, the people'.
>
> You could pretty convincingly draw an historical line from the early seventeenth-century compacts through the Revolutionary

debate into the Revolutionary period of constitution making and then into areas like the [American] Civil War where a lot of northern anger about the south's cessation was – and I've got this from my great grandfather's papers – that the south, by losing the election of 1860 and then pulling out, were breaking the compact and ought to be punished for it.

Of course, in any long historical line of descent the real meaning – why the *Mayflower* Pilgrims actually sat down and did this thing, its real cause and effects – gets pretty attenuated by the time you come to the Republican congresses of '94 and '96 and its contract with the people.

Perhaps that is why you need the mythology, sculptured, unchanging and deeply satisfying.

The frisson of proximity at Plimoth Plantation comes from a different kind of experience. This was part of a beginning, and England herself has no beginning unless, I suppose, you count the time 10,000 years ago when the sea became the Channel and an island was formed. You can go to Dover, gaze out and feel no sense of much except gratitude for the 22 miles of water. You do not even feel it at Scrooby, because the Manor House is unrecognisable, the church is like a thousand other village churches and virtually everything else of the era has gone completely.

The frisson at Plimoth is also that so much did begin there, both myth and reality. I mention to Professor Bliss that it would be utterly inconceivable in England in 1620 for a group of people to say, by signing this piece of paper I give permission to create the kind of society I accept.

'In 1620, yes, perhaps, although in the 1640s it happens with the Parliamentary army in the English Civil War.'

'But it's got to be a time of great upheaval.'

'Oh yes. It is why the history of covenanting is so rich. There is a sociology to it and there's a history to it. Let's try to think politically: what is there in common between the *Mayflower* Compact and the various English army covenants of the 1640s? More than anything else, there's upheaval, a kind of new world about all this. The radicals in the Parliamentary army felt it as strongly as the immigrants to New England. There are all these things working together, a religious tradition, some of the basic ideas of reform Protestantism, and the common law which was a way of adjudicating relationships between free individuals.'

'That's pretty deep in the American psyche, isn't it?'

'It's pretty deep in the English psyche, too! Common law was an English invention . . .'

'I mean in terms of the United States a sense of openness, that we will decide, we will not have the chains of the past, we come from somewhere else and we will not have it done to us here.'

'It's a strength and a weakness of our culture, but it is certainly a mark of our culture. I'm not sure whether I want to celebrate or bemoan it, but it's certainly there.'

And, leaving aside the openness, it is exactly what those who had waited at the ordinary place, where the brown mud dries and cracks, were going to bring; and did.

Notes

All page references to William Bradford's handwritten manuscript, *Of Plymouth Plantation*, *c.* 1646; Edward Winslow's *Mourt's Relations*, 1622, *Good News From New England*, 1624, and *Hypocrisy Unmasked*, 1646 are taken from *The Complete Works of the Mayflower Pilgrims*, Caleb H. Johnson (ed. and pub.), undated, *c.* 2003.

Prologue

1. W. Bradford, *Of Plymouth Plantation*, p. 27.
2. The number of households has been estimated at around fifty in Immingham, seventy in Killingholme.
3. Bradford, *Plymouth Plantation*, p. 27.
4. *Ibid.*
5. *Ibid.*
6. *Ibid.*
7. *Ibid.*
8. *Ibid.*

Chapter One

1. W.G. Hoskins, *The Age of Plunder, The England of Henry VIII 1500–1547* (London and New York, Longman, 1988), pp. 37, 119.
2. H. Brogan, *The Penguin History of the USA*, 2nd edn (London, Penguin Books, 1999), p. 15.
3. *Southampton in 1620 and the 'Mayflower'*, Sheila D. Thomson, City Archivist, Southampton, 1970.
4. *Catholic Encyclopedia*, www.newadvent.org/cathen/ [accessed 1 December 2004]. The Encyclopedia, published in 1911, does not necessarily reflect current thinking.
5. See www.justus.anglican.org/resources/bio/27.html [accessed 1 December 2004].
6. Dr D. Beale, *The Mayflower Pilgrims, Roots of Puritan, Presbyterian, Congregationalist and Baptist Heritage* (Greenville, S. Carolina and Belfast, N. Ireland, Ambassador-Emerald International, 2000), p. 1.
7. *Catholic Encyclopedia.*
8. J. Kardux and E. van de Bilt, *Newcomers in an Old City* (Leiden, Burgersdijk & Niermans, 2001), p. 9.

9. O. Chadwick, *The Reformation*, The Penguin History of the Church, vol. 3 (London, Penguin Books, 1990), pp. 1–2.
10. *The Concise Oxford Dictionary* (Oxford, Clarendon Press, 1990).
11. Kardux and van de Bilt, *Newcomers*, pp. 8, 9. There will be a full discussion of Puritanism in the next chapter. Here, suffice it to say that Barry Coward (in *The Stuart Age*, Harlow, Longman, 2003) writes, p. 81: 'The word "Puritan" causes so much confusion among students of the history of the period from 1558 to 1660 that it is tempting to abandon it.' This, Coward concludes, would be a mistake.
12. A.E. McGrath, *Reformation Thought, An Introduction*, 3rd edn (Malden MA, Blackwell Publishing, 2003), p. 1.
13. Hoskins, *Age of Plunder*, p. 1.
14. Adapted from Hoskins, p. 38.
15. *A History of the County of Lincolnshire*, ed. William Page (London, James Street, 1906), p. 330.
16. Hoskins, *Age of Plunder*, preface, p. xi.
17. Chadwick, *The Reformation*, p. 123.
18. Bradford, *Plymouth Plantation*, p. 22.
19. Chadwick, *The Reformation*, p. 204.
20. E. Arber, *The Story of the Pilgrim Fathers* (London, Ward and Downey Ltd, 1897), p. 72.
21. Malcolm Dolby, interview with author.
22. A.D. Mills, *Dictionary of English Place-names*, Past Times, 2nd edn (Oxford, Oxford University Press, 1998), p. 304.
23. R. McCrum, W. Cran and R. MacNeil, *The Story of English* (London, Faber and Faber/BBC Publications, 1986), p. 71.
24. F. Dillon, *A Place for Habitation* (London, Hutchinson, 1973), p. 87.
25. 'Various denominations have been used as moneys of account for which no actual coin existed e.g. the "mark" was 160 pennies or two thirds of a pound' – *Coins of England*, 32nd edn, eds S. Mitchell and B. Reeds (London, Seaby, 1997), p. xiii.
26. Arber, *Story of Pilgrim Fathers*, p. 75.
27. H. Kirk-Smith, *William Brewster – The Father of New England* (Boston, Lincs, Richard Kay, 1992), p. 52.
28. 'Sack is any one of several dry white wines imported to England from Jerez in southern Spain and from the Canary Islands. The name is a corruption of the Spanish word *sec*, or "dry". In Elizabethan times, sack was often heated (interestingly, like Japanese *sake*) and sometimes bolstered by the addition of raw eggs, although Falstaff, the most notorious literary connoisseur of sack, took his wine neat: "I'll no pullet-sperm in my brewage!"' – L. Patrick Coyle, *The World Encyclopedia of Food* (London, Frances Pinter Ltd, 1982).
29. Kirk-Smith, *William Brewster*, pp. 52, 53.
30. C. Hill, *Society and Puritanism in Pre-revolutionary England* (London, Pimlico, 2003), p. 104.
31. Bradford, *Plymouth Plantation*, p. 233.
32. *Ibid.*, p. 234.
33. Beale, *Mayflower Pilgrims*, p. 15.

34. *The Oxford Companion to British History*, ed. J. Cannon (Oxford, Oxford University Press, 1997), p. 343.

Chapter Two

1. I asked Malcolm Dolby about travelling at the time, and wondered how much traffic there would have been. 'Travelling quite rare? I don't know, because we imagine people could be very insular but we must take into account that there certainly were fayres and some degree of trade and, of course, there was migration to towns. There were people who, if they could break away from any bond and go to a town and remain non-molesters for a year, were accepted as a free townsperson. But how far it went down the social strata I don't know, and the temptation was to stay put because of family ties, occupation and so on.'
2. A litter was framework with a couch, and it was used as a means of transporting people who were ill or wounded.
3. Beale, *Mayflower Pilgrims*, p. 41.
4. Dolby interview with author.
5. As Dolby points out, the refurbishment of local churches is 'true wherever you try and make the analogy. Babworth has been thoroughly Victorianised. If Richard Clyfton were to come back these 400 years on he would probably say from the outside "that's my church" but inside "what's happened?".'
6. Bradford, *Plymouth Plantation*, p. 606.
7. Kirk-Smith, *William Brewster*, p. 68.
8. B. Coward, *The Stuart Age, England 1603–1714*, 3rd edn (London, Longman, 2003), pp. 128, 129.
9. Kirk-Smith, *William Brewster*, p. 79.
10. It is not certain that this was Squanto, but it seems very probable.
11. Kirk-Smith, *William Brewster*, p. 79.
12. *Ibid.*, p. 81.
13. I mentioned to Dolby (no disrespect intended) that Scrooby appears to be a place that's asleep now, and the natural temptation is to think it must have been even quieter then, and yet something amazing stirred there. 'The catalyst was I think Brewster, and what drove Brewster was his Cambridge background – the radical background which he brought back with him. He was able to add to that his experience in the diplomatic service in the Low Countries.' '*Presumably when you started preaching a message, the straightforward country people would have been very receptive to it?*' 'Yes, and also the fact that this was the only message that they were going to get. They weren't going to be switching on the news to find out of they had a nonconformist curate taking the services. You would just attend your church. That was the only one and that was it.'
14. Arber, *The Story of the Pilgrim Fathers*.
15. Bradford, *Plymouth Plantation*, p. 25.
16. Kirk-Smith, *William Brewster*, p. 81.
17. Dolby interview with the author.
18. Bradford, *Plymouth Plantation*, p. 25.
19. The continuing problem with Spain, and what the Spaniards might subsequently do.

20. Bradford, *Plymouth Plantation*, p. 26.
21. *Ibid.*
22. Dolby interview with the author.
23. Kirk-Smith, *William Brewster*, p. 86.
24. On Lincoln Boat Club website http://www.geocities.com/lincolnboatclub/ [accessed 21 December 2003].
25. John Cammack to the author: 'My guess is that the men and women would have travelled together but, as you know, some of the men and the women were separated when they tried again at Immingham. This could have been because they wished to avoid the womenfolk being ill-treated as they had been in Boston – but it backfired when some were left behind.'
26. Cammack to the author.
27. *Ibid.*
28. The Hanseatic League was a merchants' association, originating within northern German and Baltic cities.
29. Cammack to the author: 'These buildings and a Market Cross were removed thus creating the present open space of the Market Place. The basic layout of the centre of Boston is very little altered since medieval times. The pattern of squares with twin burgage plots [land on a yearly rent] and many narrow lanes running backwards on both sides from the Market Place still survive nearly intact. There are also some survivors in Pump Square and South Square as well as in Strait and Wide Bargate. The main blemish is the double carriageway which slices through from the south through the eastern side of the town, but it cuts through only a relatively small part of the medieval townscape.'
30. Cammack to the author, explaining if the flotilla went through the town they might have heard local accents on the quayside and nearby roads: 'One of the fen villages past Fishtoft, on the way to Wainfleet, is Old Leake – "OwdLee-ak" (as one word). Another expression I like is an old farmer's description of a well-endowed girl: "She'em-a-bungerr!"'
31. Cammack to the author: 'The memorial at Scotia Creek might well not be in the right place – some think it could have been closer to the town, nearer Skirbeck Church. However, it seems to me to be appropriate, simple but impressive. Unfortunately it does include the words "set sail"' – which is the one thing they didn't do.'
32. Bradford, *Plymouth Plantation*, p. 26.
33. Boston was sympathetic. As Kirk-Smith points out in *William Brewster*, 'later on, when John Winthrop and 900 colonists set sail for Massachusetts, several prominent Boston citizens were among them. John Cotton, Vicar of Boston, landed on the shores of America in 1633. He took with him John Leverett, who became Ruling Elder of his Church and Governor of the Colony from 1673 to 1679. Atherton Hough, Mayor of the Borough in 1628, also sailed with Cotton and was later ordained. Richard Bellingham, Recorder of Boston from 1625 to 1633, and Thomas Dudley also became governors of Massachusetts and William Coddington became governor of Rhode Island.'
34. Kirk-Smith, *William Brewster*, p. 87

Chapter Three

1. In a story like the *Mayflower*, the unknowns are tantalising – and doubly frustrating because they seem destined to remain forever unknown. Here is a prime example. Local historian Maurice Barrick points out that

   > nobody knows why history has settled on Killingholm Creek. The only true definition is that they did sail from a creek between Hull and Grimsby on the Lincolnshire coast. Nobody today can say it was Killingholm or Immingham where they sailed from. What we have is two distinct creeks 200–300 yards apart and there is no proof which one it was!
   >
   > In 1920, to commemorate the 300th anniversary, the Anglo-American Society from Hull came across to have a service of dedication and the site was picked. Four years later they started to erect a monument. Again, nobody really knows why this place was settled on. I think the Anglo-American Society just picked that as a likely site to plant this obelisk. It has never really been challenged.
   >
   > The obelisk has been removed because industry – the Immingham docks – came along wanting to expand and build storage tanks. It wasn't quite right that people would go down there for picnics, start camp fires and so on – and the development of the docks went ahead in leaps and bounds.
   >
   > I think there would have been quite a lot of creeks, particularly in this part of the Humber where large drainage and that sort of thing entered the river. Anyway, the ship was coming – we assume – from the North Sea and would not want to go up the estuary if it could avoid it. The captain would have had to pass Grimsby but he wouldn't want to get as far as Hull so logically it would make sense to have it here, where the ship could come without compromising itself and the men could gather.
   >
   > Another thing. The men who came overland from Scrooby were able to gain easy access because there were no hills to climb – very, very flat – and the women could come all the way by boat.
   >
   > Incidentally, some people say they worshipped in the Baptist chapel at Killingholm but I'm not sure that that can be substantiated. There is also a suggestion one died while he was at Immingham – a man called Hawkins.

   Certainly nobody by the name of Hawkins sailed on the *Mayflower*.
2. See www.allerton.sch.dccl.net/aboutus/immingham/immingham.htm [accessed 7 July 2003].
3. Bradford, *Plymouth Plantation*, p. 27.
4. *Ibid.*
5. The power of a North Sea storm is demonstrated in this anecdote from a former trawlerman, Michael Beecroft (in an interview with the author). 'I was on a boat and the sea bent the big steel derricks as if they were pieces of tin.'
6. Bradford, *Plymouth Plantation*, p. 27.
7. One suggestion puts the number as high as 125 but that would seem to include the groups who were already in Holland, and *that* would include the Smyth congregation from Gainsborough.

8. A deep frustration is that we know almost nothing personal about the people who are central to the story: what they looked like, their moods and anxieties, their characters and characteristics. In that sense, they remain people of the background. (Even in Caleb Johnson's compendium, there are only two portraits. Edward Winslow, a formal face with moustache, goatee beard and long, curling hair, stands stiffly holding a letter. Myles Standish has a more substantial beard but you cannot read anything much into his face and, anyway, the authenticity of the portrait is disputed.)

   When they reached the foreground, the historians who give us precious glimpses of princes and prelates simply weren't occupying themselves with an obscure group who went from an English village to a Dutch provincial town to the North American wilderness.

   However, Malcolm Dolby says this:

   > We do know they were led by a middle-class people who were well connected, well educated, worldly and had friends in fairly high places. In his diplomatic days, Brewster would have been speaking with William Davison who was close to the centre, the court. They had aristocratic contacts and this is a factor which helped to protect them to some degree from the worst of the persecution. They could perhaps rely on some friends.
   >
   > I think much of it must come down to the personalities of those who instructed them. We are talking of a movement that had a lot of adherents all over Britain *but* it was only really at Scrooby and at Gainsborough where they decided to go one step further, and it was a very radical step: 'we're not staying here. We are never going to get anywhere in terms of progressing our ideas and we're going to be increasingly persecuted. Therefore we must go to a place where there is toleration and that place is Holland.

9. In *Story of the Pilgrim Fathers*, Arber offers confirmation of this, p. 130.
10. To 'idealise' this against the toleration of today is a mistake, as Kardux and van de Bilt point out in *Newcomers in an Old City*, although it was clearly a great deal more than King James's England offered and, in practical terms, a great deal more than anywhere else offered, too. The Dutch were a trading nation. That implied a breadth of vision and openness to the world beyond their own. If you had to flee somewhere in 1608, it didn't get much better than Holland, and there was a further important consideration: it was comparatively close.
11. Dillon, *Place for Habitation*, p. 94.
12. Bradford, *Plymouth Plantation*, p. 29.
13. Dillon, *Place for Habitation*, p. 95.
14. Kardux and van de Bilt, *Newcomers*, p. 19.
15. Dillon, *Place for Habitation*, p. 97.
16. See www.karaministries.com/articles/Baptist/begin.htm [accessed 6 June 2003].
17 Dillon, *Place for Habitation*, p. 97.
18. *Ibid.*, p. 99.
19. Beale, *Mayflower Pilgrims*, p. 65.
20. Bradford, *Dialogue Between Some Young Men Born in New England and Sundry Ancient Men that Came Out of Holland and Old England*, 1648 in Caleb Johnson, *Complete Works*, p. 611.

21. Arber, *Story of the Pilgrim Fathers*, p. 102.
22. Bradford, *Plymouth Plantation*, p. 29.
23. Kardux and van de Bilt, *Newcomers*, p. 22.
24. Bradford, *Plymouth Plantation*, p. 609.
25. Kardux and van de Bilt, *Newcomers*, p. 26.
26. Arber, *Story of the Pilgrim Fathers*, p. 143.
27. Bradford, *Plymouth Plantation*, p. 609.
28. Kardux and van de Bilt, *Newcomers*, p. 29.
29. Beale, *Mayflower Pilgrims*, p. 69.
30. Kardux and van de Bilt, *Newcomers*, p. 31.
31. *Ibid.*, p. 34.
32. Beale, *Mayflower Pilgrims*, p. 71.
33. The Dutch concept of a civil registration validating a marriage would be taken to the New World and, as a result, introduced into what had been called the Anglo-American culture.
34. Kardux and van de Bilt, *Newcomers*, p. 30.
35. Bradford, *Plymouth Plantation*, p. 29.
36. *Ibid.*
37. Beale, *Mayflower Pilgrims*, p. 71.
38. Kardux and van de Bilt, *Newcomers*, p. 30.
39. C. Gill, *Mayflower Remembered, A History of the Plymouth Pilgrims* (Newton Abbot, David & Charles, 1970), p. 55.
40. Kirk-Smith, *William Brewster*, p. 126.
41. *Ibid.*, p. 124.
42. Bradford, *Dialogue*, p. 609.
43. Kirk-Smith, *William Brewster*, p. 126.
44. Arber estimates the total book production as fifteen from October 1616 to June 1619 (four in 1617, seven in 1618, four, including *Perth Assembly*, in 1619). Arber writes that 'it abundantly witnesses to the great energy' that Brewster put in – 'the secret organisation for its production could not, in any case, be a large one'.

Chapter Four

1. As Bangs points out (in Kardux and van de Bilt, *Newcomers in an Old City*), the Scrooby group did not have to make this formal application to come to live in Leiden, but once permission had been given, any orphans would not be returned to the country of their parents' origin – in this case, England, of course – but be taken in by the Leiden orphanage.
2. Kirk-Smith, *William Brewster*, p. 136.
3. Bradford, *Plymouth Plantation*, p. 33.
4. *Ibid.*
5. *Ibid.*
6. C. Cuthbert Blaxland, *'Mayflower' Essays* (London, Ward and Downey Ltd, 1896), p. 50.
7. Kirk-Smith, *William Brewster*, p. 136.
8. *Ibid.*, p. 138.

9. Quoted in Kirk-Smith.
10. Kardux and van de Bilt, *Newcomers*, p. 47.
11. Gill, *Mayflower Remembered*, p. 55.
12. Arber, *Story of the Pilgrim Fathers*, p. 290.
13. Kardux and van de Bilt, *Newcomers*, p. 47.
14. Kirk-Smith, *William Brewster*, p. 141.
15. Kardux and van de Bilt, *Newcomers*, p. 42.
16. *Ibid.*, p. 43.
17. Kirk-Smith, *William Brewster*, p. 131.
18. Caleb Johnson website www.mayflowerhistory.com [accessed 1 December 2004].
19. Blaxland, '*Mayflower*', p. 55.
20. Bradford, *Plymouth Plantation*, p. 45.
21. *Ibid.*, p. 47.
22. Arber, *Story of the Pilgrim Fathers*, p. 309.
23. Caleb Johnson website.
24. E. Winslow, *Hypocrisy Unmasked*, 1646, in Caleb Johnson's *Complete Works*, p. 565.
25. W. Sears Nickerson *Land Ho! 1620* (Boston/New York, Houghton Miflin Co., 1931), p. 19.
26. Bradford, *Plymouth Plantation*, p. 54.
27. Winslow, *Hypocrisy Unmasked*, p. 565.
28. Beale, *Mayflower Pilgrims*, p. 87.
29. Bradford, *Plymouth Plantation*, p. 54.

Chapter Five

1. *Southampton in 1620 and the 'Mayflower'*, Southampton Archives Services.
2. Gill, *Mayflower Remembered*, p. 41.
3. Dr Andy Russel, Archaeology Unit Manager, Southampton City Council, to the author: 'Judging by recent finds of a cemetery with gravegoods such as swords and pots.'
4. Russel, information to author.
5. An entry in Southampton's Book of Instruments records (in these words and spellings) that on 26 October 1606 'the building of a ship which might be the one which sailed to cross with the *Mayflower*'. It reads:

   > A certificate under the Towne Seale, that there are latelye built att the Port of South'ton three new shipps, namelye the Rose of Hampton burthen jxl*tie* tonns, the Speedwell of Hampton burthern Ix*tie* tonns, and the John of Hampton burthen I*tie* tonns belonging unto certaine merchaunts of this place, And that there is wanting unto the sayd shipps for theyr necessary provision and better defence x*en* tonn of cast iron ordinaunce vizt. ii sakers, vii*en* minions, and ix*en* fawlcones, the which peics of ordinaunces are to be obtayned att Lewis in the Countye of Sussex, and from thence transported unto the port of South'ton to be layd abourd the sayd shipps.

Incidentally, 'merchant ships were mostly armed against pirates and in time of war used as warships in sea battles'. The guns – sakers, minions, fawlcones [falcones] – are all small cannon – *Southampton in 1620.*

6. Russel, information to author.
7. Gill, *Mayflower Remembered*, p. 41.
8. Russel, information to author.
9. Dillon, *Place for Habitation*, p. 124
10. Bradford, *Plymouth Plantation*, p. 55
11. *Southampton in 1620.*
12. It is highly unlikely we shall ever know for certain if John Alden was a Southampton man, but if he was the son of George then he would have been born in about 1599 in a house in High Street whose site today is part of Owen Owens store (*Southampton in 1620*), but Caleb Johnson suggests Alden was 'probably from an Alden family found residing in Harwich, Essex that was related by marriage to *Mayflower* captain Christopher Jones and fellow passenger Richard Gardinar. However, no conclusive records have been found.'
13. Bradford, *Plymouth Plantation*, p. 55.
14. Kirk-Smith, *William Brewster*, p. 150.
15. *Ibid.*
16. Caleb Johnson, in his *Complete Works of the Mayflower Pilgrims*, writes: 'A Williams Reynolds was master of the ship *Charity* which Thomas Weston sent out in 1622, and is likely the same man.'
17. Nickerson, *Land Ho! 1620*, pp. 121–53.
18. Bradford, *Plymouth Plantation*, p. 60.
19. Gill, *Mayflower Remembered*, p. 57.
20. Nigel Overton, information to the author.
21. 'Drake's Leat [a conduit from a reservoir on the edge of Dartmoor] had arrived, bringing fresh water to the town for the population and victualling. Conduit House served the masses but, by 1608, 38 houses had a piped supply!' – Overton, information to the author.
22. Overton, information to the author.
23. *Ibid.*
24. Evidently the accent was so strong that Sir Walter Ralegh needed a translator when he was at Court – Overton, information to the author. Accents in England must have been stronger then, and remain strong today – see Note 33 in Chapter 2.
25. *Southampton in 1620.*
26. Quoted in Dillon, *A Place for Habitation*, p. 127.
27. According to Overton:

> This has been said to reflect close association with the effects of thirty years of war against Catholic Spain; in December 1600, twenty-two cases of religious books were burnt in the market place from the sack of Cadiz.
>
> Gill [in *Mayflower Remembered*] refers to many of the merchant classes having Puritan leanings. Puritan sermons were preached by local incumbents and also visiting lecturers. He cites several Puritan tracts with Plymouth dedications.

There may well have been a sympathetic welcome and treatment rolled out for the Pilgrims – once their purpose was known – over and above that received by other visitors.

Later, during the Civil War, Plymouth's Puritan leanings manifested in the town's siding with Cromwell. No doubt Charles I's ill-considered and ill-planned campaigns of *c.* 1625 compounded feelings: 10,000 hungry, badly nourished and poorly equipped troops descend for embarkation. Failed campaigns then resulted in demoralised and diseased troops and sailors.

28. Overton, information to the author.
29. E. Winslow, *Mourt's Relation*, 1622, in Caleb Johnson's *Complete Works*, p. 262. Winslow and others wrote *Mourt's Relation, A Relation or Journal of the beginning and proceeding of the English Plantation at Plymouth in New England, by certain English Adventurers both Merchants and others* and also *Hypocrisy Unmasked, By A true relation of the proceedings of the Governor and Company of the Massachusetts against SAMUEL GORTON*, 1646.
30. Overton information to the author.
31. Dillon, *Place for Habitation*, p.130.
32. Kirk-Smith, *William Brewster*, p. 153.
33. Neil D. Thompson, 'The Origin and Parentage of Francis Eaton of the *Mayflower*', *The American Genealogist* 72 (1997): 301–9 – quoted in Caleb Johnson.
34. Kirk-Smith summarising Anthony R. Wagner, 'The Origin of the Mayflower Children, Jasper, Richard and Ellen More', *The New England Historical and Genealogical Register*, 114 (1960): 163–8.
35. Kirk-Smith, *William Brewster*, p. 158.
36. K. Caffrey, *The Mayflower* (London, André Deutsch, 1975), p. 105.
37. Bradford, *Plymouth Plantation*, p. 64.
38. This date is surmise.
39. Stuart Upham, Devon boatbuilder, quoted in Caffrey, *The Mayflower*, p.105.
40. Caffrey, *The Mayflower*, pp 105–6.
41. Nickerson, *Land Ho!*, p. 119.
42. Bradford, *Plymouth Plantation*, p. 65.
43. Capt J. Smith, *New England's Trials*, 1622, in Caleb Johnson, *Complete Works*, p. 950.
44. Nickerson, *Land Ho!*, p. 59.
45. *Ibid.*, p. 119.
46. *Ibid.*, pp. 112, 116.
47. *Ibid.*, p. 119.
48. Bradford, *Plymouth Plantation*, p. 65.
49. Latitudes and longitudes had long been a part of human knowledge: Ptolemy (second century AD) had discussed them.
50. Nickerson, *Land Ho!*, p. 121.

Chapter Six

1. Bradford, *Plymouth Plantation*, p. 71. The 'other government' was the Plymouth Company, which had a patent from New Jersey northwards.

2. Winslow, *Mourt's Relation*, pp. 262–3.
3. *Ibid.*, p. 262.
4. *Ibid.*
5. As with so much about the *Mayflower*, the Compact is not straightforward. It wasn't even called that until 1793 – the earlier titles were many and varied (like 'association and agreement' by Bradford, for example). Bradford does not, in fact, tell us who signed it, although he did write the names of all the passengers on the *Mayflower*. It seems that, knowing all the free adult males did sign, Nathaniel Morton, in *New England's Memorial* (1669), used Bradford's passenger list. For a discussion on this, see *Plymouth Colony* by Stratton, pp. 411–13.
6. Kardux and van de Bilt, *Newcomers*, p. 58.
7. Nickerson, *Land Ho!*, p. 147.
8. Bradford, *Plymouth Plantation*, p. 71.
9. Kardux and van de Bilt, *Newcomers*, p. 59.
10. Caleb Johnson writes that Carver was 'likely from Yorkshire, but his exact origins have not been found'. Johnson points out that 'recent research' by Jeremy D. Bangs points to Carver first marrying Mary Delano of L'Ecluse, France and then Katherine White.
11. Gill, *Mayflower Remembered*, p. 70.
12. Winslow, *Mourt's Relation*, p. 262.
13. Nickerson, *Land Ho!*, p. 141.
14. See www.provincetown.com/plan/abouttown/history [accessed 1 December 2004].
15. Bradford, *Plymouth Plantation*, pp. 65–6.
16. Winslow, *Mourt's Relation*, p. 262.
17. *Ibid.*, p. 263.
18. *Ibid.*
19. *Ibid.*, p. 262.
20. A corslet was a piece of armour covering the trunk of the body. All men carried a sword, and most had knives and daggers as well. 'For muskets, the Pilgrims had two general types: matchlock and flintlock. The matchlock was more common because it was cheaper. Loading and firing a matchlock was quite a long and complicated procedure; flintlocks were significantly faster because a match was not required to light the firing mechanism. Most shooting was done with the muzzle resting in a stand, because the long muzzles were cumbersome and heavy.' (Caleb Johnson in members. aol. com/calebj/armor. html [accessed 18 April 2004].)

    The Wampanoags had no weapons to compete with the musket, which they called a thunderbolt and were 'deathly afraid of it'. The Wampanoags had 'bows and arrows and spears, which were used for hunting as well as protection of their territory. In addition, they had tomahawks made of stone, and knives made of shells or sharp shale.' www.teacher.scholastic.com/thanksgiving/plimoth/tscripft.htm [accessed 9 January 2004]).
21. Winslow, *Mourt's Relation*, p. 264.
22. See www.teacher.scholastic.com/thanksgiving/plimoth/tscripft.htm [accessed 9 January 2004].

23. 'The early name for brandy, from the Latin, meaning "water of life." The Italians claim, however, that the original name was not *aqua vitae* but *aqua vite*, or *acqua di vite*, the Italian for "water of the vine," referring to the colourless fluid which has been distilled as wine. Later, they say, either because of the power of liquor to stimulate and revive, or through a simple mistake in spelling, the more familiar term came into use.' (Alexis Lichine, *New Encyclopedia of Wines & Spirits*, New York, Alfred A. Knopf, 1974).
24. Winslow, *Mourt's Relation*, p. 264. In November 2001, the *Provincetown Banner* newspaper carried a long feature article by Laurel Guadazno, columnist and also visitor services manager for the Pilgrim Monument and Provincetown Museum.

    She points out that in the area the Pilgrims first drank fresh water and, some 300 years later, Dr William Rollins, a Boston dentist with a summer home in Truro, tried to find out exactly where this had happened. He 'determined to his satisfaction' that it was on the land of one Warren Small. Rollins bought 100ft round and put up a monument.

    Others disagreed.

    However, as Guadazno points out: 'perhaps the most conclusive evidence of this spring's existence comes from the fact that this spot has held the only historically known flowing spring along the route the Pilgrims followed. Truro historian Shebnah Rich corroborates the existence of a spring on the site . . . when he writes, "January 29, 1878 . . . I visited this place, and found a clear bubbling spring, sweet, cool, and crystal as that November day, 1620, when Captain Miles Standish and his wearied guard drank thereof with so much delight."'
25. Sassafras, a tree 20–40ft tall with many slender branches and smooth, orange-brown bark.
26. Winslow, *Mourt's Relation*, p. 264.
27. *Ibid.*, p. 265.
28. See www.tolatsga.org/wampa.html [accessed 11 January 2004].
29. A tribe on Cape Cod. See www.dickshovel.com/nau.html [accessed 1 December 2004].
30. Winslow, *Mourt's Relation*, p. 265.
31. *Ibid.*, p. 266.
32. *Ibid.*, p. 267.
33. *Ibid.*, p. 268.
34. *Ibid.*
35. *Ibid.*, p. 269.
36. See www.teacher.scholastic.com/thanksgiving/plimoth/tscripft.htm [accessed 9 January 2004].
37. See www.tauntonriver.org/nemasketpath.htm [accessed 1 December 2004].
38. Gill, *Mayflower Remembered*, p. 76.

Chapter Seven

1. Two English physicians had noticed by 1617 that lemon juice reduced the mortality from scurvy enormously and in 1747 a British Royal Navy officer

experimented using oranges and lemons. He found these were effective against it. The Navy preferred to use lime juice and the sailors became known as 'limeys'. See www.emedicine.com [accessed 11 January 2004].

2. In fact there is only Clark's Island, but with so many promontories a mistake would have been easy to make and perhaps unavoidable.
3. Gill, *Mayflower Remembered*, p. 79.
4. Winslow, *Mourt's Relation*, p. 275.
5. *Ibid.*, p. 274.
6. *Ibid.*, p. 275.
7. Bradford, *Plymouth Plantation*, p. 72.
8. *Ibid.*, p. 73.
9. *Ibid.*
10. Winslow, *Mourt's Relation*, pp. 275–6.
11. *Ibid*, p. 276.
12. See www.teacher.scholastic.com/thanksgiving/plimoth/tscripft.htm [accessed 9 January 2004].
13. Winslow, *Mourt's Relation*, p. 276.
14. A hogshead was about 50 imperial gallons. Meal was 'the edible part of any grain or pulse (usually other than wheat) ground to powder' – *Concise Oxford Dictionary*.
15. Many years later Edward Winslow (London, 1649) would set before the Parliament of England a description of what was happening. He began by citing *The Clear Sunshine of the Gospel, Breaking forth Upon the Indians in New England*.
16. See www.teacher.scholastic.com/thanksgiving/plimoth/tscripft.htm [accessed 9 January 2004].
17. Winslow's phrase in *Mourt's Relation* is that the gusts of wind 'caused much of the daubing of our house to fall down'. Daubing: 'Plaster, clay, etc. for coating a surface, especially mixed with straw and applied to laths or wattles to form a wall' – *Concise Oxford Dictionary*.
18. Winslow, *Mourt's Relation*, p. 277.
19. *Ibid.*
20. Bradford, *Plymouth Plantation*, p. 72.
21. *Ibid.*

Chapter Eight

1. See www.tolatsga.org/wampa.html [accessed 11 January 2004].
2. See www.dickshovel.com/nau.html
3. See www.tolatsga.org/wampa.html
4. See www.tolatsga.org/wampa.html
5. Winslow, *Mourt's Relation*, p. 277.
6. C. Mather, *Magnalia Christi Americana: or, The Ecclesiastical History of New-England from its first Planting in the year 1620 unto the year of our Lord 1698* (London, T. Parkhurst, 1702 folio), p. 9.
7. Winslow, *Mourt's Relation*, p. 278.
8. Caleb Johnson writes in *The Complete Works* that Master Williamson may have been a *Mayflower* crew member or a pseudonym for William Brewster.

9. Winslow, *Mourt's Relation*, p. 280.
10. The date of New Year's Day has a chequered history. Briefly, the Romans had it in late March, but Pope Gregory XIII moved it to 1 January in 1582 – not something the Pilgrims were likely to accept; and they didn't.
11. Shad: any deep-bodied edible fish.
12. Winslow, *Mourt's Relation*, p. 292.
13. Gill, *Mayflower Remembered*, p. 86.
14. Bradford, *Plymouth Plantation*, p. 76.
15. Gill, *Mayflower Remembered*, p. 88.

Chapter Nine

1. Winslow, *Mourt's Relation*, p. 283.
2. It is difficult to determine which particular village the settlers referred to as Nemasket. Contemporary accounts (and Bradford in particular) suggest it was about 14 miles from Plymouth – suggesting, in turn, a site just off Sachem Street in Middleboro.
3. Bradford, *Plymouth Plantation*, p. 77.
4. Winslow, *Mourt's Relation*, p. 284.
5. *Ibid.*, p. 285.
6. *Ibid.*
7. *Ibid.*
8. *Ibid.*, p. 286.
9. *Ibid.*, p. 287.
10. Quoted in Beale, *The Mayflower Pilgrims*, p. 138.
11. Bradford, *Plymouth Plantation*, p. 961.
12. *Ibid., p. 978.*
13. *Ibid.*
14. Winslow, *Mourt's Relation*, p. 288.
15. *Ibid.*, p. 289.
16. *Ibid.*
17. *Ibid.*
18. Bradford, *Plymouth Plantation*, p. 78.
19. W. Bradford, *Fragments of William Bradford's Register*, in Caleb Johnson, *Complete Works*, p. 961.
20. Bradford, *Plymouth Plantation*, p. 78.
21. *Ibid.*, p. 79.
22. There is a discussion on Thanksgiving, its history and mythology in Chapter 12.
23. Bradford, *Plymouth Plantation*, p. 79.
24. *Ibid.*
25. Quoted in Bradford.
26. Bradford, *Plymouth Plantation*, p. 81.
27. *Ibid.*
28. E. Winslow, *Good News From New England*, 1624, in Caleb Johnson, *Complete Works*, p. 321.
29. Winslow, *Mourt's Relation*, p. 294.

30. Henry Ainsworth, a noted religious figure in Amsterdam, had called Christmas one of the 'Pagan festivities' (Caleb Johnson).
31. A traditional English game, and ideal because all you needed, as the name implies, was a stool and a ball. One player tossed the ball at the stool, the other tried to stop it hitting the stool with his hand. Each time he did, it counted one. If the ball struck the stool the players changed places. The winner was the one who had hit the ball with his hand the most times.
32. Bradford, *Plymouth Plantation*, p. 82.

Chapter Ten

1. Brogan, *Penguin History of the USA*, p. 39.
2. Bradford, *Plymouth Plantation*, p. 83.
3. *Ibid.*
4. *Ibid.*, p. 84.
5. The office of an elder has been described as one of dignity and usefulness, vital to the life of the Church. An elder had to keep a close eye on the congregation, exercise government and discipline, and instruct the ignorant.
6. Winslow, *Mourt's Relation*, p. 325.
7. *Ibid.*
8. *Ibid.*, p. 326.
9. *Ibid.*
10. Bradford, *Plymouth Plantation*, pp. 91–2.
11. Written from a white man's viewpoint, of course. There would be plenty of trouble for the Indians all the way to here.
12. Bradford, *Plymouth Plantation*, p. 94.
13. *Ibid.*, p. 95.
14. N. Morton, *New England's Memorial*, 1669, in Caleb Johnson, *Complete Works*, p. 872.
15. J. and P. Deetz, *The Times of Their Lives. Life, Love and Death in Plymouth Colony* (New York, Anchor Books, 2001), p. 77.

Chapter Eleven

1. Bradford, *Plymouth Plantation*, p. 95.
2. *Ibid.*
3. *Ibid.*, p. 100.
4. *Oxford Companion to British History*, p. 780.
5. E.A. Stratton, *Plymouth Colony, Its History and People 1620–1691* (Salt Lake City, Ancestry Publishing, 1986), p. 27.
6. Stratton, *Plymouth Colony*, p. 29.
7. Beale, *Mayflower Pilgrims*, p. 151.
8. Alistair Cooke, who died in 2004 at the age of ninety-five, was a British journalist who emigrated to the United States in 1937 and became an American citizen in 1941. His weekly *Letter from America* on BBC radio ran to 2,869 programmes and explained America in a unique way. Cooke was a conduit. He

also wrote about America and made a television series *America* which brought the country's history to life.

9. Brogan, *Penguin History of the USA*, p. 43.
10. Gill, *Mayflower Remembered*, p. 130.
11. You can argue that there was a third Reformation – Wesleyanism, created by the brothers John and Charles Wesley. This one was internal because they were in the Anglican Church. They went on a missionary trip to America in 1729 and, on their return, founded a Methodist society. They 'desired to preach the need for personal faith within the Church of England' as they attemped to reform it. See www.deusvitae.com/faith/denominations/overviewpage.html [accessed 1 December 2004].
12. Bradford, *Plymouth Plantation*, p. 233.
13. Gill, *Mayflower Remembered*, p. 140.
14. Bradford, *Plymouth Plantation*, p. 236.
15. Quoted in Bradford, p. 238.
16. Gill, *Mayflower Remembered*, p. 142.
17. Beale, *Mayflower Pilgrims*. For a description of Puritanism in America, and all its ramifications, see pp. 153–9.

Chapter Twelve

1. J. Le Carré, *A Small Town in Germany* (New York, Dell Publishing Co., 1969).
2. http://www.thanksgiving.org/2us.html [accessed 1 December 2004].
3. Deetz, *Times of Their Lives*, p. 14.
4. Stratton, *Plymouth Colony*, p. 31.
5. Brogan, *Penguin History of the USA*, p. 40.
6. D.J. Boorstin, *The Colonial Experience* (A Phoenix Press paperback, The Orion Publishing Group, 2000), p. 21.
7. The Chesapeake Colonies, Jamestown and more broadly Virginia, Maryland. One resident said Chesapeake was 'an unhealthy place, a nest of rogues, whores, desolute and rooking [defrauding] persons; a place of intolerable labour, bad usage and hard Diet'.
8. Pilgrim Monument and Provincetown Museum pamphlet on 'Building the Monument', by Laurel Guadazno. The reference by Sears to the 'first white child' might be considered an unfortunate choice of words in our politically correct era but, of course, he was trying to say the first non-Indian child.
9. See www.pilgrim-monument.org [accessed 27 April 2004].
10. *Plymouth Guide, April–July 2004*, published by Greg Mellis, Memorial Press Group, Long Pond Road, Plymouth, Mass.
11. The Plantation's Self-guided Tour Map enjoins visitors not to indulge in stereotypes when meeting and greeting the Indians, who are called Native people. For what it is worth, the ones I met had a natural dignity and a certain grace about them.
12. As an aside, when I asked Professor Bliss for his personal view of whether the US feels it has a link with England through these religious exiles on the Mayflower, he said:

Culturally it's a very difficult one. There is a kind of schizophrenia in British culture where conservative Britons, and especially conservative English, people quite admired American policies, especially in the 1980s, but were still pretty snobbish and pretty distant about American culture generally. They were a little bit uncomfortable about American power. That was shared with the left.

On the other hand the British left, more so than the English left, was very anti-American in terms of policy and also had this concern about American power but was really quite pro-American in terms of our culture and liked its openness and democracy and demotic character.

If you asked Americans what we have in common with Britain – and of course most Americans would say England – you might have some trouble today. If you went back to world war one or perhaps two you would find it, but, coming forward to 2004, that sort of fairly clear conception of American debt to English culture and English ideas – of real historical connection – would be a little harder to find.

13. John Adams, born in the Massachusetts Bay Colony in 1735, was a lawyer who led the movement for independence. Ironically, while I was finishing this chapter an intriguing feature article appeared in the *Guardian* (24 July 2004), which touched upon Adams and much else. It was by noted historian and broadcaster Dr Tristram Hunt, and I quote a tract of it, with his kind permission, to show how old agreements can reach across the centuries. Hunt points out that some

> 800 years on, the messy constitutional compromise hammered out at Runnymede between King John and the barons manages to retain a profound emotional pull on the Anglo-American political psyche. But even as it is honoured in name, the principles of 1215 have rarely been more widely breached.
>
> The enduring legacy of Magna Carta lies in clauses 39 and 40, which state that 'no free man shall be taken or imprisoned or deprived . . . except by the lawful judgement of the peers or by the law of the land' and 'to no one will we sell, to no one will we deny or delay right or justice'. It was the elevation of the rule of law above arbitrary power which transformed the charter from a grudging political settlement into a constitutional milestone. Rapidly translated from Latin into French, Magna Carta became part of British public memory, frequently appealed to whenever monarchs overstepped the line.
>
> Its unique potency was revealed in the 1620s when another power-hungry king attempted to subvert the law of the land. Charles I's arbitrary use of royal authority – false use of royal authority, false imprisonments, forced loans, personal rule – was for many members of parliament a clear echo of wicked King John.
>
> [The] next group of revolutionaries to call upon the charter regarded parliament itself as the arbitrary power needing to be called to account: what the rebellious American colonists of the 1770s were concerned with was not

> initially the creation of a new republic, but respect for their rights as English subjects under Magna Carta. Westminster's arbitrary and, at times, brutal rule of the 13 colonies was, according to John Adams, 'directly repugnant to the great charter itself'. Indeed the revolutionaries' battle cry of 'no taxation without representation' claimed root in the principles of 1215. Such was their reverence for Runnymede that the US constitution's fifth amendment is a direct echo of clause 39.

Hunt concludes it was in America that Magna Carta retained a more contemporary relevance. The combination of a legalistic culture and a reverence for foundation documents meant the charter was celebrated as America's revolutionary birthright, whose abiding principles underpinned the US system. Today supreme court jurists display no embarrassment in citing Magna Carta to support their case.

Bibliography

Arber, Edward, *The Story of the Pilgrim Fathers*, London, Ward and Downey, 1897
Beale, David, *The Mayflower Pilgrims, Roots of Puritan, Presbyterian, Congregationalist and Baptist Heritage*, Greenville, South Carolina and Belfast, Northern Ireland, Ambassador-Emerland International, 2000
Blaxland, G. Cuthbert, *'Mayflower' Essays*, London, Ward and Downey, 1896
Boorstin, Daniel J., *The Colonial Experience*, London, Phoenix Press, 2000
Brogan, Hugh, *The Penguin History of the USA* (2nd edn), London, Penguin, 1999
Caffrey, Kate, *The Mayflower*, London, André Deutsch, 1975
Cannon, John (ed.), *The Oxford Companion to British History*, OUP, 1997
Chadwick, Owen, *The Reformation*, Penguin History of the Church series, London, Penguin, 1990
Coward, Barry, *The Stuart Age, England 1603–1714*, 3rd edn, Longman, 2003
Deetz, James and Scott, Patricia, *The Times of Their Lives. Life, Love and Death in Plymouth*, New York, Anchor, 2001
Dillon, Francis, *A Place for Habitation*, London, Hutchinson, 1973
Gill, Crispin, *Mayflower Remembered. A History of the Plymouth Pilgrims*, Newton Abbot, David & Charles, 1970
Hill, Christopher, *Society and Puritanism in Pre-Revolutionary England*, London, Pimlico, 2003
——, *Puritanism & Revolution*, London, Pimlico, 2001
Hoskins, W.G., *The Age of Plunder, The England of Henry VIII 1500–1547*, Longman, 1988
Johnson, Caleb H. (ed./pub.), *The Complete Works of the Mayflower Pilgrims*, 2003
Kardux, Joke and Bilt, Eduard van de, *Newcomers in an Old City*, Leiden, Holland, Burgersdijk & Niermans, 2001
Kirk-Smith, Harold, *William Brewster, 'The Father of New England'*, Boston, Lincs, Richard Kay, 1992
McCrum, R., Cran, W. and MacNeil, R., *The Story of English*, Faber & Faber, 1986
McGrath, Alister E., *Reformation Thought*, 3rd edn, Malden, Mass., Blackwell, 1999
Mather, Cotton, *Magnalia Christi Americana: or, The Ecclesiastical History of New-England from its first Planting in the year 1620 unto the year of our Lord 1698*, Folio, London, T. Parkhurst, 1702
Nickerson, W. Sears, *Land Ho! 1620*, Boston/New York, Houghton Miflin, 1931
Page, William (ed.), *A History of the County of Lincolnshire*, London, James Street, 1906
Plymouth Guide, Greg Mellis, Memorial Press Group, Plymouth, Mass., April–July 2004
Stratton, Eugene Aubrey, *Plymouth Colony, Its History and People 1620–1691*, Salt Lake City, Ancestry Publishing, 1986

Index

WITH A LITTLE LUCK

JANET DAILEY

WITH A LITTLE LUCK

G.K. Hall & Co. • Chivers Press
Thorndike, Maine USA   Bath, England

This Large Print edition is published by G.K. Hall, USA and by Chivers Press, England.

Published in 1999 in the U.S. by arrangement with Richard Curtis Associates, Inc.

Published in 1999 in the U.K. by arrangement with the author.

U.S. Hardcover 0-7838-8680-2 (Core Series Edition)
U.K. Hardcover 0-7540-3971-4 (Chivers Large Print)
U.K. Softcover 0-7540-3972-2 (Camden Large Print)

All the characters in this book have no existence outside the imagination of the author and have no relation whatsoever to anyone bearing the same name or names. They are not even distantly inspired by any individual known or unknown to the author, and all the incidents are pure invention.

The text of this Large Print edition is unabridged.
Other aspects of the book may vary from the original edition.

Set in 16 pt. Plantin.

Printed in United States on permanent paper.

British Library Cataloguing-in-Publication Data available.

Library of Congress Cataloging-in-Publication Data

Dailey, Janet.
With a little luck / Janet Dailey.
p. cm.
ISBN 0-7838-8680-2 (lg. print : hc : alk. paper)
1. Large type books. I. Title.
[PS3554.A29W55 1999]
813′.54—dc21 99-32483

WITH A LITTLE LUCK

CHAPTER ONE

"Are you sure you wouldn't like a ride home?" the Reverend Mr. Johnson inquired. "If you don't mind waiting a few minutes, I would be happy to drive you."

Mr. Johnson didn't look like a minister in his plaid shirt and khaki-colored pants. In his mid-forties, he resembled a fisherman who had strayed into church by mistake. In fact, he was an ardent angler, overjoyed that his Wisconsin parish was situated in an area with so many lakes, streams and rivers. He loved to state that while he was a "fisher of men" like the Lord, he was also a fisherman, an occupation and an avocation that he felt were ideally suited to one another.

"No, thank you, Reverend. It's a lovely evening and I'll enjoy the walk," Eve Rowland insisted as she slipped on her summer-weight coat of brown. "Besides, it isn't that far, really."

"Yes, but I don't like the idea of your walking alone after dark."

"Cable isn't Minneapolis or Milwaukee," she laughed. There were times when she even forgot to lock the front door of her parents' house, but she didn't worry unduly on those occasions.

"My city background is showing, isn't it?" he smiled at himself. "Thanks for filling in for Mrs. Alstrom at the organ tonight." She was the regular church organist. A minor crisis at home had kept her from attending choir practice and Eve had been asked to substitute for her. "I hope it didn't upset any of your plans for the evening."

"I didn't have any plans," she said, and didn't go any further in her reply. It was rare for her ever to have plans for an evening — social plans, that is.

"That's a pity." The minister's eyes darkened with sympathy, even as he changed his expression to give her an encouraging smile. "You are a warm and generous woman. Maybe I should whisper in the ears of the eligible male members of my congregation."

He meant to be kind but his offer had a demoralizing effect. Eve fixed a quick smile in place to hide her reaction. "That's a nice thought, but most of them are already semi-attached to someone else. You might as well save your matchmaking talents for another time." She started to leave. "Good night. And I'm glad I could help out."

"I'll see you in church on Sunday." Mr. Johnson lifted his hand in a saluting wave.

"Not this Sunday," she said. "We're opening the summer cottage on the lake, so neither my parents nor I will be in church."

"Oh? Which lake?" His fishing curiosity was awakened.

"Namekagon." Which was only a few miles east of town.

"Marvelous fishing there," he stated.

"I know. It's dad's favorite." She glanced at her wristwatch, a utilitarian piece with a plain leather band that made no pretense of being decorative. "I'd better be going. Good night, Reverend Johnson."

"Good night."

Leaving the church, Eve buttoned her coat against the invading night air. Although it was officially summer, the temperature in the Northwoods dipped to the cool range in the evening hours. The sky was crystal bright with stars, hundreds of thousands of them lighting the heavens. A moon, big and fat, competed with the stars; its silver globe was nearly a spotlight shining down on the earth. The streetlights along the main thoroughfare were almost unneeded.

As she walked along the sidewalk, her mind kept echoing the matchmaking offer the minister had made. Having lived in Cable for all of her twenty-six years — with the exception of four years spent at college in Madison — Eve knew virtually every single man in the area. Those she might have been interested in never noticed her; and those that noticed her she wasn't interested in. She was almost convinced she was too particular.

Her mother despaired that Eve would ever find a man who could satisfy her, and kept reminding her that with each passing year she was becoming more set in her ways. Eve had given up hope long ago that Prince Charming would ever come this far north, but she wasn't going to get married just for the sake of being married, no matter how nice and respectable a suitor might be. She didn't intend to marry unless she had, at least, a deep affection for the man. So far, no one had aroused even that. There had been boyfriends now and then. Most of them she genuinely liked, but not with any depth. It seemed she was always attracted to men who weren't attracted to her.

It wasn't because she was homely. She was attractive, in a plain sort of way. With brown hair and eyes, she had a flawless complexion, but her features were unassuming. Her figure was average, neither thin nor plump. She wasn't too tall or too short. She simply didn't stand out in a crowd. In a sea of pretty faces, hers would be the last to be noticed.

Eve was just as realistic in her assessment of her personality traits. She was intelligent, basically good-natured and possessed a good sense of humor. As a music teacher, she appreciated music and the arts. But she tended to be quiet and not quick to make friends. Her early years as a wallflower had lessened her inclination for parties. She preferred celebrating with a few close friends to attending a large social function. By nature she wasn't aggressive, although she wouldn't allow herself to be walked on.

There were some who suggested that, at twenty-six, she was too old to be living at home. When Eve considered the cost of living alone versus her salary, it became a matter of sheer practicality. Besides, she and her parents were good friends. She was just as independent as she would have been living in an apartment.

With all her thoughts focused inward, Eve didn't notice the tavern she was approaching. A window was open to let out the smoke and let in fresh air. Inside, a jukebox was loudly playing a popular song. Eve didn't hear it or the laughter and spirited voices. Her gaze was on the sidewalk in front of her feet.

Suddenly a man stepped directly in front of her. Eve didn't have time to stop or step aside. Her hands came up to absorb the shock of the collision. He evidently didn't see her, either, as he took a step forward and collided head-on. In a reflex action his arms went around to catch her, while his forward progress carried her backward two steps.

Dazed by the total unexpectedness of the accident, Eve lifted her head. She wasn't certain that the fault belonged entirely to either one of them. Too stunned yet to speak, she stared at the stranger she'd bumped into — or vice versa.

The light from the neon tavern sign fully illuminated his face. Nearly a head taller than she was, he had dark hair that waved in thick strands to fall at a rakish angle across his forehead. His eyes were blue, with a perpetual glint of humor in them. Tanned skin was stretched across very masculine features. He was handsome in a tough rakehell sort of way. A reckless smile showed the white of his teeth.

"What's this I've caught?" His mocking voice was matched by the laughing glint in his eyes as they traveled over her, taking in the brown of her hair and eyes and the brown coat. "I believe it is a brown mouse."

The teasing remark did not go down well, considering the earlier demoralizing remark by the minister. Her gaze dropped to the cream-colored pullover and the thin-striped blue-and-cream color of his shirt collar. Since he had obviously just left the tavern, Eve wasn't surprised that there was liquor on his breath. He'd been drinking, but he wasn't drunk. He was steady on his feet, and there was no glaze of alcohol in the rich blue of his eyes.

"I'm sorry," Eve apologized stiffly. "I wasn't paying attention to where I was going." Then she realized his arms were still holding her and her hands were flattened against his chest — a very solid chest. Her heart began to beat unevenly.

"I wasn't looking where *I* was going, so it seems we were both to blame, brown mouse. Did I hurt you?" It was more disturbing to listen to the low pitch of his voice without seeing his face, so Eve looked up. His half-closed eyes were difficult to meet squarely.

"No, you didn't." When he showed no inclination to release her, she stated, "I'm all right. You can let go of me now."

"Must I?" he sighed deeply. His hands moved, but not away from her. Instead they began roaming over her shoulders and spine in an exploring fashion, as if testing the way she felt in his arms. "Do you know how long it's been since I held a woman in my arms?"

The well-shaped line of his mouth held a latent sensuality as his question confirmed the direction that Eve had suspected his thoughts were taking. His hands were exerting a slight pressure to inch her closer to him. They were standing on the sidewalk of a main street a few feet away from a tavern full of people.

Surely he wouldn't try to accost her in such a place? She wanted to struggle, but she was afraid he might view it as provocation rather than resistance. Yet she recognized the inherent danger in the situation. She kept her body rigid.

"Would you please let me go?" she requested.

"I'm frightening you, aren't I?" He tipped his head to one side, regarding her lazily, while his hands stopped their movement.

"Yes," Eve admitted, because her heart was beating a mile a minute and there was a choked sensation in her throat.

He let his hands slide away to let her stand

free. She had expected an argument. It was a full second before she realized he was no longer holding her. She brushed past him and was a step beyond him when his hand snaked out to catch her arm.

"Don't scurry off into the dark, brown mouse." His voice chided her for running. "Stay a minute."

"No." His hand forced her to stop, but she lifted her arm in protest of his grip, straining against the unyielding strength of his fingers.

"What's your hurry? Are you meeting someone?"

The questions were curious, interested.

"No." Eve was confused and wary. He wouldn't release her, but he was making no move to do more than keep her there.

"Where are you going in such a rush?" Shadows fell across his face to throw the angles and planes of his features into harsh relief. They enhanced his rough virility, adding to the aura of dangerous attraction.

"I'm going home," she stated.

"I don't have any place to go but home, either," he said. "So why don't we go some place together? Then we won't have to go home."

"I want to go home," Eve insisted firmly, despite the faint quiver that was spreading up her arm from the restraining touch of his hand.

"Why? It's lonely there."

She had difficulty imagining a man like him

ever being lonely. It was obviously a line. She wasn't going to be strung along by it.

"Let me put it another way: I don't want to go with you."

"I think I'm giving you the wrong impression." A half smile slanted his mouth, casually disarming. "I want to go someplace where we can talk."

Another line, Eve guessed. "I doubt that you're interested in talking," she returned with a tinge of sarcasm.

"It's true," he insisted, and moved to stand more to the front of her, without letting go of her arm.

Eve stared straight ahead in an effort to ignore him and the strange leaping of her pulse. His other hand moved to touch the side of her silky brown hair. Instinctively she jerked away from the soft caress, preferring force to his present means of intimidating her. She turned her head to stare at him.

When she met his gaze, Eve realized he was a man who communicated by touching — with his hands or his gaze . . . or his mouth and his body. Unbidden, her mind had added the last. She didn't doubt his expertise in any area. Her composure began to splinter a little, undermined by her unexpectedly wayward imagination.

"It is true," he repeated. "Don't you know that a man can talk to a brown mouse?"

Which was hardly flattering in the light of her

own low opinion of her sex appeal.

"Would you please not call me that?" Irritation flashed through her as she refused to comment on his observation.

"I always wondered if a brown mouse would retaliate when it was backed into a corner. There is some spirit there, behind that apparent timidity." It was obvious by the look of satisfaction on his face that she had heightened his interest. Eve wished she had kept her mouth shut. "A brown mouse. That's what you are, you know. With your brown hair and your brown eyes and your brown coat."

He was baiting her, but this time she ignored him. "I am a brown mouse who is anxious to go home, so would you let me go?" She injected a weary note in her voice, as if she were finding him quite tiresome. Fleetingly it occurred to her that she wouldn't be in this situation if she had accepted the Reverend Mr. Johnson's offer of a ride home.

"If you insist that's what you want to do, I'll walk with you to make sure you arrive safely and no cat pounces on you on the way home."

"I can think of only one 'cat' that might pounce on me and that's you," Eve retorted.

"Touché!" he laughed, and she was upset with herself for liking the sound of it.

She faced him directly. "If you don't leave me alone, I'm going to have to scream."

"Mice squeak," he corrected, but his gaze had narrowed on her, judging to see how serious she was about her threat.

"This brown mouse screams," she insisted.

She could, and if she felt sufficiently threatened, she would. It hadn't reached that point yet, but this conversation had gone on long enough.

"I believe she does," he agreed after a second had passed. He released her arm and lifted his hands in a mocking indication that he wouldn't touch her again.

"Thank you." Eve wasn't sure why she said that. Immediately she began walking away, trying not to walk too fast. She could feel him watching her with those magnetic blue eyes. It was an unnerving sensation.

"Good night, brown mouse." His low voice called after her, a hint of regret in its tone.

She didn't answer him. For another ten feet, Eve wondered if he would start following her. She forced herself not to look back. A few seconds later she heard the tavern door open and close. She glanced over her shoulder, but he wasn't in sight. Since no customer had come out, he had obviously gone back inside. She didn't have to wonder anymore whether he would come after her. Instead Eve found herself wondering who he was.

It was after ten when she reached her home. Both her parents were in the living room when she walked in. Neither of them was particularly striking in his appearance. Her father was a tall spare man with hazel eyes and thinning brown hair, while her mother was petitely built, with graying brown hair and brown eyes. It was a toss-up from whom Eve had inherited her common looks.

"Choir practice must have run late," her mother observed. It was a statement of conversation, not a remark about Eve's lateness in getting home.

"A little." She shrugged out of her brown coat and wondered if she would ever wear it again without thinking of herself as a brown mouse. "Mr. Johnson offered me a ride home, but it was such a lovely evening I decided to walk. So it took a little longer."

She didn't mention the stranger outside the tavern. They were still her parents. Eve didn't want to cause them needless concern. It had been a harmless incident anyway, not worth recounting.

In the middle of the night Toby McClure rolled onto his side. His long, little boy lashes fluttered, his sleep disturbed by a faint sound. He slowly let them come open, his sleepy blue eyes focusing on the door to his bedroom, which stood ajar. Listening, he heard hushed movement in another part of the house. A smile touched the corners of his mouth and deepened when he heard the person bump into a chair and curse beneath his breath.

Throwing back the covers, Toby slipped out of his single bed and walked to the hall door.

His bare feet made no sound on the carpeted floor. He opened the door wide and waited until he saw the towering frame of his father separate from the darkness. He was walking unsteadily, trying so hard to be quiet.

The light from the full moon streamed through the window at the end of the hallway where Toby stood, including him in its path. The instant he saw the boy, his father, Luck McClure, stopped abruptly and swayed, bracing a hand against the wall to steady himself. A frown gathered on his forehead as he eyed the boy.

"What are you doing out of bed? You're supposed to be asleep," he accused in a growling voice that had a trace of a slur.

"You woke me up," Toby replied. "You always do when you try to sneak in."

"I wasn't sneaking." He emphatically denied that suggestion and glanced around. "Where's Mrs. Jackson, the lady who is supposed to be sitting with you?"

"She was going to charge double after midnight, so I paid her off and sent her home. You owe me twelve dollars."

"You —" Luck McClure clamped his mouth shut on the explosion of anger and carefully raised a hand to cradle his forehead. "We'll talk about this in the morning, Toby," he declared in heavy warning.

"Yes, sir. I'll remind you if you forget," he promised. A mischievous light danced in his eyes. "You owe me twelve dollars."

"That's another thing we'll discuss in the morning." But it was a weak facsimile of his previous warning, as a wave of tiredness washed over him. "Right now, I'm going to bed."

Luck pushed away from the wall and used that impetus to carry him to the bedroom door opposite his son's. Toby watched him open the door to the darkened room and head in the general direction of the bed. Without a light to see the exact location of his destination, Luck stubbed his toe on an end post. He started to swear and stopped sharply when Toby crossed the hall to flip the switch, turning on the overhead light.

"Why aren't you back in bed where you belong?" Luck hobbled around to the side of the bed and half sat, half fell onto the mattress.

"I figured you'd need help getting ready for bed." Toby walked to the bed with all the weary patience of an adult and helped finish tugging the pullover sweater over his father's head.

"For an eight-year-old kid, you figure a lot of things," Luck observed with a wry sort of affection. While he unbuttoned the cuffs of his shirt, Toby unfastened the buttons on his shirtfront.

"You've gotta admit, dad, I did you a favor tonight," Toby said as he helped pull his arms free of the shirt. "How would it have looked if Mrs. Jackson had seen you come home drunk?"

"I'm not drunk," Luck protested, unfastening his pants and standing long enough to slip them down his hips. Toby pulled them the rest of the way off. "I just had a few drinks, that's all."

"Sure, dad." He reached over and pulled down the bedcovers. It didn't take much persuasion to get his father under them.

"It feels so good to lie down," Luck groaned, and started to shut his eyes when Toby tucked the covers around him. He opened them to give his son a bleary-eyed look. "Did I tell you I talked to a brown mouse?" The question was barely out before he rolled onto his side, burrowing into the pillow. "You'd better get some sleep, son," he mumbled.

Shaking his head, Toby walked to the door and paused to look at his already snoring father. He reached up to flip off the light.

"A brown mouse," he repeated. "That's another thing we'll discuss in the morning."

Back in his moonlit room, Toby crawled into bed. He glanced at the framed photograph on the table beside his bed. The picture was a twin to the one on his father's bureau. From it, a tawny-haired blonde with green eyes smiled back at him — his mother, and easily the most beautiful woman Toby had ever seen. Not that he remembered her. He had been a baby when she died — six years ago today. His gaze strayed in the direction of his father's bedroom. Sighing, he closed his eyes.

Shortly after eight the next morning, Toby woke up. He lay there for several minutes before he finally yawned and climbed out of bed to stretch. Twenty minutes later he had brushed his teeth and washed, combed his hair and found a clean pair of jeans and a yellow T-shirt to wear.

Leaving his bedroom, he paused in the hallway to look in on his father. Luck McClure was sprawled across the bed, the spare pillow clutched by an encircling arm. Toby quietly closed the door, although he doubted his father would be disturbed by any noise he made.

In the kitchen, he put a fresh pot of coffee on to perk, then pushed the step stool to the counter and climbed it to reach the juice glasses and a cereal bowl in the cupboard. Positioning the stool in front of another cupboard, he mounted it to take down a box of cornflakes. With orange juice and milk from the refrigerator, Toby sat down to the kitchen table to eat his breakfast of cereal and orange juice.

By the time he'd finished, the coffee was done. He glanced from it to the pitcher of orange juice, hesitated, and walked to the refrigerator to take out a pitcher of tomato juice. Climbing back up the step stool, he took down a tall glass and filled it three-quarters full with tomato juice. When he returned the pitcher to the refrigerator, he took out an egg, cracked it, and added it to the tomato juice. He stirred that mixture hard, then added garlic and Tabasco to it. Sniffing the end result, he wrinkled his nose in distaste.

Taking the glass, he left the kitchen and walked down the hallway to his father's room. He hadn't changed position in bed. Toby leaned over, taking great care not to spill the contents of the glass, and shook his father's shoulder with his free hand.

"It's nine o'clock, dad. Time to get up." His statement drew a groan of protest. "Come on, dad."

With great reluctance, Luck rolled onto his back, flinging an arm across his eyes to shield them from the brightness of the sunlight shining in his window. Toby waited in patient silence until he sat up.

"Oh, my head," Luck mumbled, and held it in both his hands, the bedcovers falling around his waist to leave his torso bare.

Toby climbed onto the bed, balancing on his knees while he offered his father the concoction he'd made. "Drink this. It'll make you feel better."

Lowering his hands part way from his head, Luck looked at it skeptically. "What is it?"

"Don't ask," Toby advised, and reached out to pinch his father's nose closed while he tipped the glass to his lips. He managed to pour a mouthful down before his father choked and took the glass out of his hand.

"What is this?" Luck coughed and frowned

as he studied the glass.

"It's a hangover remedy." And Toby became the recipient of the glowering frown and a raised eyebrow.

"And when did you become an expert on hangover remedies?" Luck challenged.

"I saw it on television once," Toby shrugged.

Luck shook his head in quiet exasperation. "I should make you drink this, you know that, don't you?" he sighed.

"There's fresh coffee in the kitchen." Toby hopped off the bed, just in case his father intended to carry out that threat.

"Go pour me a cup. And take this with you." A smile curved slowly, forming attractive grooves on either side of his mouth — male dimples — as he handed the glass back to Toby. "I'll be there as soon as I get some clothes on."

"I'll pour you some orange juice, too," Toby volunteered.

"Just straight orange juice. Don't put anything else in it."

"I won't." A wide grin split Toby's face before he turned to walk swiftly from the room.

With a wry shake of his head, Luck threw back the covers and climbed slowly out of bed. He paused beside the bureau to glance at the photograph. *Well, pretty lady, do you see what kind of boy your son has grown into?* The blue of his eyes had a pensive look as he walked to the bathroom.

CHAPTER TWO

"Your coffee is cold," Toby accused when his father finally appeared in the kitchen.

Dressed in worn blue jeans and a gray sweat shirt, Luck had taken the time to shower and shave. His dark brown hair gleamed almost black, combed into a careless kind of order. He smiled at the reproval from his son.

"I had to get cleaned up," he defended himself, and sipped at the lukewarm coffee before adding some hot liquid from the coffeepot. He sat down in a chair opposite from his son and rested his forearms on the table. "Do you want to explain to me what happened to Mrs. Jackson last night?"

"She was going to charge you double for staying after midnight, so I paid her and sent her home," Toby said, repeating his previous night's explanation.

"And she went — just like that," Luck replied with a wave of his hand to indicate how easy it had been. "She just went and left you here alone?"

"Well . . ." Toby hedged, and squirmed in his chair.

"Why did she leave?"

"She got the impression we were broke, I think. She got a little upset thinking that you'd asked her to stay when you knew all you could afford to pay was twelve dollars."

"Why did you do it?"

"I'm too old to have a sitter, dad," Toby protested. "I can take care of myself."

"Maybe you can, but what about my peace of mind? I'm an adult. You're a child. When I leave, I want to know there's an adult with you — looking after you — yes. But mostly in case there's an emergency — if you should get sick or hurt. I'd like to know there is someone here with you to help," he explained firmly. "Do you understand?"

"Yes." It was a low admission.

"From now on, when I go out for the evening, you will have a sitter and she will stay here until I come back. Is that understood?"

"Yes."

"Good." With the discussion concluded, Luck raised the coffee cup to his mouth.

"What about the twelve dollars?" As far as Toby was concerned, the discussion wasn't over. "It's from the money I've been saving to buy a minibike."

"You should have considered that before you spent it."

"But that's what you would have had to pay her if I hadn't," Toby reasoned with the utmost logic. "You would have had to pay her that and more."

"I'll give you the twelve dollars back on one condition," Luck replied. "You call Mrs. Jackson, tell her what you did, and apologize."

There was a long sigh before Toby nodded his agreement. "Okay."

"Have you had breakfast?" Luck changed the subject.

"Cornflakes."

"Would you like some bacon and eggs?"

"Sure," Toby agreed. "I'll help."

While he set the table, Luck put the bacon in the skillet and broke eggs in a bowl to scramble them. Finished with his task before his father, Toby walked over to the stove to watch.

"Dad?" He tipped his head back to look up to his tall parent. "Do you want to explain about the brown mouse?"

"The brown mouse?" Luck frowned at him, his expression blank.

"Yeah. Last night when you came home, you said you had talked to a brown mouse," Toby explained. "I thought people only saw pink elephants when they were drinking."

"People can have all kinds of illusions when they are drinking. Evidently mine was a brown mouse," Luck murmured. "I must have had a few more drinks than I realized."

"It was because of mom, wasn't it?" Toby asked quietly.

There was a moment of silence. Then Luck gave him a smiling glance. "What do you want to do today? Do you want to go fishing?

Boating? Just name it." He deliberately avoided his son's question, and Toby knew there was no need to repeat it.

"Let's go fishing," Toby decided.

"Fishing it is," Luck agreed, and smiled as he rumpled the top of his son's brown hair.

Two hours later the dishes were washed and the beds were made and they were sitting in the boat, anchored in a cove of Lake Namekagon. A thick forest crowded the meandering shoreline, occasionally leaving room for a sandy stretch of beach. A mixture of hardwood and conifers, with extensive stands of pine and spruce, provided a blend of the green shades of summer. The unruffled calm of the lake reflected the edging wall of forest, home for the black bear, deer, beaver and other wildlife.

Their fishing lines were in the water, their rods resting against the sides of the boat in their stands. Toby was leaning back in his seat, his little-boy legs stretched out in front of him and his hands clasped behind his head for a pillow. He stared at the puffy cloud formations in the blue sky with a frown of concentration.

Luck was equally relaxed, yet suspicious of the long silence that was only broken by the infrequent lapping of water against the boat or the cry of a bird. His sidelong glance studied the intent expression of his son.

"You seem to be doing some pretty heavy thinking, Toby," he observed, and let his gaze slide skyward when his son glanced at him. "What's on your mind?"

"I've been trying to figure something out." Toby turned his head in the pillow of his hands. The frowning concentration remained fixed in his expression. "What exactly does a mother do?"

The question widened Luck's eyes slightly. The question caused him to recognize that his son had never been exposed to the life of a family unit — father, mother and children. There was only one grandparent living, and no aunts or uncles. During the school year, the weekends were the times they had to share together. Luck had often permitted his son to invite a friend over, sometimes to stay overnight, but mostly to accompany them on an afternoon outing; but Toby had never stayed overnight with any of his friends.

The question was a general one — and a serious one. He couldn't avoid answering it. "Mothers do all sorts of things. They cook, wash dishes, clean the house, take care of you when you're sick, do the laundry, all sorts of things like that. Sometimes they work at a job during the day, too. Mothers remember birthdays without being reminded, make special treats for no reason, and think up games to play when you're bored." He knew it was an inadequate answer because he'd left out the love and the caring that he didn't know how to describe.

When Luck finished, he glanced at his son.

Toby was staring at the sky, the frown of concentration replaced with a thoughtful look. "I think we need a mother," he announced after several seconds.

"Why?" The statement touched off a defensive mechanism that made Luck challenge it. "Since when have you and I not been able to manage on our own? I thought we had a pretty good system worked out."

"We do, dad," Toby assured him, then sighed. "I'm just tired of always having to wash dishes and make my bed."

The edges of his mouth deepened in a lazy smile. "Having a mother wouldn't mean you'd get out of doing your share of the daily chores."

Unclasping his hands from behind his head, Toby sat upright. "How do you go about finding a mother?"

"That's my problem." Luck made that point very clear. "In order for you to have a mother, I would have to get married again."

"Do you think you'd *like* to get married again?"

"Don't you think your questions are getting a little bit personal?" *And a little bit awkward to handle,* Luck thought as he sat up, a tiny crease running across his forehead.

"I'm your son. If you can't talk to me about it, who can you?" Toby reasoned.

"You are much too old for your age." His blue eyes glinted with dry humor when he met the earnest gaze of his son.

"If you got married again, you could have more children," Toby pointed out. "Have you thought about that?"

"Yes, and I don't know if I could handle another one of you," Luck teased.

With a sigh of exasperation, Toby protested. "Dad, will you please be serious? I am trying to discuss this intelligently with you. You wouldn't necessarily have another boy. You could have a little girl."

"Is that what this is about? Do you want brothers and sisters?" There was something at the bottom of all this interest in a mother. Sooner or later, Luck felt he would uncover the reason.

"Do you know that it's really impossible to have a father-son conversation with you?" Toby declared with adult irritation. "You never answer my questions. You just ask me another. How am I ever going to learn anything?"

"All right." Luck crossed his arms in front of him and adopted a serious look. "What do you want to know?"

"If you met the right girl, would you get married again?"

"Yes, if I met the right girl," he conceded with a slow nod.

With a satisfied smile, Toby resumed his former position stretched out in the seat, his head pillowed in his hands, and stared at the sky. "I'll help you look."

Luck took a deep breath, started to say something, then decided it was wiser to let the subject drop.

The lake cottage was built of logs, complete with a front porch that overlooked the lake across the road. The rustic, yet modern structure was tucked in a forest clearing, a dense stand of pines forming a semicircle around it.

Over the weekend, Eve Rowland and her parents had moved in lock, stock and barrel for the summer. It had been a labor of fun opening up their vacation home again and reawakening happy memories of previous summers.

Standing on the porch, Eve gazed at the azure waters of Namekagon Lake. Here in the northwoods of Wisconsin and Minnesota was where the legend of Paul Bunyan and his blue ox, Babe, was born. According to the tales, Paul and Babe stomped around a little in Namekagon, just one of the many lakes in Wisconsin. Eve could remember looking at a map of the area as a child and believing the tale. The mythical figure of Paul Bunyan had been as real to her as the Easter Bunny and Santa Claus, even if he didn't pass out presents.

Eve lifted her head to the clear blue sky and breathed in the clean pine-scented air. On a sigh of contentment, Eve turned and walked into the cottage. It was small, just two bedrooms, the kitchen separated from the living room by a table nook. She let the screen door bang shut. Her father had his fishing gear spread over the table and was working on one of his reels. Her mother was in the kitchen, fixing some potato salad to chill for the evening meal.

"Is it all right if I use the car?" Eve asked. "I want to go to the store down the road. I'm out of shampoo and I'm going to need some suntan lotion."

"Sure." Her father reached in his pants' pocket and tossed her the car keys.

"Was there anything you needed?" Eve reached to pick up her canvas purse where she'd left it on a sofa cushion.

"Maybe some milk," her mother answered, "but other than that, I can't think of anything."

"Okay. I'll be back later," she called over her shoulder as she pushed open the door to the porch.

Sliding into the driver's seat of the sedan, Eve felt as bright and sunny as the summer afternoon. She had dressed to snatch her mood that day. The terry-cloth material of her short-sleeved top and slacks was a cheerful canary yellow, trimmed with white. A white hairband kept her brown hair away from her face, framing its oval shape.

It was a short drive to the combination grocery and general store that served the resort community. The Rowland family had traded there many times in past summers, so Eve was a familiar face to the owners. She chatted with them a few minutes as she paid for her purchases.

When she started to leave, she heard a man's voice ask to speak to the owner. It sounded vaguely familiar, but when she turned to see if it was anyone she knew, the man was hidden from her view by an aisle. Since the man had business with the owner, and since it was possible she didn't even know him, Eve continued out of the store, dismissing the incident from her mind.

She'd left the car in the store's parking area. She walked toward it, but it was only when she got closer that she began to realize something was wrong. Her steps slowed and her eyes widened in disbelief at the sight of the shattered windshield and the three-inch-diameter hole in the glass.

Stunned, Eve absently glanced in the side window and saw the baseball lying on the front seat. Reacting mechanically, she opened the door and reached to pick up the ball amid the splintered chips of glass on the car seat.

"That's my ball." A young boy's voice claimed ownership of the object in her hand.

Still too stunned to be angry or upset, Eve turned to look at him. A baseball cap was perched atop a mass of dark brown hair, while a pair of unblinking innocent blue eyes stared back at her. Eve judged the boy to be eight, no older than nine. She had the feeling that she had seen him somewhere before, possibly at school.

"Did you do this?" She gestured toward the

broken windshield, using the same hand that held the baseball.

"Not exactly. You see, my dad just bought me this new baseball glove." He glanced at the oversized leather mitt on his left hand. "We were trying it out to see how it worked. I asked dad to throw me a hard one so I could tell whether there was enough padding to keep my hand from stinging. Only when he did, it was too high and the ball hit the tip of my glove and bounced off, then smashed your windshield. It must have hit it just right," he declared with a rueful grimace. "So it was really my dad who threw the ball. I just didn't catch it."

"A parking lot isn't the place to play catch." At the moment, that was the only thing Eve could think of to say. It was a helpless kind of protest, lacking the strength to change a deed that was already done.

"We know that now," the boy agreed.

"Where's your father?"

"He went into the store to see if they knew who the car belonged to," he explained. "He told me to stay here in case you came back while he was gone."

The comment jogged her memory of the man who had been in the store asking to speak to the owner. She started to turn when she heard the same voice ask, "Is this your car?"

"It's my father's." Eve completed the turn to face the boy's father.

Cold shock froze her limbs into immobility. It was the stranger she'd met outside the tavern last week. The rumpled darkness of his hair grew in thick waves, a few strands straying onto his forehead. The same magnetic blue eyes were looking at her with warm interest. The sunlight added a rough vitality to the handsomely masculine features.

Eve waited, unconsciously holding her breath, for the recognition to show in his eyes as she mentally braced herself to watch that mouth with its ready smile form the words "brown mouse." But it didn't happen. He didn't recognize her. Evidently the combination of liquor and the night's shadows had made her image hazy in his mind. Eve just hoped it stayed that way, as feeling began to steal back into her limbs.

He glanced at the baseball in her hand. "I hope Toby explained what happened." His expression was pleasant, yet serious.

"Yes, he did." She was conscious of how loudly her heart was pounding. "At least he said you threw the ball and he missed it."

"I'm afraid that's what happened," he admitted with a faintly rueful lift of his mouth. "Naturally I'll pay the cost of having the windshield replaced on your father's car, Miss —"

"Rowland. Eve Rowland." She introduced herself and was glad that between the sack of groceries in one arm and the ball in the other hand, she wasn't able to shake hands.

"My name is Luck McClure, and this is my son, Toby." He laid a hand on the boy's shoulder with a trace of parental pride. "We're spending the summer at a lake house a few miles from here."

Eve was certain she had misunderstood his name. "Did you say Luke McClure?"

"No." He smiled, as if it were a common mistake. "It's Luck — as in good luck. Although in actual fact the proper name of Luck has its derivations in the name of Luke or Lucias. It's one of those family names that somehow manages to get passed along to future generations."

"I see," she murmured, and glanced at Toby, who had obviously not been named after his father. She wondered if there were another little Luck somewhere at home. At least now she understood why the boy had seemed familiar at first. There was a definite resemblance between him and his father.

"With that windshield smashed, you aren't going to be able to see to drive home," Luck stated. "I would appreciate it if you would let us give you a ride."

Under the circumstances, Eve didn't know any other way that she could get back to the cottage if she didn't accept his offer. "Yes, thank you," she nodded.

"May I have my baseball back?" the boy spoke up.

"Of course." She handed it to him.

"Our car is parked over here." Luck McClure

reclaimed her attention, directing her toward a late-model Jaguar. "Did you say the car was your father's?"

"Yes. He's at the cottage."

"Is that where you would like me to drive you?" He walked around to open the passenger door for her, while his son climbed in the back seat.

"Yes. My parents and I are spending the summer there." Eve waited until he was behind the wheel to give him directions.

"That isn't far from our house," he commented, and Eve wished it was in the opposite direction. Any minute now she just knew he was going to recognize her, which would make things uncomfortable, if not embarrassing. "I'll make arrangements with your father about paying for the windshield."

Briefly Eve wondered if that was a slur at her sex, insinuating that she wasn't capable of making adequate arrangements because she was a woman. She doubted it, though. Luck McClure was definitely all man, but he didn't strike her as the chauvinistic type. More than likely he simply wanted to deal directly with the owner of the car. Which suited her fine. The less she saw of him, the less chance there would be that he'd remember her.

The rounded bill of a baseball cap entered her side vision as the boy leaned over the seat. "I really thought you'd be mad when you saw what we did to your car. How come you weren't?"

The question made her smile. "I was too stunned. I couldn't believe what I saw."

"I couldn't, either, when it happened," Luck admitted with a low chuckle. It reached out to share the moment of amusement with her and pulled her gaze in his direction.

With less wariness, Eve let herself forget their first meeting outside the tavern. There was an easy charm about Luck McClure that she found attractive, in addition to his looks. It had a quality of bold friendliness to it.

"Flirting" was a word that had a female connotation, but this was one time when Eve felt it could apply to a man without diminishing his virility. In fact, the gleam lurking in his blue eyes and the ready smile enhanced it. Part of her wished this was their first meeting, because she knew sooner or later he would recognize his "brown mouse." And a man like Luck McClure would never be attracted to a brown mouse.

His gaze slid from the road long enough to meet her eyes. There was warm male interest in the look that ran over her face, a look that probably had its basis in a curiosity similar to the one Eve had just experienced. She was briefly stimulated by it until she remembered how futile it was to be attracted to him. Eve glanced at the road a second before his attention returned to it.

"Our place is just ahead on the left," Eve stated.

As Luck slowed the car to make the turn into the short driveway, the boy, Toby, announced, "We go by here all the time. I didn't think anybody lived in that house. When did you move in?"

"This past weekend," she replied, then wondered if that would jog Luck's memory of the tavern incident. A quick glance didn't find any reaction. "We spend the summers here. We sometimes come here during the winter holidays to snowmobile or ice-fish and do some cross-country skiing."

"Do you like to ski?" Toby's questions continued even after the car stopped.

"With Mt. Telemark practically in our backyard, it would be a shame if I didn't." A faint smile touched her mouth as she shifted the sack of groceries to open the door. "As it happens, I enjoy it."

"Me, too. Dad took me skiing last Christmas." The boy scrambled out of the back seat to join his father. "Next year I'll be good enough to ski with him." He tipped his head back to look up at his father for confirmation. "Won't I, dad?"

"By the end of next winter, you'll be a veteran of the slopes," Luck agreed with a lazy smile, and waited until Eve had walked around the front of the car before starting toward the log cottage.

With this tall, good-looking man beside her, she felt oddly self-conscious — a sensation that had nothing to do with their previous encounter. It was more an awareness of physical attraction than an uneasiness. She failed to notice that Toby wasn't with them until the car door slammed again and the boy came running after them. Simultaneously she paused with Luck McClure to see what had delayed Toby.

"You left the keys in the ignition again, dad," the boy declared with an adult reprimand in his expression, and handed the car keys to his father. "That's how cars get stolen."

"Yes, Toby." Luck accepted the admonishment with lazy indulgence and slipped the keys into his pocket.

When they started toward the porch again, Toby tagged along.

Her parents recovered quickly from their initial surprise at the strange man and boy accompanying Eve into the house. She introduced them, then Luck took over the explanation of the shattered windshield. Exhibiting his typical understanding, her father was not angered by the accident . . . more amused than anything.

While they discussed particulars, Eve went into the kitchen to put away the milk she'd got. She remained in the alcove, satisfied to just observe the easy way Luck McClure related to her parents. It was a knack few people had. It came naturally to him, part of his relaxed, easygoing style.

With all his apparent friendliness, Eve didn't doubt that he could handle authority equally well. There was something in his presence that commanded respect. It was an understated quality, but that didn't lessen its strength.

Her gaze strayed to the boy standing beside Luck. He was listening attentively to all that was being said, possessing an oddly mature sense of responsibility for a boy of his age. His only motion was tossing the ball into his glove and retrieving it to toss it methodically again.

With the milk put away, Eve was running out of reasons to dawdle in the kitchen. Since she didn't want to take part in the conversation between her parents and Luck McClure, she took her suntan lotion and shampoo and slipped away to her bedroom. She paused in front of the vanity mirror above her dresser and studied her reflection.

The white band sleeked her brown hair away from her face, emphasizing features that were not so serene as they normally were. Eve touched the mouth that looked softer and fuller, fingertips brushing the curve. There was an added glow of suppressed excitement in the luminous brown of her eyes. The cause of it was Luck McClure and that never ending question of when he would recognize her.

With all the cheery yellow of her pants and top, Eve admitted to herself that she didn't look like a brown mouse. If anything, a sunflower was more apt — with its bright yellow petals and brown center.

"You really are a 'vanity' mirror," Eve murmured, and turned away from the reflecting glass before she became too wrapped up in her appearance.

But her subconscious made a silent resolution not to wear brown again. From now on, only bright colors would be added to her wardrobe. Drab clothing did nothing to improve her looks. "Brown mouse" — the phrase mocked her with its recollections of that night.

Eve dreaded the time when she would meet his wife, but in this small resort community it would be impossible for their paths not to cross sometime during the course of the summer. It would be foolish to try to avoid it. But what do you say to a woman whose husband tried to pick you up?

What kind of marriage did he have? He had said it was lonely at home and he wanted to talk to someone. He and his wife were obviously having trouble, Eve concluded. Or maybe he was just the type that stepped out anyway. No, she shook that thought away. Indulging in an idle flirtation would come naturally to him, but Luck McClure wasn't the type to let it go beyond the bantering of words. There was too much depth to him for that.

What did it matter? He was married. Regardless of the problems he was having, Luck was the kind who would persist until he solved them. It was ridiculous to waste her time thinking about a married man, no matter how interesting and compelling he might be.

The closing of the screen door and the cessation of voices from the front room turned Eve to face her bedroom door. She listened and heard the opening of car doors outside. The tall arresting man and his son were leaving.

It was just as well. Now she could come out of hiding — the realization stopped her short of the door. She had been hiding. Hiding because he had looked at her with a man's interest in the opposite sex and her ego hadn't wanted him to remember that she was a plain brown mouse. So what had she done? Scurried off into her hole, just like a brown mouse.

Never again, Eve resolved, and left her "hole" to return to the front room. The only occupant was her mother. Eve glanced around, noticing the Jaguar was gone from the driveway.

"Where's dad?"

"Mr. McClure drove him back to the car. They called a garage. A man's coming over to pick up our car and replace the broken windshield," her mother explained. "He should be back shortly."

An hour later her father returned, but it was the mechanic who brought him back — not Luck McClure.

CHAPTER THREE

The Rowlands were without transportation for two days. On the morning of the third day, the garage owner delivered the car, complete with a new windshield. The day had started out with gray and threatening skies. By the time the car was returned it began drizzling. And by noon it was raining steadily, confining Eve indoors.

With the car returned, her parents decided to restock their grocery supplies that afternoon. They invited Eve to come with them, but since they planned to visit some of their friends while they were out, she declined.

On rainy days she usually enjoyed curling up with a book, but on this occasion she was too restless to read. Since she had the entire afternoon on her hands, she decided to do some baking and went into the kitchen to stir up a batch of chocolate chip cookies, her father's favorite.

Soon the delicious smell of cookies baking in the oven filled the small cottage and chased away the gloom of the gray rainy day. Cookies from two sheet trays were cooling on the kitchen counter, atop an opened newspaper. Eve glanced through the glass door of the oven at the third sheet. Its cookies were just beginning to brown, a mere minute away from being done.

The thud of footsteps on the wooden porch floor reached her hearing, straightening Eve from the oven. An instant after they stopped, there was a knock on the door. She cast a glance at the oven, then went to answer the door. A splash of flour had left a white streak on the burgundy velour of her top. She brushed at it but only succeeded in spreading the white patch across her stomach. Eve was still brushing at it when she opened the door.

The slick material of a dark blue Windbreaker glistened with rain across a set of wide shoulders that turned at the sound of the opening door. Her hand stopped its motion when Eve looked into a pair of arresting blue eyes.

A tiny electric shock quivered through her nerve ends at the sight of Luck McClure on the other side of the wire mesh screen. Dampness gave a black sheen to his dark brown hair. Toby was beside him, his face almost lost under the hooded sweat shirt pulled over his head and tied under his chin. Beyond the shelter of the porch roof, rain fell in an obscuring gray curtain.

"Hello, Mr. McClure," Eve recovered her voice to greet him calmly.

An easy casual smile touched his mouth, so absently charming. "I stopped to —"

His explanation was interrupted by the oven timer dinging its bell to signal Eve the cookies should be done. "Excuse me. I have something in the oven." Manners dictated that she couldn't leave them standing on the porch, so she quickly unhooked the screen door. "Come in," she invited hurriedly, and retraced her path to the kitchen to remove the cookies before they burned.

Behind her she heard the screen door open and the shuffle of incoming footsteps. "Don't forget to wipe your feet, dad, " Toby murmured the conscientious reminder.

Opening the oven door, Eve took a pot holder and used it to absorb the heat of the metal cookie sheet while she lifted it out of the oven. Another tray of individually spooned cookie dough was sitting on the counter, ready to be put in to bake. She slipped it on the rack with her free hand and closed the oven door.

"My parents are gone this afternoon," she said, carrying the sheet of baked cookies to the counter where the others were cooling, conscious that Luck McClure and his son had followed her to the kitchen. "Was there something I could help you with?" she offered, and began removing the cookies from the sheet with a metal spatula.

"I told your father he could use my car if he had any errands to run while his was in the shop," he explained. "I stopped to see if he needed it."

"The garage delivered our car this morning." Eve half turned to answer him and felt the slow inspection of his look.

Her cheeks were flushed from the heat of the oven. The sweep of his glance left behind an odd licking sensation that heightened her already high color. It was a look he would give to any semiattractive woman — a man's assessment of her looks — but that didn't alter its effect on her.

Toby appeared at her elbow, offering her a distraction. He peered over the top of the counter to see what she was doing. Untying his hood, he pushed it off his head, tousling his brown hair in the process.

"What are you making?" he said curiously.

"Chocolate-chip cookies." She smiled briefly at him and continued to slide the cookies off the net spatula onto the newspaper with the rest.

He breathed in deeply, his blue eyes rounded as if drinking in the sight. "They smell good."

"Would you like one?" Eve offered. As an afterthought, she glanced at Luck, who had moved into her side vision. "Is it all right if he has a cookie?"

"Sure." Permission was granted with a faint nod of his head.

Toby reached for one that she had just set on the paper. "Careful," she warned, but it came too late. Toby was already jerking his hand away, nursing burned fingers.

"They're hot," he stated.

"Naturally. They just came out of the oven. Try one of those at the back." She pointed with the spatula. "They've had a chance to cool."

He took one of the cookies she'd indicated and bit into it. As he chewed it, he studied the cookie. "These are really good," he declared.

"You'll have to help your mother make some for you." Eve flashed him a smile at the compliment.

"I don't have a mother anymore," Toby replied absently, and took another bite of the cookie.

His statement sent invisible shock waves through her. She darted a troubled glance at Luck. Had his problems at home ended in divorce? Except for a certain blandness in his gaze, he didn't appear bothered by the topic his son had introduced.

"My wife died when Toby was small," he explained, and glanced at his son. The corners of his mouth were pulled upward in a smile. "Toby and I have been baching it for several years now, but I'm afraid our domestic talents don't stretch to baking cookies."

"I see," she murmured because she didn't know what else to say.

The knowledge that he was married, and therefore out of circulation, had made her feel safe from his obvious male attraction. The discovery that he was a widower caught her off guard, leaving her shaken.

"May I have another cookie?" Toby asked after he'd licked the melted chocolate of a chip from his finger.

"Of course." She'd made a large batch, so there was plenty to spare. Homemade cookies were obviously a special treat for the boy.

As he took another one, Toby glanced at his father. "Why don't you try one, dad? You don't know what you're missing."

"Go ahead." Eve added her permission and moved aside as she laid the last cookie down.

While Luck took her up on the offer and helped himself to a cookie, Eve carried the empty sheet to the adjoining counter and began spooning cookie dough onto it from the mixing bowl. The ever curious Toby followed her.

"What's that?"

"This is the cookie batter. When you bake it in the oven, it turns into a cookie." It was becoming obvious to her that this was all new to him. If he'd seen it before, it had been too long ago for him to remember clearly.

"How do you make it?" He looked up at her with a thoughtful frown.

"There's a recipe on the back of the chocolate-chip package." The teaching habit was too firmly ingrained for Eve to overlook the chance to impart knowledge when interest was aroused. She paused in her task to pick up the empty chip package and show it to him. "It's right there. It tells you all the ingredients and how to do it."

With the cookie in one hand and the package with its recipe in the other, Toby wandered to the opposite side of the kitchen and studied the printing with frowning concentration. The kitchen was a small alcove off the front room. When Luck moved to lean a hip against the counter near Eve, she began to realize how limited the walk space was.

"There is something very comfortable about a kitchen filled with the smell of fresh baking on a rainy day. It really feels like a home then," Luck remarked.

"Yes, it does," Eve agreed, and knew it was that casual intimacy that was disturbing her.

"Have you eaten one of your cookies? They *are* good," Luck said, confirming his son's opinion.

"Not yet," she admitted, and turned to tell him there was coffee in the electric pot if he wanted a cup. But when she opened her mouth to speak, he slipped the rounded edge of a warm cookie inside.

"A cook should sample her wares," he insisted with lazy inoffensive mockery.

There was an instant of surprised delay as her eyes met the glinting humor of his. Then her teeth instinctively sank into the sweet morsel to take a bite. Luck held onto the cookie until she did, then surrendered it to the hand that reached for it.

With food in her mouth, good manners dictated that she not speak until it was chewed and swallowed. It wasn't easy under his lazily watchful eyes, especially when he took due note of the tongue that darted out to lick the melted chocolate from her lips. Her heart began thumping against her ribs like a locomotive climbing a steep incline.

"I'll finish it later with some coffee." Eve set the half-eaten cookie on the counter, unwilling to go through the unnerving experience of Luck watching her eat again. She picked up the spoon and worked at concentrating on filling the cookie sheet with drops of dough.

"And I thought all along that Eve tempted Adam with an apple," Luck drawled softly. "When did you discover a cookie worked better?"

Again her gaze raced to him, surprised that he remembered her name and stunned by the implication of his words. No matter how she tried, Eve couldn't react casually to this sexual bantering of words the way he did. He was much more adept at the game than she was.

"What does 'tempted' mean?" Toby eyed his father curiously.

Luck turned to look at his son, not upset by the question nor the fact that Toby had been listening. "It's like putting a worm on a hook. The fish can't resist taking a nibble."

"Oh." With his curiosity satisfied, Toby's attention moved on to other things. He set the empty chocolate-chip package on the counter where Eve had left it before. "This doesn't look hard to do, dad. Do you think we could make some cookies sometime?"

"On the next rainy day we'll give it a try," he promised, and sent a twinkling look at Eve. "If we have trouble, we can give Eve a call."

"Yeah," Toby agreed with a wide grin.

Unexpectedly, just when Eve had decided Luck was going to become a fixture in the kitchen for what was left of the afternoon, he straightened from the counter. "Toby and I have taken advantage of your hospitality long enough. We'd better be leaving."

The timer went off to signal the other sheet of cookies was ready to come out of the oven. Its intrusive sound allowed her to turn away and hide the sudden rush of keen disappointment that he was leaving. It also permitted her to remember the reason for his visit.

"It was thoughtful of you to stop," Eve replied, taking the cookie sheet from the oven.

"It was the least I could do," Luck insisted, and paused in her path to the counter. She was compelled to look into the deep indigo color of his eyes. A half smile slanted his mouth. "I hope you have forgiven me for what happened the other time we met."

She went white with shock. "Then you do remember."

Although the smile remained, an attractive frown was added to his expression. "I was talking about the broken windshield. Was there something else I was supposed to remember?"

She felt the curious intensity of his gaze probe for an answer, one that she had very nearly given away. "No. Of course not." She rushed a nervous smile onto her face and stepped around him to the counter, her pulse racing a thousand miles an hour.

For an uneasy moment, Eve thought he was going to question her answer, then she heard him take a step toward the front room and the door. "Tell your parents I said hello."

"I will," she promised, and turned when the pair were nearly to the door.

"Goodbye, Eve." Toby waved.

"Goodbye," she echoed his farewell.

The cottage seemed terribly quiet and empty after they'd gone. The gray rain outside the windows seemed to close in, its loneliness seeping in through the walls. Eve poured a cup of coffee and sat at the table to finish the cookie Luck had given her. It had lost some of its flavor.

The following week Eve volunteered to make the short trip to the store to buy bread, milk and the other essential items that always needed replenishing, so her parents could go boating with friends that had stopped by. When she arrived at the store, she was quick to notice the sleek Jaguar sedan parked in front of it. She wasn't aware of the glow of anticipation that came to her eyes.

Luck and Toby were on their way out of the

store with an armful of groceries when she walked in. "Hello." Her bright greeting was a shade breathless.

The wide lazy smile that Luck gave her quickened her pulse. "You are safe today. Toby left his baseball and glove at the house," he said.

"Good. I was wondering whether I should stop here or not." Eve laughed as she lied, because she hadn't given the broken windshield incident another thought.

"Look what we bought." Toby reached into the smaller sack he carried and pulled out a package of chocolate chips. "We're going to make some the next time it rains."

"I hope they turn out," she smiled.

"So do I," Luck murmured dryly, and touched the boy's shoulder. "Let's go, Toby. We'll see you, Eve," he nodded, using that indefinite phrase that committed nothing.

"Bye, Eve."

The smile faded from her expression as she watched them go. Turning away from the door, she went to do her shopping.

"When do you suppose it's going to rain again?" Toby searched the blue sky for a glimpse of dark clouds, but there wasn't a sign of even a puffy white one. He sank to his knees on the beach towel that Luck was stretched out on. Grains of sand clung to his bare feet, wet like the rest of him from swimming in the lake.

"It's been almost a week."

"Maybe we're in for a drought," Luck suggested with dry humor at his son's impatience.

"Very funny." Toby made a face at him and turned to squint into the sunlight reflected off the lake's surface. "The water is pretty warm. Are you going to come in for a swim now?"

"In a little bit." The heat of the sun burning into his exposed flesh made him lazy.

A red beach ball bounced on the sand near him and rolled onto his towel. Luck started to sit up and made it halfway before the ball's owner arrived.

"Sorry," a breathless female voice apologized.

Turning, he leaned on an elbow as a shapely blonde in a very brief bikini knelt on the sand beside him and reached for the ball. Her smile was wide and totally beguiling.

"No harm done," he assured her, and noticed the amount of cleavage that was revealed when she bent to pick up the ball.

His gaze lifted to her face and observed the knowing sparkle in her eyes. Wisely he guessed that it had all been a ploy to attract his attention. It was an old game. Despite the beautiful packaging, he discovered he wasn't interested in playing.

The blonde waited for several seconds, but he didn't make the expected gambit. Disappointment flickered in her expression, then was quickly veiled by a coy smile. Rising in a graceful turning motion, she ran back to her friends.

"That blonde was really a knockout, huh, dad?"

Amused, Luck cast a glance over his shoulder at his son, who was still staring after the shapely girl. "Yes, I guess she was," he agreed blandly, and looked back to the trio playing keep-away. Then he pushed himself into a full sitting position, his attention leaving the scantily clad blonde.

"She thought you were pretty neat, too," Toby observed, a hint of devilry in his smile. "I saw the sexy look she gave you."

"You see too much." Luck gave him a playful push backward, plopping him down on the sand.

Toby just laughed. "Why don't you marry someone like her?"

Luck sighed. He'd thought that subject had been forgotten. He shook his head in a mild form of exasperation. "Looks aren't everything, son." Rolling to his feet, he reached down to pull Toby up. "Let's go for that swim of yours."

"Race ya!" Toby challenged, and took off at a dead run.

He loped after him, his long strides keeping the distance between them short. Wading into the lake until he was up to his knees, he then dived in. Powerful reaching strokes soon carried Luck into deeper water, where he waited for Toby to catch up with him.

"What do you think, pretty lady?" Luck murmured in a voice that was audible only to himself. "Have you ruined me for anyone else?"

The image of his wife swirled through the mists of his mind, her face laughing up at him as she pulled him to their bed. Her features were soft, like a fading edge of a dream, her likeness no longer bringing him the sharp stabbing pain. Time had reduced it to a beautiful memory that came back to haunt him at odd times.

Although he still possessed a man's sexual appetite, emotional desire seemed to have left him. Except for Toby, it seemed that all the good things in life were behind him. Tomorrow seemed empty, without promise.

A squeal of female laughter from the lakeshore pulled his gaze to the beach and the cavorting blonde. Her bold bid for his attention had left him cold, even though he had liked what he had seen. He found the subtle approach much sexier — like the time Eve had licked the chocolate from her lips. Strange that he had thought of her instead of the way his wife, Lisa, used to run her finger around the rim of a glass.

A hand sprayed water on his face. Luck blinked and wiped the droplets from his eyes as Toby laughed and struck out, swimming away from him. The moment of curious reflection was gone as he took up the challenge of his son.

Thunder crashed and rolled across the sky, unleashing a torrent of rain to hammer on the roof of the cottage. A rain-cool breeze rushed in through a window above the kitchen sink, stirring the brown silk of Eve's hair as she washed the luncheon dishes.

Lightning cracked outside the window. "My, that looked close," her mother murmured, always a little nervous about violent storms.

"The baseball game in Milwaukee has just been postponed because of the rain," her father sighed in disappointment and switched off the radio atop the refrigerator. "And they always have doubleheaders on Saturday, too." If her father had one passion besides fishing, it was baseball. "Maybe it will clear off later this afternoon and —" He was interrupted by the ring of the telephone in the front room. "I'll get it."

"If it's Mabel and Frank, tell them to come over," her mother called. "It's a good day to play cards."

On the third ring, he answered it. "It's for you, Eve." He had to raise his voice to make himself heard above the storm.

Grabbing a towel, Eve wiped the dishwater from her hands as she walked to the phone. "Hello?"

"Hello, Eve. This is Toby. Toby McClure."

A vague surprise widened her eyes. "Hello, Toby." Warm pleasure ran through her voice and expression.

"I'm trying to make some chocolate-chip cookies," he said, and she smiled when she remembered this was the first rainy day since he and Luck had been over. "But I can't figure out how to get cream from shortening and sugar."

"What?" A puzzled frown creased her forehead as she tried to fathom his problem.

"The directions say to 'cream' the sugar and shortening," Toby explained patiently.

Eve swallowed the laugh that bubbled in her throat. The directions probably didn't make sense to him. "That means you should blend them together until they make a thick 'creamy' mixture."

A heavy sigh came over the phone. "I thought this was going to be easy, but it isn't." There was a pause, followed by a reluctant request, "Eve, I don't suppose you could maybe come over and show me how to make them?" There was so much pride in his voice, and a grudging admission of defeat.

"Where's your father? He should be able to help you," she suggested.

"He didn't get home until real late last night, so he's lying down, taking a nap," Toby explained. "Can you come?"

It was impossible to turn him down, especially when she didn't want to. "Yes, I'll come. Where exactly do you live?" Eve knew it was somewhere close from other comments that had been made. Toby gave her precise directions. After she had promised to be there within a few minutes, she hung up the phone. "Dad, were you or mom planning to use the car this afternoon?"

"No. Did you want to use it?" He was already reaching in his pocket for the keys.

"I'm off to the McClures to give Toby his first lesson in baking cookies," Eve explained with a soft laugh, and told them the boy's problem understanding the directions. Their amusement blended with hers.

"Never mind the dishes. I'll finish them," her mother volunteered. "You'd better take an umbrella, too, and wear a coat."

In her bedroom, Eve brushed her hair and freshened her lipstick. She didn't allow herself to wonder why she was taking so much trouble with her appearance when she was going to see an eight-year-old. It would have started her thinking about his father, something she was trying to pretend not to do at this point. She hesitated before taking the brown coat out of her closet, but it was the only one she had that repelled water.

The sheeting rain was almost more than the windshield wipers could handle. It obscured her vision so that, despite Toby's excellent directions, she nearly missed the turn into the driveway. The lake house was set back in the trees, out of sight of the road. Eve parked her car behind the Jaguar.

The umbrella afforded her little protection from the driving rain. Her coat was stained wet by the time she walked the short distance from the car to the front door. Toby must have been watching for her, because he opened the door a second before she reached it. He pressed a forefinger to his lips and motioned her inside. She hurried in, unable to do anything about the rainwater dripping from her and the umbrella.

"Dad's still sleeping," Toby whispered, and explained, "He needs the rest."

The entry hall skirted the living room, paneled in cedar with a heavy beamed slanted ceiling and a natural stone fireplace. Toby's glance in that direction indicated it was where Luck was sleeping. Eve looked in when Toby led her past. There, sprawled on a geometric-patterned couch, was Luck, naked from the waist up, an arm flung over his head in sleep. It was the first time Eve had ever seen anyone frowning in his sleep.

In the kitchen, Toby led her to the table where he had all the ingredients set out. "Will you show me how to make cookies?" he asked, repeating the request he'd made over the phone.

"No, I won't show you," Eve said, taking off her wet coat and draping it over a chair back. "I'll tell you how to do it. The best way to learn is by doing."

Step by step, she directed him through the mixing process. When the first sheet came out of the oven, Toby was all eyes. He could hardly wait until the cookies were cool enough to taste and, thus, assure himself that they were as good as they looked.

"They taste just like yours," he declared on a triumphant note after he'd taken the first bite.

"Of course," Eve laughed, but kept it low so she wouldn't waken Luck in the next room.

"I couldn't have done it if you hadn't helped me," Toby added, all honesty. "You're a good teacher."

"That's what I am. Really," she emphasized when he failed to understand. "I *am* a teacher."

"What subject?"

"Music."

"Too bad it isn't English. That's my worst subject," he grimaced. "Dad isn't very good at it, either."

"We all have subjects that we don't do as well in as others," Eve shrugged lightly. "Mine is math."

"Dad is really good at that, and science, but he has to use it all the time in his work."

"What does he do?"

"He works for my grandpa." Then realizing that didn't answer her question, Toby elaborated, "My grandpa owns North Lakes Lumber. Mostly my dad works on the logging side. That way we can spend more time together in the summer when I'm out of school. He had a meeting with grandpa last night. That's why he was so late coming home."

"I thought he had a date." The words were out before Eve realized she had spoken.

"Sometimes he goes out on dates," Toby admitted, finding nothing wrong with her comment. "We like going places and doing things together, but sometimes dad is like me. I like to play with kids my own age once in a while; so does he. I imagine you do, too."

"Yes, that's true." She silently marveled at his logical reasoning. He was quite a remarkable boy.

Without being reminded, he checked on the cookies in the oven and concluded they were done. He took the cookie sheet out with a pot holder and rested it on the tabletop while he scooped the cookies off.

"We've been talking about dad getting married again," he announced, and didn't see the surprised arch of her eyebrow. "Dad gets pretty lonely sometimes. It's been rough on him since my mother died six years ago. Three weeks ago it was six years *exactly*," he stressed, and shook his head in a rueful fashion when he looked at her. "Boy, did he ever go on a binge that night!" He rolled his eyes to emphasize the point.

Three weeks ago. Eve did a fast mental calculation, her mind whirling. "Was . . . that on a Thursday?"

"I think so. Why?" Toby eyed her with an unblinking look.

The night she'd bumped into him outside the tavern. He had wanted someone to talk to, Eve remembered. A man can talk to a brown mouse, Luck had said. But she had refused, and he had gone back inside the tavern.

"No reason." She shook her head absently. "It was nothing important." But she couldn't resist going back to the subject. "You said he got drunk that night." She tried to sound mildly interested.

"I guess," Toby agreed emphatically. "He even had hallucinations."

"He did?"

"After I helped him into bed, he claimed that he had talked to a brown mouse." He looked at her, laughter suddenly dancing in his eyes. "Can you imagine that?"

"Yes." Eve swallowed and tried to smile. "Yes, I can." Her suspicions were confirmed beyond question. Now she wanted off the subject. "I'll help you spoon the cookie dough on the tray," she volunteered, letting action take the place of words.

When the last sheet of cookies came out of the oven, Eve washed the baking dishes while Toby wiped them and put them away. He leaned an elbow on the counter and watched her scrub at the baked-on crumbs on the cookie sheet.

"I don't really mind helping with dishes, or even making my bed," Toby said, and propped his head up with his hand. "But I'm going to like having a mother."

She didn't see the connection between the two statements. "Why is that?"

"Because sometimes my friends tease me

when I have to dust furniture or fold clothes," he explained. "Dad told me that mothers clean and cook and do all those kinds of things."

"That's true." Eve tried very hard not to smile. It had to be rough to have your manhood questioned by your peers when you were only eight years old. Reading between the lines, she could see where Toby had acquired his air of maturity. Responsibility had been given to him at an early age, so he didn't possess that carefree attitude typical of most children his age.

She rinsed the last cookie sheet and handed it to Toby to dry. Draining the dishwater from the sink, she wiped off the counter, then dried her hands. She glanced at the wall clock and wondered where the afternoon had gone.

"Now that we have everything cleaned up, it's time I was leaving," she declared.

"Can't you stay a little while longer?"

"No, it's late." She removed her brown coat from the chair back and slipped it on.

Toby brought her the umbrella. "Thanks for coming, Eve." He stopped for an instant as a thought occurred to him. "Maybe I should call you Miss Rowland, since you're a teacher."

"I'd like it better if you called me Eve," she replied, and started toward the entry hall.

"Okay, Eve," he grinned, and walked with her.

As she passed the living room, her gaze was automatically drawn inside. Luck was sitting up, rubbing his hands over his face as though he had just wakened. The movement in front of him attracted his attention. He glanced up and became motionless for an instant when he saw Eve.

Because of the clouds blocking out the sun, there was little light in the entry way. Eve didn't think about the dimness as she started to speak, smiling at the grogginess that was evident in his expression.

But Luck spoke before she did. "Don't scurry off into the darkness . . . brown mouse." There was a trancelike quality to his voice.

Her steps faltered. She had escaped recognition for so long that she had stopped dreading it. Now that he remembered her, she felt sick. Tearing her gaze from him, she hurried toward the front door. As she jerked it open, she heard him call her name.

"Eve!"

She didn't stop. She didn't even remember to open the umbrella until the slow rain drenched her face. There was water on the ground. It splashed beneath her running feet as she hurried toward her car.

CHAPTER FOUR

A startled outcry was torn from her throat by the hand that caught her arm and spun her around. Eve hadn't thought Luck would come after her — not out in the rain. But there he was, standing before her with his naked chest glistening a hard bronze from the rain, the sprinkling of chest hairs curling tightly in the wetness. The steady rain beat at his dark hair, driving it onto his forehead. Reluctantly, Eve lifted her gaze to the blue of his eyes, drowning in the full recognition of his look.

"You *are* the girl I bumped into outside the tavern that night," Luck stated in final acceptance of the fact.

"Yes." The hand holding the umbrella wavered, causing Luck to dodge his head and duck under the wire spines stretching the material.

His gaze swept her face, hair and eyes. "I thought I'd conjured you out of a whiskey bottle. I don't know why nothing clicked when I met you." A frown flickered between his brows, then vanished when his gaze slid to her coat. "It must have been the combination of the shadows and the brown coat . . . and the fogginess of sleep. Why didn't you say anything before?"

"And remind you that I was the brown mouse?" There was bitterness in the laughing breath she released.

"What's wrong with being a brown mouse?" The corners of his mouth deepened in an attractive smile. "I recall that I happened to like the brown mouse I met."

"A brown mouse is just a small rat. It's hardly a name that someone wants to be called." This time Eve worked to keep the bitterness out of her voice and turn the comment into a joke for her pride's sake. She succeeded to a large degree. "You certainly don't want to remind someone of it if they've forgotten."

"It's all in the eye of the beholder, Eve," Luck corrected with a rueful twist of his mouth. "You see a rat, and I see a soft furry creature. You are a strong sensitive woman, but you aren't very sure of yourself. I wish you had stayed that night. It all might have turned out differently."

How could she say that she wished she had, too, knowing what she knew now. Hindsight always altered a person's perspective.

"Dad!" Toby shouted from the opened front door. "You'd better come inside! You're getting soaking wet out there!"

"Toby's right." Her gaze fell to the rivulets of rainwater running down the muscled contours of his bare chest, all hard sinew and taut sun-browned skin. His blatant maleness spun a whole new set of evocative sensations. "You're getting drenched. You should go in the house."

"Come in with me." Luck didn't let go of her arms, holding her as he issued the invitation.

"No. I have to go home." She resisted the temptation to accept, listening to the steady drip of rain off her umbrella, its swift fall in the same rhythm as her pulse.

His mouth quirked. "That's what you said then, too."

"It's late. I —" The sentence went no farther as the wetness of his palm cupped her cheek. Eve completely forgot what she was going to say, her thoughts scattered by the disturbing caress of his touch.

"Dad!" Toby sounded impatient and irritated. "You're going to catch your death of pneumonia!"

It was the diversion Eve needed to collect her senses before she did something foolish. "You'd better go." She turned away, breaking contact with his hand and lifting the umbrella high enough to clear his head. There was no resistance as she slipped out of his grasp to walk the last few steps to the car.

"We'll see you again, Eve." It was a definite statement.

But she wasn't certain what promise it contained. "Yes." She opened the car door and slipped inside, struggling to close the wet umbrella. Luck continued to stand in the rain, watching her.

"Do you think it will be sunny tomorrow?" he asked unexpectedly.

"I haven't been paying any attention to the weather forecast," Eve replied.

"Neither have I," Luck admitted.

He was indifferent to the slow rain falling on him as he watched Eve reverse the car at a right angle to turn around in the drive. The incident had not been a figment of an alcoholic imagination. The woman he'd thought he had only dreamed about had actually been under his nose all this time.

The one good feeling he'd experienced in six years had happened when he had held her in his arms, but he hadn't believed it was real. Even now Luck wasn't sure that part hadn't been imagined. Comfortable didn't describe the feeling it had aroused. It was something more basic than that. It had been right and natural with his arms around her, feeling the softness of her body against his.

The woman had been Eve. It was strange he hadn't realized it before. She was quiet and warm, with an inner resiliency and a gentle humor that he liked. A smile twitched his mouth as Luck remembered she had a definite will of her own, as well. She wasn't easily intimidated.

"Dad!"

He turned, letting his gaze leave the red taillights of her car, and walked to the house, wet feet squishing in wet shoes. A smile curved his mouth at the disapproving expression on his son's face when he reached the door.

"You're sopping wet," Toby accused. "You wouldn't let me run out there like that with no coat or anything. You tell me I'll catch cold. How come you can do it?"

"Because I'm stupid," Luck replied, because he couldn't argue with the point his son had raised.

"You'd better get out of those wet clothes," Toby advised.

"I intend to." He left a watery trail behind him as he walked to the private bath off his bedroom where he stripped and put on the toweling robe Toby brought him. "Why was Eve here?" he asked, vigorously rubbing his wet hair with a bath towel.

"She came over to help me make cookies. They're good, too." A sharp questioning glance from Luck prompted Toby to explain. "I called and asked her to come over 'cause I was having trouble with the directions and you were asleep." Then it was his turn to tip his head to one side and send a questioning look at his father. "How come you called her a brown mouse?"

"It turns out Eve was the one I talked to that night and referred to as a brown mouse," he shrugged, and tossed the towel over a rack.

"I thought you were drunk that night."

"I had a few drinks, more after I met her than before. Which probably explains why I wasn't sure whether it had happened or I had imagined it."

"But why did you call her a brown mouse?" Toby didn't understand that yet.

"It's a long story," Luck began.

"I know," Toby inserted with a resigned sigh. "You'll tell me all about it some other time."

"That's right." A smile played with the corners of his mouth as he turned his son around and pushed him in front of him out of the bathroom. "Is there any coffee made?"

"Yeah." Toby tilted his head way back to frown at him. "I just hope you remember all the things you're going to tell me 'some other time.' "

In the kitchen, Luck filled a mug with coffee and helped himself to a handful of the cookies stacked on the table. "What did you and Eve talk about?" Settling onto a chair, he bit into one of the cookies and eyed Toby skeptically. "Did you really make these?"

"Yeah," was the defensive retort. "Eve told me how. She says you learn best by doing. She's a teacher. Did you know that? I mean a for-real teacher. She teaches music."

"No, I didn't know that," Luck admitted.

"We talked about that some and a bunch of other things." Toby frowned in an attempt to recall the subjects he'd discussed with Eve. "I told her you were thinking about getting married again."

Luck choked on the drink of coffee he'd taken and coughed, "You did what?!!" He set the mug down to stare at his son, controlling the anger that trembled beneath his disbelieving look.

"I mentioned that you were talking about getting married again," he repeated with all the round-eyed innocence of an eight-year-old. "Well, it's true."

"No, *you've* been talking about it." Luck pointed a finger at his son, shaking it slightly in his direction. "Why on earth did you mention it to Eve? I thought it was a private discussion between you and me."

"Gosh, dad, I didn't know you wanted to keep it a secret," Toby blinked.

"Toby, you don't go around discussing personal matters with strangers." He ran his fingers through his damp hair in a gesture of exasperation. "My God, you'll be blabbing it to the whole neighborhood next. Why don't you just take an ad out in the paper? Wanted: A wife for a widower with an eight-year-old blabbermouth."

"Do you think anyone would apply?" Behind the thoughtful frown, there was the beginnings of a plan.

"No!" Luck slammed his hand on the table. "If I find out that you've put an advertisement in any paper, I swear you won't be able to sit down for a week! This marriage business has gone far enough!"

"But you said —" Toby started to protest.

"I don't care what I said," Luck interrupted with a slicing wave of his hand to dismiss that argument. "I've played along with this marriage idea of yours, but it's got to stop. I'll decide *when* and *if* I'm getting married again without any prompting from you!"

"But face it, dad, you should get married," Toby patiently insisted. "You need somebody to keep you company and to look after you. I'm getting too old to be doing all this woman's work around the house."

"You don't get married just for companionship and someone to keep house." Luck regretted his earlier, imprecise explanation of a mother's role. It had started this whole mess. "There is more involved than that. A man is supposed to love the woman he marries."

"You're talking about hugging and kissing and that stuff," Toby nodded in understanding.

"That and . . . other things," Luck conceded with marked impatience.

"You mean sex, like in that book you and I read together when you explained to me how babies were made," his son replied quite calmly.

Luck shook his head and scratched his forehead. "Yes, I mean sex and the feelings you have toward the woman you marry."

"Would you consider marrying someone like

Eve?" Toby cocked his head at a wondering angle. "You said looks weren't everything."

"Why did you say a thing like that?" he challenged with irritation. "Don't you think Eve is an attractive woman?"

"Eve is all right, I like her, but —"

"No buts!" Luck flashed. "Eve is a lovely young woman and I don't want you implying otherwise with comments like 'looks aren't everything.' It's thoughtless remarks like that that hurt people's feelings." He should know. He had already wounded Eve when he called her a brown mouse, even though he hadn't meant it to be unkind. "Don't ever say anything to slight her!"

"Gee, dad, you don't have to get so hostile," Toby admonished, and defended his position. "Eve just doesn't look anything at all like the blonde we saw on the beach the other day. That blonde could have been the centerfold in *Playboy* magazine."

Luck started to ask where Toby had gotten his hands on a magazine like that, but he remembered his own curiosity at that age and decided not to pursue the issue at this time. Instead he just sighed, "I'm not interested in marrying a woman who has staples in her stomach."

Toby jerked his head and frowned. "Why would she have staples in her stomach?"

"Never mind." He lifted his hands in defeat. "The whole subject of women and marriage is closed. But you remember what I said about Eve," he warned. "I don't want to hear you making any disparaging remarks about her."

"I wouldn't, dad." Toby looked offended. "She's nice."

"Don't forget it, then," he replied less forcefully, and stood up. "I'm going to get out of this robe and put some clothes on. You'd better find something to put these cookies in."

"Yes, sir," Toby agreed in a dispirited tone.

Luck hesitated. "I didn't mean to be rough on you, Toby. I know you mean well. It's just that sometimes you make situations very awkward without realizing it."

"How?"

"I can't explain." He shook his head, then reached out to rumple his son's hair in a show of affection. "Don't let it worry you."

The rain had washed the land clean. The sky was a fresh clear blue while the green pine needles had lost their coat of dust to contrast sharply with the blue horizon. After a day's worth of summer sunshine, the ground was drying out, with only water standing in the low spots as a reminder it had rained.

Sitting on the seat in front of the upright piano, Eve let her fingers glide over the keys, seeking out the Mozart melody without conscious direction. She played from memory, eyes closed, listening to the individual notes flowing from one to another. The beauty of the song was an indirect therapy for the vague dejection that had haunted her since Luck had recognized her as his brown mouse less than two days ago.

When the last note faded into the emptiness of the cottage, Eve reluctantly let her fingers slide from the keys to her lap. The applause from a single person sounded behind her. Startled, Eve swung around on the piano seat to discover the identity of her audience of one.

The wire mesh of the screen door darkened the form of the man standing on the porch, but Eve recognized Luck instantly. An alternating pleasure and uncertainty ran through her system, setting her nerves on edge while quickening her pulse.

"I didn't hear you come." She rose quickly to cross the room and unhook the door. "Mom and dad went fishing this morning." As she pushed open the door to let him in, she noticed the only car in the driveway belonged to her parents. "Where's your car?"

"I came by boat." He stepped inside, so tall and so vigorously manly. Eve kept a safe distance between them to elude the raw force of his attraction that seemed to grow stronger with each meeting. "I tied it up at the shore. Toby's watching it."

"Oh." The knack of idle conversation deserted her. It was foolish to let that brown-mouse episode tie her tongue, but it had. She should never have allowed herself to become so sensitive about it. She should have accepted Luck's explanation the other day and let it die.

"Toby and I decided to take a ride around the lake this morning and thought you might like to come along." That lazy half smile that Eve found so disturbing accompanied his invitation.

Her delight was short-lived as she read between the lines. "It's thoughtful of you to ask, but I don't want you to feel that you're obligated to do so because you think you should make up for what happened outside the tavern that night." There was a trace of pride in the way she held her head, tipped higher than normal.

His smile grew more pronounced, bringing a gentleness to his hard-hewn features. "I'm not going to apologize for anything I said or did then," Luck informed her. "I regret that you felt slighted by the phrase of brown mouse, but I meant it in the kindest possible way. I'm asking you to come with us because we'd like your company. If you feel that I need an excuse to ask, then let's say that it is my way of thanking you for showing Toby how to make cookies." Glinting blue eyes gently mocked her as he paused. "Will you come with us?"

Eve smiled in a self-mocking way that etched attractive dimples in her cheeks. "I'd like to, yes," she accepted. "Just give me a couple of minutes to change." It would be too awkward climbing in and out of a boat in the wraparound denim skirt she was wearing.

"Sure." He reached for the screen door to open it. "We'll be stopping for lunch, probably at one of the resorts along the lake."

Eve hesitated, wondering if she was being too presumptuous, then threw caution to the wind to suggest, "If you'll give me another fifteen minutes, I can fix some sandwiches and stuff for a picnic lunch. Toby would like that."

"Toby would love it," Luck agreed. "We'll meet you at the boat in fifteen minutes."

"I'll be there," she promised as he pushed the door open and walked out.

Lingering near the door, Eve watched him descend the steps and strike out across the road toward the lakeshore, a warm feeling of pleasure running swiftly through her veins. Before he had disappeared from view, she retreated to the kitchen to take the picnic basket out of the pantry cupboard and raid the refrigerator. To go with the ham sandwiches she fixed, Eve added a wedge of Wisconsin Cheddar cheese along with some milder Colby, plus crackers and red Delicious apples. She filled a thermos cooler with lemonade and packed it in the basket, then laid a bag of potato chips on top.

Most of the allotted time was gone when she entered her bedroom. She quickly changed out of the skirt and blouse into a pair of white shorts and a flame-red halter top. At the last minute, she slipped on a pair of white canvas shoes with rubber soles and grabbed a long-sleeved blouse from the closet, in case she wanted protection from the sun.

With her arm hooked through the handle of the picnic basket, Eve crossed the road to the lake. Toby was skipping stones across the flat surface of the lake, a picture of intensity. A cigarette dangled from Luck's mouth, his eyes squinting against the curling smoke as he stood in a relaxed stance beside his son. At the sound of Eve's approach, the upper half of his body swiveled toward her. His gaze swept her in slow appreciation, setting her aglow with pleasure.

"Hi, Eve!" Toby greeted her with an exuberant welcome, the handful of stones falling from his hands so he could brush the dust from them.

"You still have two minutes to go." Luck dropped the cigarette to the ground, grinding it dead under his heel.

"Maybe I should go back to the cottage," Eve laughed in a suddenly buoyant mood.

"Oh, no, you don't," Luck denied the suggestion, a matching humor shining in his look.

She surrendered the picnic basket to his reaching hand. A line tied around a tree moored the pleasure cruiser close to the shore. Luck swung the basket onto the bow, then turned to help Eve aboard. Previously she had only guessed at the strength in the sinewed muscles of his shoulders and arms. But when his hands spanned the bareness of her rib cage and lifted her with muscles rippling to swing her up onto the bow as easily as he had the basket, she had her belief confirmed.

The imprint of his firm hands stayed with her, warming her flesh and letting her relive the sensation of his touch as she carried the basket to the stern of the boat and stowed it under one of the cushioned seats. Toby was tossed aboard with equal ease and came scrambling back to where Eve was. After untying the mooring line, Luck pushed the boat into deeper water and heaved himself on board.

"All set?" Luck cast them each a glance as his hand paused on the ignition key.

At their nods, he turned the key. The powerful engine of the cruise boat sputtered, then roared smoothly to life, the blades churning water. Turning the wheel, Luck maneuvered the boat around to point toward the open water before opening the throttle to send it shooting forward.

The speed generated a wind that lifted the swath of brown hair from Eve's neck, blowing and swirling it behind her. A little late she realized she hadn't brought a scarf. There was nothing to be done about it now, so she turned her face to the wind, letting it race over her and whip the hair off her shoulders.

Resting her arm on the side of the boat, Eve had a clear view of all that was in front of her, including Luck. He stood behind the wheel, his feet braced apart. The sun-bronzed angles of his jutting profile were carved against a blue sky as vividly blue as his eyes. The wind ruffled the virile thickness of his dark hair and flattened his shirt against his hard flesh, revealing the play of muscles beneath it. Snug Levi's outlined the slimness of his hips and the corded muscles of his thighs, reinforcing an aura of rough sexiness. Something stirred deep within her.

The instant Eve realized how openly she was staring, she shifted her gaze to the boy at his side, a youthful replica of his father. This day Toby had left behind his mask of maturity to adopt the carefree attitude that was usually so evident in Luck with that dancing glint in his eyes and easy smile.

The loud throb of the engine made conversation impossible, but Eve heard Toby urge his father to go faster. She saw the smile Luck flashed him and knew he laughed, even though the wind stole the sound from her. The throttle was pushed wide open until the powerboat was skimming over the surface of the water and bouncing over the wakes of other boats as the churning blades sent out their own fantail.

Luck glanced over at her and smiled, and Eve smiled back. For a brief moment, she allowed herself to consider the intimate picture they made — man, woman and child. For an even briefer minute, she let herself pretend that that's the way it was, until realism caught her up sharply and made her shake the image away.

After a while, Luck eased the throttle back and turned the wheel over to his son. Toby swelled with importance, his oversized sense of responsibility surfacing to turn his expression serious. Luck stayed beside him the first few minutes until Toby got the feel of operating the boat. Then he moved to the opposite side of the boat to lean a hip against the rail and keep an unobtrusive vigil for traffic that his son might not see. The position put him almost directly in front of Eve.

His sweeping side-glance caught her looking at him and Luck raised his voice to comment, "It's a beautiful day."

"Lovely," Eve shouted the agreement, because it did seem perfect to her. The wind made an unexpected change of direction and blew the hair across her face. Turning her head, she pushed it away. When she looked back, Luck was facing the front.

A quarter of an hour later or more, he straightened and motioned to her. "It's your turn to be skipper!" Luck called.

"Aye, aye, sir," she grinned, and moved to relieve Toby at the wheel.

She was quick to notice that the small boy was just beginning to show the tension of operating the boat. Wisely Luck had seen it and had Eve take over before it ceased to be fun for Toby and became onerous instead. Out of the corner of her eye, Eve saw Toby dart over to receive praise from his father for a job well done.

Then her attention was centered on guiding the boat.

Luck said something to her, but the wind and the engine noise tore it away. She shook her head and frowned that she didn't hear him. He crossed over to stand in a small space behind her.

"Let's go to the northern side of the lake," he leaned forward to repeat his suggestion.

"I'm not familiar with that area. We don't usually go up that far." Eve half turned her head to answer him and discovered he had bent closer to hear her, which brought his face inches from hers. Her gaze touched briefly on his mouth, then darted swiftly to his eyes to be captured by their vivid blueness.

"Neither am I. Let's explore strange waters together," Luck replied, his eyes crinkling at the corners.

"Okay." But there was a breathless quality to her voice.

It was some minutes after she turned the boat north before Luck abandoned his post behind her. It was only when he was gone that Eve realized how overly conscious she had been of his closeness, every nerve end tingling, although no contact had been made.

Familiar territory was left behind as they ventured into unknown waters. When a cluster of islands appeared, Eve reduced the boat's speed to find the channel through them. She hesitated over the choice.

"Want me to take over?" Luck asked.

"Yes." She relinquished the wheel to him with a quick smile. "That way if you run into a submerged log, it will be your fault instead of mine."

"Wise thinking," he grinned.

"Look!" Toby shouted, and pointed toward the waters ahead of them. "It's a deer swimming across the lake."

In the lake waters off their port side, there was the antlered head of a young buck swimming across the span of water between two islands. Luck throttled the engine to a slow idle, so they could watch him. When the deer reached the opposite island, it scrambled onto shore and disappeared within seconds in the thick stand of trees and underbrush.

"Boy, that was really something, huh, dad?" Toby exclaimed.

"It sure was," was the indulgent agreement.

With a child's lightning change of subject, Toby asked, "When are we going to have our picnic?"

"When we get hungry," Luck replied.

"I'm hungry," Toby stated.

Luck glanced at his watch. "I guess we can start looking for a place to go ashore. Or would you rather drop anchor and eat on the boat?" He included Eve in the question.

"It doesn't matter to me," she shrugged.

"Maybe we can land on one of the islands," Toby suggested.

"I don't know why not," Luck smiled down at the boy, then began surveying the cluster of islands for a likely picnic spot.

"Who knows? Maybe we'll find Chief Namekagon's lost silver mine," Eve remarked.

Toby turned to her. "What lost silver mine?"

"The one that belonged to the Indian chief the lake was named after. Legend has it that it's on one of the islands on the lake," she explained.

"Is it true?" Toby frowned.

"No one knows for sure," she admitted. "But he paid for all his purchases at the trading post in Ashland with pure silver ore. Supposedly the old chief was going to show the location of his mine to a friend, but he saw a bad omen and postponed the trip. Then he died without ever telling anyone where it was."

"Wow!" Toby declared with round-eyed excitement. "Wouldn't it be something if we found it?"

"A lot of people have looked over the years," Eve cautioned. "No one has found it yet."

"How about having our picnic there?" Luck pointed to an island with a wide crescent of sand stretching in front of its pine trees.

"It looks perfect." Eve approved the choice, and Luck nosed the boat toward the spot.

CHAPTER FIVE

The three of them sat cross-legged on a blanket Luck had brought from the boat while Eve unpacked the picnic basket. "Cheese, fruit, crackers," Luck said, observing the items she removed. "All that's missing is a bottle of wine. You should have said something."

There were too many romantic overtones in that remark. Eve wasn't sure how to interpret it, so she tried the casual approach and reached in the basket for the cold thermos.

"I guess we'll have to make do with lemonade," she shrugged brightly.

"I like lemonade," Toby inserted as she set the thermos aside to arrange a sandwich and a portion of chips on a paper plate and handed it to him. "This looks good, Eve."

"I hope you like it." She fixed a plate for Luck, then one for herself, leaving the cheese, fruit and crackers on top of the basket for dessert.

"Have you ever looked for the lost mine, Eve?" Toby munched thoughtfully on his sandwich while he studied her.

"Not really. Just a few times when I was your age."

The subject continued to fascinate him. Throughout the meal, he pumped her for information, dredging up tidbits of knowledge Eve had forgotten she knew. Toby refused the slice of cheese she offered him when his sandwich was gone but took the shiny apple.

Luck ate his. When it was gone, he used the knife to slice off another chunk. "This is good cheese."

"Wisconsin cheese, of course," she smiled. "Anything else would be unpatriotic."

"Did Chief Namekagon really have seven wives?" Toby returned to his favorite subject.

"Yes, but I guess he must have kept the location of the mine a secret from them, too," Eve replied.

"Seven wives," Toby sighed, and glanced at his father. "Gee, dad, all you need is one."

"Or none," Luck murmured softly, and sent a look of silencing sharpness at his son. "More lemonade, Toby?"

"No, thanks." He tossed his apple core into the small sack Eve had brought along for their wastepaper. Rising, Toby dusted the sandwich crumbs from his legs. "Is it okay if I do a little exploring?"

At Luck's nod of permission, Toby took off. Within minutes, he had disappeared along a faint animal path that led into the island's thick forest. For the first few minutes, they could hear him rustling through the underbrush. When that stopped, Eve became conscious of the silence and that she was alone with Luck. Her gaze strayed to him, drawn by an irrepressible compulsion, only to have her heart knock against her ribs when she found him watching her.

"More cheese?" She spoke quickly to cover the sudden disturbance that seethed through her. In the far distance, there was the sound of a boat traversing the lake, reminding her they weren't the only ones in the vicinity, no matter how isolated they seemed.

"No. I'm full." Luck shook his dark head in refusal.

Inactivity didn't suit her at the moment because she knew it would take her thoughts in a direction that wasn't wise. "I'd better pack all this away before it attracts all the insects on the island."

Eve tightly wrapped the cheese that was left and stowed it in the basket with the thermos of lemonade and the few potato chips that were left. As she added the paper sack with their litter to the basket, she was conscious that Luck had risen. When he crouched beside her, balanced on the balls of his feet, she found it difficult to breathe normally. His warm scent was all around her, heightened by the heat of the sun. She was kneeling on the blanket, sitting on her heels, aware of him with a fine-tuned radar.

"The food was very good. Thanks for the picnic, Eve." His hand reached out to cup the back of her head and pull her forward.

Lifting her gaze, she watched the sensual line of his mouth coming closer. She couldn't have resisted him if she wanted to, which she didn't. Her eyes closed an instant before his mouth touched her lips, then moved onto them to linger an instant. The kiss started her trembling all the way to her toes. Much too soon he was lifting his head, leaving her lips aching for the warm pressure of his mouth.

The very brevity of the kiss reminded her that it was a gesture of gratitude. It had meant no more than a peck on the cheek. She would be foolish to read more into it than that. Lowering her head, she struggled to appear unmoved by the experience, as casual about it as he seemed to be. Her fingers fastened on the wicker handle of the picnic basket.

"Do you want to put this in the boat now?" She picked it up to hand it to him, her gaze slanting upward.

For an instant Eve was subjected to the probing search of his narrowed eyes. Then his smooth smile erased the sensation as he took the picnic basket from her.

"Might as well," Luck agreed idly, and pushed to his feet.

Standing up, Eve resisted the impulse to watch him walk to the boat. Instead she shook the crumbs and grains of sand off the blanket and folded it into a square. Feeling the isolation again, she turned her gaze to the treed interior of the island. The blanket was clutched in front of her, pressed protectively to her fluttering stomach. Behind her Eve heard the approach of Luck's footsteps in the sand.

"Where do you suppose Toby has gone?" she wondered.

"Leave the blanket here. We'll see if we can find him," Luck suggested, and took her hand after she'd laid the blanket down.

His easy possession sent a warm thrill over her skin. Eve liked the sensation of her slender hand being lost in the largeness of his. Together they walked to the narrow trail Toby had taken, where they would have to proceed single file.

"I'll go first, in case we run into some briers. I wouldn't want your legs to be scratched up." The downward sweep of his gaze took note of the bareness of her legs below the white shorts.

Instead of releasing her hand to start up the path, as Eve had expected he would, Luck curved his arm behind his back and shifted his grip to lead her. The forest shadows swallowed them up, the ground spongy beneath the faintly marked earth, the smell of pine resin heavy in the air.

Out of sight of their picnic site, a fallen timber blocked the trail, its huge trunk denoting the forest giant it had once been. Luck released her hand to climb over it and waited on the other side to help her. The rubber sole of her shoe found a foothold on the broken nub of a limb, providing her a step to the top of the trunk. All around them was dense foliage, with only a vague glitter of the lake's surface shining through the leaves.

"I'm glad this is a small island," Eve remarked. "A person could get lost in this."

"It's practically a jungle," Luck agreed.

His hands gripped the curves of her waist, spanning her hipbones to help her down. Eve steadied herself by placing her hands on his shoulders while he lifted her off the trunk to the ground. When it was solidly beneath her, she discovered the toes of her shoes were touching his, a hand's length separating them.

Beneath her hands she felt his flexed muscles go taut, his hands retaining their hold on her waist. Looking up, Eve saw his keen gaze going over every facet of her appearance. She became conscious of the lack of lipstick and the wind-ratted hair. It caused a tension that forced her to speak so it would be broken.

"I should have brought a comb. My hair is a mess," she remarked tightly.

Luck's gaze wandered slowly over it and back to her face, the color of his eyes changing, deepening. "It looks like a man mussed it while he was making love to you."

His hand reached to smooth the hair away from her face and cup the back of her head. The idle caress parted Eve's lips in a silent breath, fastening his attention on them. While his mouth began moving inexorably closer, his other hand shifted to her lower spine and applied pressure to gather her in.

The tension flowed out of her with a piercing sweetness as his mouth finally reached its destination. It rocked slowly over her lips, tasting and testing first this curve, then another. The trip-hammer beat of her heart revealed the havoc he was raising with her senses.

This intimate investigation didn't stop there. His hard warm lips continued their foray, grazing over her cheek to the sensitive area around her ear. Growing weaker, her hands inched to his shoulders, clinging to him for support and balance in this dizzying embrace.

"Do you have any idea how good this feels, Eve?" he murmured in a rough disturbed tone.

She felt the shuddering breath he took and moaned softly in an aching reply. It turned his head, bringing it to a different angle as he took firm possession of her lips, the territory already familiar to him from the last exploration. Now Luck staked his claim to it and made a driving search into the dark recesses of her mouth.

Eve curved her arms around his neck, seeking the springing thickness of his hair. His hands began roaming restlessly over her shoulders and back, left bare by the red halter top she wore. The softness of her curves was pressed and shaped to his hard bone and taut muscle. The kiss deepened until Eve was raw with the hot ache that burned within her.

Gradually she felt the passion withdrawing from his kiss. It ended before his mouth reluctantly ended the contact. Breathless and dazed, she slowly lowered her chin until it was level. She was conscious that Luck was trying to force his lungs to breathe normally. She tried to get a hold of her own emotions, but without his success. His head continued to be bent toward her, his chin and mouth at a level with her eyes.

"We'll never find Toby this way," he said finally.

"No, we won't," Eve agreed, and self-consciously brought her hands down from around his neck.

He loosened his hold, stepping back to create room between them. She slid a glance at him, trying to obtain a clue as to how she was expected to treat this kiss. Luck was half-turned, looking down the trail. Something was troubling his expression, but it smoothed into a smile when he glanced at her. Yet Eve was conscious that a faint puzzled light shaded his eyes.

"Toby can't be far. The island is too small," he said, and reached for her hand again before starting up the trail.

Twenty yards farther, they reached the opposite shore of the island and found Toby sitting on a waterlogged stump at the lake's edge. He hopped down when he saw them.

"Are we ready to go?" he asked with an unconcern that didn't match the bright curiosity of his eyes.

"If you are," Luck replied.

Toby's presence brought back the easygoing

friendly atmosphere that had marked the beginning of the excursion. Not once did Eve feel uncomfortable, yet an uncertainty stayed with her. She couldn't tell whether Luck regarded her as a woman or a friend.

He beached the boat on the shore in front of her parents' cottage and gave her a hand to dry land. There was nothing in his manner to indicate he would accept an invitation to come to the house for a drink, so Eve didn't issue one.

"I enjoyed myself," she said instead. "Thanks for asking me to come along."

"It was our pleasure. Maybe we'll do it again sometime." It was a noncommittal reply, indefinite, promising nothing.

Eve tried not to let her disappointment show as she clutched the picnic basket and the blouse she hadn't worn. After waving goodbye to Toby aboard the boat, she struck out for the road and the log cottage opposite it.

Since he'd left Eve, the frown around his forehead and eyes had deepened. As he walked the path from the lake to his house, Luck tried to recall the last time he'd felt as alive as he had those few brief moments when he'd held Eve and kissed her. The deadness inside him had gone. He worried at it, searching for it in some hidden corner, barely conscious of Toby ambling along behind him.

"Dad?" Toby requested his attention and received an abstract glance. "Why do people kiss?"

That brought Luck sharply out of his reverie. He shortened his strides to let Toby catch up with him and raised a suspicious eyebrow. "Because they like each other." He gave a general answer.

Toby turned his head to eye him thoughtfully. "Have you ever kissed anybody you didn't like?"

Luck knew it was a loaded question, but he answered it anyway. "No."

"If you only kiss people you like, then you must like Eve," Toby concluded. The sharply questioning look couldn't be ignored, and the boy admitted, "I saw you and Eve. I was coming back to see if you were ready to leave, but you were so busy kissing her that you didn't hear me."

"No, I didn't hear you," Luck admitted grimly. The hot rush of emotion had deafened him to everything but the soft sounds of submission she made. He was bothered by a vague sense of infidelity. "And, yes, I like Eve."

"Why don't you marry her?"

"Liking isn't loving." Luck cast an irritated glance at his son. "And I thought it was understood that that subject was closed."

There was a long sigh from Toby but no comment.

Later that night Toby was sprawled on the

floor of the living room, arms crossed on a throw pillow, his chin resting in the hollow of his fists while he watched television. At a commercial, he turned to glance at his father in the easy chair — only he wasn't there.

Frowning, Toby pushed up on his hands to peer into the kitchen, but there was no sign of him. His father hadn't been acting right since the boat ride. That fact prompted Toby to go in search of him.

He found him in a darkened bedroom. The hallway light spilled in to show him sitting on the bed, elbows on his knees and his chin resting on clasped hands. Toby paused in the doorway for a minute, confused until he saw that his father was staring at the framed photograph of his mother on the dresser.

Toby walked up to him and laid a comforting hand on his shoulder. "What's wrong, dad?"

Bringing his hands down, Luck turned his head, paused, then sighed heavily. A smile broke half-heartedly. "Nothing, sport."

But Toby glanced at the picture. "Were you thinking about mom?"

There was a wry twist to his father's mouth. "No, I wasn't." Pushing to his feet, he rested a hand on Toby's shoulder. Together they left the room. As they walked out the door, Toby stole a glance over his shoulder at the picture of the smiling tawny-haired blonde. He slipped his small hand into his father's, but he knew it was small comfort.

The next day Toby's stomach insisted it was lunchtime. Entering the house through the back door, he walked into the kitchen. His arrival coincided with his father saying a final goodbye to an unknown party on the telephone extension in the kitchen.

"I'll tell him. Right . . . I'll be there," Luck said, and hung up.

His curiosity overflowed, as it usually did. "Who was that? Tell me what? Where will you be?" The questions tumbled out with barely a breath in between.

"Your granddad said hello," Luck replied, answering two questions.

"Why didn't you let me talk to him?" Toby frowned in disappointment.

"Because he was busy. Next time, okay?" his father promised, and glanced at the wall clock. "I suppose you want lunch. What will it be? Hamburgers? Grilled cheese? How about some soup?"

"Hamburgers," Toby chose without a great deal of interest or enthusiasm. Hooking an arm around a chair back, he watched his father take the meat from the refrigerator and carry it to the stove, where he shaped portions into patties to put in the skillet. "You said you'd be there. Be where? When?"

"I have to drive to Duluth this Friday to meet with your grandfather," Luck replied, and half turned to instruct, "Put the ketchup and mustard on the table."

"I suppose you're going to ask Mrs. Jackson to come over to stay with me," Toby grumbled as he went about setting the table and putting on the condiments.

"You are absolutely right. I'm calling her after lunch."

"Oh, dad, do you have to?" Toby appealed to him. "Sometimes Mrs. Jackson is a real pain."

"Has it ever occurred to you that Mrs. Jackson might think you are a real pain?" his father countered.

"She always thinks I'm making up stories."

"I wonder why?" Luck murmured dryly.

Toby let the silverware clatter to the table as a thought occurred to hm. "Why couldn't you ask Eve to come over? If I *have* to have somebody sit with me, I'd rather it was Eve."

Luck hesitated, and Toby studied that momentary indecision with interest. "I'll ask her," his father finally agreed.

"You'll call her after lunch?" Toby persisted for a more definite agreement.

"Yes."

Eve was halfway out the door with her arms full of suntan lotion, blanket and a paperback for an afternoon in the sun when the telephone rang. She ended up dropping everything but the lotion onto couch cushions before she got the receiver to her ear.

"Rowlands," she answered.

"Hello, Eve?" Luck's voice responded on the other end of the line.

She tossed the suntan lotion on top of the blanket and hugged her free arm around her middle, holding tight to the pleasure of his voice. "Yes, this is Eve."

"Luck McClure," he needlessly identified himself. "Are you busy this Friday?"

"No." She and her mother had tentatively talked about a shopping expedition into Cable, but that certainly could be postponed.

"I have a large favor to ask. I have some business I have to take care of on Friday, which means I'll be gone most of the day and late into the evening. Toby asked if you would stay with him while I'm gone instead of the woman who usually sits with him."

Swallowing her disappointment, Eve smoothly agreed, "I don't mind in the least looking after Toby. What time would you like me to come?"

"I'd like to get an early start. Would eight o'clock be too early?" Luck asked.

"I can be there by eight."

"Thanks. Toby will be glad to know you're coming," he said. "We'll see you on Friday."

"On Friday," Eve repeated, and echoed his goodbye.

Toby would be glad she was coming, he'd said. Did that mean that Luck wouldn't? Eve sighed wearily because she simply didn't know.

On Friday morning her father dropped her

off at the lake house a few minutes before eight. As she got out of the car, he leaned over to remind her, "If you need anything, you be sure to call us. Your mother or I can be over in a matter of minutes."

"I will. Thanks, dad." She waved to him and hurried toward the house.

Toby had obviously been watching for her because the front door opened before she reached it. He stood in the opening, a broad smile of welcome on his face.

"Hi, Eve."

"Hello, Toby." Her gaze went past him to the tall figure approaching the door as she entered.

The fluttering of her pulse signaled the heightening of her senses. Eve had never seen Luck in business clothes, and the dark suit and tie altered his appearance in a way that intensified the aura of male authority, dominating and powerful.

"Right on time." He smiled in an absent fashion. "I left a phone number by the telephone. You can reach me there if you have an emergency."

"Which I hope I won't," she replied, trying to respond with her usual naturalness.

After a glance of agreement, he laid a hand on Toby's head. "Behave yourself. Otherwise Eve will make you stand in a corner."

"No, she won't." Toby dipped his head to avoid the mussing of his father's hand.

His smile held a trace of affection and indulgence toward his son when Luck turned to Eve. "I shouldn't be too late getting back tonight."

"Don't worry about it," she assured him. "Toby and I will be all right."

"You know how to reach me if you need me," Luck reminded her, and she tried not to be disappointed because the remark held no underlying meaning. It was a straightforward statement from a father to a sitter. "I have to be going," he addressed both of them and smiled at his son. "See you later."

"Tell granddad hi for me," Toby instructed.

"I will," Luck promised.

To get out the door, Luck had to walk past Eve. His arm inadvertently brushed against hers, sending a little quiver through her limbs. When she breathed in, she caught the musky scent of his male after-shave lotion, potently stimulating as the man who wore it. The essence of him seemed to linger even afer he'd walked out the door.

With Toby standing beside her on the threshold, Eve watched him walk to the car. She returned his wave when he reversed out of the driveway onto the road and felt a definite sensation of being part of the family — standing at the doorway with her "son" and waving goodbye to her "husband."

Eve shook the thought away. It was that kind of dangerous thinking that would lead to heartbreak. It was definitely not wise. She was a baby-sitter — that's all.

Fixing a bright smile on her mouth, she looked down at Toby. "What's on the agenda this morning?"

He shrugged and tipped his head back to give her a bright-eyed look that reminded her a lot of his father. "I don't know. Do you want to play catch?"

"Do you think we'll break a window?" Eve teased.

"I hope not," Toby declared with a grim look. "I had to spend half the money I was saving for a minibike to pay my share of the damage to your windshield. Dad paid for most of it 'cause it was mostly his fault for throwing the ball too high, but he wouldn't have been playing if it hadn't been for me. We share things."

"Yes, I can see that," she nodded, because the two seemed to have a remarkable relationship, unique to anything she'd come across in her meetings with parents at school.

"Do you want to play catch?" he repeated his suggestion.

"Sure," Eve agreed, even though she didn't feel obligated to entertain him. The idea of being active appealed to her. "Go get your ball and glove."

"I'll bring dad's for you," he offered. "Sometimes I throw it pretty hard —" Toby warned "— and it stings your hand when you catch it."

The driveway seemed the safest place to play catch since there weren't any windows in the line of fire. When Toby tired of that, they walked down by the lake, where he gave her lessons in the fine art of skipping stones on the lake's surface.

At noon they returned to the lake cabin. "What would you like for lunch?" Eve asked as they entered through the kitchen door.

"A peanut butter sandwich and a glass of milk is okay." He didn't sound enthused by his own suggestion.

"Is that what you usually have?" she asked.

"It's easy," Toby shrugged. "Dad and I aren't much for cooking."

"How about if I check the refrigerator and see if there's anything else to eat?" Eve suggested, certain that Toby would like something more imaginative if she offered to fix it.

"Go ahead," he agreed, then warned, "There's not much in there except some frozen dinners in the freezer section of the icebox."

When she opened the refrigerator door, she discovered Toby was right. The shelves were nearly bare, except for milk, eggs, bacon and a couple of jars of jam.

Toby watched her expression. "I told you," he reminded her. "Dad fixes breakfast and sometimes cooks steaks on the grill. Otherwise we eat out or have frozen dinners. They're pretty good, though."

Eve found a package of cheese in the dairy drawer of the refrigerator. "Do you like grilled cheese sandwiches?" she asked.

"Yeah," he nodded.

While the skillet was heating to grill them, Eve searched through the cupboards and found a lone can of condensed tomato soup. She diluted it with milk and added a dab of butter. When she set the lunch on the table, Toby consumed it with all the gusto of the growing boy that he was.

"Boy, that was good, Eve!" he declared, and leaned back in his chair to rub his full stomach. "You sure are a good cook."

"Grilling a sandwich and opening a can of soup isn't exactly cooking," she smiled. "I was thinking that I might call my father and see if he would drive us to the store this afternoon and pick up some groceries. I'll cook you a *real* dinner tonight. Would you like that?"

"You bet!"

CHAPTER SIX

After a few inquiries Eve was able to discover some of Toby's favorite dishes. Being a young boy, he had simple tastes. Dinner that evening consisted of fried chicken, mashed potatoes and gravy and some early sweet corn-on-the-cob. For dessert she fixed fresh strawberry shortcake with lots of whipped cream.

"I can't ever remember eating food that good," Toby insisted. "It was really delicious, Eve."

"Why, thank you, sir." With her hands full of dirty dishes to be carried to the sink, she gave him a mock curtsy.

"I'll help wash the dishes," he volunteered, and pushed away from the table. "Dad usually dries them."

"You don't need to help." She had already learned while she was preparing the meal that Toby was accustomed to doing household chores. His sense of duty was commendable, but he was still very young and needed a break from it once in a while. "You can have the night off and I'll do them."

"Really?" He seemed stunned by her offer.

"Yes, really," she laughed.

"I'll stay and keep you company." He dragged a chair over to the kitchen counter by the sink.

"I'd like that," Eve said, and let the sink fill with water, squirting liquid soap into it.

Kneeling on the chair seat, Toby rested his arms on the counter and propped his chin on an upraised hand to watch her. "You know, it'd really be great to have a mother. It's getting to be a hassle cleaning the house, washing dishes and all that stuff."

"I can imagine." She smiled faintly as she began washing the dishes and rinsing them under the running faucet, then setting them on the draining board to dry.

"I'd sure like to figure out how to find someone for dad to marry." Toby sighed his frustration. "I thought about putting an ad in the paper, but dad really got upset when I mentioned it to him."

Her initial pang of envy came from the knowledge that she coveted the role of Toby's mother — and Luck's wife. It wouldn't take much encouragement to fall head over heels in love with Luck. She was already more than halfway there now.

But after the brief envy came amusement and sympathy for Luck's plight. The idea of advertising for a wife had to have come as a shock to him.

"It would have been a little embarrassing for your father, Toby," Eve murmured, the corners of her mouth deepening with the smile she tried to contain.

"Dad seemed to think that, too." He grimaced in resignation to the decision. "I told dad that you'd make a good mother and he should marry you."

"Toby, you didn't!" She nearly dropped the dish in her hand, a warm pink flooding her cheeks.

"Yes, I did," he assured her innocently. "What's wrong with that? He likes you. I know he does. I saw him kiss you."

Eve became very busy with the dishes, trying to hide her agitation and embarrassment with her work. "Just because you kiss someone doesn't necessarily mean you want to marry them, Toby."

"Yeah, that's what dad said," he admitted.

She hated the curiosity that made her ask, "What else did your dad say when you suggested he should marry me?"

"Nothing. He told me the subject was closed and I wasn't supposed to discuss it anymore, but we need someone around here to take care of us." The comment revealed he hadn't let go of the idea. "There's too much work for a boy like me to do, and dad's busy. Somewhere there's a girl that dad will marry. I just gotta find her."

"Toby McClure, I think you should leave that to your father," Eve suggested.

"Yeah, but he isn't *trying* to find anybody,"

Toby protested. "I thought I'd have better luck." Then he laughed. "I made a joke, didn't I? Better luck for Luck."

"Yes, you did." Her smile widened into a grin.

"That's my name, too, you know," he declared, and settled his chin on his hand once more.

"No, I didn't know that." Her brown eyes widened in vague surprise. "I thought it was Toby — Tobias," she corrected it from the shortened version.

"That's my middle name," Toby explained. "My real first name is Luck — like my dad's. My mom insisted on naming me after him when I was born, but dad said it was too hard growing up with a name like that. He said I'd wind up getting called Little Luck, and he didn't like the idea of being Big Luck. So they called me Toby instead."

"I think that was probably best," Eve agreed with the decision.

In her experience at the school, she'd seen how cruel children could be sometimes when one of the members had an unusual name. Sometimes they teased him unmercifully. As a rule children didn't like being different. It wasn't until later, when their sense of individuality surfaced, that they showed a desire for unique names.

Yet she couldn't help remembering when she had first been introduced to the father and son, and Luck had explained the family tradition of his name. At the time she had wondered if there was a "little" Luck at home to carry it on. It was slightly amusing to discover it had been Toby all along.

After the dishes were done, she and Toby went into the front room and watched television for a while. At nine o'clock she suggested that it was time he took a bath and got ready for bed. He didn't argue or try to persuade her to let him stay up until Luck came home.

Spanking clean from his bath, Toby trotted barefoot into the living room in his pajamas. He half flopped himself across the armrest of the chair where Eve was sitting.

"Are you going to tuck me into bed?" he asked.

"I sure am." Eve smiled at the irresistible appeal of his look. Toby was just as capable of twisting her around his finger as his roguish father was.

Toby led the way to his room while Eve followed. He made a running leap at the bed, dived under the covers and was settled comfortably by the time Eve arrived at his bedside. A white pillowcase framed the mass of dark brown hair as a pair of bright blue eyes looked back at her.

She made a show of tucking the covers close to his sides while he kept his arms on top of them. Then she sat sideways on the edge of the mattress.

"You don't have to read me a story or anything," Toby said. "I'm too old for that."

"Okay. Would you like me to leave the light on for a while?" Eve asked, referring to the small lamp burning on the bedside table. She already suspected he was "too old" for that, too.

"No." There was a negative movement of his head against the pillow.

Her glance had already been drawn to the night table, where it was caught by the framed photograph of a beautiful blond-haired woman with sparkling green eyes. A vague pain splintered through Eve as she guessed the identity of the smiling face in the photograph.

"Is this a picture of your mother?" she asked Toby for confirmation, her throat hurting.

"Yes. Her name was Lisa." Toby blithely passed on the information.

"She's very beautiful," Eve admitted, aware that Luck would never have called this woman a "brown mouse." She was golden — all sunshine and springtime. Eve despised herself for the jealousy that was twisting inside her. But she didn't have a prayer of ever competing with someone as beautiful as this girl — not even with her memory. It was utterly hopeless to think Luck would ever love her.

"Dad has a picture just like that in his room," Toby informed her. "He talks to it a lot . . . although he hasn't lately," he added as an afterthought.

"I'm sure he loves her very much." She tried to smile and conceal the awful aching inside. "It's time you were going to sleep."

"Will you kiss me good-night?" he asked with an unblinking look.

"Of course." There was a tightness in her throat as Eve bent toward him and brushed his forehead with a kiss. She longed for the right to do that every night. She straightened, murmuring, "Have a nice night, Toby."

"Good night, Eve." With a contented look on his face, he snuggled deeper under the covers.

Her hand faltered as she reached past the framed photograph to turn out the light. Standing up, she moved silently out of the room. Bitter tears burned the back of her eyes. She regretted more than she ever had in her life that she had been born plain.

In the living room Eve turned down the volume on the television set and picked up a magazine lying on the coffee table. Curling up in the large armchair, she tried to force herself to read the articles it contained. The clock on the fireplace mantel ticked away the time.

It was after midnight when Luck pulled into the driveway, much later than he had anticipated. Switching off the engine, he grabbed his briefcase and his suit jacket from the rear seat. The briefcase he carried in his hand as he climbed out of the car; the jacket he swung over his shoulder, held by the hook of a finger.

His tie was draped loosely around his neck, the top buttons of his shirt unfastened.

The tension of a long drive and the mental fatigue from a full day of business discussions cramped the muscles in his shoulders and neck. Weariness drew tired lines in his tough rakehell features.

As Luck walked to the front door of the cabin, he noticed the light burning in the window. The edges of his mouth lifted in a faint smile at the welcoming sight. When he opened the door, he heard the muted volume of the television set. There was a warm run of pleasure as he realized Eve must have waited up for him to come home.

Setting his briefcase down just inside the door, he walked into the living room and paused. Eve had fallen asleep in the big armchair, with a magazine in her lap. His smile lengthened at the sight of her curled up like a velvety brown mouse. Luck tossed his suit jacket onto the sofa along with his tie and walked over to turn off the television set.

Silence swirled through the room as he approached the chair where she was sleeping. He intended to wake her, but when he looked down at her, the tiredness seemed to fall away from him. In repose, her serene features reminded him of the gentle beauty of a madonna — or a sleeping beauty waiting to be wakened with a kiss. The latter was a tantalizing thought.

Leaning down, Luck placed his hands on either armrest of the armchair. He felt alive and whole, renewed by her presence. He lowered his mouth onto her lips, stimulated by their sweet softness. At the initial contact, they were unresponsive to the mobile pressure of his kiss. Then Luck felt her lips move against his. Raw emotions surged through him, an aching pressure building inside him.

Eve stirred with the beginnings of wakefulness and he pulled back, not straightening but continuing to lean over her. The desire was strong to pick her up and carry her into his bedroom where he could give rein to those feelings that swept him.

Her lashes slowly drifted open and he watched the dawning light of recognition flare in her brown, nearly black eyes. His blood was warmed by the pleasure at seeing him that ran wild in her look.

"You're home," she murmured in soft joy.

"Yes," Luck answered huskily, because it seemed he had come home. It was a sensation he couldn't quite explain, not even to himself.

One minute he could see the welcome in her eyes and in the next it was gone, as a sudden rush of self-consciousness hid it from him. She lowered her chin, a vague agitation making her restive.

"I must have fallen asleep." She brushed a hand across her eyes, then reached for the opened magazine in her lap.

Faintly irritated by her sudden remoteness, Luck pushed himself erect, withdrawing physically from her as she had withdrawn from him. He saw the flicker of her hurt in the velvet darkness of her eyes. Luck regretted the day he'd ever called her a brown mouse. Her sensitive nature had found the phrase offensive when he had actually used it with teasing affection.

All Eve knew about what he was feeling she saw in the displeasure written on his features. There was a vague sensation that he had kissed her, but she thought she had dreamed that.

"What time is it?" There was a crick in her neck from sleeping in the chair. She rubbed at the stiffness as she uncurled her legs.

"It's nearly one." His answer was abrupt. "I'm sorry I was so late getting back."

"It's all right." Eve smiled in his direction without actually meeting his gaze.

"You didn't have to wait up for me." It almost sounded like a criticism. "You should have lain down on the couch."

"I didn't plan to fall asleep. I was reading and . . . I guess I dozed off," she explained self-consciously.

"Let me check on Toby, then I'll drive you home," he said.

Luck disappeared into the darkened hallway leading to the bedrooms as Eve forced her cramped body out of the chair. She noticed his suit jacket and tie on the sofa when she retrieved her purse from the coffee table. She remembered how incredibly handsome he'd looked when she'd opened her eyes and seen him standing there, bent over her to wake her. He must have seen the rush of love she'd felt. There didn't seem to be any other explanation for the way he'd withdrawn from her — his sudden shortness. He probably thought she was going to start fawning all over him and didn't want the embarrassment of her unwanted attentions. She resolved not to let him see the way she felt toward him, not again.

When he returned to the living room, Eve managed to appear very calm and controlled — and very casual. Yet there wasn't any approval in his inspecting glance.

"Ready?" he asked.

"Yes." She had to look away from him before she was affected by his blatant masculinity. "Is Toby all right?"

"He's sound asleep," Luck replied. "He'll be okay alone until I get back."

"Of course," she murmured, and moved toward the front door.

Outside, a full moon bathed the night with its silvery light and the sky was a twinkle with stars. A breeze whispered through the pines, scenting the air with their freshness. Eve paused beside the passenger side of the car while Luck opened the door for her.

Nervousness made her say, "It's a lovely evening, isn't it?" The ambience seemed too romantic for her peace of mind.

"Yes, it is," Luck agreed, and waited until she was inside before closing the door.

Her gaze followed him as he walked around the car and slid behind the wheel. When he started the motor, Eve faced the front. Her nerve ends quivered with his nearness, making the silence intolerable.

"How did your business go today?" she asked, to make conversation.

"Fine." It was a noncommunicative answer, but Luck made it easier by asking, "Did Toby give you any trouble today?"

"None," Eve assured him. At this time of night there was no traffic on the road to her parents' lake cottage. They had it all to themselves. "We played catch — and didn't break a single window," she added with feigned lightness.

"You're luckier than I am." He slid her a brief glance, one side of his mouth lifting in a half smile, his voice dry with amusement.

"We were careful about the area we picked," she explained, relaxing a little under the humorous overtones of the subject matter.

It was a short drive to the cottage. Part of her regretted the quickness with which they covered the distance, and another part of her was relieved. When they drove in, Eve noticed her parents had left the porch light burning.

"I hope they weren't worried about you," Luck commented as he stopped the car.

"I doubt it," she replied. "They've accepted that I'm a big girl now. My hours are my own."

Letting the engine idle, he shifted the gear into the park and half turned in the seat to face her. "How much do I owe you for staying with Toby?"

She stiffened at the offer of payment for her services. "Nothing," Eve insisted.

"I didn't ask you to stay with Toby with the intentions of getting a free baby-sitter. If you hadn't come, I would have had to pay someone else," Luck reasoned.

"Please don't ask me to take money for this," she appealed to him, not wanting to be paid for something she had done gladly. "Just consider it a favor from a neighbor."

"All right." He gave in reluctantly. "I won't argue with you."

"Thank you." Eve looked away to reach for the door handle, but she was kept from opening it by the staying hand that touched her arm.

Almost against her will, she looked back at him. The sheen of the moonlight bronzed the masculine angles and planes of his face, giving them a rugged look. A hunger rose within her that she couldn't deny.

"Thank you for staying with Toby." His voice was pitched disturbingly low, vibrant in its rich tone.

"You're welcome," Eve whispered the reply, too affected by his touch and his nearness to speak normally.

Nor could she draw away when his head bent toward hers. She trembled under the possession of his hard lips, her resolve shattering into a thousand pieces. His hand spanned her rib cage just below the uplift of her breast and silently urged her closer.

Eve arched nearer, trying to satisfy the hunger she tasted in his kiss. The blood pounded in her ears with a thunderous force as she let him part her lips to savor the completeness of her response. A soft moan came from her throat at the ache Luck aroused in her.

He was everything. Her senses were dominated by him. The feel of his rock-hard muscles excited her hesitant hands, which rested lightly on his chest, warmed by the heat generated from his male body. That combination of scents — tobacco smoke, musky cologne and his own male scent — filled her lungs with its heady mixture. And the taste of him was in her mouth.

The world was spinning crazily, but Eve didn't care — as long as she had him to cling to. Kissing him was both heaven and hell. But regardless of the consequences, she seemed to be condemned to loving him.

Luck dragged his mouth from her lips and let it moistly graze over her cheek, trailing fire. Her breath was so shallow, it was practically nonexistent. He combed his fingers into her hair as if to hold her head still.

"And thanks for waiting up for me, Eve," he

murmured thickly against her sensitive skin. "It's been a long time since anyone has done that. I can't explain how good it made me feel."

"Luck, I. . . ." But she was afraid to say the words. Then he kissed her again and she didn't need to say anything.

But this time it was brief, although she had the consolation of sensing his reluctance when it ended and he drew away.

"I've got to get back. Toby's alone," Luck said, as if he needed to explain.

"Yes." This time he made no move to stop her when she opened the door. "Good night," she murmured as she stepped out of the car.

"Good night, Eve," he responded.

She seemed to glide on air to the lighted porch, conscious that Luck was waiting to make sure she got safely inside. Opening the door, she turned and waved to him. She watched the red taillights of his car until they disappeared onto the road.

It would be so easy to read something significant into his kisses. Eve tried desperately to guard against raising false hopes. Thinking about the photograph of his late wife helped. That, and the memory of the time when he had intimated he was lonely.

As she undressed for bed, Eve berated herself for being such a fool as to let herself love him. It was very difficult to listen when she felt so good.

This time there were no lights burning to welcome him home when Luck entered the cabin. He didn't bother to turn any on as he made his way down the hallway in the dark.

"Dad?" Toby's sleepy voice called out to him.

"Yes, son, it's me." He paused by the doorway to his son's room.

"Did you take Eve home?" Toby asked.

"Yes. I just got back," he explained. "Are you okay?"

"Yeah." There was the rustle of bedcovers shifting. "How was granddad?"

"He's fine," Luck assured him. "It's very late. You go back to sleep, Toby. We'll talk in the morning."

"Okay, dad," he replied in the middle of a yawn. "Good night."

"Good night, Toby." Luck waited until he heard silence from the room, then entered his own.

The moonlight shining in through the window illuminated the room sufficiently, allowing him to undress without the need of turning on the bed lamp. Unbuttoning his shirt, he pulled it free from the waistband of his pants and shrugged out of it to toss it into the clothes hamper.

He sat down on the edge of the bed to take off his shoes. The moon laid its light on the framed photograph sitting on his dresser. Luck stopped to gaze at it.

"We had a good thing, Lisa," he murmured. "But it was a long time ago." There was an amused lift to his mouth, a little on the wry side. "Why do I have the feeling that you don't mind if I fall in love with someone else?"

But she didn't answer him. It had been quite a while since she had. Luck wasn't haunted anymore by images from the past. And he didn't feel any guilt that it was so.

CHAPTER SEVEN

The afternoon sun burned into her oiled skin as Eve shifted her position in the reclining lounge chair. Dark sunglasses blocked out most of the glare, but the scarlet swimsuit exposed her body to the sun's tanning rays. The straps were unfastened so that they wouldn't leave any white strips on her shoulders.

When she reached for her glass of iced tea sitting under the chair in the shade, Eve held the bodice in position with her hand so that the top wouldn't fall down when she bent over. The sip of tea momentarily cooled and refreshed her. She'd promised herself to walk down to the lake for a swim, but so far she hadn't found the energy.

The front screen door creaked on its hinges and Eve turned her head toward the lake cottage as her mother stepped onto the porch. She saw Eve and smiled.

"There you are," she declared. "I was ready to hike down to the lake. You're wanted on the telephone."

"Me?" She almost forgot about the untied straps of her swimsuit as she sat up abruptly. A quicksilver run of excitement sped through her nerves. "Who is it?"

"It's Luck McClure," her mother answered.

"Tell him I'll be right there," Eve urged.

Her fingers turned into thumbs as she tried hurriedly to knot the straps behind her neck. While she struggled with that, the leather thongs refused to cooperate with her attempts to slip her bare feet into them. She heard the screen door swing shut behind her mother.

The message was being passed to Luck that she was on her way to the phone, but Eve was afraid he'd get tired of waiting if she took too long. When she finally had the straps tied and the shoes on, she ran to the cottage.

The telephone receiver was off the hook, lying beside the phone on the table. Eve grabbed it up, mindless of the amused glances exchanged by her parents.

"Hello?" She was winded from her panicked rush to the phone — and the breathless excitement she couldn't control.

"Eve? You sound out of breath," Luck's voice observed, and she closed her eyes in silent relief that he hadn't hung up.

"I was outside." She swallowed in an attempt to steady her breathing.

"Your mother told me that she thought you were down by the lake," he admitted.

"Actually, I wasn't," Eve explained. "I was out front, sunbathing."

"Wearing a skimpy little bikini, I suppose," Luck murmured.

"No." She half smiled. "I have on a very respectable one-piece bathing suit."

"I should have guessed." His voice was dry with contained amusement.

The reply stung her sensitive ego. She knew exactly what he was thinking. A one-piece suit was precisely what a brown mouse would wear. After all, they weren't very daring creatures.

"Why are you calling, Luck?" She supposed he wanted her to stay with Toby again. It was really quite a bargain when baby-sitters could be paid with a kiss. After last night what else could he think?

"I called to ask you to have dinner with us tonight. Since you wouldn't let me pay you anything for staying with Toby, I thought you might accept an invitation to dinner," he explained.

If he hadn't added the explanation, she would probably have leaped at the invitation, but he stole the pleasure from it.

"I told you last night that I was just being a friendly neighbor," Eve reminded him stiffly. "I don't expect anything in return. And you certainly aren't obligated to take me to dinner."

"I'm not asking out of any sense of duty," Luck stated on a note of tolerance. "Toby and I *want* you to come over for dinner tonight."

"Thank you, but I —" She started to refuse politely for her pride's sake, but he interrupted her.

"Before you turn me down, you'd better hear

the terms of the invitation." A faint thread of amusement ran through his voice.

"Terms?" Eve repeated with a bewildered frown.

"Ever since Toby got up this morning, he's been bragging about what a great cook you are," he informed her. "It's been a long time since I've had a home-cooked meal, so I decided to ask you over to dinner tonight and find out if Toby knows what he's talking about."

She was a little stunned by the implication of his reply, and faintly amused. "Do you mean you're asking me to dinner and you're expecting me to cook it?"

"Only part of it," Luck assured her. "I've got some steaks, so I'll take care of the meat course. The rest of the menu I'll leave to you."

"You have a lot of nerve, Luck McClure." But she couldn't help laughing.

"What do you say?" he challenged. "Is it a deal? Will you come tonight?"

"What time?" she asked, and smiled at the mouthpiece of the receiver.

"I'll pick you up at six o'clock. Is that all right?" he asked.

"That's fine," Eve nodded. "I'll be ready."

"I'll see you at six," Luck promised, and rang off.

Her smile lingered as she replaced the receiver on its cradle and turned away from the phone. She happened to glance at her father and caught the merry twinkle in his hazel eyes.

"I take it that you're going out to dinner with Luck," he guessed from the one side of the conversation he'd heard. "You've been seeing quite a bit of him lately. Maybe I should have a chat with him when he comes to pick you up tonight and find out his intentions."

He was only teasing, but Eve reacted just the same. "Don't you dare," she warned, and he laughed.

As part of her new image to rid herself of the brown-mouse label, Eve wore a white blouse of eyelet lace that scalloped to a vee neckline and buttoned down the front. With it she wore a pair of cornflower-blue slacks in a clingy material.

Promptly at six o'clock, Luck drove up to the cottage, accompanied by Toby. Ready and waiting, Eve bolted from the cabin before her father had a chance to tease her further by carrying out his threat to "have a little talk" with Luck.

Toby whistled like an adult wolf when he saw her. Eve flushed a little. She hadn't thought the different style and color of clothes made that much difference in her appearance — enough for an eight-year-old to notice.

When Toby hopped into the rear seat so Eve could sit in front beside Luck, she was subjected to a wickedly admiring rake of his blue eyes. Her cheeks grew even warmer.

"Not bad," Luck murmured his approval.

Compliments from him were something she couldn't handle, so she tried to turn it aside with a self-effacing remark. "You mean, it's not bad for a brown mouse," Eve corrected.

"No, not a brown mouse anymore. A blue one," he declared with a glance at her slacks. After checking for traffic, Luck reversed onto the road.

"Did dad tell you we're going to have steaks tonight?" Toby leaned over the top of the front seat.

"Yes, he did," she admitted.

"How do you like yours cooked?" Luck asked.

"Medium rare." Her sensitive nerves felt just about that raw at the moment, ultraconscious of the man behind the wheel.

"I guessed you were the red-blooded kind." He allowed his gaze to leave the road long enough to send a mocking glance at her. The innuendo seemed to hint she had a passionate nature, which only served to heighten her awareness of him.

"That's the way we like ours, too, isn't it, dad?" Toby said, unconscious of any hidden meaning in the talk.

"It sure is," Luck agreed, a smile playing at the edges of his mouth.

"You have to watch him, though," Toby told Eve. "Or he winds up burning them."

"Now wait a minute," Luck said in protest. "Who's the cook around here?"

"Eve," his son was quick to answer.

A low chuckle came from Luck's throat. "That's a point well taken." He slowed the car as they approached the drive to the cabin.

Preparations for the evening meal became a family affair. Luck started the grill in the backyard and cooked the steaks, while Toby took care of setting the table and helping Eve. She fixed a fresh spinach salad and wild rice to go along with the steaks. There were enough strawberries left over from the previous night's shortcake dessert to add to other fruit for a mixed fruit sauce as a light dessert.

When they sat down at the table, the meal seemed flawless. Eve wasn't sure whether it was the food or the company that made it all taste so good, but all three of them ate every bite of food on their plates.

"Didn't I tell you Eve was a good cook?" Toby stayed at the table while they lingered over their coffee.

"You certainly did," Luck agreed. "And you were right, too."

"Your father deserves some of the credit," Eve insisted. "I don't know about yours, but my steak was perfect."

"Thank you." Luck inclined his dark head in mocking acceptance of the compliment. Thick strands of rich brown hair fell across his forehead, adding to his rakish air.

"Mine was good, too," Toby assured him, then took away the compliment. "But all you had to do was watch them so they wouldn't burn. Eve really did the cooking."

"And an excellent job, too." He didn't argue with his son's summation. The magnetic blue of his eyes centered on her, lazy and disturbing. "You certainly know the way to a man's heart."

All her senses went haywire at that remark, throwing her into a state of heady confusion. She struggled to conceal it, quickly dropping her gaze and busying her hands with the dessert dishes still on the table.

"Don't bother with the dishes," Luck instructed. "We'll just stack them in the sink for now."

"Nonsense." There was an agitated edge to her voice that betrayed her inner disturbance. "It will only take a few minutes to do them and they'll be out of the way."

"In that case, we'll all help." He pushed out of his chair. "You can clear the table and stack the dishes by the sink, and Toby can wash them while I dry."

They seemed to get them done in record time. Eve finished wiping the stove, table and counter tops a little before Toby and Luck were through.

As the trio entered the living room, Toby turned to walk backward and face them. "Why don't we start a fire in the fireplace, dad?"

"It's summer, Toby," Luck reminded him with an indulgent look.

"I know, but it would be fun," he shrugged.

"We could toast marshmallows."

"You can't still be hungry," Eve laughed.

"No, but I'll eat them anyway," he replied, and she understood that most of the pleasure came from toasting them, rather than eating them. "Please, dad. Just a little fire."

"Okay," Luck gave in. "Just a small one."

While Toby dashed back to the kitchen for the bag of marshmallows and a long-handled toasting fork, Luck built a small fire in the stone fireplace. When it was burning nicely, the three of them sat on the floor in a semicircle around the hearth.

Toby did the actual toasting of the marshmallows, passing around the finished product in turns. Half a bag was consumed — mostly by the fire — before he finally tired of the task. All of them had to wash the sticky gooey residue from their hands. Once that was done, the flickering flames of a fading fire drew them back to their former positions.

A contented silence settled over the room, broken only by the soft crackle of the burning wood. Outside, darkness had descended and the soft glow of the fire provided the only light in the front room. Sitting cross-legged between them, Toby yawned loudly.

"Gosh, I'm tired," he declared. "I think I'll go to bed."

Luck wore a look of vague surprise that his son was actually volunteering to go to bed. A little thread of self-consciousness laced its way through Eve's nerve ends at the prospect of being alone with Luck.

"I guess it is your bedtime," Luck remarked as his son pushed to his feet with apparent tiredness.

"Yeah." Toby paused to look at Eve. "Thanks for cooking dinner tonight. It was really good."

"You're welcome." Her mouth trembled a little in its smile.

"Good night," he wished her.

"Good night," she returned.

"I'll be in shortly," Luck promised.

"You don't need to. You can stay with Eve," Toby said, then partially turned to hide the frowning look of reproval he gave his father from her. She heard him whisper, "I'm big enough to go to bed by myself. Don't embarrass me in front of her."

A slow smile broke over Luck's features at his son's admonition. "Get to bed." He affectionately slapped Toby on the behind to send him on his way.

When he'd gone, Luck slid the lazy smile in Eve's direction, encompassing her with the warmth of its casual intimacy. There had been an ease between them. Eve had definitely felt it, yet without Toby's presence to serve as a buffer, it started to dissipate. She became conscious there was only the two of them in the room. The silence that had been so pleasant and comfortable began to grow heavy. She'd never had the knack for making idle conversation, but the situation seemed to demand it.

"He's quite the boy," Eve remarked under the strain of silence.

"Unfortunately he's grown old before his time." His smile twisted into a regretful grimace that held a certain resignation.

"I don't think he's suffered too much from it," she replied, because Toby did appear to have achieved a balance between his boyhood and his sense of responsibility.

"I guess he hasn't." Luck stared at the fire and seemed to lose himself in the tiny yellow flames darting their tongues over the glowing log.

Eve couldn't think of a response, and the silence lengthened. She supposed that he was thinking about his late wife, probably remembering past moments shared.

No more sounds came from the direction of Toby's bedroom, and the tension ran through her system. Her legs were becoming cramped by her curled sitting position, but Eve was reluctant to move and draw attention to herself. She didn't want Luck to look at her and mentally compare her to the beautiful blonde in the photograph.

At that moment he seemed to rouse himself and become aware that he wasn't alone. "That fire is becoming hypnotic," he said, explaining away his preoccupation.

"Yes." Eve pretended she had been fascinated by it, too, when the only fascination that existed within her was for him.

Luck made a move as if to stand, then paused. "Was there any coffee left?"

"Yes." She rose quickly to her feet. "I'll heat it up for you. It will only take a minute."

"I can get it." But Luck didn't protest too stridently, willing to let himself be persuaded to remain where he was.

"No, you stay here," Eve insisted. "I've been sitting so long I'm starting to get stiff. I need to move around a bit." Which was the truth, although the greater truth was a need to be alone and get herself together. She had to stop being torn apart by this unrequited love for him.

"Okay." Luck didn't argue the point further, remaining by the fire. "If you insist."

Activity helped as she buried herself in the kitchen, turning the coffee on to warm it through and setting out cups for each of them. Yet she couldn't forget that another woman had once brought him coffee and kissed his son good-night as she had done the previous evening. The latter thought prompted Eve to check on Toby while she waited for the coffee to heat.

When she entered the hallway, it was at the precise moment that Luck entered it from the living room. Eve stopped, a little guiltily.

"I thought I'd see if Toby was all right," she explained.

The slight curve to his mouth captivated her with its male charm. "That's where I was headed, too," Luck replied, lifting a dark brow in arching inquiry. "Shall we go together and both be satisfied?"

He took her agreement for granted, linking an arm around her waist to guide her down the darkened hallway. The sensation was much too enjoyable for Eve to resist. She was becoming satisfied with the crumbs of his attention — something she had believed her pride would never let her do.

The doorway to his room stood open and they paused in its frame, standing side by side. In the semidarkness they could see his shining face, all youthful innocence in sleep. His dark hair waved across his forehead like a cap. Deep affection for the sleeping child tugged at her heartstrings.

"That's about the only time he's quiet," Luck murmured softly.

A faint smile touched her mouth as Eve turned her head to look up at him in silent understanding. Toby was always doing, saying or up to something. She could well imagine the wry truth in Luck's comment.

When she met his downward glance, something warm and wonderful shone in his blue eyes. There was a caressing quality in the way they wandered over her upturned face. It started her heart pounding at a rapid speed.

He bent slightly toward her, brushing her lips in a light kiss that stirred her senses and left her wanting more. That desire trembled within her, not letting itself be known. Nothing invited it to show her wants, and Eve lacked the aggression and confidence to assert herself.

"Do you suppose the coffee's hot yet?" Luck murmured, not lifting his head very far from hers.

"It should be," she whispered, and doubted if her voice had the strength to speak louder.

As they turned to leave the doorway, neither of them noticed the little boy in bed cautiously open one eye, or the satisfied smile that smugly curved his mouth.

Luck accompanied her to the kitchen and carried his own cup of hot coffee into the living room. He walked past the sofa and chairs to the fireplace, lowering himself to sit on the floor in front of the dying fire. Reaching out, he pulled a couple of throw pillows from the sofa closer to his position and patted them to invite Eve to join him. She sat on one, bending her legs to the side and holding her cup in both hands.

"Toby likes you a lot, Eve," Luck remarked, eyeing her with a sidelong glance.

"I like him a lot, too," she admitted. "So I guess it's mutual."

"Toby and I have led a bachelor's life for a long time," he said, continuing to regard her steadily. "I always thought we managed very well." He paused for a brief second. "Tonight I realized there were a lot of things we've been missing. I'm glad you came to dinner this evening."

"I'm glad you asked me," Eve replied, and

guessed at his loneliness.

His actions and words had proved that he liked her, that he even regarded her as reasonably attractive. She knew she should be happy about that, but there was a part of her that wished he could be insanely in love with her, wanting her above all other women. It was silly to wish for the moon when she had the glow of the firelight.

"What I'm trying to say is that meeting you has been one of the best things that has happened to us in a long while." Luck appeared determined to convince her of something, but Eve wasn't sure what it was.

She couldn't help noticing the way it was always "we" or "us," never "I" or "me." He was coupling himself with Toby. It was her effect on "them" — not "him." She lowered her gaze to the cup in her hands.

"I'm handling this badly, aren't I?" His voice held a sigh of self-amusement.

"I can't answer that because I don't know what you're trying to handle," Eve said, attempting to speak lightly but unable to look at him.

"It's really very simple." He curved a hand under her chin and turned it toward him. "I want to kiss you. I've been wanting to do it all evening, but I never found the opening. So I was trying to make one."

Her heart fluttered at the disturbing hint of desire in his blue eyes. Luck had finally said

"I," and her senses were on a rampage, wild with the promise that the word held. With a total lack of concern for the deliberateness of his actions, he took the coffee cup from her hands and set it on the stone hearth beside his.

Her composure was so rattled that she wondered how Luck could go about this all so calmly. Anticipation had her trembling on the brink of raw longing for his embrace. The sensation was becoming so strong that Eve didn't think she could hide it.

When his hands closed on her arms to draw her to him, Eve abandoned herself to the emotional needs and wants searing within. The fire in the hearth was dying, but the one inside her was kindled to a full blaze by the sure possession of his hard male lips.

His hand burrowed into the thickness of her brown hair, holding its mass while he supported the back of her head as his driving kiss forced it backward. Her arms went around his middle, her sense of touch excited by the solidness of his muscled body, so hard and firm and virile.

A mist of sensuality swirled itself around her consciousness and made any thought of caution a hazy ill-defined one. His hand roamed along her spine, alternately caressing and urging her closer. Eve strained to comply and arched nearer. The unyielding wall of his body flattened her breasts, but it wasn't enough.

Her breathing was so shallow it was almost

nonexistent when Luck dragged his mouth from her lips to nibble at her throat and trail its way up the pulsing vein to the sensitive hollow below her ear. Eve quivered with the intensity of the passions he was arousing.

"I've needed this for so long, Eve," he declared in a voice thick with desire, the heat of his breath inflaming her skin. "I've been so empty. Fill me up, Eve. Fill me up."

But she didn't need to be urged. Her hunger and emptiness had been as great as his. Her eagerly parted lips were already seeking his when his mouth came back to claim them. The whole weight of him was behind the kiss, bending her backward farther and farther until she slipped off the pillow onto the carpeted floor.

Within seconds they were lying together, and the hard pressure of his male body was making itself felt on every inch of hers. No longer needing to hold her, his hands were free to explore the soft curves that had been against him.

When Luck shifted his position to make a more thorough discovery, a shirt button caught in the eyelet lace of her blouse. He swore under his breath, impatient with the obstacle as Eve was. There was a reluctant delay as Luck paused to free the button. When his knuckles rubbed against a breast, Eve couldn't help breathing in sharply at the inadvertent contact, a white-hot rush of desire searing through her veins.

Her reaction didn't go unnoticed. The instant he had rid himself of the impediment, his hand covered her breast and a soft moan of satisfaction trembled from her throat. He kissed the source of the sound and unerringly found the pleasure point at the base of her neck that sent excited shivers over her skin.

With her eyes closed to lock the delirious sensations of supreme joy forever in her memory, Eve caressed the taut muscles of his shoulders. His deft fingers unfastened the front of her lace blouse and pushed the material aside. When his hand glided inside her brassiere and lifted a breast from its confining cup, she was a churning mass of desire.

Her clamoring needs were almost beyond endurance as his mouth traveled downward from her collarbone to nuzzle the slope of her breast. His leg was hooked across her thighs, and she was rawly conscious of his hard need outlined against her hip. The ache in her loins ran wild when his mouth circled the sensitive peak of her breast. She was writhing inside.

"I thought you told me only married people did that, dad."

CHAPTER EIGHT

Toby's voice shattered the erotic moment into a thousand pieces. Both of them froze at the sound of it. Then her fingers dug into his muscled arms in embarrassed panic when her suddenly widened eyes saw the pajama-clad boy leaning casually over the back of the couch.

Luck reacted swiftly, using his body as a shield to hide her nakedness while he quickly pulled her blouse over her breast. Eve had a glimpse of the savage anger that took over his hard features before he turned his head to glare at Toby.

"What the hell are you doing out of bed?" he demanded harshly.

"I woke up 'cause I was thirsty, so I came out to the kitchen to get a drink," his son explained, unabashed by the intimate scene he had interrupted and apparently oblivious to the awkward situation he was causing. "How come you were doing that if you and Eve aren't married?"

"You've got two seconds to get into your bed," Luck warned. "Or, so help me, you won't be able to sit down for a month!"

"But I was only wondering —" Toby began

to protest, frowning in bewilderment.

"Now!" Luck snapped the word and brought a knee up as if to rise and carry out his threat.

Toby pushed off the couch and started toward the hallway, grumbling to himself. "You keep telling me I should ask questions when I don't understand. I don't know why you're yelling at me for doing it."

"Go to your room and stay there." The line of his jaw was iron hard.

The response from Toby was a loud sigh that signaled compliance. The instant he was out of sight, Luck sat up and combed a hand through his hair before casting a grimly apologetic glance at Eve's reddened face. She sat up quickly, half turning from him to button her blouse, nearly mortified to death by the incident.

"I'm sorry, Eve," Luck sighed heavily.

"It wasn't your fault," she murmured self-consciously, and tried to restore some semblance of order to her tousled clothes.

She wasn't sure which embarrassed her more — what Toby had seen or what he might have seen if he'd come a few minutes later. She had been lost beyond control, her sense of morality completely abandoned.

"I'm going to have a talk with that boy." Irritation vibrated through his taut declaration.

"You shouldn't be angry with him." Despite the embarrassment Toby had caused, Eve defended his innocent role in the scene. She scrambled to her feet the minute she was decent, and Luck followed to stand beside her. She was too disconcerted by the incident to meet his eyes squarely, so her sidelong glance fell somewhere short of his face. "Toby didn't mean to do anything wrong."

"I wouldn't be too sure about that," Luck muttered, more to himself, as he sent a hard glance toward the hallway to the bedrooms.

Then he was bringing all of his attention back to her. She stiffened at the touch of his hand on her shoulder. There were still yearnings within her that hadn't been fully suppressed and she didn't want things to get out of hand twice.

"Eve —" he began in a low tone that seemed to echo the buried wants inside her.

She knew she didn't dare listen to what he wanted to say. "I think you'd better take me home, Luck," she interrupted him stiffly.

Even without looking at him, she sensed his hesitation and trembled inwardly at the thought of trying to resist him if he decided to persuade her to change her mind. She didn't think she'd have the strength of will for a long struggle.

"All right, I will." He gave in grudgingly and removed his hand from her shoulder.

"I think it's best," Eve insisted faintly.

"Of course." There was a clipped edge to his voice. "Give me a minute to tell Toby where I'm going."

"Yes," she murmured.

He moved reluctantly away from her and Eve shuddered uncontrollably when he was out of the room. She had known she loved him, but she hadn't guessed at the depth of that emotion. She had nearly lost all sense of morals for the sake of the moment. It was sobering to realize she would probably do it all over again, given the opportunity.

When Luck entered the bedroom, Toby looked at him with affronted dignity. The urge to grab the boy by the shoulders and shake him hard still rang strong within Luck. It was all he could do to hold onto his temper and not let it fly.

"I'm taking Eve home." The anger was there in his abrupt tone of voice. "When I get back, you and I are going to have a talk."

"Okay," Toby agreed with equal curtness. "But I don't see what you're so uptight about."

"Don't say another word," Luck warned. "Or we'll have that talk now."

Toby pressed his lips together in a thin straight line that showed his resentment for the browbeating tactics. Pivoting, Luck walked from the room.

His anger came from an unbridled instinct to protect Eve. It had run strong and hot within him, imposing the need to shelter her body with his own and later to lash out at his son for the mental harm he'd caused.

When he rejoined her in the living room,

Luck noticed how much further she had withdrawn into her shell. His senses remembered the way she had responded to him without inhibition. They craved it again, but after the way his own son had embarrassed her, he couldn't bring himself to impose his desires on her to know again that wild feeling she had aroused.

Without a word she turned and walked to the door, avoiding his look. Left with no choice but to follow her, he turned his head to the side in a grim kind of despair. Powerful feelings began to make themselves known to him. Uppermost remained the need to right whatever damage had been done to her sensitive nature.

A raw tension dominated the drive to her parents' lake cottage. Eve sat rigidly in the passenger seat, staring straight ahead. Luck had made a couple of attempts at conversation, but her short one-word answers had ended it. She felt that she didn't dare relax her guard for a second or all her inner feelings would spew forth.

She could only thank God she was adult enough to recognize that Luck could want to make love to her without being in love with her. Her embarrassment would have been doubled otherwise.

Luck stopped his car behind her father's sedan. This time he switched off the engine and got out to walk around the hood and open her door. He silently accompanied her to the front porch.

"Good night, Luck." Eve wanted to escape inside the cabin without further ado, but he wasn't of the same mind.

His hand caught her arm near the elbow. "I'm not letting you go inside feeling the way you do," he said.

"I'm all right," she lied.

His other hand cupped the side of her face, a certain grimness in his expression. "I don't want Toby's interference spoiling those moments for us."

"It doesn't matter." Eve tried to evade the issue.

"It does matter," Luck insisted. "It matters a great deal to me."

"Please." It was a protest of sorts against any discussion of the subject.

His hand wouldn't let her move away from its touch. "I'm not ashamed of wanting to make love to you, Eve," he declared. "And I don't want you to be, either."

His bluntness seemed to weaken her knees. After avoiding his gaze for so long, she finally looked at him. His steady regard captured her glance and held it.

"Okay?" Luck wanted her agreement to his previous statement.

"Okay." She gave it in a whisper.

He kissed her warmly as if to seal the agreement, then lifted his head. "You and I will talk about this tomorrow," he said. "In the mean-time, I've got to go back and have a little father-to-son chat with Toby."

"All right." Eve wasn't sure what he wanted to talk about, and that uncertainty was in her voice.

Luck heard it and seemed to hesitate before letting her go. "Good night, Eve."

"Good night." She called softly after him as he descended the porch steps to his car.

Returning to the cabin, Luck went directly to his son's bedroom. He switched on the light as he entered the room. Toby sat up and made a project out of arranging his pillows to lean against them. When Luck walked to the bed, Toby crossed his arms in a gesture that implied determined tolerance.

"Sit down, dad," he said. "I think it's time we talked this out."

Luck didn't find the usual amusement in his son's pseudo-adult attitude and had to smother a fierce rush of irritation. "I'll sit down," he stated. "But I'm going to do the talking and you're going to listen."

"Whatever you say." Again there was an exhibition of patience with his father.

"Do you have any idea how much you embarrassed Eve?" Luck demanded, taking a position on the edge of the bed.

"You kinda lost your cool, too, dad," Toby pointed out calmly.

"I said I was going to do the talking," Luck

reminded him sternly. "It wasn't so bad that you walked in when you did, Toby. The part that was wrong was when you stayed."

"I wanted to find out what was going on," he explained with wide-eyed innocence.

"It was none of your business," Luck countered. "There are certain times when a couple wants privacy."

"But you told me that happened when the two people were married." A faint light gleamed in Toby's eyes, betraying his supposed naiveté.

"That is beside the point." The line of his mouth became grim as Luck's gaze narrowed on his son. "Right now, I want you to understand that what you did was wrong and you owe Eve an apology."

"Was what you and Eve were doing wrong?" Toby inquired.

"Toby." There was a warning in his father's voice not to sidetrack the conversation with his own questions.

"Okay," he sighed with mock exaggeration. "I'll apologize to Eve," Toby promised. "But since you like Eve and you want to do things with her that married people do, why don't you marry her? Did you find out if she has staples in her stomach?"

"Staples?" Luck frowned, briefly avoiding the first question.

"Don't you remember when we met that real sexy blonde on the beach and you said you didn't want to marry anyone with staples in her stomach?" Toby reminded him.

It took Luck a minute to recall his reference to the centerfold type. "No, Eve isn't the kind with staples," he replied.

"Then why don't you ask her to marry you?" Toby argued. "I'd really like it if she became my mother."

"You would, huh?" He tilted his head to one side in half challenge. "After what you pulled tonight, she might not be interested in becoming your mother even if I asked her."

A look of guilty regret entered Toby's expression. "She was really upset, huh?" He was worried by the question.

"Yes, she was. Thanks to you." Luck didn't lessen the blame.

"If I told her I was sorry, maybe then she'd say yes if you asked her," Toby suggested.

"I've already told you that you're going to apologize to her in the morning," he stated.

"Are you going to ask her to marry you after that?" Toby wanted to know.

"I don't recall even suggesting that I wanted to marry Eve," Luck replied.

"But you do, don't you?" Toby persisted.

"We'll talk about that another time." He avoided a direct answer. "Tonight you just think about what you're going to say to Eve tomorrow."

"Will you think about marrying her?" His son refused to let go of the subject as Luck straightened from the bed. Toby slid under the covers to lie down once again while Luck tucked him in.

"I'll think about it," he conceded.

"Good night, dad." There was a satisfied note in Toby's voice.

"Good night."

Luck was absently shaking his head as he walked from the room. After checking to make sure the fire in the fireplace was out, he went to his own room and walked to the dresser where Lisa's photograph stood. He picked it up and studied it for a minute.

"You know it isn't that I love you any less," he murmured to the picture. "What we had, I'll never lose. It's just that my love for Eve is stronger. You would have liked her."

He held the photograph for a minute longer, saying a kind of farewell to the past and its beautiful memories. With deep affection he placed the picture carefully inside one of the dresser drawers. He had not believed it possible to fall in love twice in a lifetime, but he had. Once as a young man — and now as a mature adult. By closing the drawer, he turned a page in his life.

A round beverage tray was precariously balanced on Toby's small hand as he quietly turned the knob to open his father's door. The orange juice sloshed over the rim of its glass, but he miraculously managed not to spill the hot coffee. With both hands holding the tray once more, he walked to the bed where his father was soundly sleeping.

When he set the tray on the nightstand, Toby noticed something was missing. His mother's photograph was gone from the dresser. A smile slowly began to curve his mouth until he was grinning from ear to ear. He tried hard to wipe it away when he turned a twinkling look on his father.

"It's time to get up, dad." He shook a bronze shoulder to add action to his summons.

His father stirred reluctantly and opened a bleary eye. He closed it again when he saw Toby.

"Come on, dad." Toby nudged him again. "Wake up. It's seven-thirty. I brought you some orange juice and coffee."

This time both sleepy blue eyes opened and Luck pushed himself into a half-sitting position in the bed. Toby handed him the glass of orange juice and crawled onto the bed to sit cross-legged.

After downing the juice, Luck set the glass on the tray and reached for the pack of cigarettes and lighter on the nightstand.

"You are certainly bright-eyed this morning." There was a trace of envy in his father's sleep-thickened voice as he lit a cigarette and blew out a stream of blue gray smoke.

"I've been up awhile," Toby shrugged. "Long enough to make the coffee and have some cereal."

Luck picked up the coffee cup and took a sip from it. "After last night, I think it would be a good idea if you started knocking before walking into somebody's room."

"You mean, so I won't embarrass Eve when she starts sleeping in here after you're married," Toby guessed.

"Yes —" The affirmative reply was out before he realized what he'd admitted. The second he heard what he had said, he came instantly awake.

Toby laughed with glee. "You did decide to marry her!"

"Now, you wait just a minute," Luck ordered, but there wasn't any way he could retract his previous admission. "That doesn't mean Eve is willing to marry me."

"I know." Toby continued to grin widely. "You haven't asked her yet. When are you going to propose to her?"

"You will have to apologize for last night," Luck reminded him. "You aren't getting out of that."

"We can go over there this morning, just like we planned." Toby began laying out the strategy. "I'll apologize to her, then you can ask her to marry you."

"No, Toby." His father shook his head. "That isn't the way it's going to happen. We'll go over there and you'll apologize. That's it."

"Ahh, dad," Toby protested. "You're going to ask her anyway. Why not this morning?"

"Because you don't ask a woman to be your wife while there's an eight-year-old kid standing around listening," his father replied with mild exasperation.

"When are you going to ask her, then?" Toby demanded impatiently.

"I'm going to invite Eve to have dinner with me tonight," he said. "You're going to stay home and I'll have Mrs. Jackson come over to sit with you."

"Mrs. Jackson?" Toby cried with a grimace of dislike. "Why does she have to come over?"

"We've been through this before, " Luck reminded him. "You aren't going to stay here by yourself."

"Well, why do you have to go out to dinner with Eve?" he argued. "Why can't she come over here like she did last night? I'll leave you two alone and promise not to listen."

His father sighed heavily and glanced toward the ceiling. "How can I make you understand?" he wondered aloud. "When a woman receives a marriage proposal, she has a right to expect a few romantic touches along with it — a little wine and candlelight. You don't have her come over, cook dinner, wash dishes, then propose. It just isn't done like that."

"It sure sounds like an awful lot of fuss to me," Toby grumbled. "Eve wouldn't mind if you just asked her without going through all that."

"I don't care whether she doesn't mind. I

do," Luck stated, and crushed the half-smoked cigarette in the ashtray. "Off the bed," he ordered. "I want to get dressed."

"Are we going to Eve's now?" Toby hopped to the floor.

"Not this early in the morning," Luck told him. "We'll wait until later."

"But it's Sunday. She might go to church," he protested.

"Then we'll drive over there the first thing this afternoon."

"Aw, dad." Toby sighed his disappointment and left the bedroom dragging his feet.

It was noontime when Eve and her parents returned to the lake cottage from Sunday church services. Dinner was in the oven, so they were able to sit down to the table in short order. By one o'clock the dishes were done and Eve went to her room to change out of her good dress.

"Eve?" The questioning call from her mother was accompanied by a knock on the door. "Your father and I are going for a boat ride on the lake. Would you like to come with us?"

Zipping her jeans, Eve went to the door and opened it. "No, thanks, mom." She smiled at the woman with graying brown hair. "I think I'll just stay here and finish that book I was reading."

She didn't mention that Luck had indicated he would see her today. No definite arrangement had been made. Eve preferred that her parents didn't know that she was staying on the off chance he might come by or call.

"Is Eve coming with us?" her father asked from the front room.

"No," her mother answered him. "She's going to stay here."

"I'll bet she's expecting Luck McClure," he declared on a teasing note, and Eve felt a faint blush warming her cheeks.

"Don't mind him," her mother declared with an understanding smile. "He's remembering the way I sat around the house waiting to hear from him when we were dating." She made a move to leave. "We probably won't be back until later this afternoon."

"Have a good time," Eve said.

"You, too," her mother called back with a wink.

CHAPTER NINE

Toby was slumped in the passenger seat of the car, a grimly dejected expression on his face. "Boy, I wish Mrs. Jackson had been busy tonight." He grumbled the complaint for the sixth time since Luck had phoned her to sit with him.

"She's coming and there's nothing you can do to change that," Luck stated, looking briefly away from the road at his son. "I don't want you pulling any of your shenanigans, either."

Toby was silent for a minute. "Have you thought about how expensive this is going to be, dad?" He tried another tactic. "You not only have to pay Mrs. Jackson to stay with me, but you've also got to pay for Eve's dinner and yours. With the money you're spending tonight, I'd have enough to buy my minibike. It sure would be a lot cheaper if you just asked her this afternoon."

"I don't want to hear any more about it." They had hardly been off the subject since this morning, and his patience was wearing thin.

"But don't I have some say in this?" Toby argued. "After all, she is going to be my mother."

"I wouldn't bring that up if I were you,"

Luck warned. "You haven't squared yourself with Eve about last night. She might not want to be the mother to a boy who doesn't respect other people's private moments."

"Yes, but I'm going to apologize for that," Toby reasoned. "Eve will understand. I'm just a little kid."

"Sometimes I wonder about that," Luck murmured to himself.

Taking the ice-cube tray out of the freezer section of the refrigerator, Eve carried it to the sink and popped out a handful of cubes to put in the glass of tea sitting on the counter. The rest she dumped into a plastic container and set it in the freezer for later use. She turned on the cold water faucet to fill the ice-cube tray. The noise made by the running water drowned out the sound of the car pulling into the drive.

As she carried the tray full of water to the refrigerator, she heard car doors slamming outside. Her heart seemed to leap at the sound. In her excitement, Eve forgot about the tray in her hands and started to turn. Water spilled over the sides and onto the floor.

"Damn," she swore softly at her carelessness, and set the tray on the counter.

Hurriedly Eve tore some paper towels off the roll and bent down to sop up the mess. Her pulse raced with the sound of footsteps approaching the cottage. Her haste just seemed to make it take longer to wipe up the spilled water.

A knock rattled the screen door in its frame. She carried the water-soaked wad of paper towels to the sink, a hand cupped under them to catch any drips.

"I'm coming!" Eve called anxiously, and dropped the mess in the sink.

Her glance darted to the screen door and the familiar outline of Luck's build darkened by the wire mesh. She paused long enough to dry her hands on a terry towel and run smoothing fingers over her gleaming brown hair.

There was a wild run of pleasure through her veins as she hurried toward the door. Reflex action adjusted the knitted waistband of her carnation-red top around her snug-fitting jeans.

Eve didn't notice the shorter form standing next to Luck until she was nearly to the door, and realized he'd brought Toby with him. Not that she minded; it was just that Luck had indicated he wanted to talk to her privately. Toby's presence negated that opportunity. And there was the embarrassing matter of last night's scene. She was naturally modest, so there was a sense of discomfort in meeting Toby today.

"Hello." She greeted them through the screen and unlatched the door to open it. There was a nervous edge to her smile until she met the dancing warmth of Luck's blue eyes. It eased almost immediately as a little glow started to build strength. "Sorry it took so long, but I had to mop up some water I spilled."

"That's all right. We didn't wait that long," Luck assured her. The admiring run of his gaze over her face and figure seemed to give her confidence. She could tell he liked what he saw, even if she wasn't the type to turn heads.

"Hello, Toby." Eve was able to smile at the young boy without any strain as he entered the cottage at his father's side.

"Hi." His response seemed a little more subdued than normal, as if his mind were preoccupied with other matters, but his bright eyes were just as alert as they always were.

"Come in," Eve invited. "I just fixed myself a glass of iced tea. Would you two like some?"

Refusal formed on Luck's mouth, but Toby was quicker with his acceptance. "Yeah, I'd like a glass."

"And some cookies, too?" Eve guessed.

"Chocolate chip?" he asked hopefully, and she nodded affirmatively. "I sure would."

"What do you say?" Luck prompted his son to show some manners.

"Thank you," Toby inserted, then frowned. "Or was it supposed to be 'please'?"

"It doesn't matter," Eve assured him with a faint smile. "You've got the idea." Her glance lifted to the boy's father. "Did you want a glass of tea and some cookies?"

"I'll settle for the tea," he replied, changing his mind in the face of his son's acceptance.

The pair followed her into the small kitchen. Toby crowded close to the counter to watch her while Luck stayed out of her way, leaning a hip against a counter top and lighting a cigarette. Eve never lost her awareness of his lean masculinity, even though he wasn't in her line of vision. Her body's finely tuned radar was aware of his presence.

She fixed two more glasses of tea without any mishap and even managed to put the ice-cube tray filled with water in the refrigerator's freezer section without spilling any. Lifting the lid of the cookie jar, Eve took out three chocolate chip cookies and placed them on a paper napkin for Toby.

"Here you go, Toby." She turned to give them to him.

"Wait a minute," Luck stated, and laid a hand on his son's shoulder to stop him from taking them. "Before any refreshments are passed around, there's something Toby wants to say to you, Eve. Isn't there, Toby?" There was a prodding tone in his voice when he addressed his son.

A big sigh came from Toby as he lowered the hand that had reached for the cookies. "Yes," he admitted, and turned his round blue gaze on Eve. "I'm sorry for embarrassing you last night. I didn't mean to."

"I know you didn't." She colored slightly at the reference to the incident.

"Dad explained about respecting other people's privacy," he said. "I was wrong to stay without you knowing I was there. I'm really and truly sorry, Eve. All I wanted to do was find out what was going on. I never meant to embarrass you."

Toby possessed more than his share of natural curiosity. She had known all along that he hadn't meant any harm. It was obvious he wasn't shocked by what he'd seen, which allowed her to feel that the scene between herself and Luck had been natural and right.

"It's all right, Toby," Eve promised him. "You're forgiven, so we can all forget about it."

His blue eyes widened in a hopeful look. "Then you aren't mad or upset about it?"

"No, not at all," she replied with a shake of her head.

Tipping his head back, Toby turned it to look up at his father. "See?" he challenged. "I told you she wouldn't be."

"I know you did," Luck admitted. "But she deserved an apology just the same."

"Now will you ask her to marry you instead of —" Toby didn't get the question finished before Luck clamped a hand over his mouth to muffle the rest of it.

An electric shock went through Eve as her gaze flew to Luck's face. Her own complexion had gone pale at Toby's suggestion. His ruggedly virile features held grim impatience and displeasure in their expression, and Eve knew she had been right to doubt that Toby knew what he was talking about. It seemed she had been catapulted from one awkward situation into another.

"Toby, I could throttle you," Luck muttered angrily, and took his hand from the boy's mouth. "Don't you dare say another word."

"But —" Toby frowned his lack of understanding.

"I mean it," Luck cut across his voice with stern reproval. "Get your cookies and iced tea and go outside," he ordered. "I don't want to hear so much as a peep out of you."

"Okay," Toby grumbled, and moved to the counter to take the napkin of cookies and a glass of iced tea. Eve was too frozen to help him.

"You stay outside and don't come walking back in," Luck warned. "Remember what you promised me about that."

"Yes, dad," he nodded, and trudged toward the screen door.

Eve continued to stare at Luck as he snubbed the cigarette butt in an ashtray on the counter. There was regret in the hard line of his mouth and a grim apology in his eyes when he finally looked at her. She heard the door bang shut behind the departing Toby.

"I'm afraid my son has a big mouth," Luck said.

A terrible pain wrenched at her heart. She turned away to hide it, clasping the edge of the counter with both hands. Dredging deep into the well of her reserve strength, she found a little piece of composure.

"Don't worry about it," Eve declared with forced lightness. "I'm not going to hold you to Toby's suggestion, so no marriage proposal is expected."

Her pulse raced as Luck moved to stand behind her. His hands settled lightly on the rounded points of her shoulders. At the moment she wasn't up to resisting his touch. A tremor of longing quivered through her senses.

"Why not?" he murmured, very close to her.

She pretended not to understand. "Why not what?" Her voice wavered.

"Since Toby has already let the cat out of the bag, I might as well ask you to marry me now, instead of waiting," Luck replied.

She half turned to look at him over her shoulder. He couldn't possibly be serious, but his steady gaze seemed to imply that he was. She was afraid to believe it. She loved him so much that it didn't seem possible her wildest dream might come true.

"Luck, you don't have to do this." She gave him a chance to retract his semiproposal.

That lazy half smile lifted a corner of his mouth, potent in its male charm. "I know I don't," he agreed.

"Then. . . ." Eve continued to hesitate.

"I want you to be my wife," Luck said in an effort to make it clear to her that he was serious. It wasn't any kind of cruel joke. "And

Toby wants you to be his mother — although I wouldn't blame you if you have second thoughts about taking on that role. He talks when he shouldn't — he sees things he shouldn't — and he knows things he shouldn't. It isn't going to be any bed of roses."

"I don't mind." She breathed the reply because she was beginning to believe that he meant all this.

"You'd better be sure about that." He turned her around to face him and let his hands slide down her back to gather her closer to him. "We haven't known each other long. I don't want to rush you into something. If you want to think it over, I'll wait for your answer."

Spreading her hands across the front of his shirt, Eve could feel his body warmth through the material. The steady beat of his heart assured her that this was all real. It wasn't a dream.

"It isn't that." Eve hadn't realized that she hadn't got around to accepting his proposal until that minute. "I'd like to marry you."

Luck tipped his head toward her. "Did I hear a but at the end of that?" he questioned.

"No." She hadn't said it, not in so many words; yet it was there — silently. "It's just so sudden. I can't think why you'd want to marry me," she admitted at last.

"I want to marry you for the usual reason." A warm dryness rustled his voice. "I love you, Eve."

The breath she drew in became lodged in her throat. She hadn't realized what beautiful words they were until Luck uttered them. An incredulous joy misted her eyes.

"I love you, too," she declared in a voice choked with emotion.

His mouth closed on hers and there was no more need for words. Her hands slid around his neck and into the thickness of his dark hair as his molding arms crushed her to his length. Eve reeled under the hard possession of his kiss, still dazed that he actually wanted her. But he seemed determined to prove it with action as well as words.

When her parted lips were at last convinced, Luck showered her face with rough kisses. Her eyes, her brows, her cheeks, her nose, her chin, her jaw — no part of her was exempted from his hungry foray. It left her so weak she could hardly breathe. Her racing heart threatened to burst from the love swelling within her.

The searing pleasure of it all was a sweet ache that throbbed through her limbs. His hands leisurely roamed her shoulders, back and hips to caress and arouse her flesh to a fever pitch of delight. For Eve there was no holding back. She gave him her heart and soul in return, and anything else he wanted — her pride, her dignity, her self-respect. It was all his.

A faint tremor went through him when Luck lifted his head an inch or so from hers to study her with a heavy-lidded look of desire. "I thought it would take more convincing than this to persuade you to marry me," he admitted huskily.

"Hardly." Eve smiled at that, knowing she had been his for the taking a long time now.

He withdrew a hand from her back to cup her upturned face. She turned into its largeness and pressed a kiss in its palm. His fingers began a tactile examination of her features from the curve of her cheekbone to the outline of her lips.

"That night I bumped into you outside the tavern, I knew I didn't want to let you go," Luck murmured. "But I didn't dream that I'd eventually marry you."

Even though their first meeting was a special and vivid memory, Eve wished he hadn't mentioned it. She didn't want to remember that he had regarded her as a brown mouse. She closed her eyes to shut it out.

"I thought you were a figment of my imagination," he went on, and slid his hand to her neck, where his thumb stroked the curve of her throat. "Until I finally recognized you that rainy afternoon you came to help Toby bake cookies. And there you were, right in my own home."

"I remember," Eve admitted softly, but she wasn't enthused about the subject.

Luck drank in a deep breath and let it out slowly. "Before I met you, I was beginning to think I wasn't capable of caring for another woman."

There was an instantaneous image in her mind of the photograph of his first wife. A painful sweep of jealousy washed over her because she would never be first in his life. She loved him so much that she was willing to settle for being second as long as it meant she could spend her life with him.

"Toby has been wanting me to get married for some time," Luck told her. "He even chose you before I did. I have to admit my son has very good taste."

Eve smiled faintly. "He's still outside — and probably dying of curiosity."

"Let him." His arm tightened fractionally around her waist. "It's what he deserves." Then Luck sighed reluctantly. "I suppose we should let him in on the news, although he was positive you'd agree to marry me."

"He was right." She basked in the blue light of his unswerving gaze.

"He's never going to let us hear the end of it. You know that, don't you?" he mocked lightly.

"Probably not," Eve agreed with a widening smile.

"We might as well go tell him," Luck finally agreed with her suggestion.

As he turned to guide her out of the kitchen, he kept his arm curved tightly around her and her body pressed close to his side. It was a very possessive gesture and it thrilled Eve.

When they walked outside, they found Toby sitting on the porch steps waiting patiently —

or perhaps impatiently, judging by how quickly he bounded to his feet to greet them. His bright glance darted eagerly from one to the other.

"Did she say yes?" he asked Luck with bated breath.

"What makes you think I asked her?" Luck challenged.

He cast an anxious look at Eve, who was trying not to smile. "You did, didn't you?" Again the question was addressed to his father.

"I did." Luck didn't keep him in the dark any longer. "And Eve agreed to be my wife."

"Whoopee!" Toby shouted with glee and practically jumped in the air. "I knew she would," he rubbed it in to his father. "I told you that you didn't have to wait until tonight, didn't I?"

Luck glanced at Eve to explain. "I was going to do it up right. I had it all planned — to take you out to dinner, ply you with champagne, sway you with candlelight and flowers. Then I was going to propose. Unfortunately, blabbermouth jumped the gun."

"Now you don't have to do that," Toby inserted. "And I don't have to stay with Mrs. Jackson. Eve can come over to our place tonight and we'll all have dinner together."

"No, she can't," Luck stated, shaking his head.

Toby frowned. "Why can't she come?"

"Because I'm taking her out to dinner just

the way I planned," he said. "And Mrs. Jackson is coming over to stay with you just as we arranged it."

"Dad," he protested.

"I'm going to have to share her with you a lot of evenings in the future, but on the first night of our engagement, I'm going to have her all to myself," Luck declared.

"I'd stay in my room," Toby promised.

"That isn't the same," he insisted, and looked again at Eve. "You will have dinner with me tonight if I promise you you won't have to cook it?"

"Yes." Even if she had to cook it, she would have agreed.

"I'll come over early, around seven, so I can talk to your parents." Luck smiled as he realized, "I haven't asked you how soon you'd like the wedding to be?"

His phrasing of the question — not "when" but "how soon" — nearly took her breath away. For a second she could only look at him, a wealth of love shining in her eyes.

"The sooner the better, don't you think?" she suggested, a little tentatively.

"Absolutely." His answer was very definite as he bent his head to claim her lips once more.

What started out as a brief kiss lingered into something longer. Eve leaned more heavily against him, letting his strength support her. Before passion could flare, they were reminded that they weren't alone.

"I have a question," Toby said, interrupting their embrace.

"What is it?" But Luck was more than a little preoccupied with his study of her soft lips.

"Am I supposed to leave you two alone every time you start kissing?" he asked.

"Not necessarily every time. Why?" Luck dragged his gaze from her face to glance curiously at his son.

"If I did, it just seems to me that I might be spending an awful lot of time by myself," Toby sighed. "And I'd really kinda hoped the three of us could be together like a family."

"We *will* be a family," Eve assured him. "And you won't be spending much time alone."

"Eve's right." Luck reached out to curve an arm around his son's shoulders and draw him into their circle. "Part of the plan was for you to have a mother, wasn't it?"

"Yep." Toby smiled widely.

CHAPTER TEN

The three of them spent the afternoon together, partly to allay Toby's concern about his position in the new family unit and partly because Luck and Eve enjoyed Toby's company and shared a mutual desire to include him. Eve knew she was just imagining it, but the sun seemed to shine brighter and the air smelled fresher than it ever had before.

Her parents hadn't returned from their boat ride by the time Luck and Toby left to go home. Eve had some time alone to think over the unexpected proposal and all that had been said. She finally came out of the wonderful daze that had numbed her to a few home truths.

Luck had asked her to marry him for many reasons. He had said that he loved her, and she didn't doubt that in his own way he did. But she realized he didn't love her as much as she loved him. Another factor was Toby: he had needed and wanted a mother, and he had liked her. He'd undoubtedly had a lot of influence on Luck's decision. That was only natural.

Plus Eve had known he was a lonely man. He wanted the company of a woman — and not just in a sexual way, for she was sure he could find that type of feminine company. That night in front of the tavern, Luck had said he wanted to talk to her — that she was the kind he could talk to. He needed that in a woman, just as she needed to be able to talk to him. But part of his reason for proposing had to be the desire for companionship.

Then there was the bachelor existence he and Toby led. They needed someone to cook and clean house for them. How much more convenient it would be to have live-in help. Cooking and cleaning would be part of her new role, although naturally both Luck and Toby would help.

There was nothing wrong with any of his reasons. None of them were bad. As a matter of fact there were a lot of couples starting out their wedded life with less solid foundations than theirs. But the realizations brought Eve down out of her dreamworld to face the reality of their future. Luck wanted to marry a comfortable, practical Eve, not a starry-eyed romantic. It was better that she knew that.

It didn't alter the special significance of the evening to come. It was still their engagement dinner. Eve took extra care in choosing a dress to wear and fixing her hair and makeup. The results weren't too bad, even to her critical eye. The rose color of the dress was a little drab, but its lines flattered her slender figure. The soft curls of her chestnut hair glistened in the light.

True to his word, Luck arrived promptly at

seven, with a bouquet of scarlet roses for Eve. She hadn't mentioned anything to her parents about his proposal, waiting until he came so they could tell them together.

They were overjoyed at the news, especially her mother, who had despaired that Eve would ever find a man to satisfy her. Her father seemed to take pride in Luck's old-fashioned gesture of asking his permission to marry his daughter. It was granted without any hesitation.

By half-past seven the congratulations were over and they were on their way to the restaurant. Eve realized how difficult it was to keep both feet on the ground when she was with Luck. Her hand rested on the car seat, held in the warm clasp of his.

"Are you happy?" he asked.

"Yes." She could say that without any doubt, even with the facts before her concerning his reasons for wanting to marry her.

"I thought we could drive to Duluth tomorrow," he said. "I need to buy you a ring, but I want to be sure you like it. We'll pick something out together. Is tomorrow all right?"

"Yes, it's fine," Eve nodded.

"I want you to meet my father while we're there. We'll have dinner with him," he stated.

"That would be good," she agreed. "I'd like to get to know him."

"You'll like him." He sent her a brief smile. "And I have no doubt that he'll like you."

"I hope so." But she was secretly concerned that his father would compare her with Luck's first wife and wonder what his son saw in such a "plain Jane." A lot of his friends who had known his first wife would probably wonder about that, also. She wouldn't blame them if they did.

"Would you mind if Toby came with us tomorrow?" Luck asked as he slowed the car to turn into the restaurant parking lot.

"Of course I don't mind," Eve assured him. "If we don't include him, he'll probably become convinced he's being neglected."

"That's what I thought, too," he agreed, and parked the car between two others.

After climbing out of the car, Luck walked around it to open her door and help her out. He lingered on the spot, holding her hand and smiling at her.

"Have I told you that you look very lovely tonight?" he asked.

"No, but thank you." Eve smiled, but she wondered if he was just being kind. Perhaps it was a nice way of saying she looked as good as she could look.

Bending his head, he let his mouth move warmly over hers. The firm kiss didn't last long, but it reassured her of his affection. Eve doubted if that brief kiss disturbed him as much as it disturbed her, though.

When it was over, he escorted her to the restaurant entrance, his hand pressed against the back of her waist. Inside they were shown to a small table for two in a quiet corner of the establishment.

"Didn't I promise you candlelight?" Luck gestured to the candle burning in an amber glass when they were both seated in their chairs across from each other.

"Yes, you did," she agreed with a remembering smile. "You neglected to mention the soft music playing in the background." Eve referred to the muted strains of romantic mood music coming over the restaurant's stereo system.

"I saved that for the finishing touch." The corners of his mouth deepened in a vague amusement.

A young and very attractive waitress approached their table. With her blond hair and blue eyes, she seemed the epitome of everything sexy, without appearing vulgarly so. She smiled at both of them, yet Eve jealously thought she noticed something other than professional interest in the girl's eyes when she looked at Luck.

"Would you like a drink before dinner?" she inquired.

"Yes, we'd like a bottle of champagne," Luck ordered with a responding smile.

Eve would probably have checked his pulse to see if he was sick if he hadn't noticed the blonde's obvious beauty. Yet when he did she was hurt. It made no sense at all. Somehow she managed to keep the conflicting emotions out of her expression.

The waitress left and came back with the bottle of champagne. After she had opened it, she poured some in a glass for Luck to sample. He nodded his approval and she filled a glass for each of them.

When she'd gone, Luck raised his glass to make a toast. "To the love of my life, who is soon to be my wife."

It was a very touching sentiment, but Eve knew it was an exaggeration. He had promised her a romantic evening and he was trying to give it to her, but she would rather their relationship remained honest and did not become sullied with false compliments.

"That was very beautiful, Luck," she admitted. "But it wasn't necessary."

"Oh?" His eyebrow arched at her comment. "Why isn't it necessary?"

"Because —" she shrugged a shoulder a little nervously "— I didn't expect you to pretend that you are wildly and romantically in love with me. You don't have to make flowery speeches."

"I see." The line of his jaw became hard, even though he smiled. "And it doesn't bother you if I'm not wildly and romantically in love with you?" There was a trace of challenge in his question.

Eve assured him, "I've accepted it." She didn't want him to act the part of a romantic lover when it wasn't what he truly felt.

"I'm glad you have," he murmured dryly, and motioned for the waitress to bring them menus. "I understand the prime rib is very good here."

The dinner conversation was dominated by mundane topics. The meal was very enjoyable, yet Eve sensed some underlying tension. Luck was pleasant and friendly, but sometimes when he looked at her she felt uneasy. He'd always been able to disturb her physically, yet this was different — almost as if he were angry, though he didn't appear to be.

The dinner had stretched to a second cup of coffee after dessert before Luck suggested it was time to leave. Eve accepted his decision, still unable to put her finger on the source of the troubling sensation.

In silence they crossed the parking lot to the car. Luck assisted her into the passenger seat, then walked behind the car to slide into the driver's seat. He made no attempt to start the car.

"Is something wrong?" Eve frowned slightly.

"There seems to be," he said with a nod, and half turned in the seat to face her.

"What is it?" She wasn't sure if he meant something was wrong with the car or something else.

"You," Luck answered simply.

"What have I done?" She drew back in surprise.

"Where did you get this ridiculous notion

that I'm not wildly in love with you?" he demanded.

"Well, you're not," Eve stated in defense, then faltered under his piercing gaze. "I believe you when you say you love me, but —"

"That's good of you," he taunted dryly. "If I'm not madly in love with you, maybe you should explain why I want to marry you. I'm sure it has something to do with Toby."

"Why are you asking me?" Eve countered. "You know the reasons as well as I do."

"Perhaps better, since they happen to be mine." Luck stretched an arm along the seat back and appeared to relax. "But I'd like to hear you tell me what they are."

"I can provide some of the things that are missing in your life," she said uneasily, not sure why he wanted her to explain, unless it was to make sure she understood.

"Such as?" he prompted her into elaborating on the answer.

"You need a mother for your son, someone to take care of your house and do the cooking, someone to care about you and be there when you want company. . . ." Eve hesitated.

"You left out bed partner," he reminded her coolly.

"That, too," she conceded.

"I'm glad. For a minute I thought I was hiring a full-time housekeeper instead of acquiring a wife." This time some of his anger crept into his voice.

"I . . . don't understand," Eve stammered.

"You silly fool. There is only one reason why I'm marrying you. I love you and I don't want to live without you!" Luck snapped.

"But Toby —"

"I haven't done too bad a job raising him alone. If he has managed without a mother this long, then he can make it the rest of the way," he retorted. "Believe me, I'm glad the two of you like each other, but I wouldn't give a damn if he hated you as long as I loved you."

"But I thought —" Eve tried again to voice her impressions, and again Luck interrupted her.

"As for the cooking and cleaning, I could have that done. I know you haven't inquired, but I could afford that if it were what I wanted."

"You admitted you were lonely," she inserted quickly before he could cut her off again. "You said it was lonely at home that night outside the tavern."

"So I did," Luck admitted. "Eve, a man can have a hundred women living in his house and still be lonely if none of those women is the right one."

"Please." She turned her head away, afraid of being convinced by him. "I know how much you loved your first wife."

"Yes, I *loved* Lisa —" he stressed the verb "— but it's in the past tense, Eve. I *did* love her, but I love *you* now. It's completely different."

"I know that," she murmured with a little ache.

"Do you?" Luck sighed behind her, then his hands were turning her into his arms. "I loved her as a young man loves. I'm not the same person anymore. I've changed. I've grown up. I'm an adult male, Eve, and I want you and love you as only a man can — wildly, deeply and romantically."

"Luck." Eve held her breath, finally beginning to believe it could be true.

"Come here." He smiled and began to gather her into his arms. "I want to prove it to you."

She could hardly argue when his mouth was covering hers with such hungry force. And she didn't want to anymore.

We hope you have enjoyed this Large Print book. Other G.K. Hall & Co. or Chivers Press Large Print books are available at your library or directly from the publishers.

For more information about current and upcoming titles, please call or write, without obligation, to:

All our Large Print titles are designed for easy reading, and all our books are made to last.